ECONOMIC DEVELOPMENT IN EAST-CENTRAL EUROPE IN THE 19TH AND 20TH CENTURIES

IVÁN T. BEREND *and* GYÖRGY RÁNKI

Economic Development in East-Central Europe in the 19th and 20th Centuries

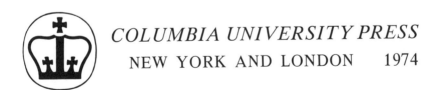

COLUMBIA UNIVERSITY PRESS
NEW YORK AND LONDON   1974

Library of Congress Cataloging in Publication Data

Berend, Ivan T., 1930–
  Economic development in East-Central Europe in the
19th and 20th centuries.

  Translation of Közép-Kelet-Europa gazdásagi fejlődése
a XIX-XX. [tizenkilencedik-huszadik] században.
  1. Europe, Eastern—Economic conditions. I. Ránki,
György, 1930–   joint author. II. Title.
HC244.B38913   330.9'47   73-6542
ISBN 0-231-03013-4

Foreword

It is our good fortune that two such outstanding Hungarian economic historians as Iván T. Berend and György Ránki have undertaken an analysis of East Central European economic developments. The economic history of Europe, and especially the economic history of East Central Europe, is a neglected art in the United States. Here is a monograph which combines a fine sense of detail and a superior understanding of major trends. It was first published in Hungarian in 1969, and it now appears in a specially prepared English version. The Hungarian edition was an instant success. Berend and Ránki form a famous team and, although they are relatively young historians, they have been working together for over two decades. Their many books and articles have appeared in Hungarian, German, French, Russian and English, with topics ranging from Hungarian industrial developments before World War I to socialist Hungary's central economic planning. Their close friendship and assiduous collaboration is the envy of their colleagues: they are each other's best mentors and critics. Their openness, objectivity, and the readability of their style have made them well-known and admired figures in their own country. They have also published individually, with Berend showing a particular interest in urban problems and in economic planning, and Ránki pouring out an astonishing number of learned essays on contemporary political and diplomatic history. How they find the time for all this is a mystery. They both teach at their own universities, guide several doctoral candidates, head important scholarly associations, sit on too many committees, and are frequent guest lecturers abroad, especially in Oxford, in Paris, and in the United States.

The volume they have prepared is based heavily on archival material; the sections on the former territories of the Habsburg Monarchy understandably benefit more from archival sources than do other sections. But, then, it is impossible to know equally well all the regions of that bewilderingly complex area that extends from the Baltic Sea to Macedonia, and from the Elbe River to the Ukraine. The authors tell the exciting story of how, in the nineteenth century, the Habsburg Monarchy, a partitioned Poland, and the Balkan possessions of the Ottoman Empire—all once somnolent—gradually came to life and then sped, one after the other, from near-feudalism to advanced agrarian and industrial capitalism. They also explain how rapid economic progress made inevitable the political self-assertion of Poland, Czechoslovakia, Austria, Hungary, Rumania, Yugoslavia, and Albania in the twentieth century.

The story is dramatic even when told through statistical figures and seemingly cold data on exports-imports and capital accumulation. For behind every new factory, bank, and railroad is the often heartbreaking story of forced migration, social dislocation, cultural crisis, and political upheaval. People have always had to pay a heavy price for modernization: in East Central Europe the price was especially burdensome and it still has not been completely paid. But no one can doubt, particularly after reading this book, that modernization would have to come and would be worth the effort. What is more, the job was apparently not done too badly by the regimes and entrepreneurs of the past century and half.

The expert reader will probably quarrel with one or another point in the book. This will most certainly be welcomed by the authors.

István Deak
Professor of History
Director, Institute on
East Central Europe

Preface

"Habent sua fata libelli." The well-known Latin saying is valid not only for the future but also for the antecedents of any book. This one has had a rather long pre-history. In the early 1950s while still university students we started to work together on modern Hungarian economic history. Spending almost fifteen years on research in Hungarian economic history of the nineteenth and twentieth centuries, we always had to contend with the particular problems of the East-Central European economic model. We particularly felt the lack of comprehensive and comparative studies, especially in view of the rich literature on the West.

The idea of writing a comparative East-Central European economic history was evolving in our thoughts in the mid-1960s. It was furthered by our academic and personal experiences, which clearly revealed the inseparability of the fate of nations and peoples in this region from their economic development.

Our work was given impetus by the growing trend toward comparative studies in the social sciences, especially in the discipline of economic history. A paper at the Third International Congress of Economic History in Munich in 1965 was the first step. We received great encouragement from Professor Shepard Clough, who after the Congress invited us to write a book on this topic. We are very grateful to him not only for strengthening our intention but for initiating the publication of this book by Columbia University Press. Professor István Deak also helped us through the difficulties of publication.

This study could not have been carried on without the generous help of the Hungarian Academy of Sciences and the Ministry of Education in Hungary. Their grants made it possible as well to do research in the various Eastern European countries. We are also very much indebted to the Ford Foundation and the École Pratique des Hautes Études for their grants which gave us the opportunity to broaden our knowledge by providing access to the immense resources of American and French libraries.

In a short preface it is impossible to list the names of all our Hungarian colleagues and the Eastern and Western scholars who helped us by their publications, and often with their advice and comments. We acknowledge our appreciation to all of them.

Our main aim was not to elaborate a detailed economic history of this region, country by country, but to try to search out the main tendencies, the common features, and the special peculiarities of economic growth in order to delineate an East-Central European economic model.

This book was published in Hungarian at the end of 1969. An English translation was submitted in mid-1970 but a rather long time was needed to "translate" the Hungarian English into an American one. The major merit for this task belongs to Mrs. Ruth Rocker, whose thorough copy editing made the publication actually possible. We should like to acknowledge her valuable help. We are grateful to Mr. Bernard Gronert, executive editor of Columbia University Press, for his assistance in preparing the way to publication.

Iván T. Berend and György Ránki

Budapest, March 15, 1972.

Contents

Tables

Introduction

At present the term "East-Central Europe" appears in Western literature chiefly as a political notion, referring collectively to the group of European socialist countries which emerged after World War II. However, this category coincides with the East-Central Europe of the interwar years, on which was focused a vast literature growing out of the political transformation following World War I. Of course, the term also has a geographic meaning. It embraces the eastern region of the European continent from roughly the River Elbe to the Russian plains and from the Baltic Sea to the Black Sea and the Adriatic.*

In the present work the notion of East-Central Europe is applied with neither a political nor a geographic meaning, though both are valid. Thus, in the period following World War II the political application of the term was beyond argument, for most of the countries in this area set up identical socio-economic structures and similar political institutions. The geographic interpretation is also possible, not only because East-Central Europe forms a special region with definite physical and climatic traits but because under the particular historical circumstances these traits exerted a similar influence on the development of the countries in the region. It is important to remember that this region has been affected by its immediate proximity to Asia and the Middle East and its remoteness from the oceans at the same time that it has been an organic part of the most developed continent of the world.

It is our view that not only can historical circumstances not be disregarded but that they take precedence. It is in history that we find the decisive factors which caused Eastern Europe to diverge from the path followed by the Western countries of the Continent. Hence, East-Central Europe is first of all a historical concept, evolving primarily from the peculiar course of historical-economic development.

In tracing this evolution it is not necessary to go back to ancient times or search for special features ascribable to the migration period or the

---

*Our study covers the territory of the Austro-Hungarian Monarchy and its successor states, the Polish territories, and the Balkans except Greece, which belongs more to the Mediterranean sphere.

Byzantine Empire. The clue to our investigation, notably the rise of the modern economy, is to be found in the fifteenth and sixteenth centuries when the two halves of the Continent went separate ways. Although differences existed before that time in economic and social levels, there was also much similarity, particularly in tendencies of development. If the countries of the eastern regions often lagged behind, they nevertheless tended to follow the French or German states. The sharp and irrevocable split came in the fifteenth and sixteenth centuries.

From the sixteenth to the eighteenth century the western regions of Europe underwent a radical change as a consequence of the gradual but significant transformation of world trade. There was both a shift in trade routes and a change in the structure of merchandise. Connected with these changes was the disintegration of feudal agrarian conditions, signs of which had already become evident. Thus the gradual disappearance of serfdom gained a strong impetus in the sixteenth century, particularly in England. Narrow, local markets began a rapid expansion to national, even world, dimensions. With the rapidly growing production of goods, the Western European agrarian structure was characterized increasingly by two principal types of change. On the one hand, the earlier manorial rent in kind gave way to a new form: payment in money by peasants who owned their own plots of land (the French *censitaire*). On the other hand, wealthy elements rose from the peasantry: tenants paying a capitalist land rent (England). In England the transformation in the forms of manorial rent was only the first expression of the radically changing agrarian structure from the sixteenth to the eighteenth century. By the process of enclosures, present ownership of property for the most part disappeared and was replaced by extensive capitalist farming based on the leasing of land. In France the land remained the property of the landlord until the close of the eighteenth century although the rights of the peasantry to use the land were quite extensive, virtually including the possibilities of free sale and succession. Peasant farming became the chief agent in the expansion of agricultural commodity production.

The transformation of agriculture, the weakening or disappearance of serfdom, was abetted in Western Europe by the transformation of industry. The emergence of manufacturing altered the division of labor. Owing to the pressure of increasing demand and to the investment in industry of rapidly accumulating capital, rural handicrafts and production by urban guilds gave way in Britain and France to large industrial works (based on manual labor) and to increasing division of labor.

Thus, in the countries of Western Europe the seventeenth and eighteenth centuries witnessed the disintegration of the old socio-economic framework and the development of new capitalist conditions. Burgeoning industry, flourishing trade, the transformation of agriculture, ever more extensive urbanization, and the strengthening of the bourgeoisie in the towns created the foundations for building central state power to replace feudal disunity.

The countries of Eastern Europe were unable to tread the same path of development at that time or later. The factors operative in the West were either absent in the East or had opposite effects. The eastern regions of the Continent became an agrarian reserve of the increasingly industrialized West. The traditional economic system, serfdom and manorial rent, persisted. In these three decisive centuries the possibility of independent statehood vanished in much of Eastern Europe, especially in the Balkan Peninsula. Instead of the centralized independent state power realized in the Western countries came the Turkish conquest. Although Turkish rule and its consequences lasted longest and weighed most heavily on the Balkan countries, the effects were not confined to the Peninsula. From about the middle of the sixteenth century the central and southern parts of Hungary also came under Turkish occupation, and for a century and a half the unoccupied parts of the country became the scene of permanent warfare. The effects of the Turkish onslaught were felt far beyond these borders and significantly altered the political map of East-Central Europe.

This was the age when the earlier independent states were replaced by the formation (or the acceleration) of increasingly powerful empires. A clear indication of the effect of the Turkish wars was the elevation of Ferdinand of the House of Hapsburg to the throne of the unoccupied parts of the Hungarian Kingdom—an important step in the development of the Hapsburg Empire in Central Europe. The absence of independent states and later the absence of independent national domains became a general feature of these regions after the fifteenth and sixteenth centuries.

It was these conditions that determined the radically dissimilar development of Eastern and Western Europe from the sixteenth century on. They were effective in checking the dissolution of the old feudal order, the transformation of agriculture, and industrial-urban development along Western lines. Traditional forms were preserved, causing stagnation for several centuries and permitting no more than a very feeble and slow breakthrough of modernization.

While these conditions applied in general to the whole of Eastern Europe, there were essential differences between the parts of Southeastern Europe occupied by the Turks and the other parts of East-Central Europe. The degree of feudal stagnation and backwardness in the two regions was so unequal as to be more than a quantitative difference. In the provinces of Southeastern Europe annexed by the Ottoman Empire military oppression and the merciless exaction of ransoms and levies by the Turks weighed heavily on the population. Unlike other countries of Europe which had lost their independence, in these subjugated countries the conquerors not only settled down but also transformed the existing socio-economic system. Traditional forms of class and economy partly disappeared, and the typical system of Turkish feudalism preserved many elements of the ancient forms from the early Middle Ages. The principal feature was maximal centralization of the state, based on the concentration of landownership in the hands of the state. The landlord-serf relationship assumed thereby a special nature. The Turkish spahi-landlords appointed by the sultan exercised only a controlling function, securing an income fixed and demanded by the state. Under this system the peasant masses became a state peasantry, the serfs of the ruler. The landlord was only a state official without ownership and without the possibility of holding a hereditary estate for life or inheriting land by way of succession.

The development of the towns also took a peculiar turn under the sultan's direct supremacy. Although clinging to medieval forms of industry, they were able to attain relative freedom of agrarian development and some commerce.

Considering that under the Turkish system of feudalism commercial agriculture did not develop on the large estates, that urban advance was exceedingly slow, and especially that the system of governmental taxation and finance was extortive and exploitative, it is natural that socio-economic development stagnated in the Balkans for several centuries. In fact, Turkish feudalism was marked not only by backwardness but also by excessive rigidity and little capacity for response to any external challenge. Hence, the general European advance beginning with the fifteenth century created little if any stir in the parts of Europe occupied by the Turks. The Turkish type of feudalism was irreconcilably antagonistic to capitalist development. Around the end of the eighteenth century when minimal steps of capitalist development appeared, they did not find any support; on the contrary, they clashed against every obstructive barrier of the extortive system.

In other parts of East-Central Europe the picture was by no means so unfavorable, although here too the aforementioned circumstances inevitably caused development to deviate from that in the West. Ancient feudal conditions survived. Serfdom persisted; the transformation of agriculture was very slow; and there was hardly any industrial-urban progress. However, in the countries of East-Central Europe deviation from the West did not lead to feudalism of the Turkish type but to the establishment of a new, special system of serfdom. In the areas east of the Elbe River there developed during the sixteenth to eighteenth centuries what may be denoted as "the second edition of serfdom" (using Engels' well-known term). In the fifteenth century bondage had begun to slacken in these parts of Europe; as in the West statute labor and payment in kind were being replaced by the payment of rent in money. But these new forms were discontinued and superseded by a system recalling an earlier stage of serfdom and reestablishing the bondage of serfs. This was manifest in successive laws in the sixteenth and seventeenth centuries that once again tied the peasant to the land by abolishing the right of migration in Prussian, Hungarian, and Russian territory.

This was not merely a legal change, nor was it retribution for the violent German, Hungarian, Polish, Bohemian, and Russian peasant revolts which took place at the time and grew into wars spreading over extensive parts of the countries involved. It was a development closely connected with the new demands of the Eastern European economies. In Western Europe, under the influence of favorable conditions, agricultural commodity production could proceed within the framework of a peasant or capitalist lease of land and be linked with urban-industrial advancement. In peripheral Eastern Europe the preconditions of capitalist advancement failed to materialize. It was rather the effect of

Western Europe's rapidly developing markets that was felt in the economy of Eastern Europe.

The most important reason for the renewal of serfdom was to secure the labor required by the large estates. Step by step these estates restored the big demesne farms typical of earlier centuries which provided for the cultivation of the land by praedial services. Of the Western tendency toward commodity production based on wage work by peasant farmers or by capitalist tenants, only isolated traces of secondary importance existed in Eastern Europe.

The obstruction of incipient capitalist development, the consolidation of serfdom, and the strengthening of the large estates as producers of commodities exerted a powerful influence on the position of the towns. The landlords gained the upper hand in both politics and economy, prevailing over the urban bourgeoisie. The towns stagnated at the level of trades and guild crafts, and henceforth the main line of urban advancement rested not on industrialization but on the development of market towns of agrarian character. Industry was sparse and weak; commercial capital was confined to narrow limits and its inflow into industry did not even begin. The towns therefore remained in their medieval state for lack of the dynamism of modern urban development.

The slow rate of urban development, the partial agricultural self-sufficiency of the towns, and the consequently small dimensions of town markets in turn affected the commodity production of the landlords and limited the natural domestic agricultural market. There were, it is true, differing levels of markets among the various countries in the region under review. For instance, the more successful industrialization of the Bohemian towns presented a contrast to the agricultural structure of Hungarian towns and created a wider domestic market for agricultural products. While the size of the respective urban home markets appears to be striking here, it was the favorable opportunities afforded by sea transport to some countries (the Eastern rather than East-Central) that were of real significance. Relatively inexpensive water transportation provided a fairly safe connection with Western European markets and greatly improved the chances for sale of goods, thereby promoting commodity production. In the last analysis, notwithstanding the differences, in the East-Central European countries large-estate commodity production was realized mostly through reliance on foreign markets.

Thus, in East-Central Europe the period from the sixteenth to the eighteenth centuries cannot be regarded as an era of transition from feudalism to capitalism but rather a peculiar, belated feudalism. Medieval conditions, instead of waning, were consolidated. But this did not take the same form as the process in the Balkans under the sway of Turkish feudalism. While backward conditions in Eastern Europe continued and the rate of economic advancement was slow, the system was by no means as rigid and unreceptive to progress as in the parts under Turkish rule. The second serfdom and capitalist development were in opposition, but not in the form of an irreconcilable, implacable antagonism as in the Balkans. Finally, the economic development in Western Europe, the steadily increasing dimensions of manufacturing industry, and later, the gathering force of industrial revolution from the close of the eighteenth century to the middle of the nineteenth, had some impact on the countries of East-Central Europe. Susceptible to the influences exerted by more advanced areas, these economies, though barred from modern economic growth, traveled a peculiar road of capitalist development, chiefly from the last third of the eighteenth century to the beginning of the twentieth. This road was, of course, roundabout and rocky, rendering advance slow and complicated. Yet, the gradual modernization of agriculture, commodity production based on hired labor, the step-by-step change-over of villein-worked large estates to extensive capitalist farming—a process with many contradictory elements—could nevertheless be initiated. Thus, by the start of the nineteenth century in some parts of East-Central Europe socio-economic trends heralding a transition from feudalism to capitalism began to emerge.

What were the principal factors and processes of capitalist economic development? First, an increase in commodity production resting on the social division of labor and on the progress of urbanization, accompanied by a transformation of the social structure, cessation of the serf-landlord relationship, and establishment of a system of wage work. This development did get under way, very slowly, within the traditional economic-social framework, though the persistence of inveterate laws and institutions raised heavy barriers to progress. The appearance of capitalist forms of organization, the regular introduction of paid work instead of villein services, and the rising capitalist commodity production of the large estates in the first half of the nineteenth century, all helped the new system to gain ground gradually in the agriculture of East-Central European countries. In the Balkans, under Turkish rule, the obsolete economic structure became increasingly apparent when Turkish military power began to show signs of tottering and yielded to a very tentative germination of capitalist conditions by a series of primitive reforms and concessions. Thus, the beginnings of capitalist commodity production also appeared in the peasant economy of the Balkans after its partial relief from the heavy yoke of Turkish feudalism.

At the same time industrial production started in this part of Europe, disrupting the guild system, where it existed, or the primitive forms of peasant domestic industry. Workshops with large numbers of laborers were set up in the towns, where craftsmen employed by a single proprietor often performed the same work side by side; but there also appeared industrial works, sometimes in the towns but more often in villages, whose activities were based on buying up the products of peasant handicraft, dividing the process of production into stages, and creating new, modern forms of industry with local division of labor. Beginning in the eighteenth century these so-called factories sometimes employed several hundred, even as many as a thousand, workers, in the more advanced countries of East-Central Europe.

This two-directional advancement was mutually helpful to agriculture and industry, creating markets for each at home and promoting foreign trade. This early stage of capitalism gave rise to new and acute demands, calling, among other things, for better means of transport and modern forms of credit, and especially afforded opportunity for strengthening the merchants, those exceedingly mobile and increasingly important figures in the economy. In fact, the introduction of capitalism in agriculture and industry was connected with ever more lively commercial activity. In countries which needed to export agrarian products and import industrial goods the principal source of accumulation of capital was through the local and international exchange of supplies of merchandise.

All these steps in economic development during the first half of the nineteenth century clashed more and more violently with the rigid and anachronistic traditional laws and instititions. The development of capitalist economy was thwarted by the lack of modern property law, by feudal laws on opening mines, by aristocratic prerogatives, by medieval rules barring the development of a modern credit system, by the obligation of serfs to pay rent, primarily in the form of statute labor, by the outlawry of the Jews, by the curtailment of municipal rights, and by a number of other feudal institutions and medieval laws.

In truth, the development of capitalism was badly hampered and very slow in the first half of the nineteenth century. Progress was frustrated further to the extent that the inadequacy of the ancient forms, their unsuitability for further progress, and the bankruptcy of the economic system of serfdom became blatantly manifest. The awareness of bankruptcy undermined the pillars of the old economic-social order—the nobility and landowners—and their efforts to find some solution created a much stronger disruptive force than did the appearance of the still modest bourgeoisie. The steadily widening and deepening mass movement of the serfs made matters worse; this movement became the chief agent for change, as an expression that the masses suffered most from the bankruptcy of the feudal order and from the tortures of a transformation which showed little promise of realization.

These economic processes of the first half of the nineteenth century, the beginnings of modern economic development, were also accompanied in East-Central Europe by the idea of national states and its rapid spread. In the West the endeavor to establish a national market and a national domain was a concomitant of the achievement of bourgeois status; therefore it was the truly free historical road of capitalism which led to the emergence of national states. With only partial realization of capitalism in agriculture, oriented mainly toward supplying external markets, in East-Central Europe modernization did not arouse such strong nationalist aspirations as in the West. Nevertheless nationalism and the idea of national independence struck increasingly strong roots in the eastern parts of the Continent.

The countries of East-Central Europe presented a peculiar paradox. On the one hand, the advance of capitalism, even in a slow, contradictory, and inconsistent form, created the minimum maturity required for national aspirations. On the other hand, the very backwardness was the main factor in the rising nationalist feelings. In other words, in the West the bourgeois national state was born of the advancement of bourgeois civilization; in the East it was rather the failings, the contradiction and impediments, of this development which fostered nationalism and strengthened independent national endeavors.

The strata of landlords who had reached the rudimentary stage of capitalist development necessarily came up against the innumerable problems arising out of the need to improve their farms and make them thrive. At the same time they found themselves face to face with the obstacles emanating from the economic and social backwardness of the country. It was comparison with Western Europe, the sensation of backwardness and poverty in the first place, which promoted nationalism. This strengthened the effects at modernization which coincided with the idea of nationalism, particularly since the economic and social backwardness in these countries of Europe was closely related to the partial or complete lack of national independence under the multinational empires inherited from the Middle Ages.

Thus the national aspirations that went hand in hand with the demand for transformation of the socio-economic structure constituted the chief driving force behind all the changes brought about in the nineteenth century—recurring, failing, then attaining results and determining the whole course of development in East-Central Europe, particularly in the second half of the century. In some countries the explosive force of contradictions led to the outbreak of revolutions; in others, and more often, the pressure was relieved by partial and gradual reforms. Notwithstanding the differing degrees of realization and the widely dissimilar solutions, a slow and halting, yet continuous and definite, process of bourgeois transformation occurred in the entire area.

In the first half of the nineteenth century modern economic and social development made inevitable the elimination of traditional institutions and medieval laws. After certain preliminaries and half measures, this task was accomplished roughly at mid-century by revolutions and revolts and by a series of reforms extorted by force or granted and executed by the supreme authority. In two or three decades the serfs were emancipated in the countries of East-Central Europe; the prerogatives of the nobility, including exemption from taxation, were abolished; the free acquisition of land and bourgeois ownership of property were made possible, implying the separation of the landlords' estates from the peasants' holdings, a part of the former being added to the latter. Decrees were issued, laying down as well as regulating the execution of the laws of bourgeois loans and providing in general for the many attributes of the modern state.

These modern bourgeois institutions and legislation—though partial and contradictory—gave a new and significant impetus to economic and social development. The modern capitalist transformation of agriculture in the second half of the nineteenth century as a result of revolutions, revolts, and reforms was accompanied by the development of the infrastructure and a modern organization of credit service. The transformation of agriculture in turn created new possibilities while stimulating and promoting the earlier initiated capitalist development of industry. After the so-called handicraft-manufacture period of the first half of the century, the last decades of the nineteenth century and the opening years of the twentieth saw the establishment of modern, power-driven, large-scale industry.

These changes, however, properly belong to the industrial revolution, to the extensive socio-economic transformation within the framework of which the historical processes of transition to capitalism were completed. In this book we have concentrated on these processes and on the industrial revolution. However important modern capitalist agrarian development may have been, the traditional economic and social structure could be broken up, and the transition from the feudal system to capitalism accomplished, only by the industrial revolution.

Part One
The Rise: Transition
to Modern Capitalist
Economy and the
Industrial Revolution

Prologue

The economic literature dealing with the industrial revolution offers many and varied interpretations and applications of the term. We belong to the school of historians who give it a broad meaning as did Marx in first defining the term or Toynbee in his writings on the subject. In this view, the industrial revolution is the combination of economic, social, and political changes—the transformation of the whole economy and society.

We believe that this economic and social process, having spanned such a long historical period, should be regarded as a major revolution in economic history. We do not accept a restricted use of the term, whether to the whole of industry or to certain technical problems of a certain branch of industry. Nor do we find altogether satisfactory the broader interpretation which regards the process not only as the "home affair" of industry but as a force pervading the entire national economy —transforming agriculture, industry, transport, trade and various other fields—but does not correlate these changes with the social processes to which they are linked. On the evidence of the eighteenth and nineteenth centuries technological and economic developments, accompanied by the growth of productive forces, sooner or later bring about a change in the socio-economic framework, transforming traditional medieval society into modern capitalist society and leading to the emergence of new production relations. Therefore there is close correlation between the transition from feudalism to capitalism and the processes of industrial revolution. Without the start of the industrial revolution the transition to capitalism cannot be complete, and without the development and establishment of capitalist conditions the industrial revolution cannot get under way or penetrate the whole of economic life.

In the first part of this book, dealing with the nineteenth century beginnings of modern economic growth in East-Central Europe until World War I, one of our main endeavors is to throw light on the peculiar course of the industrial revolution and outline the contrasting patterns of modern economic development in the countries of East-Central Europe.

1 The Demographic Preconditions of Modern Economic Development

In the most dynamic stage of the emergence of capitalist conditions, in the period of industrial revolution, extremely important demographic changes took place as the concomitant of economic growth—and strangely enough also as the precondition and consequence of economic growth. Not infrequently a sort of "demographic revolution" is claimed to have occurred, and with justification, inasmuch as the population changes in the eighteenth and nineteenth centuries are without precedent in earlier times. The most striking feature was the phenomenal increase. The total population of Europe increased by 14 million from 1600 to 1700, by 70 million from 1700 to 1800, and by 206 million from 1800 to 1900. It is particularly noteworthy that in the course of a century, from 1800 to 1900, the population of Great Britain increased nearly fourfold, from 10.5 million to 38 million; that of Germany more than doubled, from 24.5 million to 50.6 million. In Belgium and Sweden, too, the number of inhabitants more than doubled; in France it nearly doubled. In the period before the industrial revolution average annual population growth was little more than 0.5 per cent, but by the nineteenth and twentieth centuries the annual population growth approached 2 per cent.

This rapid increase was due to a sudden fall in the death rate. The most striking instance is Great Britain where the number of births per 1,000 ranged between 37.7 and 36.6 from 1740 to 1830, declining to 32.6 between 1841 and 1850, while the death rate of about 36 per 1,000 in the 1730s fell to 21 per 1,000 by the 1810s, and to as low as 14 per 1,000 by the outbreak of World War I. Before the advent of capitalism, in addition to the normally high death rate, populations were from time to time decimated by severe epidemics. The increased supply of meat in winter resulting from the introduction of forage, the increased consumption of vegetables, better personal hygiene, improved housing, running water, and particularly the progress in medical care saved millions of people from early death. The dramatic change in mortality is clearly illustrated by the fact that from the Roman Age to 1800 there was hardly any change in the life span in Europe; it remained at about 25 years. However, during the next hundred years and by the early twentieth century life expectancy rose to about 45 years. (In 1905 in Germany the life span was 45 years for men, 48 years for women; in France it was similar, while in Italy it was 44 and 45 years, respectively.)

Although the increase in population had diverse causes, its effect on the European economy was generally beneficial: it promoted rapid growth. In other words, the notable population growth was itself an important productive force.

The demographic upsurge gave considerable impetus to production and resulted in a permanent and significant widening of the inner market. The greater number of people speeded up social mobility, since the limited quantity of land forced the surplus population to leave the villages. This increased social mobility was a dynamic element. Furthermore, the changes connected with population growth enlarged the gainfully occupied share of the population.

Population growth also had many indirect effects. Some stress the correlative growth in knowledge and experiences. With twice as many people there is thought to be twice as much potential for invention and innovation. Others emphasize the challenge of demographic growth to technical development: the surplus goods to supply the needs of a growing population can only be obtained by permanent technical improvement.

But the effects of demographic change on economic growth were by no means free from contradictions. At a time when stimulating effects take place, there can be adverse tendencies as well. Rapid development of population can give rise to a labor surplus, leading to a decline in the price of labor and to restraint in technical progress. In the long run the changed age structure also has some braking effects—above all, in the larger and steadily growing share of aged and inactive in the population. Population growth also leads to an increase in unproductive expenditures; for example, the cost of social investments, causing a relative decline in directly productive investment. And the exploitation of natural resources may not be as rapid as the population growth, so that the quantity of raw materials per head diminishes.

Whether the stimulating or the braking effects prevail depends mainly on the economic level of the given country. At a primitive stage the negative effects of population growth are stronger.

What was the course of the demographic revolution in East-Central Europe and what were its effects?

Statistical information on demography was obtained later than in the West. For the first half of the nineteenth century or earlier, apart from sporadic data, practically no records are available, and even for the second half of the nineteenth century the information is often incomplete and scanty. Therefore we are unable to compare the demographic trends of the eighteenth and nineteenth centuries; nor do we have the necessary data concerning nineteenth-century demographic changes in this region as we do for Great Britain and Western Europe. However, the principal trends can be discerned.

Even from the incomplete data presented in Table 1-1 it is obvious that in the nineteenth century population growth showed a roughly similar tendency in the countries of East-Central Europe and Western Europe. A particularly rapid increase in population was characteristic of Russia and also of the Polish Kingdom. The number of inhabitants of Russia rose approximately fourfold. According to available Polish records, from 1810 to 1910 the population increased from 3.3 million to 12.1 million, or nearly fourfold, while according to a census referring

Table 1-1. Population Growth in East-Central Europe, 1800–1910 *(in millions)*

	c.1800	1850	1865	1880	1910
Austria[a]	13.9[b]	17.6	19.9	22.1	28.4
Hungary	9.3[c]	13.8	15.4[d]	15.7	20.9
Russia	35.5	68.5	73.6[d]	97.7	160.7
Bulgaria	—	—	—	2.8	4.3
Rumania	—	3.7[e]	4.1	4.6	7.0
Serbia	—	0.9	1.2	1.7	2.9

Source: Based on miscellaneous national statistics.

[a] In the cis-Leithan parts of the Hapsburg, i.e., Austro-Hungarian, Monarchy.
[b] Data from the years 1819–20.
[c] Data from 1787.
[d] Data from 1869.
[e] Data from 1859.

Table 1-2. Population Growth in Europe, 1800–1900 *(in per cent)*

	1801–20	1821–30	1831–40	1841–50	1851–60	1861–70	1871–80	1881–90	1891–1900
European average	6.5	9.4	7.1	5.8	6.2	7.7	8.3	9.0	9.9
Austria-Hungary	5.3	9.8	5.3	3.6	6.8	7.5	4.4	9.1	9.6
Balkans	4.2	3.3	6.3	6.3	5.2	6.2	4.6	11.0	10.5

Source: D.V. Glass and E. Grebenik, "World Population, 1800–1950," in *The Cambridge Economic History of Europe,* Vol. VI, Part I, Cambridge, 1965, p. 62.

to the entire Polish territory the population increased from 9 million to 29 million between 1800 and 1910, or more than threefold. This rate of growth equaled that of the most rapid demographic increase in Great Britain. Austrian and Hungarian records bear witness to a much slower growth, but even in these countries the number of inhabitants nearly doubled in the course of the nineteenth century. Thus the rate of growth was not far behind that in the Western countries of the Continent.

As regards the Balkan countries the picture is somewhat different. Table 1-2 shows that the populations of most of these countries approximately doubled from the 1860s to the opening years of the twentieth century. The distinctive feature is the fact that this growth, instead of marking the whole of the nineteenth century, took place only in the second half, after a slow increase in the first half.

It is noteworthy that, as shown in Table 1-2, until 1880 the population growth of the Balkan countries—apart from an exceptional decade—remained behind the European average. Moreover, the rate of growth did not exceed the approximately 0.5 per cent level typical of precapitalistic societies. However, after the 1880s there was a leap forward in the Balkans, which raised the growth rate in these countries above the European average. The rate of growth doubled over the preceding period, surpassing 1 per cent annually.

In considering population growth, close attention should be paid to *emigration*. The population figures reflect the consequences of the outflow of people which was taking place in this period. Around the end of the nineteenth century in many countries of East-Central Europe emigration on a large scale became a typical demographic feature.

As early as the last decades of the nineteenth century, but especially after the turn of the century, emigration from the Austro-Hungarian Monarchy increased steadily. There was a particularly high rate of outflow from the Austrian provinces of the Monarchy (not including Hungary), particularly from Galicia, Bukovina, and Dalmatia. Between 1871 and 1910, 1.8 million inhabitants left this region, chiefly for overseas destinations. The net loss—after allowing for repatriation—was 1.3 million. Emigration became a drain amounting to 28.4 per cent of the population growth at the beginning of the twentieth century.

In these decades Hungary also ranked high in emigration. In the last decades of the nineteenth century about 0.5 million inhabitants, and about fifteen years later 1.4 million, left the country. When repatriations are taken into account, the net loss was 1.3 to 1.4 million. Thus emigration absorbed approximately one-fifth to one-fourth of the population growth in the decades from the 1870s to World War I.

In the Russian Empire by comparison the process of emigration was relatively less extensive; altogether, there were 1.5 million emigrants in the period from 1871 to 1906. Of these the largest exodus was from the Polish districts overseas: between 1901 and 1913 more than 1.1 million. As a matter of fact Polish emigration was the largest outflow from East-Central Europe if the Polish territories belonging to Germany and to the Austro-Hungarian Monarchy are included. The number of Poles who emigrated up to World War I is estimated to have been about 3.5 million.

Until the turn of the century, emigration from the Balkan countries was still quite insignificant, not more than about half a million. But already at the beginning of the present century a significant part of the population growth was lost through emigration, though the outflow remained far behind that in the Polish territories or Hungary. Owing to their more backward socio-economic development, the Balkan peoples were much less mobile. The peculiar Balkan path of agrarian development and the influence of peasant farming on a stationary life also contributed to their immobility.

In the strongest wave of emigration a total of about four to five million inhabitants left East-Central Europe to find new homes abroad, chiefly in the United States. This region furnished a preponderant share of immigrants in the early twentieth century. Thus in 1906, 25.9 per cent of the immigrants to the United States came from the Austro-Hungarian Monarchy, 21 per cent from Russia (including the Polish Kingdom), and another 2 to 3 per cent from the Balkan countries. (Of the total of 1.1 million immigrants in that year those of Turkish, Greek, Bulgarian, Rumanian, and Serbian nationality numbered 44,000. Turkish and Greek immigrants may have made up half of this number.) Therefore in the main immigration movement of the early twentieth century—the inflow to the United States—approximately half of the immigrants came from the countries of East-Central Europe. This was the peak period of emigration from Eastern Europe. Of those coming to America between 1861 and 1870 only 0.5 per cent were from this region; between 1871 and 1880, 4.5 to 5 per cent; between 1881 and 1890, 12 per cent; and between 1891 and 1900, 33 per cent.

Mass emigration thus became an important drain on population growth in East-Central Europe at the close of the nineteenth and especially at the beginning of the twentieth century, primarily from the backward provinces of the Austro-Hungarian Monarchy, including Hungary, and from Polish territories belonging to the various empires.

In general the emigration movement in Eastern Europe did not exceed similar movements in other European countries; in fact, it remained far behind the dimensions of emigration from Southern Europe (Italy and Spain), Great Britain, and Germany. However, the outflow from the latter countries culminated in earlier decades of the nineteenth century and abated by the time emigration hit its stride in the East. From 1820 to 1860, 2.8 million emigrants left the British Isles for North America; from Germany, 1.5 million. About 84 per cent of the immigrants to the United States came from these two sources. Between 1860 and 1890 the figures were 3.5 million and 3.0 million respectively, in all 62 per cent of the immigrants to the United States. From 1890 to World War I, the 2 million English and Irish and 1 million German settlers accounted for only 16 per cent of the immigrants, with Eastern Europeans making up most of the remainder.

Demographic tendencies and population growth in the nineteenth century and up to World War I were roughly similar in East-Central Europe and the other European countries. Notwithstanding the basic similarities, however, there were conditions peculiar to certain East European countries which caused deviations in these trends.

Hungary is a case in point. Figures cited earlier indicate that the population increased by 35 per cent between 1869 and 1910—or below that of countries with the most dynamic increase of population. The rate of growth was strongly influenced in this period by the last great epidemic (cholera) in the early 1870s which claimed a minimum of 0.3 million victims, according to contemporary sources. Actually population growth between 1869 and 1880 failed to reach even the level typical of traditional societies and virtually stagnated (the yearly increase being 0.13 per cent). However, after 1880 the actual increase rose to 1 per cent and even slightly higher. Moreover, since the great wave of emigration from the country was about the turn of the century and the years following, the yearly natural increase may be put at 1.3 per cent between 1880 and 1910.

No special circumstance can be detected regarding the source of the increase. The birthrate did not display any essential change though some reduction took place, evidently ascribable to the progress of urbanization. The rate of 37 per 1,000 between 1900 and 1910 was nevertheless still fairly high. The death rate was reduced significantly from about 37 to 25 per 1,000. However, the latter figure was still considerably higher than in most European countries. The explanation probably lies in the relatively backward medical care in the country, the high infant mortality, and the ravages of tuberculosis—a widespread disease. (In incidence of tuberculosis, Budapest was at the top of the list of the most important European cities in 1905.)

No essential difference is found between Hungarian and Austrian conditions with respect to actual population growth. In a period of four decades the yearly increase in the Austrian population was around 1 per cent, much higher than in Hungary, but between 1890 and 1910 the Austrian birthrate was slightly lower. In the Balkan countries the annual rate of natural increase reached a peak of 1.5 per cent about the turn of the century. The death rate corresponded to Hungary's but the birthrate was higher, around 40 per 1,000. Equally high birthrates were characteristic of Russia where (including Polish territories) the figure reached 50 per 1,000.

Available records also shed light on the increase in average life expectancy. From 1900 to 1910 in Hungary expectancy increased from 36 to 39 years for males, from 38 to 40 years for females. Those over 60 years of age increased from 5 per cent of the total population in 1869 to 8.2 per cent by 1910. In Austria in 1875 average life expectancy was 31 years for males and 34 years for females, and in 1905, 39 and 41 years respectively. Russian records of 1895 put life expectancy at 31 and 33 years, respectively. Presumably in the Balkan countries the span was similar to that in Russia, or slightly shorter.

Though records are deficient for the Balkan countries, it is evident that by the first decade of the twentieth century life expectancy considerably increased in the eastern parts of Europe, and the life span was prolonged to between 30 and 40 years. This advance was not insignificant when compared with conditions in the 1860s and 1870s or with the average European level of 28 years at the turn of the century, if we accept this as valid for East-Central Europe. On the other hand, the persistent lag behind Western Europe is striking. Whereas in East-Central Europe the average life expectancy was between 30 and 40 years, in Western Europe it had moved to around 45 to 50 years, a minimum difference of ten years.

Probably the difference was due to the greater economic and cultural maturity in Western Europe. Actually the difference between the two halves of Europe in economic and cultural maturity was much greater than might be inferred from the data presented. The demographic development of a country, it should be noted, is not directly dependent on its economic maturity and civilization. For instance, in the reduction of mortality an extremely important role is played by the general achievements of civilization and culture which, though produced by the highly developed countries, make themselves felt in less advanced regions, provided these regions are not too backward. The advances in the nineteenth century in the East-Central European countries had produced the minimal development required for them to be receptive to some of mankind's scientific and cultural achievements.

Though progressing at a more moderate rate than in Western Europe, the prolongation of life expectancy had important economic consequences. In addition to the quantitative growth in manpower, the longer life span added qualitative factors: the number of experienced laborers and craftsmen increased considerably, offering possibilities for more intensive work and more modern organization of production. Consequently, the marked demographic tendencies of the nineteenth century, notably population growth and longer life span, were accompanied by a rapid advance in the stage of civilization and a rise in the cultural level, the effect of which in reducing the death rate has been pointed out previously. These decades saw the beginnings of mass education and the rapid spread of literacy. This radical transformation enhanced the efficiency of the available manpower and came to form an increasingly essential precondition for the use of machines.

At the beginning of the nineteenth century 60 per cent of the population of Western Europe was illiterate. By the opening years of the twentieth only a small part of the population could not read and write. In France illiteracy fell to 17 per cent by 1900. In Belgium one-third of the population was still illiterate in 1866; in 1900 only one-fifth. The figure was below 1 per cent in Great Britain and Holland in 1900, while in Germany, Switzerland, and the Scandinavian countries only 1 to 2 per cent of the school-age population was illiterate. Mass education and literacy were not anywhere near as widespread in the countries of East-Central Europe. However, we have to make a clear distinction in that region between the modern Austro-Hungarian educational system as a whole and the Balkans, and also within the Monarchy between Austro-Bohemian and Hungarian education.

The first step in establishing a modern educational system in Austria was as early as December 6, 1774, when Maria Theresa ordered every village with a parochial center to establish village schools *(Trivial-schule)*. After several reorganizations, the real turning-point in modern education was the 1869 decree, which was the beginning of free and compulsory mass education from the ages of 6 to 14. By 1880 the reorganization in the Bohemian and Austrian territories was completed, with about 95–99 per cent of school-age children attending school. In Dalmatia and Bukovina only 67 and 36 per cent respectively attended. As a consequence of these reforms, illiteracy quickly began to disappear. The share of illiterates in the whole of Cisleithania (including the backward eastern territories of Galicia, Bukovina, etc.) fell to one-third in 1880 and to one-fourth in 1900. The western region approached the highest levels elsewhere on the Continent. On these foundations there developed a well-organized, fairly widespread and thorough secondary school system similar to that of Germany's and the university training equaled Western European standards.

The development of the modern Hungarian educational system cannot be separated from the school system of the Hapsburg Empire. The first steps were also taken in the last third of the nineteenth century and the real turning-point took place after the Compromise. The 1868 decree, worked out by J. Eötvös, adopted the modern educational system of Europe based on the principle of free and obligatory education. In 1870 there were more than 14,000 schools and 18,000 teachers, but of the 2.2 million children of school age, only 50 per cent were enrolled in the new school system. In the school year 1900–1901, the number rose to 82 per cent. Although the progress was rather impressive and resulted in a sudden decline of illiteracy (68 per cent in 1869, 33 per cent in 1910), it could not produce a higher cultural level. The educational resources were rather low, as indicated by the fact that in the Hungarian schools every teacher had to deal with twice as many pupils as in Austria. The average number of pupils per teacher approached 80. This was the basis of the secondary education, rather good in content but extremely narrow and selective. At the beginning of the twentieth century only 4 per cent of the students of secondary school age were actually enrolled in secondary school. As for the universities, the 10,000 students in the 1900–1901 school year shows the continuing tradition of high academic achievements. On the other hand, the structure of the university training kept the universities from fulfilling modern needs: 66 per cent of university students studied law or theology, only 8 per cent medicine, and 14 per cent technology.

Thus in parts of the Austro-Hungarian Monarchy the population increase was accompanied by a rather rapid rise in the general cultural level, though at a slower pace than in Western Europe. The situation was quite different, however, in the most backward provinces of the Monarchy, in Russia, or in the Balkans. For instance, in Bosnia-Hercegovina as late as 1908 there were not enough primary schools to admit more than 15 per cent of the school-age population. In Russia—without Poland—70 per cent of the population was illiterate about the turn of the century.

In the Balkans after the birth of independent states there were several proclamations covering the adoption of a modern continental school system. In Rumania the right of free and obligatory elementary education was declared in 1864. But no effective measures were taken to ensure the realization of these rights. Only after the new 1883 and 1893 decrees were some changes instituted in the elementary education. In 1899, 78 per cent of the population over the age of 7 was still illiterate; in 1912, 61 per cent. The secondary school system was established only after the 1898 decree and was still in its infancy prior to World War I.

In Bulgaria the 1878 decree was more a theoretical framework than an efficient measure. At the beginning of the 1880s there were only 2,211 elementary schools in the country. After the regulations of the 1890s were instituted, development was more rapid. In 1898 the school system included almost 5,000 schools with 8,000 teachers and nearly 350,000 pupils. Illiteracy declined from 72 per cent of the population in 1900 to 66 per cent in 1910. The secondary school system remained at a backward stage. At the turn of the century there were only about 140 schools with 30,000 students. The first institution of higher education was opened only in 1888 and reorganized as a university in 1904. Furthermore the size of the student body (400) showed clearly the low commitment to university training. The situation was similar in Serbia where illiteracy remained at an even higher level—79 per cent in 1900.

From these figures it can be seen that the countries of Central Europe did follow the Western tendency though lagging behind, whereas the 70 to 80 per cent illiteracy encountered in Russia and the Balkan countries at the beginning of the twentieth century was far below the level of Western Europe in the early nineteenth century and presented a picture of almost medieval conditions.

In conclusion, the available but incomplete data clearly demonstrate that in the nineteenth century the East-Central European rate of population growth did not differ on the whole from that of Western Europe. However, the components of the increase varied in part. In the area under review the widening gap between the roughly unchanged birthrate and the falling death rate became the principal source of growth, but this difference appeared at dissimilar levels of development. In the West the early nineteenth-century death rate of about 36 per 1,000 sank to a yearly average of 15 to 20 per 1,000 by the beginning of the present century, while in the East the fall was much smaller, the mortality rate remaining about 25 per 1,000. That even in the most backward regions of East-Central Europe the population increase reached the average European level could come about only because high birthrates (approximately 40 to 50 per 1,000) accompanied the relatively high death rates. However, the high birthrate was not the consequence of development; in part, it was due to the low stage of civilization in precapitalistic societies and the almost complete lack of urbanization.

Finally, it was only in a few countries of Central Europe that numerical increase in population went hand in hand with rapid elevation of the cultural level. This did not happen in the Balkans. Here the increase could hardly have created the cultural background which was indispensable for the modernization of the economy.

2 Agrarian Transformation and Modern Agrarian Development

In view of the complex course of social-economic-cultural transformation, the "demographic revolution" of the nineteenth century would not have been possible had it not been preceded or accompanied by a sharp increase in the efficiency and output of agricultural goods. Since agriculture was dominant in the economies of Europe until the end of the eighteenth century, the transformation of the traditional economic structure could not be carried out without a radical change in agriculture. Modern agrarian advancement allowed the release of large masses of the rural population from farm work and their entry into nonagrarian spheres. At the same time agriculture became able to take care of the needs of independently expanding industrial regions. (It is also true that transformation and modernization of agriculture could not have got under way without the markets of these industrial centers.) In this sense the agrarian basis of the industrial revolution, referred to by some writers as the "agrarian revolution," has been recognized as a very important precondition of industrialization. This concept has been widely accepted in the literature on economic history ever since the work of P. Mantoux.

The capitalist agrarian transformation or "agrarian revolution" consisted of two closely interrelated processes: first, the social changes, in the ownership of land (and its legal forms); secondly, the simultaneous technical changes—interacting with one another—which modernized the forms and instruments of farming.

Great Britain was the first European country where these correlated processes took place. In the Introduction, mention has been made of their antecedents in conjunction with the start of the industrial revolution. Feudal ownership of the land had long since ended and so had the associated form of communal farming. As a result of enclosure large amounts of land passed into the hands of capitalist landowners and tenants of large estates. During the eighteenth century agricultural production also underwent radical changes. Three-course rotation farming was widely replaced by modern crop rotation; modern techniques of housing and feeding animals became widely diffused, ending the previously inevitable slaughter of a considerable part of the livestock at the end of each year.

In France and in the western half of the Continent in general (perhaps with the exception of Holland where, as in Great Britain, modern transformation ran its course much earlier), though feudal bondage had already begun to loosen, the real change came with the French revolution. The feudal ownership of land was abolished and most of it was made the civil property of the peasantry which actually owned and farmed the land. Unlike England, in France, Belgium, and the western parts of Germany (and for the most part also in the Scandinavian countries) the smallholder peasant became the bearer of modern capitalist agricultural development. In these countries, too, the major technical changes came much later, culminating chiefly in the middle of the nineteenth century. From this time the system of modern crop rotation gained widespread acceptance in the Western European countries; at the same time canalization and drainage, soil amelioration, and improved techniques of farming led to a rapid increase in productivity.

Intertwined with the concurrent beginnings of the industrial revolution, these processes were among the radical changes which affected every sector of the economy. The agricultural revolution of Western Europe was nevertheless unable to meet the food demands created by the exceedingly rapid industrialization of the most progressive Western countries. Despite its quick transformation and development, agriculture gradually diminished in importance, forfeiting its dominant role by the middle of the nineteenth century. In Western Europe, which had been compelled to import agricultural products from the time when handicraft industry began to flourish, regular imports became still more indispensable.

It was these broadened Western European markets and the Western agrarian revolution which exerted decisive influence on the backward agrarian countries in the eastern half of the Continent. This was the challenge which elicited response from the socio-economic systems of East-Central Europe, which had been unable by themselves to move from the stagnation of traditional economy. Slowly and painfully they now started on the course of capitalist transformation. By the middle of the nineteenth century the development of Western Europe provided a principal impetus to the modern agrarian transformation of East-Central Europe.

The crisis in the socio-economic systems of East-Central Europe became steadily more acute because of the delay in finding solutions. There were some attempts at reform in the first half of the nineteenth century, but only inconsistent and partial measures were possible because of the power of the conservative, privileged class of landowners. From the end of the eighteenth century to the second third of the nineteenth century, starting in the western areas of the region and spreading eastward, serfdom and other traditional institutions were abolished and feudal ownership of property was replaced by bourgeois ownership through partial reforms, revolutions, revolts, and general regulations.

In the western (Austrian and Bohemian) provinces of the Hapsburg Empire the emancipation of serfs and the elimination of the related feudal ownership took place in connection with the revolutionary events of 1848. Indeed, the decrees and orders issued by Maria Theresa and especially those signed by Joseph II were an integral part of the antecedents of these events.

Maria Theresa's urbarium in 1767 was intended to regulate the increasingly unlimited exaction of statute labor by landlords. At this time, in accordance with feudal conditions, the whole of the estate was in principle the property of the landlord; only about 40 per cent was regarded as domanial, that is to say, land farmed under the management of the landlord. The Patent of 1769, which prohibited the reduction of land held by the peasantry, was grossly violated and the various decrees of the 1770s restricting villein services also failed to effect any change in the situation of manorial tenants. However, the Patent of Joseph II, which provided for the emancipation of serfs, abolished personal dependence and ensured the right and possibility of free migration and the liberty to choose one's place of abode and profession. The inheritance of peasant holdings by direct lawful intestate succession and the introduction of a uniform land tax may be regarded as steps leading to the civil ownership of land. However, the last decrees issued by Joseph II in 1789 providing for the complete abolition of serfdom and the payment of all villein services in money were not executed.

In the first half of the nineteenth century corvée was not too exacting in most of the Austrian provinces; the inflicted burden of payment in products and money weighed more heavily on the serfs. Notwithstanding the numerous feudal services, however, the husbandry released from personal bondage and actually owning about two-thirds of the land gave evidence of substantial progress toward capitalism. The spread of capitalist conditions, coupled with the development of the means and methods of production, is reflected in the strong differentiation among the peasantry itself, in the rapidly growing number of landless cotters and serfs with dwarf holdings.

According to some estimates, agricultural production in the Austrian provinces increased by approximately 70 per cent between 1789 and 1847. Characterized, however, by the domination of the traditional three-course rotation system with relatively little livestock, poor yields (4.5 fold), and traditional structure of production, the level of agriculture could not be said to have been high. It was mainly the relatively slow improvement of agricultural production which repeatedly directed attention in the 1830s and 1840s to the desirability of completely abolishing serfdom, at least in the form of obligatory manumission compensation. So it was natural that the emancipation of the serfs and the indemnity of statute labor were among the most urgent targets of the revolution of 1848. After the revolution—when the peasants had actually ceased to render villein services—resolutions at assemblies of various Austrian and Bohemian provinces brought only half-measures, until at last on September 7, 1848, a bill was carried providing for the final emancipation of serfs. This law abolished serfdom as well as all the connected rights and obligations. For the most part it was not only the land that had earlier been held by tenants in return for fixed payment or other stated nonmilitary services (socage) which passed to the ownership of the peasants, but also the manorial estates which were in the possession of the serfs at the time of the emancipation. However, neither cotters nor agricultural laborers were allotted any land. The law of the emancipation of serfs ordained manumission compensation, the details of which were laid down in 1849. Certain earlier services were cancelled without any compensation, while compensation was to be paid for the services due the landlord as owner of the tenure held in socage. This compensation was paid partly by the state and partly by the peasant, but the amount paid by the peasant was not to exceed 40 per cent of the cadastral value of the acquired land.

Thus by the end of the nineteenth century a relatively strong, but not absolutely dominating, system of large estates emerged or remained valid in Austria and Bohemia (Table 2-1).

During the second period of serfdom established and consolidated in Hungary from the sixteenth century, the principal tendency was a steady increase in manorial land and the implied statute labor. The position of the Hungarian serfs was first regulated by Maria Theresa's urbarium providing protection against the attempts of landlords to lay excessive claim to manorial services and limiting statute labor. However, the results were only partial and rather transient. Moreover, since the most important decrees of Joseph II concerning serfdom applied to Hungary only in part, the system of personal bondage was still largely in force there in the first half of the nineteenth century.

At this time a dual tendency may be observed in Hungary. On the one hand, the landlords persisted in their powerful efforts to extend their manorial properties by diverse legal and illegal means, and to increase villein services in order to secure the necessary manpower. On the other hand, they soon found that the boom in wheat, and later in wool, could only be partially exploited owing to the low productivity of statute labor. Thus, the idea of abolishing feudal conditions came not only from the peasantry but also from some of the landlords who were conscious of the need for reform and sought an expedient alternative to the existing situation. The solution still appeared to be the old method of exacting increased villein services, but after the 1830s the Diet of nobles also began to look into the possibilities of partial compensation for socage service. Manumission compensation was, however, not made

Table 2-1.   Land Distribution in Austria and Bohemia,
Late Nineteenth Century*

Size of Holdings (in hectares)	Per Cent of Farms		Per Cent of Land Area	
	Austria	Bohemia	Austria	Bohemia
0–5	58.0	71.6	5.9	14.7
5–50	39.2	27.5	40.9	49.0
50–100	1.7	0.4	7.2	3.5
over 100	1.2	0.5	46.8	32.8

*Mostly not private property.
Source: Based on *Ergebnisse der landwirtschaftlichen Betriebszahlung vom 3. juni 1902. Österreichische Statistik LXXXIII.*

compulsory, and only an insignificant number of Hungarian serfs could avail themselves of the possibility of free compensation. It was the revolutions of 1848 which rescued the issue of Hungarian serfdom from the stagnation created by the deadlock of negotiations and contradictions. On March 18, 1848, the bill providing for the emancipation of serfs was passed by the Diet, and the law abolishing villein bondage and laying down the right of compensation was sanctioned in April.

The law having made an end to villein socage, the land formerly worked by statute labor passed into the ownership of the peasantry. However, the earlier manorial estates remained the property of the former landlords. Therefore, the emancipation of the serfs was carried out while retaining the system of large estates. According to not fully reliable estimates, 53 per cent of the land remained in the hands of the big landowners. After the great adjustment a considerable number of peasants were still without land or acquired holdings of insignificant size. In addition to this favorable solution for the big landowners, many more or less important remnants of feudal legal relations were also salvaged and preserved. Thus, in Hungary too, capitalist agrarian development was carried out primarily for the benefit of the large estates. The relation of large estates and peasant farms in Hungarian agriculture at the close of the nineteenth century is shown in Table 2-2.

In developments beginning with the sixteenth and seventeenth centuries in the course of which the farms of Eastern Europe became the grain suppliers of the advancing, urbanizing countries of Western Europe, an outstanding role was assumed by Polish areas where the advantage of sea transport offered more favorable conditions for export. Consequently the development of Polish agriculture was more

Table 2-2. Land Distribution in Hungary, 1895

Size of Holdings (in cadastral holds) (1 hold = 0.57 hectares)	Per Cent of Farms	Per Cent of Land Area
0–5	53.6	5.8
5–100	45.4	46.5
100–1,000	0.8	15.4
over 1,000	0.2	32.3

Source: Based on Hungarian agricultural statistics of 1895.

rapid, especially in the nineteenth century when the demand for agricultural goods was enhanced by the expanding industrial revolution in Western Europe. The growth of agricultural production and the increase in livestock were based mainly on manorial farms, which were enlarged again and again by the addition of new stretches of land after 1807 when the peasants gained personal liberty. As suggested by certain estimates, 40 per cent of peasant holdings passed, through various procedures, into the hands of big landowners in the period from 1816 to 1846, and after further confiscations barely 16 per cent of the arable land was in the possession of peasants in the 1860s.

The expansion of manorial farms increased the demand of the large estates for statute labor, which soon proved to be inadequate both in quantity and quality. The landlords contrived to evolve a peculiar mixture of wage work and labor service. As the possibilities for large-scale export raised commodity production and furthered a money economy, in addition to statute labor, payment in money was extensively practiced. According to certain records, 40 per cent of peasant farmers received money payments in the 1850s. However, this did not overcome the contradiction which existed because of feudal bondage and which grew particularly acute, especially after 1848, with the emancipation of serfs in neighboring Prussia as well as in the Polish parts belonging to Austria. The problem was aggravated by the very strong differentiation among the Polish peasantry even under the old conditions, when large numbers of landless peasants joined in the agrarian struggle not only for the abolition of diverse services but also for the redistribution of land by carving up the large estates.

After the emancipation of serfs in Russia in 1861 the situation worsened, all the more so as the fight for the elimination of feudal conditions was coupled with a fight for national independence in Poland. Although the leaders of the war of independence which broke out in 1863 were far from agreement concerning the radical elimination of feudalism, the decree issued on January 22, 1863, allotted the land to the peasants, abolished all connected services and held out the prospect of compensation by the state to the former owners. This project was to bring full satisfaction to peasants who possessed land, but gave little to the landless cotters. Owing to the inner conflicts of the landowners who headed the revolt, the execution of the reform proceeded very slowly and, strangely enough, it was realized only by the decree of 1864, issued by the Russian Czar who put down the Polish revolt. (Also included in this conscious endeavor to stir up discord between the Polish nobility and peasantry was the fact that a reform of serfdom had been enacted in Russia in 1861. Incidentally, this reform, the detailed treatment of which lies outside the scope of our present work, was of a still more moderate nature and left nearly two-thirds of the land in the hands of the big landowners.)

This decree of 1864 abolished all villein services, passed the land held by peasants into their possession, and declared that the lands confiscated since the year 1846 were subject to restoration upon the rightful claimant's demand, which meant approximately a million hectares of land to the peasants. Moreover, all the prerogatives of the landowners were annulled without any compensation. Though some favors were shown to the landlords in the execution of the decree, the emancipation of the Polish serfs was nevertheless quite radical: 695,000 families of feudal tenants acquired approximately 4.4 million hectares of land, 30 per cent of the plots being under 2 hectares, 40 per cent between 2 and 9 hectares, and 30 per cent over 9 hectares.

In the principalities of what was later Rumania, most of which remained under Turkish rule until the close of the eighteenth century, the second stage of serfdom was instituted at a relatively late date. Manorial farming had gathered strength as early as the seventeenth century, but the measures taken in conjunction with the process, notably confiscation of land, the increase of statute labor, and the exaction of other services, did not become apparent before the second half of the eighteenth century. As the foreign grain markets became accessible owing to the improvement of transportation to the Rumanian boyars and landowners, they strove to enlarge their farms by depriving peasants of their holdings and demanding increased villein services. Statute labor, though fixed at twelve days yearly in 1775, may have been exceeded in practice, but at the beginning of the nineteenth century it was raised to 43 days a year in some decrees. In practice this was so far exceeded that in 1831–32 when the so-called Reglement Organique in effect totaled the various labor dues as 68 days, it curbed rather than extended the prevailing practice. However, the Reglement Organique—deemed by some writers to have been the codification of the second serfdom—

plunged the peasantry into an exceedingly adverse position by further restricting the right of free migration and by providing latent possibilities for augmenting the dimensions of manorial estates.

According to the statute, the peasants were entitled to hold two-thirds of the landlord's estate with only one-third remaining under the landowner's management, but this decree was violated more often than not. The demand for villein services by landowners and their efforts to add land to the manor under their own management increased along with the possibilities for favorable marketing of their products. After the Peace of Adrianople in 1829—which lifted the earlier Turkish restrictions on trade in the principalities of later Rumania—grain exports rose rapidly. In the period between 1831 and 1877 the grain exports of the principalities more than doubled, while the area of land sown with grain greatly increased.

It is important to note, however, that the economic expansion did not alter the position of the peasantry, and not surprisingly, the mid-nineteenth century was marked by numerous peasant movements and much antagonism between the serfs and the landlords.

Under the impact of the revolutionary events of 1848, the issue of emancipation of the serfs was widely raised, particularly in the more economically advanced region of Wallachia. But the committee formed to investigate the question did not get beyond conferences and proposals.

In the 1850s the attention of the Great Powers interested in the international position of the Rumanian principalities was drawn to the grave situation of the peasantry and the anachronistic existence of serfdom. The Paris Convention of 1859, which regularized the status of the principalities, decreed the abolition of serfdom in Clause 46. However, the question was whether the peasants were to be left with or without land. The landowners in power naturally pressed for the latter solution, and the long-drawn-out negotiations—in the course of which church lands were secularized by the government—finally led to the elaboration of the new agrarian law of 1864. According to this law the ancient feudal services ceased and the peasants became the owners of the land they held and of the land allotted by the law. Two-thirds of the landowners' estates were to be handed over to the peasants as property entailed for thirty years. The landowners were to be compensated in bonds the total value of which corresponded to fifteen times that of the formerly rendered services.

The law having been put into operation, 467,840 peasant families obtained 1.8 million hectares of land, of which 1.2 million hectares had been the property of boyars and 0.6 million hectares had been owned by the state. This implied that the big landowners remained in possession of approximately 60 per cent of the land, while the peasants were allotted straggling plots with poor soil. By abolishing serfdom while leaving the bulk of the landed estates in the hands of the big landowners, thereby creating an extremely unfavorable property structure as demonstrated in Table 2-3, the Rumanian agrarian reform was the starting point of capitalism in agriculture.

Thus the development of capitalist agriculture which took place in Rumania chiefly under the leadership of the commodity-producing large estates followed the pattern in the countries east of the Elbe instead of displaying any similarity to that in the Balkan countries.

While there was some relationship between the fight for the abolition of feudal conditions and the struggle for national independence in Poland and Hungary, the two processes completely coincided in Serbia and Bulgaria. Here feudalism was definitely a Turkish institution. Turkish feudalism remained largely unchanged by time, and in the Balkans the commodity-producing large estates, characteristic of the conditions prevailing in the second edition of serfdom, failed to take shape. There was merciless feudal exploitation coupled with the most primitive productive forces.

The liquidation of ancient Turkish feudalism began in the early eighteenth century. The so-called *chiflik* estates were the first to be wound up; the other pillar of the Turkish system of ownership, the *spahi*

Table 2-3. Land Distribution in Rumania, 1897

Size of Holdings (in hectares)	Per Cent of Holdings	Per Cent of Land Area
0–5	77.2	25.9
5–10	18.2	14.7
10–100	4.0	11.1
over 100	0.6	48.3

Source: J. Evans, *Agrarian Revolution in Rumania,* Cambridge, 1924, p. 76.

estates, survived much longer. In Serbia the dissolution of Turkish feudalism took place for the most part between 1815 and 1839. The laws of Hatti Sherif Gülhana, which came into force in 1839 and provided for the protection of Christian property, put the land into the possession of the peasants not only in fact but also legally. No direct compensation was paid for the land taken from the Turkish landowners although part of the money paid by Serbia to Turkey was compensation for the confiscated land. The situation differed slightly in the districts joined to Serbia after 1878, following the Congress of Berlin. In these parts Turkish feudalism had remained in force until the Congress of Berlin, and the Turkish law issued in 1858 regulated the ownership of land in this spirit. After 1878 the Turkish landowners had to be indemnified here too for the expropriated land, and this was also effected through the Serbian state. Hence in Serbia the abolition of Turkish feudalism was carried out directly in favor of the Serbian peasantry, and the developing capitalist agrarian structure was marked by the full domination of peasant farmers.

Although Turkish rule lasted much longer in Bulgaria, the breakdown of obsolete Turkish feudalism nevertheless started here too in the 1830s and 1840s. The abolition of the spahi system of landownership was initiated by the Turkish state itself. Apart from those in the western region of Bulgaria, most of the spahi estates passed into the possession of the Turkish state in the 1840s. The wide strata of peasantry thus formed, subject to the state alone, paid their dues to the treasury, were mostly exempt from statute labor, but could not regard their tenure as their own property. However, it was only for a short time that the new order promoted agrarian production and relieved the hard lot of the peasantry. The inner crisis of the Turkish state created a grave financial situation which the government tried to overcome by imposing new taxes. The burden of taxation weighed ever more oppressively on the peasant smallholders who were unable to meet their obligations. By the 1870s a new, severe inner tension made itself felt, induced by the obsolete socio-economic conditions and the problems of subjection by the Turks. In 1878, when, as a result of the Russo-Turkish Wars, not only Turkish landowners but also the majority of Turkish peasants fled from the country, the Bulgarian peasants were freed from the vestiges of feudal conditions and could easily acquire new plots of land. Furthermore, in the areas where the Turkish landowners did not leave their estates, the new Bulgarian state compelled them to hand their landed properties over to the Bulgarian peasants. Thus the large Turkish feudal estates ceased to exist in the 1880s and most of the land passed into peasant ownership, so that in Bulgaria agrarian capitalist development rested on a base of smallholdings (Table 2-4).

In the first half of the nineteenth century, in its early stage, capitalist agrarian development clashed with medieval traditional institutions, especially serfdom, and with the medieval legal system. This, together with other factors, primarily the influence of events in Western Europe, led to the emancipation of serfs by the latter part of the nineteenth century. By this time the feudal institutions which formed the strongest obstacles to modern capitalist development had been demolished by the revolutionary movements, revolts, and reforms in East-Central Europe. Although the remnants of feudalism proved to be exceedingly tenacious in most countries and continued to restrict progress, the establishment of modern capitalist agriculture was nevertheless made possible.

While the emancipation of serfs and the concomitant institutional and legal changes created the fundamental internal preconditions of transformation in every country of East-Central Europe, capitalist agrarian transformation did not take place promptly and automatically. Also required were the broadening of markets and the consequent activation of economic incentives to stimulate agriculture. With rare exceptions, expanding local markets could be found only in Austrian and Bohemian areas which were in the process of vigorous industrialization and urbanization. As pointed out before, in most of the East-Central European countries the impetus came from the swift widening and intensification of Western European commercial activities.

Table 2-4. Land Distribution in Bulgaria, 1897

Size of Holdings (in hectares)	Per Cent of Farms	Per Cent of Land Area
0–10	87.3	49.0
10–100	12.6	44.5
over 100	0.1	6.5

Source: Z. Natan, *Stopanska istoria na Bulgaria* (The economic history of Bulgaria), Sofia, 1957.

As the industrial revolution of Western Europe advanced and ran its course, it furnished an unprecedentedly powerful impulse to agricultural production in Eastern Europe by the promise of markets. But in its old backward condition Eastern European agriculture was unable to take advantage of these possibilities. As a matter of fact, supplies for export had earlier been provided mainly by cheaper statute labor and very low domestic consumption. The process of discarding the medieval handicraft character of farming and becoming an "industry" based on modern techniques could not progress within the framework of the petrified system of serfdom. In these agrarian countries no increase of agricultural productivity came about until the middle or latter part of the nineteenth century. It was then that the system of wage work gained ascendancy, the use of machines was initiated, and the ancient feudal organization of work was replaced by new forms of capitalist management.

While following a similar course throughout the eastern regions of Europe, the processes were not identical from country to country. The different preconditions in the area produced two main types of capitalist agrarian development—with numerous regional variations.

One variant, that typical of the Hapsburg Empire (the Austro-Hungarian Monarchy), the Russian Empire, and Rumania, was marked by the gradual transformation of former feudal manorial estates into capitalist enterprises. As pointed out before, in these countries large masses of the liberated peasantry were allotted no land, 50 per cent were given dwarf holdings, while the latifundia of the big landowners remained practically untouched. However, after the emancipation of serfs, those farms which had previously pursued extensive commodity production exhibited many elements of capitalism and were gradually transformed from estates run with statute labor into capitalist enterprises based on wage work. This transformation (termed agrarian advancement, evolving from *Gutswirtschaft*) has been defined in the Marxist lierature—after Lenin—as the Prussian pattern of agrarian development. It took place in the second half of the nineteenth century.

The essential differences existing between certain countries of the region do not contradict the general validity of the Prussian pattern in characterizing agrarian development in this area. In Russia, for example, as compared with the Hapsburg Monarchy, there was more significant obstruction of capitalist development of the large estates, so that real progress could not take place even as late as the end of the nineteenth century. On the other hand, there was also a great difference between the western and eastern parts of the Hapsburg Empire. In the Austrian and Bohemian areas where industrialization was accelerated by the aid of eighteenth-century mercantile protectionism, owing to a strong handicraft industry and speedier, more extensive industrial revolution, the large estates advanced more rapidly toward capitalism. Moreover, in addition to the large estates, peasant farmers also had much better chances, and peasant farming was much more vigorous and successful than in Hungary, Russia, or Rumania. In some parts of Austria, chiefly in the Tyrol, free peasant development of the Western type also occurred. Thus we see that regional peculiarities have to be taken into account. It is beyond the scope of the present work to go into these special features and types of development. Our purpose is merely to present a general picture of the progress of capitalist development and of the chief tendencies.

In the second half of the nineteenth century the traditional forms of the organization of work gradually disappeared—sometimes at a rapid rate, sometimes more slowly—yielding to modern capitalist forms. In most countries of East-Central Europe the development of these processes was facilitated by the earlier disappearance of rural communes, collective forms of using the land, the periodic redistribution of land, and the traditional framework of organization, from compulsory rotation to collective peasant labor. In most parts of the Hapsburg Empire the decrees of Maria Theresa and Joseph II put an end to the activities of land communes, which were, in fact, already in a process of disintegration as early as the last third of the eighteenth century.

The discontinuance of the redistribution of land, the protection of permanent villein tenures, the subsequent introduction of civil ownership of land, as well as the elements of modern taxation, wiped out the rural communes not only in Austria, Bohemia, and Moravia, but at the beginning of the nineteenth century also in the more backward regions of the Monarchy. In Bukovina, for example, numerous half-measures and reforms were finally followed in 1819 by a decree which abolished community of land. The situation was very similar in the Polish Kingdom where communal land shrank to negligible importance by the time the serfs were emancipated, amounting to no more than about 15 per cent of the land held by peasants. The Polish situation was almost unique in the Slav areas where land communes (obshchina, mir, za-druga, etc.) actually flourished as late as the nineteenth century. The surviving rural communes in the Slav areas constituted a serious obstacle to the spread of modern capitalist reorganization of work. Whether the precapitalistic forms of rural communes disappeared wholly or partially or survived generally, the capitalist development finally created the corresponding forms of land ownership.

But the form of landed property with which the incipient capitalist mode of production is confronted does not suit it. It first creates for itself the form required by subordinating agriculture to capital. It thus transforms feudal landed property, clan property, small-peasant property in mark communes—no matter how divergent the juristic forms may be—into the economic form corresponding to the requirements of this mode of production.[1]

Organization of work in forms suitable for capitalist methods of production and "agriculture subordinated to capital" could of course be evolved only gradually. Even villein services, which had constituted the basis of farming, could not be dispensed with abruptly, but temporary forms were devised and their remnants were integrated into the new system. After the emancipation of serfs the masses of landless peasants furnished an abundant labor supply. But for periods of varying length, depending on the general level of economic advancement, there was a more or less serious lack of capital required for the employment of hired labor.

The required capital had to cover not only the wages fund but also the landowners' purchases of equipment after the sudden loss of villein services performed by the serfs with their own implements. The indigent peasantry, free to trade their labor and unable to procure another livelihood (particularly in regions where industry could absorb only an insignificant fraction of them), along with the large estates deprived of statute labor but incapable of changing over to wage work, evolved the so-called *otrabotochnaia sistema (otrabotka)*—the system of labor service. In this form of management the peasants either farmed the

---

[1] Karl Marx, *Capital,* Vol. III, Moscow, 1966 edition, p. 617.

owner's land with their own tools and their own draught animals (if they possessed any), or, in the height of seasonal work, they did the harvesting, hoeing, and the like in return for loans, the allotment of plots for share-farming, and numerous other preliminary allocations.

These typical forms of transition from statute labor to capitalist wage work prevailed for a long time in Rumania and, of course, in Russia; but for briefer periods and temporarily they played an important role in Hungary—between the War of Independence of 1848 and the Compromise of 1867—as well as in nearly all the other countries of East-Central Europe.

In the 1880s the labor-service system prevailed in seventeen of the forty-seven European provinces of Russia. In Hungary some sources refer to the 1850s and 1860s as the time when *Ledolgozás* (labor service) was predominant; however, this appraisal appears to be exaggerated and without proper foundation. There is evidence of the labor service system having been applied extensively in the category of medium-sized farms and as a complementary method in the production of hoed plants on large estates. In view of the dimensions of medium-sized farms and the widespread cultivation of hoed plants, the area farmed under the labor service system would seem to be more accurately estimated at about one quarter of the arable land. After 1867 the percentage rapidly decreased. On the large estates this transitory system was almost completely superseded, and subsequently it was found to have survived only as a characteristic of undeveloped medium-sized farms.

In Rumania, on the other hand, transitory forms were much more significant. At the close of the nineteenth century Rumanian villages presented a strange mixture of the past and the present.

The agrarian system fell into a peculiar compound of serfdom and capitalism; from it landlords and their tenants secured all the advantages of both, while the peasants were saddled with all the burdens of both. From serfdom the landlords had all the facilities of servile labour without any of the feudal obligations towards it; while from capitalism they had the freedom to bargain with labour without the restraint of a free labour market. The peasants, however, were subjected to servile labour without its counterpart in land rights; and from capitalism they had all the trials of wage earners without being really free to trade their labours where they willed.[2]

[2] D. Mitrany, *The Land and the Peasant in Rumania,* Oxford, 1930, p. 80.

Many of these unfortunate Rumanian peasants ran into heavy debts which they paid off by installments of labor services in the typical form of the old system. Often they were compelled to render services over periods of two or three years to clear off their liabilities.

Thus these elements of transition persisted rather extensively in certain countries as late as the end of the nineteenth century. But even in these countries they did not hinder the acceptance and widening use of wage labor, which appeared as the most important element of modern capitalist organization of work. In the Austro-Hungarian Monarchy the adoption of wage labor may have been much quicker and less hampered.

The establishment of new capitalist economy, and the gradual elimination of the transitory forms, may have depended in the first place on the investment of capital. In East-Central Europe domestic economic development provided no possibilities for raising the necessary capital through domestic saving. In the most advanced countries of Western Europe, especially in Great Britain but partly also in Holland, such large sums of capital were accumulated by some businessmen as to make the capitalist tenants of large farms into central figures in the development of modern capitalist agriculture. They paid rent to the landlord and completely transformed all the methods of farming with huge investments. In Great Britain at the beginning of the present century 88 per cent of farms were leased to tenants, and about 85 to 87 per cent of the land was farmed by tenants. In Holland approximately half of the cultivated land was in the hands of leaseholders.

In most of the Western countries of the Continent leasing could not play such a prominent role. The required capital could not be obtained in such amounts from the accumulated wealth of businessmen. Therefore, the role of the capitalist tenant was in general filled by the much more impersonal bank which, while pooling the capital made available by the economy, provided agriculture with capital on mortgage. The rapid acceptance and extensive use of the system of mortgage loans became one of the dominant features of modern agrarian development in nineteenth-century Europe.

In East-Central Europe—similarly in this respect to conditions in the western half of the Continent—leasing did play a certain role, but it was not the principal line of capitalist development. Not infrequently it was a capitalist leaseholder, and not the former feudal landlord himself, who changed over gradually to the new methods of farm management. However, in most cases, landowners did not let all of their property but only a part of it in order to use the rent they collected for the economic development of the land farmed by themselves. In the second half of the nineteenth century in Hungary of the medium-size estates from 500 to 1,000 cadastral hold (1 cadastral hold = 0.57 hectare) the entire property was leased in 25 per cent of the cases, a part of the property in 22.5 per cent. In the category of large estates of over 1,000 cadastral hold, the entire property was leased to tenants in 22 per cent of the cases, while in another 18.6 per cent only a part of the property was let. In all, slightly less than one-fifth of the total of Hungarian landed property was farmed by leaseholders.

A smaller role was played by tenure of land in other countries of Eastern Europe. In the eastern regions of Germany, even in Mecklenburg where leasing out land was the most customary, 70 per cent of the estates of over 200 hectares were farmed by their owners. In Russia the role of leaseholders remained almost negligible, although after the reform until the mid-1880s in the European provinces the proportion of rented land increased by 25 per cent; in the belt of rich black soil by 50 per cent.

Among the countries which followed the Prussian-Russian pattern of agrarian development a peculiar situation may be noted in Rumania in the farming of rented land. Around the turn of the century, 60 per cent of the farms of more than 100 hectares—a total of 2.3 million hectares—were farmed by tenants. In the largest properties of over 3,000 hectares, 73 per cent of the land was in the hands of leaseholders. In Rumania lease farming differed widely from the European pattern of tenancy as well as from the type familiar in East-Central Europe. The bulk of the land was not leased by big businessmen intending to introduce modern, large-scale capitalist farming. Owing to the general lag of capitalist development, no commercial or other capitalist strata emerged which had the means and were willing to go in for capitalist farming on a large scale. On the other hand, landowners were badly in need of capital for modernization. A considerable part of their land could not be managed with wage work, and their own equipment and machines. The Rumanian tenant system was a transition economy of extensive cultivation. In most instances the landowner let his land or a considerable part of it, but the speculator or tenant did not start to farm it himself. Instead he sublet it to peasants on usurious terms. An investigation of twenty large estates about the turn of the century revealed the astonishing fact that nearly half of the land was leased to peasants. This was partly typical of the turn of events in Russia, too. Hence in Rumania there was no extensive capitalist tenant farming, but the peculiar forms of transition noted above survived in wide circles.

In accordance with Continental practice, mortgage credit played a much more important role in East-Central Europe than did the leasing system. The credit activities of the banks became most decisive in Central European regions—in the countries of the Austro-Hungarian Monarchy. In Austria (including the Bohemian parts), as well as in Hungary, mortgage loans increased rapidly in the second half of the nineteenth century. In Austria mortgage credits amounted in 1858 to 2.2 billion crowns, in 1889 to 7.2 billion, and in 1907 to 13.4 billion. During the same period in Hungary mortgage credits totaled 0.1 billion crowns in 1858, 0.9 billion in 1889, and 2.8 billion in 1907. About 30 per cent of mortgage loans were raised on houses, about 70 per cent on land.

The more than sixfold increase in Austrian mortgage credits in half a century—and the even greater increase in Hungary of more than threefold just in the years around the turn of the century—clearly demonstrates the significance of bank credit in financing agriculture. It becomes even clearer when the amount of credits is compared to the value of land. In the early years of the present century the total amount of the bank loans granted on landed property was 33 to 40 per cent of the value of arable land in Hungary. In Austria the ratio was still higher.

The supply of funds to agriculture was partly solved, even if the peasant farmers did not profit from the new arrangements in equal measure. At any rate, the big landowners acquired the capital necessary to modernize their farms. However, this was not so in Rumania. Here, owing to the lower level of capital accumulation and banking activities, the capital made available to agriculture was incomparably smaller. In Rumania around the turn of the century, mortgage loans amounted to approximately one-tenth of the value of land in private ownership. In 1913 total mortgage credit was 450 million lei. Of this about 60 per cent was given by banks.

These data confirm our earlier observations from another aspect:

disadvantageous conditions for changing over to capitalist economy and the unfavorable supply of capital greatly contributed to the survival of traditional institutions, to the invariably prominent role of obschina, and to the vigorous and lasting domination of transitory forms such as the labor service system and peasant tenancy.

Nonetheless, in the countries of this region the establishment of agriculture on a modern capitalist basis finally came about in varying measure and at dissimilar levels in the decades prior to the First World War by the aid of home saving, mortgage loans, and to a lesser degree by the complementary support of capitalist leasing. Two indicators of this process were the steadily increasing use of hired labor and the installation of machines.

Following the War of Independence of 1848 progress was much more rapid in Hungary. Since 64 per cent of the serfs were emancipated either without being allotted any land or getting only strips of land and the division of land did not undergo any change during the more than half a century until the outbreak of World War I, acquisition of holdings by the landless, emancipated peasants was a rare exception. In the second half of the nineteenth century 1.1 million families became wage workers. In the period following the Compromise, on the big estates which were being granted large bank credits and Austrian loans, hired labor increased rapidly. This development was further promoted by extensive public works, regulation of waterways, and the building of roads and railways where members of the agrarian population found employment as laborers. Around the turn of the century the number of servants and agrarian laborers employed on large estates increased more rapidly than did the population itself. Whereas in the half century between 1850 and 1900 population growth was 45 per cent, the number of agricultural wage workers increased by 73 per cent. By 1900—counting only wage earners—they numbered 1.9 million (in 1890 the figure was 1.7 million). Thus in the second half of the nineteenth century not only the landless peasants but also other strata of the population, evidently some of those with dwarf holdings, became agricultural laborers. Finally, 39 per cent of the gainfully occupied agrarian population were wage workers in Hungary.

In Austria and Bohemia a larger proportion of the landless peasantry was absorbed by industry, but here too the landless who remained in farming soon became wage workers. The peasants who did not own land

and could not find employment in industry turned to farm labor in the second half of the nineteenth century. In Austria (in Austrian territory alone) 29.5 per cent of the agrarian population, and in Bohemia 36 per cent, found a livelihood as wage workers in 1900.

As pointed out before, the spread of hired labor, the central factor in the development of modern capitalist organization of work, was closely connected with the acquisition of farming equipment by the landowners. Thus, in 1863 hardly any farm machines were used in Hungary. At the time of the first comprehensive statistical survey, 194 steam engines (totaling 1,600 horsepower) were found in Hungarian agriculture. Less than a decade later, by 1871, the number was nearly 3,000 (with a total capacity of 30,800 h.p.), including 7 steam ploughs, 2,416 threshing machines, and 504 other diverse kinds of power-driven machines. The number of horse-drawn sowing machines approached 7,000; the number of threshers working by horses was over 3,000. There were another 1,800 horse-drawn harvesting and mowing machines.

By 1895, at the next agricultural census and the last until the First World War, the number of steam ploughs had jumped from 7 to 159, steam-operated threshing machines 3.5 times (to 8,920), while other steam-driven machines had nearly doubled (982). Horse-drawn sowing machines had increased nearly sevenfold (over 44,000); threshers working by horses 1.5 times (to approximately 47,000). Horse-drawn harvesting and mowing machines increased nearly threefold (to about 5,000). Only partial records are available concerning the progress in the early years of the present century. These reveal that on the eve of World War I the number of steam-operated threshing machines reached 20,000, so that 90 per cent of the threshing was done with steam engines.

The rapid growth of machine capacity may be inferred also from the increase of agricultural machine imports in the first decade of the century to more than double the figure recorded in the above-mentioned statistics of 1895. When one takes into consideration that home production also displayed a marked upswing in this period, the increase in agricultural machine capacity between 1895 and 1913 may reasonably be put at double or more than double.

In Russia there was a sixfold increase in agricultural machine imports from 1869 to 1872 and from 1893 to 1896. Simultaneously, home production of agricultural machines also made headway. In 1862 agricultural machines were produced in only 52 factories; by 1879 such machinery was made in as many as 340 factories. Between 1871 and 1901 the number of steam engines actually increased from 1,351 to 12,091. In Rumania 55 steam ploughs, 4,339 traction engines, and 4,585 threshing machines were in operation at the beginning of the present century. In addition, about 12,500 horse-drawn sowing machines indicated the start of mechanization. The comparison of Hungary and Rumania with France and Germany (Table 2-5) illustrates the difference in the level of mechanization between Eastern and Western Europe.

The widening use of hired labor and machines provides incontrovertible evidence of the transformation of large estates, which formerly relied on statute labor, into capitalist farms.

Agrarian development in the Balkans differed considerably from the pattern of agricultural capitalist transformation in Central Europe (the Prussian variant). The main reason for the dissimilarity was the radical difference in the way the emancipation of the serfs had been realized. In Southern Slav regions, as explained before, feudal ownership of land was identical with the military-feudal system of the occupying Turkish power, and liberation from the Turkish rule was followed by the complete collapse of the ancient feudal estates. In the struggle of the Balkan states for independence, the peasants became the owners

Table 2-5. The Level of Agricultural Mechanization c.1900

Country	Steam Ploughs		Steam Threshing Machines		Steam Sowing Machines	
	No. of ploughs	Area per plough (in thousand hectares)	Threshers (in thousands)	Area per thresher (in hectares)	Sowers (in thousands)	Area per sower (in hectares)
Hungary	159	50.54	8.9	945	44	153
Rumania	55	99.6	4.6	1,194	12.5	437
France	—	—	29.8	156	52.4	492
Germany	1,696	16.9	25.9	111	169.5	170

Source: Michael Serbian, *Rumäniens Agrarverhaltnisse,* Berlin, 1913, p. 10, and miscellaneous national agricultural statistics. The figures for Hungary and Germany are from 1895, those for Rumania from 1905, those for France from 1892, referring to grain-producing areas.

of all the land. Therefore, in the 1860s and 1870s the domination of peasant farming was the most characteristic trait in these countries. As stated by an expert in the history of the peasantry in Eastern Europe: "It is here that we can find, if we wish to, the perfect counterpart of the development which took place in Great Britain: instead of the declining peasantry and the expanding large estates, a sharp contrast is created by the vanishing of vast landed properties and by the peasantry which has seized every bit of land."[3]

The decline of Turkish military-political power and the breakup of large feudal estates were, however, by no means accompanied by the abolition of all forms and institutions of traditional economy. Moreover, the fact that the land passed into peasant ownership did not imply that the preconditions of agrarian capitalist development took shape as in the West where the two processes went hand in hand.

Consequently, the capitalist development of the newly formed peasant farms released from the feudal system could get under way only very slowly. A change-over to modern farming was inevitably more protracted than was agrarian development in Eastern Europe based on the capitalist farming of large estates. For a long time after liberation there was hardly any change in the ownership and farming methods of the peasantry. This is indicated by the widespread adherence to communal farming in the villages. In accordance with the customary law, the Southern Slav *zadruga* was in reality collective family property incorporating the typical features of common property and settlement under primitive economic-social conditions. The voluntarily discharged duties within the communal forms of work imposed by the *zadruga* (including the so-called *moba* and *pozaimitza*) proved to be conservative elements that preserved the traditional organization of work and the old methods of cultivation. Communal peasant labor performed without payment or compensation prevented wage work from gaining ground, rendering it unnecessary and even impossible.

The gradual disintegration of traditional institutions, beginning in the middle of the nineteenth century, cleared the way for the establishment

---

[3] E. Niederhauser, *A parasztság Európában: A parasztság Magyarországon a kapitalizmus korában, 1848–1914* (The Peasantry in Europe: The Peasantry in Hungary in the Age of Capitalism, 1848–1914), ed. by István Szabó, Akadémiai Kiadó (Publishing House of the Hungarian Academy of Sciences), Budapest, 1965, Vol. II, p. 657.

of capitalist conditions, and the disappearance of obsolete forms by the beginning of the present century allowed the very gradual emergence of modern agriculture.

The slow advancement in the modernization and capitalist development of peasant farming followed unmistakably from the existing circumstances: the peasants who gained ownership of the land possessed no capital and were unable to acquire adequate loans to carry out modernization. Instead of being helped by modern capitalist credit, the peasants were victims of medieval usury that extorted payment of as much as 200 per cent interest a year. According to an appraisal referring to 1,200 villages of Bulgaria at the beginning of the present century, 300 were in debt for the whole, 400 for half, of the expected value of the crop.

These loans did not in fact serve the advancement of farming but were meant only to keep the families alive, providing as they did for a minimal livelihood from one crop to the next and preserving the bankrupt state of the peasantry. Earnings from the new crop went to settle old debts, and the remainder was used for "indispensable" purchases.

The peasant holdings operated at an extremely low level and could take little advantage of opportunities to produce for market sale. Furthermore, the peasants were heavily burdened by steadily increasing taxation. On the one hand, they had to pay substantial compensation for the land taken over from the Turkish proprietors, sums which were usually far beyond the capabilities of their low-level peasant production; on the other hand, they had to contribute through taxation to the increasing expenditures being incurred by the modern state apparatus. Between 1879 and 1911 peasants were compelled to pay 15 to 20 per cent of their earnings as taxes in Bulgaria. In most instances peasant farmers ran into heavy debt and often became bankrupt. At best, they just scraped along, and the great majority were unable to progress so far as to change over to actual capitalist agriculture.

Typically, the instruments of production applied on peasant farms at the beginning of the present century were still on the level of preceding centuries. In Serbia there was absolutely no livestock on nearly one-third of peasant holdings, and over 40 per cent of the farmers did not own any vehicle of transport. In Bulgaria there were altogether 155 steam-driven threshing machines in operation, or one machine for 15.6

thousand hectares of tillage land (fifteen times the area per machine in Rumania); 257 horse-drawn sowing machines—one machine for 9.4 thousand hectares—had to serve over twenty times the area per machine in Rumania. By the twentieth century machines had therefore not come into general use in Southern Slav agriculture. Moreover, no improvement can be said to have ensued until the outbreak of the First World War, for even iron ploughs had not superseded wooden ploughs. In the year 1900 only 10 per cent of the 435,000 ploughs used in Bulgaria were made of iron. By 1910 the number had in fact more than doubled, but the 114,000 iron ploughs were still hardly more than one-fifth of the total number of ploughs used in farming. The proportion of wooden and iron ploughs was approximately the same in Serbia.

The use of better means of production and the introduction of modern forms of capitalist farming were all the more indispensable to the improvement of peasant farms as the time for acquiring new stretches of uncultivated land soon passed. In both of these Balkan countries the breakup of properties into small or dwarf holdings was spurred by demographic pressure. The exceedingly high birthrate, the very poor absorption of population by urbanization and industry, and the very low social mobility in general rapidly increased the absolute size of the agrarian population. As the law of inheritance provided for equal division of the land among all the children, small and dwarf holdings yielding low income, scarcely above the level of simple subsistence, mushroomed. These farms could take little or no part in production for the market. According to available records, a maximum of 30 to 40 per cent of the Bulgarian agricultural output was marketed. In Serbia, on farms under 10 hectares about 80 per cent of the yield was consumed by the peasant family which cultivated the land.

Under such conditions, agriculture based on peasant ownership of the land after the Balkan pattern experienced little in the way of advances. On the contrary, the standard of agricultural production was for the most part far inferior to that in the countries following the Prussian model, and the persistently patriarchal atmosphere hampered the emergence of villages. Capitalist development started at a slower rate and later, and noteworthy advance took place only after the turn of the century.

The changes in agriculture, mirroring significantly unequal standards, the gradual disappearance of traditional institutions and farming methods, the introduction of modern capitalist farming and organization of work (machinery and the wide acceptance of hired labor) lifted the countries of East-Central Europe out of their century-long stagnation and led to a powerful upswing in agricultural production. The agrarian boom—in spite of declining prices—was to set in first in the Austrian and Bohemian parts owing to the rapidly widening domestic markets, but the advancing industrialization of the Western countries—including the western regions of the Austro-Hungarian Monarchy—produced such prosperity as to make huge demands on—and offer unprecedented opportunities to—the agriculture of the eastern provinces of the Monarchy and to the Balkan countries in general.

Despite the rapid development of Austrian and Bohemian agriculture these regions became less capable of satisfying the needs created by industrialization, while the cis-Leithan parts of the Monarchy assumed an increasingly industrial character and were compelled to import agricultural products. Hence Hungarian—and also Russian, Rumanian, and Balkan—cereals, meat, fruit, and other kinds of food found an almost unlimited market after the industrial revolution in the countries of Western Europe.

Under these influences the area of cultivated land rapidly increased in East-Central Europe and the stretches of fallow ground were steadily reduced. In Austria, between 1867 and 1894 arable land lying fallow was reduced from 14.1 per cent to 9 per cent in Upper Austria, from 25.7 per cent to 20.1 per cent in Lower Austria, from 17.4 per cent to 2.5 per cent in Bohemia, and from 14.8 per cent to 3.4 per cent in Moravia. In Hungary the tilled land amounted to 10.9 million hectares in 1873; by 1906 it was 13.5 million hectares. Between 1871 and 1875, 21.9 per cent of the arable land was left fallow; between 1901 and 1905, 10.5 per cent.

In Rumania and especially in the Balkan countries one of the most striking features of agrarian development in these decades was the substitution of agriculture, particularly the growing of corn, for the earlier semi-nomadic raising of livestock. The amount of cultivated land, of arable land, grew enormously. In Rumania this process set in earlier. In Moldavia the area of tillage nearly doubled between 1833 and 1859 (from 440,000 to 800,000 hectares). In the Rumanian principalities the area in grain fields increased tenfold from 1829 to 1840. The rapid extension of sown land continued without letup in the second half of the nineteenth century: The total area cultivated was 2.5 million hectares in 1860 and 5.2 million after the turn of the century.

The great change-over in agriculture took place in the second half of the nineteenth century in Serbia and Bulgaria. With the decline in livestock raising, the figure of 1,498 head of cattle in 1859 was estimated to have fallen to 695 head by 1895 (number of animals per thousand inhabitants). In the meantime agriculture was pursued on ever more extensive stretches of land. Wheat fields covered 130,000 hectares in 1880 and by the turn of the century more than 400,000 hectares, while the area of maize fields doubled. In Bulgaria the 5.6 million hectares of arable land recorded in 1889 grew to nearly 8 million hectares by the year 1912.

The expansion of tillage and the reduction of fallow land were accompanied by technical change, by the progress of agrarian technology. The diminution of fallow ground in itself resulted partly from the fact that the system of three-course rotation from the Middle Ages, practiced as late as the middle of the nineteenth century even in the most advanced countries of the region, for example Austria, was abandoned. By the beginning of the twentieth century modern forms of agriculture had made extensive gains. In addition to the use of machines, as mentioned before, modern forms of fertilization and soil amelioration were also introduced. In the second half of the nineteenth century in the advanced countries of the region the systematic use of manure became a regular activity (as a concomitant of modern stable livestock breeding). In 1896, 18 kg. of farmyard manure fell to each cadastral hold of ploughed land in Hungary, which permitted the dressing of fields with manure every nine years (instead of the four-year repetition of the process held to be desirable).

In the 1890s, only a few decades later than in Western Europe, the use of chemical fertilizers was introduced. Though lagging far behind the level of the Western European countries, the regular use of fertilizers by advanced farmers is evident from records of the early twentieth century. In 1907, 17 kg. phosphorous fertilizer was applied per cadastral hold in Austria, 5 kg. in Hungary, 1.3 kg. in Russia. (In the same year the respective figures were 98 kg. in Belgium, 83 kg. in Great Britain, and 54 kg. in Germany.) The increased use of fertilizers can be observed quite closely in this period. From 1897 to 1901 and again from 1902 to 1907 the use of fertilizers more than doubled in Hungary, while in the period between 1907 and 1913 it rose nearly fivefold.

The effects of soil improvement by irrigation in its first, rudimentary form, by the regulation of waterways and by drainage were also felt. In the period under examination these steps were accompanied by the widening of the area of cultivated land and by a general increase in yields. In Rumania the average yield of wheat per cadastral acre was 5 quintals between 1881 and 1885, 6.7 quintals between 1903 and 1912. (In Bulgaria and Serbia the corresponding figures for the latter period were 6.2 and 5.2 quintals respectively.) During the same years the average yield in Hungary increased from 6.3 to 7.4 quintals, in Austria from 6.6 to 7.7 quintals, and in Russia from 3.4 to 4.2 quintals.

In the countries of East-Central Europe the growth in the area of arable land and the advance in agrarian techniques led to a swift increase in cereal production, as illustrated in Table 2-6.

Apart from Austria and Bohemia there was a remarkably rapid increase in crops after the 1880s. Within approximately three decades wheat production nearly doubled in Hungary, increased two and a half times in Bulgaria, approximately threefold in Rumania, and almost fourfold in Serbia.

No accurate comparable records are available for earlier years, but

Table 2-6. Wheat and Corn Production in East-Central Europe, 1880–1884 and 1903–1912 *(in million quintals)*

Country	1880–84		1903–12	
	Wheat	*Corn*	*Wheat*	*Corn*
Austria with Bohemia	11.2	4.0	15.5	4.0
Hungary	27.3	20.0	45.5	41.0
Rumania	7.7	17.0[a]	22.3	23.0
Serbia	1.1	4.8[b]	4.0	5.9
Bulgaria	4.0	4.8[c]	10.6	6.4

Source: Compiled from the sources indicated in the relevant section of the Bibliographical Summary for chapter 2.

[a] Yearly average in 1886–90.

[b] Figures from 1901.

[c] Figures from 1889.

in Russia, which exhibited slower development after the 1880s, the level in 1864–66 and 1885–94 still indicates rapid growth. By 1894 grain production had increased 73 per cent. In the Polish districts under Prussian rule grain production doubled in the fifteen years from the early 1890s, and by the outbreak of World War I another increase of 30 per cent was attained.

In most countries of the region grain production dominated the agricultural scene, occupying 90 per cent of the tilled land in Rumania, 80 per cent in Russia, slightly more than 60 per cent in Hungary, and more than half of the arable land in Serbia, Bulgaria, and even Bohemia.

In some countries there was a considerable advance in the production of root crops and industrial plants. Sugar beets were cultivated in Bohemia; potatoes in Austria and Russia; tobacco and essence of roses in Bulgaria.

In addition to cultivation of the land the other important factor in agricultural development was modern livestock breeding. Though open-air stock raising was still continued in these decades, the breeding of more valuable strains, based on stabling and fodder production, that is to say, modern livestock farming, was steadily gaining ground. The significant increase in the number of animals is a fair though approximate indicator of the advance achieved—not reflecting the improvement in quality. Thus in Austria, from 1850 to 1890 the number of cattle increased from 5.1 million to 8.6 million; by 1910 the figure rose to 9.2 million, or nearly double the 1850 figure. In the same period hogs increased from 2.2 million to 3.6 million, then to 6.4 million, or nearly threefold.

In Hungary the 4.5 million head of cattle in 1850 rose to 6.7 million by 1895, and to 7.3 million by 1910. The improvement in quality is shown by the fact that the value of livestock doubled between 1850 and 1910, though the rise in prices was only about 35 per cent. A similar increase is noted in hogs: the total of 4.9 million registered in 1850 rose to 7.6 million by 1910.

As pointed out before, livestock breeding lost some of its preponderance in the Balkan countries in favor of farming during the decades under review. For instance, in Rumania the number of cattle slightly decreased between 1860 and 1909, while the stocks of pigs increased from 1.1 million to 1.7 million. The similar course of events in Serbia has been mentioned before. However, livestock breeding nevertheless continued to remain the most important branch of rural economy in the Balkan countries.

The figures at the turn of the century show the level and significance of livestock breeding in the countries of East-Central Europe (Table 2-7).

The figures for Serbia are striking, but in nearly every other country as well the relative number of animals was well above the European average.

As remarked before, the modernization of agriculture and the large increase in tillage and livestock breeding were closely related to the rapidly growing export of agricultural products to industrial European markets. Before World War I the wheat produce of the countries of East-Central Europe amounted to 20 per cent of European wheat production; together with Russia, to nearly 50 per cent. In these years more than half of Rumanian wheat production and more than one-third of Rumanian corn production were exported. Hungarian wheat and flour exports amounted to more than one-third of the total Hungarian production. These countries, without Russia, supplied 13 per cent of the world's wheat exports.

The export of livestock was also considerable. Serbia, first in the world in number of pigs per head and second in cattle to the United States and Denmark alone, sold part of her livestock on foreign markets, and Rumanian as well as Hungarian livestock exports were also significant.

In the exports of the Balkan countries agricultural products predominated, constituting about 80 per cent of the total value. In Russia and

Table 2-7.   Livestock in East-Central Europe About 1900 *(per thousand inhabitants)*

Country	Cattle	Pigs	Sheep	Horses
Austria	387	123	173	66
Hungary	335	288	629	132
Rumania	366	165	690	85
Serbia	623	988	2,516	—

Source: Compiled from the sources indicated in the relevant section of the Bibliographical Summary for chapter 2.

Hungary the figures were 73 per cent and 58 per cent, respectively.

As a result of their rapid agrarian development in the second half of the nineteenth century and the beginning of the twentieth, the Eastern countries of the Continent emerged from their traditional economic stagnation for the first time and reached the level of dynamic capitalist development—with, however, noteworthy differences. Owing to their rapid agrarian advance through the realization of modern capitalist economy, they could partly keep pace with the increased demand of the Western countries of the Continent. But this could be accomplished only because the level of home consumption remained extremely low, owing to the generally lower standard of development.

Nonetheless the good results achieved by agriculture and foreign trade became decisive for the aggregate growth of the economy and opened up new opportunities for the basic development of other branches of the economy.

3 The Establishment of Modern Credit and a System of Transport

The capitalist transformation of agriculture in the second half of the nineteenth and the beginning of the twentieth century was closely correlated with the establishment of modern banks and a system of transport and communications. Earlier, in the Western parts of the Continent, these processes had not been so closely interwoven. Because modern agrarian development in Eastern Europe took place much later, it was actuated chiefly by external inducements (foreign markets): hence its tendency to prosper by concentration on exports.

As pointed out before, in Great Britain and to some extent in Holland agricultural transformation was launched long before modern banking or a system of transport and communications could have played a role. Moreover, in these countries the revolution in transport, i.e., the development of a railway system, had been preceded by the industrial revolution. The British situation was unique in this respect. The modern transformation of the economy was possible without any revolution in transport and communications because of the geographical features of the country, specifically, the possibilities provided by its waterways. On this small island (and similarly in Holland) inexpensive transport could be carried on not only by coastal shipping but also by inland waterways, particularly by the extensive network of canals built after 1761. By 1800 a 1,600-mile system of canals was in service, and by 1835, 2,200 miles of canals; 1,800 miles of navigable river lines were in use.

Nor was the need for modern banks as strong in England as elsewhere. Owing to the early onset of the industrial revolution and its more primitive technical level, the transformation did not call for investments of such magnitude as were required a few decades later on the Continent. Moreover, extensive overseas trade and the exploitation of colonies afforded ample means of procuring the required capital, while Britain's role as the "world's industrial workshop" in the eighteenth and early nineteenth centuries led to unparalleled domestic accumulation. Under these favorable conditions the mobilization of accumulated capital could be managed easily.

In the other Western European countries events took a quite different turn. The capitalist transformation of agriculture and the subsequent industrial revolution did not precede the development of adequate transport and communications or the introduction of modern banking; on the contrary, the agricultural and industrial revolution could not have taken place without these levers. In Continental Western Europe the agricultural and industrial revolution was paralleled by the revolutionary changes in transport and a system of credit.

The building of a modern system of transport and a network of railway lines began in the 1830s, more or less simultaneously with the great prosperity in agriculture and the spread of the industrial revolution. The opening of the Liverpool-Manchester line in 1830, proclaiming the advent of the railway era in England, was soon followed by the Western countries of the Continent. In France the Lyon–Saint Étienne line was opened in 1832, and the next year railways appeared in Belgium. In Germany the rapid construction of railways was initiated in 1835 by the opening of the Fürth–Nürnberg Line. By 1860 the construction of the main lines in the advanced countries had been accomplished, and about 90 per cent of all railway lines in Western Europe and the United States had been built.

Although the first lines were intended to satisfy the demands of the mining districts and industry for inexpensive transport of large quantities of bulky goods, the railway system soon affected the whole economy, interacting with all sectors and activities. In accordance with the opportunities created by the railway era, economic modernization followed a different course from that in England. Because domestic accumulation of capital was at a much lower level and there was much less available for investment, the institution of modern Crédit-Mobilier type banking was essential in the Western countries of the Continent. Indeed, the new system of banks was destined to resolve the dilemma of larger requirements of capital and smaller accumulation by collecting, concentrating, and investing mobilizable capital. Hence, the banks played a decisive role in the economic revolution of Western Continental Europe.

The birth and function of modern banks and the spread of railway transport in the western parts of the Austro-Hungarian Monarchy, or more accurately in Austria and Bohemia, were not essentially different, in timing or character, from developments in the Western part of the Continent, particularly Germany and France. This was due in no small measure to the fact that Vienna—the political, administrative, and financial center of the Hapsburg Empire—played an important role not only in the Monarchy but in the whole of Europe. As far back as the seventeenth century a few representatives of the early banks were active in Vienna, engaged chiefly in the management of the financial affairs of the court and the Empire. (We need mention here only the Wiener Stadt Bank and the Universal Bankalität.)

Private banking houses and exchange offices became more important in the first half of the nineteenth century in the Hapsburg Empire. By 1847 the number rose to 92. Along with the exchange of money, their activities were concentrated mainly on the placement of government bonds and were rarely extended to granting loans in support of business interests. Short-term credits were limited, and loans to cover production costs were unknown. It was nevertheless from these organizations of credit service that a few banks emerged whose activities soon led to modern credit operations. Of these it was the Vienna branch of the House of Rothschild which rose to a position of special eminence.

The revolutionary change in the Austrian system of banking and the replacement of traditional credit operations by the typical forms of capitalist loans came about in the middle of the century, as in France and Germany. Here too, the huge demand for loans which the existing banking system was unable to satisfy, created a need for joint-stock investment banks (Crédit-Mobilier type). In the period which witnessed the establishment in France of the Crédit-Mobilier, the Union Générale, and the Banque de Paris et des Pays Bas, Germany founded the Bank of Prussia, the Schafhausenscher Bankverein, the Darmstädter Bank, and the Discontogesellschaft.

In Austria at the beginning the brothers Pereire offered to assist and cooperate, but finally it was the influential House of Rothschild which gained the upper hand. The new era began with the foundation of the Creditanstalt in the year 1855. The establishment of the Bodencreditanstalt in 1864, the Anglo-Austrian Bank in 1864, the Wiener Bankverein in 1869, the Union Bank in 1870, and later the Länderbank was a sign of the growing acceptance of modern capitalist banks. Besides the leading banks, minor local credit banks, chiefly savings banks, mushroomed and became important in collecting the capital available in the country. Around the turn of the century 63 big banks (joint-stock companies), 559 savings banks, and approximately 5,000 cooperative credit associations with more traditional functions of commercial credit and exchange formed the network of banking institutions in Austria and Bohemia. (Of these, 20 big banks, 142 savings banks, and about 2,270 cooperative associations were situated in Bohemia.)

The share capital of these active banking institutions totaled 510 million crowns, while special reserves amounted to another 500 million. In addition to this capital, the total deposits collected by the network of banking institutions amounted to 3.8 billion crowns. This figure is of special interest because it clearly indicates the fundamental function of the Continental banking system. It must be emphasized here that not only was the total of deposits nearly four times as large as the banks' own capital, but the increase in deposits formed the principal source of the strengthening of banking institutions. In 1880 bank deposits totaled 1.5 billion crowns; by 1890 they amounted to 2.6 billion. At the same time it is noteworthy that around the turn of the century Austrian deposits surpassed slightly, by about 10 per cent, savings deposits in France, were three times higher than those in Italy, but amounted to no more than 40 per cent of the sum total of deposits in German banks.

The advanced state and the capital strength of the Austro-Bohemian banks formed the principal source for the financing of the economy. In the first period of their activity, the 1850s to 1870s, they played an extremely active part in promoting infrastructure investments, far exceeding the scope of traditional bank credits. The large-scale transport enterprises of the House of Rothschild were especially noteworthy, the foremost being the Dunagözhajózási Társaság (Danube Steamship Company) and the Österreichische Staatseisenbahn Gesellschaft (Austrian State Railways Company). The construction of the main lines, the Südbahn, the Elisabethbahn, the Nordbahn, and the Ferdinandbahn, was financed chiefly by the Creditanstalt.

After 1855, railway building passed almost entirely from the state into the hands of private firms and banks, and until the 1880s, when the system of state railways again came into prominence, railway construction formed one of the principal fields of the activities of the big banks. From the 1880s on the banks were involved ever more extensively in the financing of industrial enterprises, thus becoming the most important factor of industrial development. As in Germany, so also or even more in the cis-Leithan parts of the Monarchy, banks may be said to have been the primary force in financing economic development and the modern economic transformation. The famous Austrian *haute finance* actually became the master of the economy.

In the 1880s networks of steadily growing industrial concerns developed around the largest syndicates of banks. The biggest concern, the Creditanstalt, the Wiener Bankverein, and the Niederösterreichische Escompte Gesellschaft gained influence mainly in branches of heavy industry—in mining, metallurgy, and machine production—as well as in the paper, textile, chemical, and glass industries; the Länderbank, the Anglo-Österreichisches Bank, and the Bodencreditanstalt were interested chiefly in the newly developed chemical and electrical industries. In these fields of financial activity, mortgage loans played a very important role during the whole of the period in question. The financing of the large estates, in the process of modernization, eliminated the activities of the modern capitalist organization of credit service. Around the turn of the century the total of mortgage loans amounted to more than half of the total assets of the Austro-Bohemian network of banking institutions. (About two-thirds, 70 per cent, were lent on landed property.)

Until the turn of the century Vienna retained its lead in the bank capital controlling Austro-Bohemian domains. In 1900 Austrian bank capital, based on own sources, was preeminent in the sum total of Austro-Bohemian bank capital by a 3:1 ratio. After the turn of the century Bohemian capital greatly increased; its expansion was manifested by a considerable shift in the ratio, which by World War I had declined to 2:1.

In the parts of the Austro-Hungarian Monarchy outside the cis-Leithan region, particularly in Hungary, the establishment of a modern network of banks shows a strong resemblance to the process described above.

The development of modern Hungarian banking started in the 1830s. The Pesti Hazai Elsö Takarékpénztáregyesület (First Hungarian Savings Bank Association of Pest) was founded in 1836 with capital paid in by big landowners; soon after, savings banks were founded in most of the provincial towns. The first commercial bank was called into existence chiefly by merchants in 1841 under the name of Pesti Magyar Kereskedelmi Bank (Hungarian Commercial Bank of Pest). By 1848, 36 banking institutions were active in the country. After the stagnation of the 1850s, from the beginning of the decade of the Compromise, a number of new banks were founded. In 1860 there were already 80 banks and saving banks operating in the country.

The true period of prosperity in Hungarian banking came after the Austro-Hungarian Compromise of 1867. Local deposit and savings banks were founded in quick succession; by 1873 as many as 637 banking institutions were opened in the country. Among them were big banks by Hungarian standards. The Magyar Általános Hitelbank (General Hungarian Credit Bank) belonging to the Rothschild interests, the Anglo-Magyar Bank (Anglo-Hungarian Bank), the Franco-Magyar Bank (Franco-Hungarian Bank), and the Földhitelintézet (Mortgage Bank) transacted business on a large scale. The shocks sustained in the crisis of 1873 brought ruin, and most of the big banks collapsed. However, in the 1880s and the 1890s a new wave of investment activities revived in the capital and the provinces alike, so that by the turn of the century the number of banking institutions rose to over 2,000. The small number of big banks gathered new strength through investments by groups of foreign financiers. Besides the General Hungarian Credit Bank the leading banks were the Hungarian Commercial Bank of Pest, the Magyar Leszámitoló és Pénzváltó Bank (Hungarian Discount and Exchange Bank) and the Pesti Hazai Elsö Takarékpénztár (First Hungarian Savings Bank of Pest).

The numerical growth itself does not give the full picture. The increase in the sum total of the capital handled by the banks, presented in Table 3-1, permits deeper insight into developments.

The rapid growth of bank assets became the principal source for financing transactions in the second half of the nineteenth century. The banks and savings banks, which controlled huge amounts of money coming not only from foreign capital but also from the collection of capital accumulated in trade, industry, and agriculture and the personal savings of the population, supported the interests of agriculture in the first place. Mortgage loans that provided the large estates with capital formed a leading branch of business. In 1848 mortgage loans

Table 3-1.   Capital Resources in the Hungarian Banking
System, 1848–1900

	Capital Resources (in thousand crowns)			
Year	Share Capital and Reserve Fund	Deposits	Total	Index of Capital Growth
1848	3,724	19,138	22,862	100
1867	28,874	143,126	172,000	750
1873	199,588	348,416	548,004	2,380
1880	192,734	610,524	803,258	3,500
1890	348,532	1,104,595	1,453,127	6,340
1900	833,381	1,773,631	2,607,012	11,380

Source: *Magyar Statisztikai Közlemények* (Hungarian Statistical Publications), Budapest, 1913, Vol. 35.

amounted to 17,250,000 crowns; in 1867 the figure was 94,200,000; in 1873, 264,878,000; in 1880, 374,754,000; in 1890, 769,526,000; in 1900, 1,668,346,000; and in 1913 about 3.5 billion.

In the second half of the nineteenth century total mortgage loans in Hungary thus amounted in general to 50 to 60 per cent of the capital resources of banking institutions, slightly exceeding the Austro-Bohemian level. Compared to mortgage credits, bill transactions (i.e., commercial and industrial credits) remained relatively lower throughout. A glance at Russian developments gives a more complete picture of the Eastern European banking system. A modern system of banks was established in the Russian Empire later than in the Austro-Hungarian Monarchy. From the time of the foundation of the Kupechesky Bank (Commercial Bank) in 1754, several commercial banks were certainly active. However, their credit business was confined to a very narrow scope and in essence hardly overstepped the range of medieval credit transactions. The emergence of a modern banking system can be observed only after the reform. The foundation of the Gosudarstvenny Bank (Bank of Russia) in 1860 was followed four years later by the establishment of the first modern commercial bank, the Kommerchesky Bank (Commercial Bank) of St. Petersburg. By 1873 as many as 33 joint-stock company banks were in business. The share capital of the banks amounted to 104 million roubles in 1874. Further advance until the turn of the century is demonstrated by the rise in the sum total of share capital to 275 million roubles by 1900. Besides the big banks, an important role was played by the network of savings banks, which increased from the 75 banks active in 1880 to nearly 1,000 by the year 1900. During this period their deposits increased from 9 million to 500 million roubles.

The beginnings of the Polish network of banks go back to the crisis precipitated by the end of the Napoleonic wars. The first mortgage companies for the solution of agricultural credit problems were set up after the model of the Silesian *Landschaften*—at Poznan in 1821, and in the Polish Kingdom in 1825. The Bank of Poland, a state institution which went in for extremely vigorous financial activities, was founded in 1828.

The establishment of a modern network of banks in the form of joint-stock companies occurred in the 1870s. The foundation of the Commercial Bank of Warsaw and of numerous cooperative banking institutions took place in the years 1870 to 1873. (It is sufficient to mention here the Bank of Industrial Credits, the Urban Cooperative Credit Association, and the Cooperative Credit Association of Lodz.) Before World War I, 38 private banks were operating in the Polish Kingdom.

Thus the establishment and activities of a modern system of banking in the countries of Central Europe and in a sense in Russia as well show much similarity to the development of the credit system elsewhere on the Continent. However, the unequal levels of economic development produced dissimilarities which cannot be disregarded. The most striking difference was the more dominant, more central, more initiating role of the banks. The relative economic backwardness of the Western countries of the Continent compared with Great Britain induced them to create banks whose purpose was to finance economic growth. The backwardness of East-Central Europe, compared with the Continental countries of Western Europe, limited any domestic, spontaneous solutions through self-financing both in agriculture and in industry, and thereby enhanced the significance of banking activities.

However, it is not enough to state these facts. In the Austro-Hungarian Monarchy, except for the cis-Leithan region, the central role of the banks was particularly prominent because another peculiar difference distinguished this area from the West. The Monarchy—except for the Austrian and Bohemian parts, as pointed out before—did not experience virtually simultaneous and interactive revolutionary changes in various fields of the national economy. In the Western countries of the Continent the development of a modern banking system was accompanied by the roughly simultaneous revolution of agriculture and industry. In Eastern Europe, on the other hand, one-sided agrarian advance constituted the dynamic and decisive process; it was not connected with an extensive economic development carrying everything along with it. Since the modern transformation, still in its initial stage, had also been triggered mostly by external factors, agricultural transformation itself could not have been accomplished before developing a modern credit system. Therefore, in building up a modern system of banking, the leading forces were agrarian interests and the related necessity of realizing export.

The banking system of the Balkan countries continued to display significant differences from developments in the Austro-Hungarian Monarchy, or, in general, in the countries mentioned above. To begin with, there was the considerable delay in the rise of a modern banking system. Before the end of the nineteenth century only initial, tentative steps had been made in Rumania, Serbia, and Bulgaria. No more than a few small banking institutions had been founded.

In Rumania the first private banks, including the Marmorosch Blank Company, which was to acquire a wide reputation, and the Banca Naţional ă Moldavie, were established in the 1840s. The first modern bank was established at Jasi in 1857, but the epochal event was the opening of the Banca Naţională României (National Bank) in 1860. Progress, heretofore extremely slow, was promoted in the 1860s by a few domestic and foreign foundations. Of these the Banca României, established in 1863, and the Ottoman Bank, under British control in 1865, deserve special mention. Private banks began to spread only in the 1880s. In the period between 1866 and 1880 altogether 4 new banks were founded; in the years from 1881 to 1900 only another 23. However, from the turn of the century to the start of World War I, 197 banking institutions were opened, including the most important Rumanian banks such as the Banca Commerciale Română (1907) and the Banca Românescă (1911).

In these years, again particularly after the turn of the century, the sum total of capital rapidly increased. The share capital of Rumanian banking institutions was 10 million lei in 1865 and 22 million lei in 1881; the first major increase came by the turn of the century when the amount reached 49 million lei. Thereafter, until the outbreak of World War I, and particularly after 1910, total capital soared fivefold, reaching 228 million lei. During this period deposits increased to nearly twice the amount of share capital, approximately 450 million lei. Of course, compared with the bank capital of the countries of the Austro-Hungarian Monarchy, even with this rapid growth the amounts were quite insignificant. It is a mark of backwardness and not of high concentration that at the beginning of the present century only a few banks provided with truly solid capital, suitable for large-scale banking activities, were operating in the country. Half of the total share capital and 70 per cent of the sum total of deposits were in the possession of two banks.

In Serbia the Prva Srpska Banka (First Serbian Bank), founded in 1869, was ruined two years later; but at this time the Serbian Credit Bank was set up with French and Austrian cooperation, and in 1883 the Narodna Bank (National Bank) began to operate. Until the early 1880s only two banks, with 3.3 million dinars of capital, were functioning in the country. Here too, the real upswing came about after the turn of the century: From 80 in 1900, the number of banks increased to 187 by 1912, while the total capital rose from 16.7 million dinars to 51.2 million. Outstanding among the new institutions—founded with foreign capital—were the Srpska-Franco Banka (Franco-Serbian Bank) and the Andrejevich Bank. The principal enterprise of domestic capital was the Commercial Bank of Belgrade. However, the rapid increase of capital was at a much lower level than in Rumania. This is evidenced also by the modest amount of deposits. In the 1910s the deposits accumulated at Serbian banks totaled about 44 million dinars.

In Bulgaria the first bank (Bank Napredak), a joint-stock company, was established in 1867, and by 1887 five banks operated with a total share capital of 26.4 million leva. The very slow growth of a modern network of banking institutions is shown by the increase in the number of banks from 29 in 1900 to only 36 by 1905, with the capital rising nearly threefold. It was certainly a significant event in the development of banking when the first major bank was founded in 1901 with foreign capital, Blgarska Generalna Banka (General Bulgarian Bank). This was followed by the opening of several other fairly large banks such as the

Balkanska Banka and the Blgarska Kreditna Banka. By the outbreak of World War I, 52 banks were active. In the years preceding the First World War the capital of the Bulgarian banks rose from 100 to 150 million levas, while the liabilities amounted to approximately three times the latter figure.

Thus, the development of banking institutions in the Balkans started later than in Central Europe and remained at a lower level. However, the difference is not fully illustrated by the number of banks and their capital. The banking system of the Balkans had a much weaker, more backward economic basis. The injections of foreign capital were undoubtedly helpful in stimulating economic activity in the feeble Balkan economy. However, they did not produce a network of banking institutions which would become an integral part of the economic system, occupying a central position not only in financing business but also in stimulating saving and investment.

Under the very limited possibilities of accumulation, deposits remained negligible and, as shown before, could not play any role in financing the economy. Until the turn of the century the banks in operation hardly promoted modernization. They were unable to supersede the typical medieval forms of credit, not even usury. They failed to become an important factor in railway construction and in the financing of industry. The modern capitalist economy actually remained a tiny enclave in the Balkan socio-economic system, which retained innumerable feudal, even patriarchal, elements.

The principal sphere of bank activities was in maintaining relations between state finances, the budget, and groups of foreign financiers. The main economic importance of the banks derived from their task of satisfying demands for agricultural credits as fully as possible. In the agricultural domain their chief business was mortgage loans, though certain modern transactions of financing industry and acquiring industrial interests also existed—more markedly in Rumania than in Serbia and especially Bulgaria. The boom following the turn of the century invested Balkan banks with a truly influential force, but the brief period of less than a decade and a half until World War I did not suffice to raise them to a position of central significance in the European sense of the term as applied to Western banks.

In the countries of East-Central Europe the introduction of modern banking was virtually inseparable from agrarian development. At the same time the agricultural demands created by modernization, particularly the needs of capitalist agrarian development based on foreign markets, called for a rapid realization of modern transport. The revolution of transport and the spread of railways in Western Europe took place at a time when, as a result of the industrial revolution, the regions involved assumed an industrial character and the demand for the import of agrarian products was increasing. Moreover, this was a period marked by the building of modern colonial empires, by sharp competition among the European powers, and by the formation of military alliances.

All these developments lent economic, political, and strategic importance to the extension to the entire Continent of a modern network of railway lines, which also promised to be an excellent investment. At the same time the great powers of East-Central Europe themselves regarded it as a political and strategic task of primary significance to build systems of modern transport which would help to unify these empires. Therefore railway construction became virtually a state affair, carried on with varying forms of state cooperation. Thus the establishment of modern transport lines in East-Central Europe started at almost the same time as, or hastily followed, the boom in railway construction in Western Europe.

Railway construction was all the more important for economic life in Eastern Europe as it was not preceded in this region by any noteworthy improvement of roads. In 1860 there were 4.72 miles of roads per square mile in Great Britain and 4.84 miles in France, whereas in Austria there were only 1.6 miles, in Russia 0.01 mile. (The mileage was much the same in the Balkan countries.) Although road building was naturally stepped up everywhere after the 1860s, it remained far behind railway construction in importance. Road building did not affect so directly other sectors of the economy and did not have as great a multiplier effect on economic activity as did railway construction. While better roads were important in order to connect local markets, their effect on the national economy as a whole was less perceptible.

Thus, other forms of modernizing transport were relegated to the background by the dynamism of railway construction, particularly in the Hapsburg Empire where the initial steps were taken in the Austrian and Bohemian regions. In addition to the aforementioned economic, political, and strategic interests, here railway construction was given impetus by a highly developed industry unique in East-Central Europe, and by the demands of processing industries and of handicraft and manufacturing centers for the transport of raw materials and merchandise.

The decision to convert a line originally meant for horsecars into a railway for steam engines—the Linz-Budejevicze (Budweiss) line—was taken almost simultaneously with the opening of the first German and French railway lines. It was with the intention of emphasizing the significance and economic importance of railways that in 1841, when a track of 493 km. had been laid down, railway construction was declared to be the task of the state and the previous system of privately owned railways was abandoned.

During the 1840s another 800 km. of railway lines were built by the state. Although this was far behind the contemporaneous new lines of 2,500 km. in France, 5,400 km. in Germany, and 7,300 km. in Great Britain, Austria still belonged to that group of countries where the revolutionary progress of transport began.

The severe financial difficulties of the state in the 1850s and the intensified efforts of financial groups of great capitalists to acquire the concessions for railway construction for private firms induced the Austrian government to return to the system of privately owned railways in 1854. Indeed, the law issued on September 14 actually encouraged contractors by providing for a guarantee of interest on capital invested in railways as well as for a series of other state premiums and preferences. This passing of railway construction into private hands almost completely coincided with the prosperity in Austrian financial life following the foundation of the Creditanstalt. Hence it was not surprising that in the great wave of railway construction in the latter part of the fifties the Creditanstalt and the Rothschild group excelled, although various other concerns joined in the sharp fight for the concessions. Until the fifties the Austrian railways concentrated their energies on the Vienna-Prague line, but there was still no connection with the coast and the Alpine industry district, and the connection of the industrial region of Moravia with the river Elbe was also waiting to be realized.

In 1856 two momentous projects were on the point of execution. The first was to lay down the line from Vienna to Trieste. This line, later called the southern railway (Südbahn), was first sold by the state to a French concern, but the financial power of the Rothschilds was so strong at the time in the Hapsburg Empire that the government was persuaded to reconsider its decision. In 1858 the concession for the partly constructed line, 2,500 km. in length, was handed over to the Creditanstalt.

It was about the same time that the Vienna-Linz-Passau line and the Salzburg line were built, connecting Austria with the Western countries. The early sixties saw a slight slackening in the rate of railway construction because the low price of government securities brought high interest with which railway profits could not compete. But after the Compromise consolidated conditions, bumper crops and a fever of new enterprise induced an unprecedented wave of railway construction as a result of which tracks of 10,000 km. ran over the western parts of the Monarchy. This period witnessed the opening of the Franz Josephs Bahn which connects Vienna with the Saxonian industrial districts through Pilsen (Plzň). The crisis of 1873 affected the whole of economic life, causing a break in railway construction. In the second half of the seventies no new lines were built, and those in operation were faced with numerous financial obstacles.

This again gave rise to the proposal that the state should take railway construction into its own hands, implying the nationalization of existing lines and the building of new ones by resorting to state resources. Of the 11,379 km. installed in 1879 only 950 km. were built by the state. However, in 1890, when the construction of the principal network was accomplished, 6,600 km. of the 15,278 km. were nationalized. The last stage of Austrian railway construction, started in 1890, was concentrated on local lines. The approximately 7,500 km. constructed until 1910 were built and managed by the state. As a result of further nationalization of the 22,981 km. in Austria—of which 9,542 km., or 41 per cent, were in Bohemia—only about 4,000 km., or barely 20 per cent, remained in the possession of private railway companies.

Guided by imperial considerations and the demands of food export, Hungarian railway construction was started as an extension of the railway system built in the cis-Leithan regions of the Hapsburg Monarchy. The first railway line was opened to traffic at a relatively early date, in 1846, but it was only very slowly that this first section of 46 km. was followed by new lines. The railway connection between Vienna and Budapest was realized in the 1850s, after the suppression of the Hungarian

War of Independence. However, noteworthy construction may be observed chiefly in the second half of the decade. By 1866 a network of 2,160 km. was finally built, connecting the most important centers of the agricultural parts with the capital and so also with Vienna. The Vienna-Pest-Szeged-Temesvár line meant a connection with the most important grain-producing southern regions, the Vienna-Pest-Szolnok-Debrecen line with the center of livestock breeding beyond the river Tisza.

The railways constructed before the Austro-Hungarian Compromise with Vienna as their center were so obviously built to complete the Austrian railway network as to rouse the resentment of the contemporaneous Hungarian bourgeoisie. Thus Pester Lloyd declared on January 9, 1869: "As regards the railways from the time before the restoration of the constitution all that can be said is that they do not deserve the name of a railway system or a railway network . . . so many railways, so many blind alleys, mere branch-lines of the cis-Leithan railways . . . Hungary should be connected with the outside world through Vienna and Triest."

The period following the Compromise of 1867 lent a new and very strong impetus to railway construction. In a few years—by 1873—the length of railway lines grew threefold in Hungary, reaching 6,300 km. As the great railway boom lasted in Hungary from the mid-fifties to the mid-seventies, in precisely the years when the policy of state-supported privately owned railways (guarantee of interest) prevailed in Vienna, Hungarian railways were also private enterprises. (Of the railways opened to traffic up to 1873 only 16 per cent were state-owned.) State support of private railway companies assumed the form of granting a concession for 90 years (usually) and guaranteeing 5 per cent interest on invested capital, should profitability prove to be under that figure.

The main lines of the Hungarian railways were built in the years following the Compromise. The first were those constructed for industrial purposes: in 1867 the Pest-Hatvan-Salgótarján line, in 1870 the Hatvan-Miskolc line, and in the next year the Salgótarján-Losonc and the Miskolc-Bánréve lines. At the time when the main lines were laid down, the industrial lines of approximately 300 km. nevertheless accounted for no more than 10 per cent of the total railway network. After a few years' stagnation, from the early eighties, Hungarian railway construction proceeded with renewed vigor and few lapses so that in the period until World War I a dense network of local lines was opened to traffic. The

length of the railway network operated in Hungary was 17,000 km. in 1900; by the year 1913 it increased to over 22,000 km.

The railway system built to European standards in the Austro-Hungarian Monarchy represented the highest level among the countries of East-Central Europe. However, railway construction gathered momentum in every country of the region, though not on such an elevated plane of development.

In Russia railway building was initiated before the reform, chiefly for strategic reasons, but only 1,500 km. of track had been laid up to 1860. From the sixties, construction of the main lines was started and pursued at a rapid rate with Moscow as the center. The opening of the Moscow-Kursk, Moskow-Voronyezsh, and Moscow-Nizshnii-Novgorod lines to traffic in the seventies ensured rapid progress in the construction of further lines, notably those connecting Kursk-Charkov-Odessa, Charkov-Rostov, Caricin-Riga, Moscow-Yaroslave, and Perm-Yekaterinburgh. The principal railway construction of the eighties served to connect the major sites of raw material sources, mines, and industrial centers, as demonstrated by the train service connecting the Donyetz Basin, Krivoirog, and the Urals. By 1890 the length of the railway network was over 29,000 km. The first boom period in Russian railway construction in the sixties and seventies was followed in the late nineties by another great wave of building. Whereas in the years between 1865 and 1875, an average of 1,500 km. of lines were opened to traffic every year, in the period between 1893 and 1897 the annual average was 2,500 km. By 1900 a railway network of 56,000 km. was in use. After the turn of the century further important railway construction was carried on in the Russian Empire, and by 1913 the length of serviceable lines had reached 70,000 km.

The first step in the construction of a network of railway lines in Polish areas was the opening of the Wroclaw-Myslowice line in 1847, followed by its extension to Krakow in 1852. In 1855 Warsaw was connected with Vienna, in 1861 with Lwow; by 1912 railway lines of 3,748 km. were in operation on the territory of the Polish Kingdom. At this time lines of over 4,000 km. were built in Galicia, and more than 12,000 km. in Prussian Poland.

The first railway line of nearly 200 km. was finished in Rumania in 1869, but by the close of the eighties the network of railway lines grew to 2,500 km. The length of lines finished by 1914–15 was 3,500 km. Railway construction in Rumania served to connect agricultural regions with the harbors, since agrarian exports were of preeminent importance to the economic life of the country.

Notwithstanding the aforementioned imperial and strategic incentives and the foreign initiatives, the railway systems built in the Central European countries and in Russia fully answered their economic demand and served the economic modernization of these countries. This cannot be said without qualification for the Balkan countries. It was not long before modern railways were built in the Balkans, for strong activity developed in this field from about the 1860s. However, in these parts the introduction of modern transport was influenced even more by foreign strategic-political aims, and remained more nearly the affair of the Great Powers than anywhere else in Eastern Europe. It was, therefore, less closely interwoven in the Balkans with domestic economic transformation.

The desire of the Western Powers to create a railway connection with Turkey and thereby a continental line to the Near East was a decisive factor in the construction of the Balkan railways. In the spirit of this intention the Turkish government, backed by a British syndicate, had built a line in the 1860s along the Danube from Varna to Rustchuk, from Kustendil in a western direction. This line was to be connected with the railways of Central Europe. To further this project another line of 2,500 km. was to be constructed, running from Varna to the Austrian border. Having obtained from the Turkish government a guaranteed profit of 8,000 francs per kilometer, the Austro-French Company headed by Baron Hirsch began the construction of the connecting line in 1870. However, by the time the Balkan countries became independent, only three separate sections had been completed.

Henceforth, the realization of a railway connecting Europe with the Near East was no longer feasible without the cooperation of the independent Balkan countries. Thus, in 1883 negotiations took place between Turkey and the delegates of the three Balkan countries and an agreement was reached concerning the construction of the connecting lines. In 1888 contact was established between Vienna and Constantinople through the company Orientalische Eisenbahnen. From the 1890s the network of Balkan railways was further completed by groups of German and French financiers. The Deutsche Bank continued to develop the Macedonian railway line (west of Saloniki to Monastir), the network of the Orientalische Eisenbahnen. The line of 550 km. east of Saloniki to the coast was built under the auspices of the French Banque Imperiale Ottomane. Until the year 1913 the Deutsche Bank was in the vanguard of Eastern railway construction, conspicuously manifesting the expansive aspirations of Germany.

The railway network of the Balkan countries was mainly the result of these constructions. In Serbia the first railway line was built in 1878. Between 1880 and 1883 a 460 km. track was built as the Serbian section of the Vienna-Constantinople line. By 1912 another 400 km. were added, mostly narrow-gauge railways. In Bulgaria the first railway was the fruit of a Turko-British enterprise in 1860. In this instance the backbone of the country's railway network was the 697 km. Bulgarian section of the Vienna-Constantinople line. From 1885, after the nationalization of the railways, the railway network was further developed under state management, and by 1912, 1,948 km. were open to traffic.

The large-scale building of railways became a force of central significance for mobilizing capital. Railways created an enormous demand for capital. In the middle of the nineteenth century railway construction cost £ 57,000 a mile in Great Britain, which was extremely high, but even in the German states expenditure came to £ 10,000 to £ 20,000 per mile. When the Hungarian Eastern Railway was built in the seventies, the construction of one mile cost approximately 1 million crowns, or about £ 50,000. It would have been impossible to raise such capital through purely private enterprise. That is why railway building became the hunting-ground of powerful international syndicates and why the cooperation of the state, in the form of investments or guarantee of interest, also became indispensable. However, these conditions simultaneously rendered railway building one of the most corrupt fields of business in the second half of the nineteenth century. A company formed for the construction of a certain line became the hotbed of bribery and fraudulent practices. Special branches of business came into existence for wangling state concessions, and for getting hold of concessions acquired by others.

After the Austro-Hungarian Compromise, for instance, the Hungarian Parliament offered chances for more lucrative business than did the stock exchange. Characteristically, when it came to the frequent debates on the issue of railway concessions, Francis Deak, a puritan of the old school, the contemporary leader of Hungarian liberalism and the architect of the Compromise, ostentatiously left the chamber. In these years railways and graft came to be regarded as virtually identical in East-Central Europe.

The case of the Hungarian Eastern Railway furnishes convincing proof that this view was not unfounded. The issue of the concession for the construction of the Nagyvárad-Kolozsvár-Brassó line was pending for six years. Finally the prize was carried off by Charles Warring, an English businessman, in 1868, because, as it turned out later, he had found high patronage among landowner-governmental circles in return for offering 4 per cent (6 million crowns) of the planned building costs. The state concession itself was of high value, for it gave a guarantee of 7.5 per cent interest on the invested capital. However, instead of beginning the work himself, Warring sold the advantageous concession to the Anglo-Austrian Bank. Then he floated the Eastern Railway Company Ltd. There were numerous Hungarian politicians and aristocrats among the members of the board of directors who pocketed 14 million crowns by selling the promoters shares of companies on a higher course of exchange. Warring was appointed to organize and execute the construction, but in a few years, when 90 per cent of the amount planned to cover the total costs had been spent—as revealed by an investigation— not even half of the planned line had been completed.

After the scandal created by the exposure of such gross speculation— Warring having fled to Turkey for fear of legal proceedings—the company raised an advance on the guarantee of interest and continued the construction of the line, financing the work by issuing new state-guaranteed bonds. Since no one would buy these, they were pawned and, the company being incapable of reimbursement, the state finally had to pay the debts. "All the individuals standing at the head of the company are brigands and thieves," stated an opposition paper in 1872. "The whole Eastern Railway is nothing but theft, which theft is committed with the knowledge of the government."[1] After several more years and repeated interventions by the government, the state finally bought the shares of the company in 1876, making payment to the owners in government

---

[1] *Szabadság, mint a nép zászlója* (Liberty as the Banner of the People), 1872, p. 243.

securities good for 5 per cent of the company's precarious shares. Sub-sequently the construction of the line was finished by the state.

The immense gains promised by railway building were very tempting to capitalists and contributed to the construction of the railway network of Eastern Europe. The development of this network in the nineteenth century compared with that in Western Europe can be seen in Table 3-2. In the 1890s the density of railway lines in Eastern Europe and the Balkans was far behind that achieved in the same period in the West. However, it might have roughly corresponded to the level of railway development in Western Europe in the 1860s and 1870s.

A comparison of the tabulated values shows that in East-Central Europe the revolution of transport began in the second half of the nineteenth century. The level of development attained in the Monarchy was close to that prevailing in Western Europe. Although it was accomplished a few decades later than in the West, a relatively dense network of railways extended over the entire Empire, connecting all parts—though not with equal efficiency.

As pointed out before, railway construction was correlated with the

Table 3-2. Density of Railway Lines in 1850 and 1896–1897 in Eastern and Western Europe

	1850: Length of Railway Lines		1896–97: Length of Railway Lines	
	Per 100,000 inhabitants	Per 100 square km.	Per 100,000 inhabitants	Per 100 square km.
Great Britain	39.3	3.4	86.0	10.8
Germany	16.6	1.1	91.0	8.8
France	8.5	0.6	106.0	7.6
Austria and Bohemia	7.8	0.5	70.0	5.8
Hungary	1.7	0.1	86.6	4.8
Russia	1.0	0.01	33.3	0.8
Polish Kingdom	–	–	29.3	2.9
Rumania	0.0	0.0	46.3	2.2
Bulgaria	0.0	0.0	29.0	1.0
Serbia	0.0	0.0	25.0	1.2

Sources: For 1850: N. Gross, Industrialisation in Austria in the Nineteenth Century, unpublished doctoral dissertation, University of California, Berkeley, 1966, p. 20. For 1896: A. Matlekovits, Das Königreich Ungarn, Leipzig, 1900, pp. 663–65.

modernization of agriculture. Thus, in Russia, in the first great wave of railway building in the 1860s and 1870s, grain accounted for 30 to 40 per cent of the goods transported by rail; it was only by the turn of the century, with the second boom in railway construction, that the proportion of grain carried was reduced to 20 per cent.

In Hungary, in the first wave of railway building between 1868 and 1872, grains made up 35 to 40 per cent of the traffic. By 1897 grain consignments were reduced to 20–25 per cent of the total commodity traffic.

In addition to its close connection with agrarian prosperity, railway building became a decisive element in the general economic advancement in this period. As in Western Europe, the construction of railway lines exerted a profound influence on the whole of economic life, especially by its many-sided contribution to the creation of new markets in various quarters.

The huge quantities of industrial products required for railway building could not be supplied by the home industries in the countries of East-Central Europe, particularly in the first stages of development. When railway construction first began, the bulk of the necessary material had to be imported. In Hungary, for example, most of the required rails were brought in from other countries. In the late 1870s it was estimated that home-made rails were used in 20 per cent of the total length of tracks constructed; 12 per cent of the material utilized came from Austria, 16 per cent from France, 20 per cent from Belgium, and 26 per cent from Great Britain. The requirements of railway construction created such a strong demand in mining and metallurgy products and also in railway vehicles as to contribute considerably to the onset of the technical revolution in heavy industry. By no means confined in its effects to fields producing railway materials or connected indirectly with their production, railway building had a multiplier role, bringing prosperity to the whole of economic life.

Thus, in the second half of the nineteenth century, extensive railway building in Central Europe became an important starting-point for the transformation of traditional economy, affecting every aspect of modern capitalism in Austria and the Bohemian areas as early as the 1850s, and in Hungary from the 1860s (in Russia chiefly from the 1890s).

With regard to the Balkan countries, it is not enough to point out the relatively undeveloped state of the railways. The very circumstance of their insignificant role in the economic life of these countries had broad implications. In Western Europe, even in Central Europe, railway building and the economic processes induced by it were the focus of rapid economic development for several decades and the most important factor in their prosperity. In the Balkan countries, where such internal construction failed to take place, the system consisted mainly of international lines which did not provide for a comprehensive connection of domestic markets. Still less did it become the motive force for a tremendous boom as in Western Europe and also in the Monarchy. Hence, railway construction in this area did not produce decisive economic change nor did it perform the same functions as elsewhere in the process of growth. It was thus for a time both a symptom and a cause of economic backwardness.

In this connection we must not overlook the transient negative effects of railway building on the Balkans whereby the growing importation of industrial goods caused serious damage to nineteenth-century forms of manufacture and handicraft industry. The immediate effect of the railways on these local crafts and manufactures was to set back rather than enhance prosperity. At this time the railway system had less of a domestic function and more the function of establishing connections in the world economy, with the Balkan countries serving in the international division of labor as exporters of agrarian products to, and importers of consumer goods from, Western Europe. In this sense their economy was promoted only in part by railway building; it gave no true incentive to extensive industrialization or to the development of domestic factors of production. Its economic impact was one-sided and external, contributing to the elimination of preindustrial conditions in some areas, while preserving them in others.

4 The Role of the State

The transition to modern capitalist economy described thus far—the transformation of agriculture, the establishment of a banking system, and the construction of a network of transport—has stressed various traits peculiar to East-Central Europe. The revolution of transport, however, touches on an issue often emphasized in the literature as central to development in Eastern Europe, that is, the role of the state. It was precisely the direct role assumed by the state in railway building that supported the arguments of those who claimed that state activity was a trait peculiar to modern economic transformation in Eastern Europe. The representatives of this view, of course, refer to the role of the state not only in transport but in the industrial revolution in a wider sense.

A. Gerschenkron, who was the first economic historian to deal with the problem, sheds light on all its aspects in his excellent volume of studies entitled *Economic Backwardness in Historical Perspective.*[1] He distinguishes three main types of modern economic transformation in Europe.

In the first type, exemplified by Great Britain, the process came about quite spontaneously, without any inducement by outside factors, as a result of high development and domestic accumulation of capital.

The second type, characteristic of the Western and some central European countries, relied chiefly on a system of banks and financing by banks.[2] According to Gerschenkron, these countries—France, and particularly Germany, Switzerland, Italy, and the western parts of the Austro-Hungarian Monarchy—were backward compared with Great Britain, but only moderately so. Whereas in Great Britain the level of accumulation was so high as to encourage and finance spontaneous processes of transformation, in the Western and central Continental countries this was not possible. Instead, the available capital was collected through banks, and the investment of these funds served to modernize the economy, bringing about rapid industrialization.

[1] Cambridge, 1962.
[2] "The Continental practice of effecting industrial investments through banks should be regarded as the special means of industrialization of backward countries." *Ibid.,* p. 14.

The third type of transformation took place in East-Central Europe, including Russia, Bulgaria, the eastern provinces of the Austro-Hungarian Monarchy, and Hungary. Here, the collection and investment of existing capital were insufficient, and much more energetic intervention was necessary. The principal feature was therefore active intervention by the state.[3]

In examining dissimilarities in the general preconditions of development, it would seem to be an acceptable approach to appraise the differences in the methods of industrialization in relation to the existing level of development (the capacity to accumulate capital). However, in considering the third type of transformation encountered in Eastern and East-Central Europe, it is debatable whether state intervention should be emphasized as the special and most important trait. We would suggest that Gershenkron and others espouse a one-sided view when they discuss state activity *only* in connection with the third type, and utterly disregard its universal role. As a matter of fact, the state played an important role in modern economic transformation in the whole of Europe either directly, by promoting industrialization where preconditions were not favorable enough, or indirectly, by providing for the preconditions of industrialization.

From this viewpoint it is immaterial that the above-mentioned dissimilarities occurred at different points of time in the two European areas. In countries where the state had to intervene directly in the development of industry, to counterbalance adverse preconditions, this intervention became particularly important in the nineteenth and the early twentieth centuries. Indirect forms of intervention that helped to create favorable preconditions for the industrial revolution were employed in the preceding centuries, and were replaced in the nineteenth century by the ideology and practice of free competition and the negation of the role of the state. It is this trend that prevailed in the Western areas. But the significance of state activity is certainly not diminished by this difference in timing.

It would be difficult to deny that in England where the industrial revolution was carried out with capital procured by domestic accumulation,

---

[3] "Industrialization of the Russian type is clearly differentiated from its German or Austrian counterpart by the role of the state." *Ibid.*

this accumulation was so great because, among other factors, the state had previously been extremely active in creating favorable circumstances for it. The outstanding role of the state in the Elizabethan Age in the advancement of navigation and trade and in the acquisition of colonies is common knowledge. There was also the enclosure movement and the intervention of the state to strengthen that process, as well as the notorious poor law, which helped to provide industry with manpower and to establish the discipline demanded by wage work. In the Western countries of the Continent, too, various manifestations of state intervention are evident. One notable instance was the construction in France of a network of roads by the state. Mercantilist economic policies are another manifestation, as is the protection of domestic industries. Similar provisions occurred in the Hapsburg Monarchy, particularly from the time of Maria Theresa.

It was these early and forcible measures which helped to smooth the way for industrialization in England and Western Europe, rendering the direct forms of intervention unnecessary. Therefore, the economic role of the state *itself* can by no means be regarded as a trait peculiar to Eastern Europe. The distinction to be stressed is that in Western Europe in general intervention came earlier and in an indirect form. That is to say, state intervention furthered the possibilities of accumulation of capital, while in Eastern Europe state intervention occurred later and assumed more direct forms, concentrating on the construction of a modern network of transport and on promoting industrialization. This difference affords no ground for a theory about the peculiar role of the state unless, in addition to divergent forms (and points of time), the *dimensions* of state intervention were also special in Eastern Europe, that is, of extraordinary magnitude.

What, then, was the extent of state support, chiefly in the fields of transport and industry? An examination of the applied forms of intervention referred to before in connection with railway building deserves priority in considering this question.

In the most important countries of the region, in the cis-Leithan parts of the Austro-Hungarian Monarchy as well as in Russia, railway building was, in the main, initiated as a state enterprise. The imperial Austrian decree of December 23, 1841, proclaimed railway construction to be a task devolving on the state. Yet no more than 1,355 kilometers were built in the era of state railways, until 1854; and most of this (924 km.) was really owned by the state. Thereafter, Austria abandoned the system of state railways, and major construction was carried 'on by private contractors. As previously mentioned, substantial railway building was started in Hungary when Austria had given up the state railway system; therefore construction was from the outset in the hands of private companies. In contrast to the 2,158 km. built by private enterprise until 1867, the length of the state-owned railways was altogether 125 km.

The situation was similar in Russia where—apart from the first 27 km. of the St. Petersburg–Tzarskoieselo line—the construction of the St. Petersburg–Moscow line was also undertaken by the state in accordance with a decree issued by Czar Nicolas in 1842. However, after inspection the finished line was handed over in 1868 to a joint-stock company for operation for twenty years. Finally, in 1880, 99.7 per cent of the lines open to traffic were in the hands of private companies. But even in these years the role of the state was far from insignificant; as explained before, contribution to the financing of railway construction continued in the form of a guarantee of the rate of return.

At the close of the first great wave of railway building, and after the initial period of transition to modern transport, the system of private railways became dominant in Central Europe and Russia. The situation was slightly different in the Balkan countries where railway building began much later and progressed at a much slower rate. The few lines constructed in the 1860s and 1870s were mostly the fruit of ventures by private companies in these countries as well. Projects of major importance were undertaken in the eighties, and this decade brought a decisive change in the whole of East-Central Europe, state railways gaining ground in the area. It was in these years that privately owned railways were nationalized in Austria, Hungary, and Russia; and the majority of the new lines were built as a matter of course under state management.

As decreed by the law which came into force on December 12, 1877, all the railway lines of the cis-Leithan parts of the Austro-Hungarian Monarchy which had drawn more than 50 per cent of the state guarantee of interest in the preceding five years were to pass into state ownership. This decree clearly indicates that the restoration of the state railway system was induced by the severe economic crisis of 1873 and particularly by its disastrous financial consequences. From the 1880s on the nationalization of privately owned railways accelerated, so that by 1910 about 80 per cent of the lines were in the possession of the state.

In Hungary, too, the process of nationalization started with financial rehabilitation by the state of those railway companies shaken by the crisis. The nationalization of the Tisza railway in 1880 marks the switch to a policy of energetic nationalization. In the opening years of the twentieth century, in addition to the more than 15,000 km. of state railways, only about 3,000 km. under private companies were open to traffic in the country.

In Russia return to the state railway system in 1881 was a result of the report presented by the Baranov Committee, which had been set up in 1878. An energetic policy of nationalization was approved, and by 1906 no more than 32 per cent of the railways were left in private hands out of a network owned almost exclusively by private companies in 1880.

In the Balkan countries the state railway system evolved by a similar turn of events, railway building accelerating under an increasing preponderance of state management. In Rumania private railway construction ceased in 1888, and the state assumed full control. In Serbia the state bought the Orient Railway shares between 1889 and 1892, and from that time railway building was carried on by state institutions alone. In Bulgaria all the railway lines owned by private companies were nationalized in 1885, whereafter lines were built only by the state. Thus, in the Balkans the more important stage of railway building came when the state had taken over.

According to the available records, the state did, therefore, play a highly important role in the revolutionizing of transport in the countries of East-Central Europe. This is evidenced by the payment of guaranteed interest, and by subsequent nationalization and further railway construction within the framework of organizations set up by the state apparatus. In this connection it should be emphasized that the forms and methods of state intervention described are characteristic not only of Eastern Europe. The institution of guaranteed interest was derived from the methods of railway building in the Western part of the Continent. The difference was the scale and scope of state support.

Except for Great Britain and France, the nationalization of railways was carried out almost simultaneously on the whole Continent. The first country was Germany, and the energetic nationalization which took place there made its influence felt all over Europe from the 1880s on. The expansion of state railways was provided for by law in 1897 in Belgium, in 1885 in Italy, and in 1880 in Denmark. Early in the twentieth century the breaking up of the monopoly of railway companies began in Holland and in France.

Moreover, and this is of special importance, railway building should not be regarded as a unique state activity in Eastern Europe. The highly significant role of the state in railway construction in these countries would be incomprehensible without considering the problem of the national debt; for state activity in revolutionizing transport rested on the foreign loans raised by these governments. As will be shown later, the state was extremely important in mobilizing and securing foreign financial resources; it acted as the negotiator of foreign capital.

The other, and perhaps the most typical, direct form of state activity serving economic development in Eastern Europe was the promotion of industrialization. Peculiar to this area was the intervention by the state to develop industry by legislation. The first such law was issued in Hungary in 1881, granting exemption from taxation for fifteen years to all factories with modern technical equipment producing goods not previously manufactured in the country. In a few branches of industry—the food industry, the production of agricultural machines, the textile industry—these favors were conferred on existing factories as well as on new ones under construction. Between 1882 and 1888, 236 new factories and 187 already in operation availed themselves of these advantages. Of those enjoying immunity from taxes, 81 per cent were distilleries, while in the textile branch three factories came into the favored category.

A law enacted in 1890 widened the sphere of state support. In addition to existing favors, the granting of interest-free loans was introduced (limited by law to a total of approximately 3 million crowns). Subsequently a change-over to state subsidies occurred, amounting to one-tenth to one-third of the capital to be invested by the newly founded factory. Under the provisions of the new law, it was still chiefly the distilleries (some 177 agricultural distilleries) which enjoyed the advantages of state support.

By this legislation to promote industrialization the state paid out an average of 126,000 crowns yearly in Hungary from 1880 to 1890, and an average of 487,000 crowns yearly between 1891 and 1898, under the second law. An enhanced contribution by the state to the advancement of industry was made by the third law, enacted in 1899. In accordance with its provisions 9 million crowns were paid out as state subsidies between 1899 and 1906. Of the 198 new works granted support, 45 were in the textile branch, 34 in the chemical industry, 37 in iron and machinery. The number of agricultural distilleries that benefited amounted to no more than 28.

Still another law in 1907 opened wider the gates to state support. This law provided for a practically free hand in subsidizing the production of articles serving "economic interests," the development and enlargement of existing factories in addition to the founding of new ones. Besides the payment of subsidies for a period of fifteen years, the law authorized the Minister of Commerce to subscribe to shares for the state upon the establishment of a factory that was to receive support.

In the first three years after the 1907 law came into force 10.6 million crowns were paid out to industry—more than the total amount expended during the preceding nine years. Of the subsidies, 57 per cent went to the textile industry, another 12 per cent to iron and machinery, and 6 per cent to the chemical industry.

In the case of Hungary, increasing support of industry was obviously connected with customs tariffs. In the Europe of the 1870s and 1880s isolation through protective tariffs reappeared as an indispensable instrument of successful economic competition. The customs regime of the Austro-Hungarian Monarchy, introduced in 1887, provided for an average 15 to 30 per cent protection, which was reduced by one-fourth to one-fifth as a result of the agreements concluded in 1891. The differentiated clauses of the customs tariff of 1906 embraced more than 2,000 articles: while granting exemption from duty on 101 articles, 10 per cent ad valorem duty was imposed on 880 items, 10 to 20 per cent on 553 items, 20 to 40 per cent on 450 items, and over 40 per cent on 260 items.

The union of customs areas in force within the Austro-Hungarian Monarchy and renewed every ten years by a new decree rendered it impossible for Hungary to apply protective tariffs at her own borders. Moreover, the tariffs exacted by the Monarchy did not offer any protection to Hungarian industry, for they were calculated to serve the interests of the considerably more advanced industry of Austria and Bohemia. Therefore, Hungarian economic policy deliberately tried to make up for protective tariffs at the Hungarian border by enacting laws for the support of industry. This was manifested most clearly by the 1907 law, which provided much more important advantages than the preceding ones. It was enacted soon after very strong political opposition to maintenance of the customs union was demonstrated at the negotiations of economic compromise, held in 1906 at the regular ten-year interval.

It was decided at this time (1907) to demonstrate enhanced support for industry, which was to be much more efficient than ever before. "The law providing for the development of domestic industries" stated Act III of 1907, "is destined to compensate in some degree the means of promoting industry which would otherwise be offered by the expedient forming of an independent customs area and by the rational use of the latter for the protection of industry."

The situation was similar in the Balkan countries. The international agreements intended to serve the creation of independent Balkan states constrained these states in economic spheres and in their commercial policy. For a long time they were deprived of the right to avail themselves of the weapons of customs policy that were applied against them by incomparably stronger European powers and by their neighbors. For instance, in Bulgaria the old Turkish trade agreements remained valid until 1890, and it was only in the mid-nineties that the possibility of a customs policy suited to the country's interests came under consideration. However, there was hardly any progress until the beginning of the present century.

In Serbia the terms of the peace of Pozsaveratz (Passavoritz) of 1718 were valid until the mid-1880s, according to which a maximum of 3 per cent in customs duty could be imposed on merchandise from the most important partners, Austria and the Austro-Hungarian Monarchy.

Economic conditions themselves exerted a compelling influence on the more backward countries of East-Central Europe. For instance, the trade agreement concluded in 1875 between the Austro-Hungarian Monarchy and Rumania allowed free import into Rumania of all goods not produced there, that is to say, the bulk of industrial products. When Rumania asked for a slight modification of this clause, the Monarchy launched a tariff war. A similar situation arose in Serbia in 1906.

Thus, the Balkan countries could make scarcely any use of the weapon of protective tariffs until the close of the nineteenth century. As in Hungary, this circumstance spurred the policy of direct state support to industry. The first law in the Balkans providing for the promotion and support of industry was issued in Rumania in 1887, immediately after the customs act of 1886 and the consequent involvement in tariff war. According to the new law every factory with a minimum capital of 50,000 lei and employing more than 25 workers was to be granted favors in taxation, customs and tariffs, free premises, and prerogatives in supplies to the state. In 1902, out of the existing 625 big works, 192 enjoyed the advantages offered by state support; by 1911 the number rose to 495. The new law to promote the development of industry issued in 1912 broadened the measure of support, particularly for factories using domestic raw materials, and favors were extended to smaller works.

In Serbia the first law supporting the development of industry came into force in 1893, but truly effective state assistance dates chiefly from the law of 1898. According to that statute every factory employing a minimum of 50 workers was entitled to duty-free import of machinery, building materials, raw materials, and semifinished products, as well as to favors in taxation and tariffs. These advantages were granted also to foreign firms provided that at least half of the workers were Serbians. Of the 470 factories operating in 1910, only 94 made use of these advantages.

In Bulgaria the first rather general, and not very efficient, law for the support of industry appeared in 1894, followed by others in 1897, 1905, and 1909. These provided for the usual favors in taxation and tariffs as in other countries, and secured a priority in obtaining state orders. According to records from the year 1909, state support was given to 266 factories of which 100 were in the food industry and 61 were textile works.

Thus, it is evident that the intention of these laws for the aid of industry was to offer widespread state support in the economic development of Eastern Europe. But is is also true that these intentions were far from realized. No more than a few hundred factories had been granted state support by 1914. In Hungary and Bulgaria the relation of state subsidies to capital invested in industry and the value of production is a matter of record. At the peak of state support in Hungary between 1900 and 1914, when capital invested in industrial joint-stock companies alone increased by 800 million crowns, state subsidies were only approximately 5.9 per cent of that figure. In relation to the increase in industrial output between 1900 and 1914 state support amounted to only about 2.5 per cent.

In the same period in Bulgaria state subsidies to industry amounted to 4.3 per cent of the total investment in industry and to 3.5 per cent of industrial production. With reference to these figures, calculated and published by Gerschenkron, the author himself declares that the impact of state intervention, and the contributions of the state to the development of industry, may be denoted as having been "modest." In reality, as shown by the Hungarian figures, industry-supporting measures did not exceed modest limits in any country of the region.

All this bears witness to the rather peripheral role of state intervention in the promotion of industry, notwithstanding its "spectacular" character. However, these intervening activities of the state should not be viewed as unimportant. It would be erroneous to estimate the effect of state subsidies simply by their nominal value, for state support implied official guarantees which were conducive to more favorable conditions of credit and helped to open up previously unapproachable private resources. The direct influence of the state support of industry in Eastern Europe, from guaranteed interest on capital invested in railway construction to the grants made available for the establishment of factories around the turn of the century, was probably far less important than the indirect influence exerted on foreign capital, which was attracted by better conditions and by reassuring guarantees. It is not too far-fetched to assume a relationship between the timing of the promulgation of the laws providing for the support of industry and the increasing involvement of western capital in Eastern Europe around the turn of the century.

In Hungary it can be accurately demonstrated that the laws supporting industrial development at the beginning of the twentieth century strongly attracted Austrian and Bohemian businessmen and encouraged them to found textile works. In the period 1870 to 1900 altogether 80 textile factories, and from 1900 to 1913 more than 220, were established in Hungary. As stated with some exaggeration at a meeting of the National Association of Manufacturers in May 1908 nine-tenths of the textile factories were founded with foreign capital. "After the enactment of the Factory Act," declared an eyewitness, "visitors from Hungary aroused the interest of big Austrian textile works for industrial colonization by their tempting offers. In a few weeks lawyers from Budapest, presidents of provincial chambers of commerce called at numerous

Austrian factories and held out prospects of large subsidies, exemption from taxation, and favourable tariffs. Most of the Austrian manufacturers accepted these offers and founded textile works in Hungary."[4]

Many such documents may be found in the archives of the Ministry of Trade of Vienna, as, for instance, those referring to the Vienna manufacturer Karl Wolf. By virtue of the Factory Act of 1898, this Vienna manufacturer obtained in 1900 a concession embracing all the favors granted by the Serbian state for a period of ten years for the founding of a factory to produce hempen and flaxen yarn. Wolf could import his machines and the necessary dyes custom free; he was also granted complete exemption from taxes, as well as water supply free of charge, a 25 per cent reduction in the railway tariff, and freedom from stamp-duty for the factory to be put into operation. In return the factory was to be founded with a capital of half a million francs, to be increased to one million within five years. It was furthermore stipulated that at least half of the workers were to be Serbians.

Unquestionably the laws to promote the development of industry — like the guarantee of interest in railway building — tempted foreign capitalists to establish industrial plants and make investments in Eastern Europe. Hence, here too, state intervention exerted a significant influence by luring foreign capital into the country.

Thus, though admitting that the state played an important part in the modern economic transformation, we would deny that this activity was the principal peculiar factor of economic modernization in the countries of Eastern Europe, determining the nature of the process. As everywhere, the state promoted modernization also by other means and forms, perhaps less by making available its own resources, since they were scanty, than by stimulating investments and by guaranteeing their safety. In this connection it would, however, be wrong to emphasize these methods of enticement as an essential feature. The provenance of the capital invested as a result is far more important.

It is precisely with reference to Gerschenkron's definition of the types of industrialization in Europe that the most essential trait may be stressed. By using resources afforded by particularly high accumulation, Great Britain could follow the course of spontaneous industrialization

---

[4] R. Keller, *Die Industrieförderung in Ungarn,* Prague, 1906, p. 97.

without any special expedient. The countries of the Continent which were backward compared with Great Britain, though only relatively backward, were able to collect unused capital by the aid of a network of banks and with these funds to finance required economic investments. In Eastern Europe, notwithstanding the important role of banks, these institutions were insufficient because the countries were at such a backward stage. The amount of capital, though varying from country to country, was small; in some it was negligible in relation to the enormous demands of transformation.

This grave stage of backwardness could not, of course, be counterbalanced by the economic activity of the state alone. However, state intervention was instrumental in mobilizing and procuring the necessary sources of capital. It helped to encourage an ample inflow of foreign capital. Hence, it is not the peculiar and specific role of the state, but the import of capital, promoted and motivated by state activity, which may be regarded as the feature distinguishing Eastern Europe from the rest of the Continent in the modern transformation of the economy.

5 Investments and Foreign Capital

Every country on the European Continent relied upon factors of production imported from more advanced areas—capital and skilled manpower—in the development of modern capitalist conditions. Only Great Britain, the pioneer, was able to accomplish a total industrial revolution without importing factors of production. In the Continental countries, which embarked on the industrial revolution at a much lower level of accumulation and of development of production factors, the participation of more advanced countries was significant. In France and Belgium it was initially British capital and technical cooperation which played such a role. In Germany there was considerable activity by British and French capital, and in Austria, by French as well as German capital.

The importation of factors of production in modern economic transformation followed not only from the backwardness of the Continental countries, even the Western ones, relative to Great Britain, but also from the different demands of transformation, owing to the lag of several decades and the technical progress achieved in the meantime in Great Britain and elsewhere. On the Continent the transformation demanded by the industrial revolution appeared almost simultaneously in every branch of the economy, and modernization ensued in the railway period. Therefore, the scale of investments and the capital requirements were much larger. Similar processes occurred in industry itself where the bigger factories and newly developed branches made greater demands on capital. Consequently, in the middle of the nineteenth century economic growth called for larger investments in Continental Western Europe than had been needed at the end of the eighteenth century in Great Britain. In other words, with the passage of time the industrial revolution required a higher capital/output ratio.

Thus, in the first stage of economic transformation in Western Europe, particularly when modern transportation networks were built, practically every country raised some foreign loans. France used English capital chiefly in the 1830s in the initial stage of railway construction. Nearly half of the 30 million pounds invested in French railways in the late 1840s came from a group of British financiers. In Germany the railway construction of the 1840s offered the most important field for French capital, but foreign investments were also made in industry and banking. In Sweden and other Scandinavian countries the means of building up modern transport were provided by substantial state loans marketed abroad, especially in the 1860s when over half of the bonds were placed abroad.

When the industrial revolution was in full swing, foreign capital soon withdrew, usually after diminished activity for a decade or two; and the countries in question financed their investments mainly by drawing on their own resources. When the industrial revolution had run its course, the Western countries of the European Continent themselves became increasingly important exporters of capital.

The export of capital from the highly developed capitalist countries steadily gained in significance to the end of the nineteenth century. This was closely related to the requirements of domestic economy. The realization of the industrial revolution called for the creation of extensive foreign markets and for the importation of raw materials and agrarian products. This, in turn, made investments in less developed areas indispensable: Mines had to be opened, plantations started, and the production of agrarian countries increased by the aid of loans. Above all, modern transportation was needed to connect isolated, inaccessible regions with international economic life. The accelerated capitalist development following upon the industrial revolution raised the leading powers to such a level of economic maturity as to make the export of capital an immanent necessity.

It was to the colonies that the highly developed Western capitalist countries directed their export of capital. Here Great Britain ranked foremost. After moderate export of capital in the middle of the nineteenth century, chiefly to Europe, England's intensified financial activities in the last third of the century were with the colonies overseas. Between 1875 and 1913 the amount of British investments in Europe fell approximately one-half, while investments in other parts rose fivefold. In 1854, 60 per cent of British foreign loans went to Europe, but by 1913 only 6 per cent.

At the same time East-Central Europe provided a very important market for the export of capital from Western Europe. As British interest turned to overseas areas, a large part of the rapidly increasing foreign investments of France and Germany found a market in the less developed countries of Europe.

Beginning with the last third of the nineteenth century French investments increased at an extremely rapid rate. Having abandoned extensive export of capital in the period of the Second Empire, France granted hardly any credit in the fifteen years following the Franco-Prussian War. In 1870 her foreign investments amounted to 12 to 14 billion francs, but in 1880 the figure was 15 billion and in 1890 it was not more than 20 billion francs. However, by 1905 French investments increased to 34 billion and by 1914 they soared to 45 billion. Thus, while in the middle of the nineteenth century the export of French capital averaged only 82 million francs yearly, and from 1871 to 1885 the export of capital was quite insignificant, from the mid-1880s to the turn of the century capital exports rose to 500 million francs and between 1898 and 1913 to 1.35 billion francs yearly.

German export of capital showed a similar tendency. In 1883 it amounted to no more than 5 billion marks, increasing to 10–13 billion marks by 1893, and reaching 22–25 billion by 1914. Approximately two-thirds of the French capital and slightly more than half of the German capital was exported to European countries.

The industrial revolution, starting in Great Britain and spreading to Western Europe, soon reached the countries of Central Europe, including the Hapsburg Empire, or more accurately, the cis-Leithan parts of the Austro-Hungarian Monarchy. In Austria and Bohemia, as in the West, the beginnings of the elimination of traditional economy and modern capitalist transformation go back to the end of the eighteenth century; and here too significant achievements in transport and industry resulted from the considerable resources afforded by domestic accumulation. But the huge demand for capital required to get the industrial revolution really under way could not be entirely covered by home resources; and foreign, particularly French, capital was crucial in financing the process.

A notable event in the Austrian economic history of the 1850s was the extensive activity of the Pereire Brothers in founding banks and initiating the construction of railway lines. Along with the House of Rothschild, it was the Crédit Mobilier and other French banks which cooperated in the foundation of the Bodencreditanstalt, which was destined to play a central role. The establishment of the Anglo-Austrian Bank bears witness to the activity of British capital. The construction of the Austrian state railways and the lines of the Südbahn was executed chiefly with French capital. A considerable portion of the financial resources of the state also came from government loans raised on the money market of Paris.

Nor was foreign capital absent from major projects in the later decades. The foundation of the Länderbank, an Austrian undertaking of the Bonteux group, was carried out two years after they established the Union Générale. Other interests included the Alpine Montan Gesellschaft and the Böhmische Montan Gesellschaft.

Simultaneously with these new operations of French capital, German capital also found an important sphere of activities in the Austrian economy, chiefly by entering into increasingly close relations with the Rothschild group and by financing newly built railway lines.

However, the operations of foreign capital in financing the Austrian economy cannot be identified automatically with the same process in Western Europe. In addition to having less significance in the initial period, British capital in France and French capital in Germany lost much of their importance when the industrial revolution reached the stage of realization; and foreign capital was reduced to insignificant proportions by the rapidly widening sources of domestic accumulation. Moreover, in France and Germany economic growth was so rapid that before long they could not only do without imported factors of production (i.e., capital, labor, know-how) but had become the most important exporters of capital after Great Britain.

Austria, on the other hand, notwithstanding increasing accumulation of capital, remained in need of imported capital. Her state loans, railway construction, and industrial investments—all her credits—continued to depend on the goodwill of the masters of the Frankfort-Paris money markets. Owing to the peculiar economic laws of Austria—which hampered rather than promoted the launching of joint-stock companies and as late as the turn of the century continued to bestow weighty advantages on individual or family firms—the distribution of shares and bonds in various spheres of the economy failed to furnish reliable information about the actual economic roles of domestic and foreign capital. Table 5-1 presents a picture which must be accepted with certain reservations.

Table 5-1.   The Role of Foreign Capital in the Austrian Economy
in 1900

	(1) *Total Value* *of Shares* *and Securities* *(in thousand crowns)*	*(2)* *Value of Shares* *and Securities* *in Foreign* *Ownership* *(in thousand crowns)*	*(3)* *Column (2)* *as Per Cent* *of Column (1)*
Government securities	8,741,415	2,697.497	30.8
Public bonds	772,734	80,116	10.4
Mortgage loans and other			
obligations	2,320,172	77,026	3.3
Priority railway bonds	4,237,737	3,074,457	71.6
Other transport bonds	75,448	29,217	38.7
Industrial obligations (bonds)	54,080	17,445	32.1
Other securities	229,067	8,068	3.5
Transport shares	1,060,942	609,843	57.4
Bank shares	807,600	168,437	20.8
Shares of insurance companies	41,650	13,930	33.4
Industry shares	735,139	80,554	10.9
Total	19,075,081	6,856,590	35.0

Source: *Tabellen zur Währungsstatistik*. Pt. II, p. 1920. Vienna, 1901.

It shows that a considerable part of the bonds and shares issued in Austria, about one-third, were held outside the country at the turn of the century.

While the table clearly demonstrates the still prominent role of foreign investments at the close of the nineteenth century, it also indicates, indirectly, that this role was diminishing. Foreign capital was actually concentrated in two fields, state loans and transport, which had a declining part in capital consumption. Of the total sum of roughly 6.9 billion crowns of foreign capital, 6.4 billion crowns were sunk in these branches. At the same time the two principal new fields of development in the 1870s and 1880s, banking and industry, advanced independently of foreign capital. This is evidenced not only by the small number of industrial shares in foreign hands, the ratio being still smaller in the case of private companies (especially in industry), but also by the sum total of foreign investments, which amounted to no more than 3 to 4 per cent in these spheres.

Although the role of foreign capital in Austria cannot be regarded as transient, as it was in the Western countries of the Continent, a certain similarity is nevertheless observable. Foreign capital was used chiefly in the initial development of modern economy, with a dominant function in building up the infrastructure. In branches which were increasingly dynamic, foreign capital was of less significance.

There were other similarities between Austro-Bohemian development and the growth of capitalist economy in Western Europe. Austria too soon became an exporter, as well as an importer, of capital. Certain differences existed, however: in France and Germany, initial imports of capital were *replaced* by the export of capital. In Austria, decreasing imports of capital went on *simultaneously* with the export of capital, which was steadily increasing. Furthermore, the export of capital from Vienna differed from such transactions in the Western European countries insofar as the bulk of it went to more backward countries and areas of the Austro-Hungarian Monarchy and only a relatively small part to countries outside the Monarchy.

At the beginning of the present century the foreign debts of Austria ran to 7 billion crowns. Austrian capital invested in Hungary totaled 4.7 billion crowns and investments of approximately 0.5 billion crowns beyond the borders of the customs union, chiefly in the Balkans, must also be taken into account. (The latter figure refers to the year 1903.) Therefore, in the years before the outbreak of World War I capital investments outside the Monarchy may be put at roughly 1 billion crowns.

The level of exports of Austrian capital was much lower than corresponding figures recorded for the Western European countries. Before World War I, exported capital per inhabitant was 1,250 francs in France, 450 francs in Germany, but only 180 francs in Austria. This amount, low in itself, remained behind the sum total of capital imported into Austria—about 80 per cent of that figure. Hence, in Austria there can hardly have been any surplus accumulation of capital. The import and export of capital were practically balanced.

Thus, the same thing may be said about the role of Austrian capital in foreign investments as about other economic developments in transport, banking, and agriculture. Austria was in a special state of transition between Western and Eastern European forms of development. Her growth, while marked by many traits of Western development, also displayed those typical of the countries of Eastern Europe.

A radically different picture is presented by Eastern Europe and the eastern parts of the Austro-Hungarian Monarchy. As pointed out before in connection with the role of the state, the huge capital required for the economic transformation in these countries was in sharp contrast to the paucity of domestic accumulation. This lack of accumulation was due not only to the more pronounced economic backwardness but also to the fact that the large estates, inherited from traditional conditions of farming, partly continued their wasteful consumption patterns. Therefore, the principal economic activity could provide only a very meagre source of accumulation of capital. This particularly low level of accumulation was all the more insufficient in view of the investments needed for an industrial transformation at the end of the nineteenth century.

The importance of a lag of several decades behind Great Britain has been mentioned before in connection with the countries in the western and central parts of the Continent, and so has the consequently much larger demand for capital. Obviously, the need for capital for this peculiarly late modernization of Eastern Europe was further augmented by the technological progress achieved in the meantime. Building of the infrastructure was commenced at a time when industrialization did not supply any means for such major investments. Incomparably larger requirements arose in industry by the end of the nineteenth century. As stated before, in Great Britain the amount of invested capital per workman came to four to five months' wages in the early years of the nineteenth century; a few decades later in France the figure was six to eight months' wages. At the end of the nineteenth century, when industrialization began to flourish in Hungary, the capital invested in manufacturing industry per workman corresponded to three and a half years' wages.

The costs of industrialization were further increased because the less developed countries were compelled to compete with the highly developed ones. Thus, at the beginning of the industrial revolution poorer countries in Eastern Europe with less accumulation of capital faced much harder tasks than had the countries of Western Europe. Consequently, the strongly enhanced export of capital from Western Europe in the closing decades of the nineteenth century became the principal factor in the economic transformation of these countries.

In Hungary, which formed part of the Hapsburg Empire, and then the Austro-Hungarian Monarchy, extensive foreign investments flowed in from the middle of the nineteenth century. The first major Austrian investments were made directly after the suppression of the War of Independence of 1848, chiefly in railways, navigation, and mining. In the 1850s, 100 per cent of bituminous coal mining and 75 per cent of lignite production were in the hands of Austrians. Thus, mining was practically started with Austrian capital. The situation was similar in the sugar industry. These circumstances call attention to certain peculiar features which mark the export of capital to Hungary, and, above all, to its early start.

The first major investments of Austrian capital not only preceded by several decades the extensive financial activities of the West in Eastern Europe but virtually coincided with foreign investments in Austria, Germany, and the Scandinavian area. Moreover, the forms of investment also differed considerably from the usual concentration of foreign capital in transport and in government loans. The import of capital played an unusually prominent part in the foundation of industrial plants. This was due to the existing situation, notably within the Hapsburg Empire. There was no export of capital in the true sense of the term, but more advanced centers of the empire made investments in the less developed regions. Therefore, when it came to the construction of transport lines, the opening up of the coal mines in the vicinity of the Hungarian railways was a natural step.

Of course, these mines were opened up on the initiative of the Austrian transport companies which began the transformation of communications. For instance, bituminous coal mining was started in southern Transylvania by the Austrian State Railway Company, while exploitation of the bituminous coal basin of Pécs was taken in hand by the Danube Steamship Company, also a Rothschild concern.

The incentive to establish sugar factories came from the Austrian manufacturers, who not only wanted to export their finished goods to Hungary but soon thought of setting up branch establishments to benefit from the very low price of raw materials and labor.

A new stimulus was given to foreign investments in Hungary by the increasing prosperity in economic life in the years following the Compromise of 1867. The powerful boom of the late sixties, accompanied by a veritable fever of enterprise until the crisis of 1873, was marked by a massive inflow of foreign capital to the money market and the market for long-term securities. The stepped-up railway construction, the costs of the modern Hungarian state apparatus and the government loans it required, the rapid establishment of a credit service, and, to a certain degree, even part of the investments of an industry still at the stage of slow development—all were covered by imported capital. Thus, in this brief period—of great importance for economic progress—the foreign capital of approximately 1.5 billion crowns in fact exceeded the total of domestic accumulation by 50 per cent. (See Table 5-2.)

By the turn of the century this ratio had certainly diminished. Between 1873 and 1900 the proportion of domestic sources and foreign investments in financing the Hungarian economy was roughly 55:45. Although 63 per cent of Hungarian government securities and 65 per cent of railway bonds were still foreign-owned around the turn of the century, in the export of capital to Hungary a change was clearly discernible—particularly from the eighties—in the financial transactions of the leading countries.

To begin with, the rise of Hungarian credit service, particularly the strengthening of the big banks of Budapest, was inseparable from foreign financial activities. One base of the Hungarian credit service, the Magyar Atlalános Hitelbank (Hungarian General Credit Bank), had been founded directly after the Compromise by the Rothschild group of Vienna and the Creditanstalt. Later, the Hungarian Credit Bank became much too independent to be regarded simply as an affiliate of the Creditanstalt, but the shares held by the Rothschilds and

Table 5-2. Distribution of Investments in Hungary, 1867–1913 *(in per cent)*

	Foreign Capital	Home Accumulation
1867–73	60	40
1873–1900	45	55
1900–13	25	75

Source: Iván T. Berend and György Ránki, *Nemzeti jövedelem és tökefelhalmozás Magyarországon, 1867–1914* (National income and capital accumulation in Hungary, 1867–1914), Történelmi Szemle, Budapest, 1966, No. 2.

groups of Viennese financiers remained a source of strong influence. In the 1880s the Pesti Magyar Kereskedelmi Bank (Hungarian Commercial Bank of Pest) rose to first place financially with the aid of foreign capital, chiefly the Wiener Bankverein. It was with the support of foreign loans and invested share capital that it could become the second center of Hungarian economic life about the turn of the century. In the case of the Magyar Leszámitoló—és Penzváltó Bank (Hungarian Discount and Exchange Bank)—which grew into the third largest bank of the country—its very foundation can be traced to Austrian concerns, since it was established under the auspices of the Länderbank.

Thus it seems fair to say that a minimum of 55 per cent of the shares of the big banks of Budapest were owned by foreign groups. In this period industrial investment of foreign capital became more common. According to our calculations, about half of the industrial investments of the time may be ascribed to the activities of foreign capital. Considering that foreign capital dominated the industrial investments of the 1850s and, furthermore, that it was unnecessary to possess all the shares, sometimes even the majority, in order to gain control over and dominate a firm, it is an acceptable assumption that around 1900, 42 per cent of the share capital of Hungarian manufacturing industry was completely under the control of foreign capital, while another 18 per cent was in concerns owned jointly by foreign entrepreneurs and Hungarians.

By the turn of the century, 1.5 billion crowns of foreign capital was invested in Hungarian railways, and government securities of 2.2 billion crowns were held by Austrians, and later in increasing measure by Germans and French. Municipal bonds valued at about 1 billion crowns, mortgage deeds, and approximately 600 million crowns invested in banks and industry complete the list of foreign-held Hungarian capital.

After the turn of the century the relative participation of foreign capital in financing the economy was seriously reduced. The large amounts of capital which flowed into Hungary in the last third of the nineteenth century induced a stronger accumulation of home capital and, in a wider sense, promoted prosperity. This import of capital helped to change the growth of the Hungarian economy into an autonomous process, rendering domestic factors of production increasingly capable of supplying the capital required by the economy.

The relatively smaller role of foreign capital in the early years of the present century was due to the decrease of investments in infrastructure (amounting to 60 per cent between 1867 and 1873, 50 per cent between 1873 and 1900, and 40 per cent after 1900). Moreover, the growth of processing industries, needing less capital, accelerated; the average capital/output ratio diminished; and despite the rapid increase of investments a greater part of it was covered by the domestic accumulation of capital.

Consequently, relatively smaller amounts of new foreign capital flowed into the country than before, totaling about 1.75 billion crowns from 1900 to 1913. Only an insignificant fraction of this amount went into local railways and government securities. In fact, about one billion crowns was invested in municipal bonds and debentures, and nearly 600 million crowns went to the banks and industrial concerns. In this period the share of foreign capital in financing the Hungarian economy was only 25 per cent.

Between 1867 and 1914, 6.8 billion crowns of foreign capital flowed into the country, covering 40 per cent of the investments for the economic development of Hungary. As late as 1913 foreign capital held 55 per cent of Hungarian government securities, 44 per cent of the priority bonds of railways not owned by the state, and 56 per cent of debentures and municipal bonds. In all these fields German capital pushed forward alongside Austrian capital. The former owned 37 per cent of railway bonds and 25–30 per cent of government securities. In addition, German capital played an increasingly important role in the big banks of Hungary. German banks appeared successively to back the Austrian patrons of the leading Hungarian banks: the Disconto Gesellschaft backed the Hitelbank (Credit Bank), the Deutsche Bank, the Kereskedelmi Bank (Commercial Bank). The Magyar Bank and Kereskedelmi R.T. (Hungarian Bank and Trade Company), which improved its position after the turn of the century, entered into relations with the Darmstädter Bank, but not on an equal footing.

The share of foreign capital diminished also in industry, declining from 60 per cent at the turn of the century to 36 per cent in 1913, but in some key branches of industry—machinery, leather, and chemicals— foreign capital still controlled more than 50 per cent, and also played a decisive role in mining and metallurgy.

Thus, during the whole period of the modern economic development

of Hungary, Austrian capital was highly instrumental, while home accumulation remained insufficient throughout to provide the requisite capital. The reduction in foreign capital, noticeable in the early twentieth
century, cannot be compared to that in Austria. Nor can the export of
capital by Hungary be compared to that of Austria. By virtue of the
position of the Austro-Hungarian Monarchy as a great power, leading
Hungarian groups of financiers found opportunities to take part in transactions in the Balkans of the German and Austrian big banks. For
instance, the Hungarian Commercial Bank of Pest shared in the foundation of the Marmorosch Blank Bank of Bucarest and the Blgarska Generalna Bank, in the rice refinery and cellulose works of Braila, the steam
mill of Galați, and the weaving-mill of Jași. The Hungarian General
Credit Bank cooperated in the issue of Rumanian government loans and
in the foundation of several industrial works. These modest parcels of
shares implied a moderate export of capital: the total of exported
Hungarian capital was under 100 million crowns in the early years of the
present century, rising to 184 million crowns by the year 1913. The
volume of these transactions is illustrated by the fact that Hungarian
export of capital amounted to approximately 5 per cent of the foreign
credits raised by Hungary in the same period. Before World War I
Hungarian capital invested in the Balkans amounted to only 3 per cent
of the total Hungarian national debt.

In many respects the role of foreign capital was similar in Russia.
From the 1880s about 25 per cent of all French foreign investments went
to Russia. The rapid growth in capital inflow is indicated by the fact that
in 1892 only 12 per cent of the Russian national debt derived from
foreign sources, while in 1907 the figure was 51 per cent. Foreign capital
invested in private railways ran to 85 per cent by the early 1890s and had
risen to 93 per cent by the end of the first decade of the twentieth century. The modernization of the Russian economy was not feasible
without considerable cooperation by groups of foreign capitalists, for,
as in Hungary, home accumulation was insufficient to cover the mani-
fold investment requirements.

According to certain estimates, during the wave of Russian economic
advancement between 1892 and 1908 about 40 per cent of the economic
needs were covered by domestic saving. This level was lower than that

of contemporaneous Hungary, showing a lag in Russia of several decades.

Export of capital to the Balkans began relatively late, during the 1890s, becoming a more certain flow after the turn of the century. Accumulation of capital was extremely low in these countries which had for the most part become independent in the last third of the nineteenth century while barely emerging from their state of traditional economy. Besides the low rate of accumulation, owing to the complete lack of a capitalist credit service and to an inert social and economic structure, home resources could not be mobilized, and there was little or no possibility for savings to be used for fixed capital investment. Usually savings were utilized for usurious consumer loans. The political, social, and institutional conditions of modern economy were potentially present, but adequate economic conditions were lacking. Therefore the import of capital and know-how was much more necessary for growth than in the case of Hungary.

However, in these countries the demands of modern economy appeared first and foremost as issues of power politics and strategy. As pointed out before, either the great powers insisted on the construction of certain railway lines for strategic reasons and were willing to provide the required capital, technique, machines and experts, or the requirements of the state apparatus—mostly not of a directly economic nature —called for the acquisition of foreign capital.

After the turn of the century the foreign capital flowing to the Balkans became an organic part of modern imperialist world politics. The various great powers, especially Germany and France but partly the Monarchy as well, granted to these countries loans and credits which brought them into a close relationship with the creditors' foreign policy and their spheres of interest. Thus the export of capital to the Balkans was more important in its military-political aspects than its economic.

This applied in general to all Balkan countries, including Rumania. Rumania, however, displayed a form of transition between the type of economy in Central Europe and that in Russia and the Balkans; and the state of transition was manifested also by the activities of foreign capital. In Rumania one of the principal forms of activity of foreign capital was the granting of government loans. Rumania was the Balkan country which raised the biggest government loans. First Austrian and German and then, from the 1890s on, groups of important French financiers gave credits amounting to about 1 billion francs by the turn of the century. This figure increased to 1.7 billion francs by the outbreak of World War I (52 per cent being paid out by Germany, 32 per cent by France). More than half of these loans were spent on railway construction (or the purchase of lines in possession of private companies); another third went into harbors, roads, and agriculture. The remaining 20 per cent served to cover military expenditure. Thus, the investments of the government loans raised by Rumania were primarily of an economic nature, and therefore no problem arose when it came to repayment.

The investment of productive capital in the Rumanian economy differed markedly from the activity of foreign capital in Central Europe. This becomes clear from the volume of investments. Of the eight leading big banks operating at the beginning of the twentieth century, representing three-fourths of the total bank capital, only three were founded with Rumanian capital (Banca Agricolâ, Banca de Scont, and Banca Româneascâ). The rest (for instance, Banca Naţionalâ, Banca Generalâ a Tarii Românesti, and Banca de Credit Român) were founded completely or partly (in the case of the Banca Marmorosch Blanc) with foreign capital. Of the permanent capital and reserve fund of the eight big banks, representing 176.4 million lei in 1914, foreign investments amounted to 106.9 million lei. These came from the well-known European banks—the Disconto Gesellschaft, the Bleichröder Bank, the Länderbank, the Darmstädter and Berliner Handelsgesellschaft, the Deutsche Bank, and the Crédit Mobilier.

Rumanian manufacturing industry was almost completely built with foreign capital. Around the turn of the century 92 per cent of Rumanian industrial shares were owned by foreigners. This unprecedentedly high ratio was reduced only to 80 per cent on the eve of World War I.

In industrial investments Rumania is an example of virtually direct domination by foreign economic interests, with relatively little relationship to domestic economic development. Most of the investments were in branches of exploitation which had scarcely any connection with domestic economic advancement, and merely served the raw material needs of the investors. This is evidenced by the concentration of 60 per cent of the sum total of foreign capital in the oil industry until 1914. Before the outbreak of World War I, only 4.5 per cent of the capital invested in the Rumanian oil industry was home capital, while 27.5 per cent was German, 23.7 per cent was British, and 20 per cent was Dutch. (Until 1905 the Germans controlled a 65 percent interest, while the British and Dutch share was only 9 per cent, the French 10 per cent, the American 6.3 per cent, the Belgian 3.8 per cent, the Austrian 2 per cent, and a small portion was in Italian and Swiss ownership.) The situation was roughly similar in gas and electric power production (95.5 per cent foreign capital) and in the sugar industry (94 per cent foreign capital). In the chemical and timber industries conditions were similar, foreign capital constituting 72.3 per cent in the former and 70 per cent in the latter.

In Serbia and Bulgaria the import of capital presented a still more clear-cut picture. Serbia emerged as an independent state in 1878 as a result of the Treaty of Berlin. "When the new-born state first opened its eyes"—writes an eminent researcher of the problem—"its glance fell on the creditors surrounding its cradle."[1] To this witty and pertinent remark it may be added that the first loans were raised when Serbia was still in its embryonic stage. Here we allude to the Russian loans of 1867 and 1876, which served to finance the war against the Turks. The stream of French, German, and Austrian credits began in the late 1870s. The first loans served the international cause of railway construction, for, in accordance with clauses of the Treaty of Berlin, the above-mentioned powers began to build the Serbian sector of the Vienna-Constantinople railway line, financed from the joint loan of the Länderbank and the Union Générale. This was followed by two more new railway loans, in 1885 and 1886. In 1882, the Serbian state having obtained an enormous loan from the Anglo-Austrian Bank in return for the monopoly of salt import, the whole amount was spent on rearmament. Another loan raised in the same year covered the indemnity to be paid for the Turkish land handed over to the peasantry. A loan of 1884 served to balance the adverse budget. In the next year, in addition to the above-mentioned

[1] H. Feis, *Europe: The World's Banker, 1870–1914,* New York, 1964.

railway loan, a large tobacco loan was acquired. By the year 1895 Serbia collected credits amounting to 350 million francs.

The annuities of approximately 17 million francs to be paid as amortization of these enormous credits were beyond the financial means of the Serbian state and plunged the country into bankruptcy. A solution was hoped for from a new and massive consolidating loan raised in 1895. The precondition of this credit was the issue of a law providing for a new administration of state monopolies. Accordingly, a council of six members was set up which included two appointed Serbian members, the president and the vice-president of the National Bank, as well as two representatives of the owners of the bonds (the delegates of the Banque Impériale Ottomane and the Berliner Handelsgesellschaft respectively). This committee, particularly the French delegate, came to play a prominent role in Serbian politics, exercising control over the public revenue, with the authority to regulate policy concerning state monopolies. From this time the government could not dispose freely of the public revenue, whereby the repayment of the debts was ensured, regardless of an adverse budget in case of deficit.

Finally Serbia raised twenty-six loans until the outbreak of World War I, of which ten served to settle unfunded debts (in the value of 316.5 million dinars), eight were spent on the army and on rearmament (443.5 million dinars), and another eight loans served the purpose of promoting the economy (304 million dinars).

All these loans were burdened with relatively high interest, 7 to 8 per cent, and the average value of issue was particularly unfavorable (72 per cent). Thus, at the outset of World War I interest on the national debt of over 900 million francs accounted for 30 per cent of the public expenditures. In the long run this heavy indebtedness did little to promote Serbian economic development. As shown above, most of the loans were granted to support strategic aims and the budget; it was only between 1904 and 1910 that sizable foreign loans were raised for private investment purposes. A few enterprises of the generally insignificant Serbian industry were the fruits of these investments. For instance, the first major iron works (Metallurgic Combine Smederlovo) was founded with British capital; the copper mines of Maidanpek with French capital. French capital was also active in coal mining and in the cement industry. (The Industrie de la Houille et du Ciment Franco-Serbe was founded in 1909.) Belgian capital was also very strong in coal mining (Société des Mines et Charbonnages d'Alexinats, 1903; Usine Minières et Fonderies Associées).

Foreign capital showed considerable interest in raw material exploitation; the Mines de Cuivre Saint Georges, a company for the exploitation of the copper mines of Bor, was founded in 1905 by groups of French financiers. Chromium, lead, and zinc mining elicited the participation of British capital. Some interest was evinced by foreign capital in the chemical industry and in timber. The branches of processing were far less attractive to foreign entrepreneurs; only a few sugar factories were established with German or Austrian capital just before World War I. The sum total of capital invested in 470 Serbian manufacturing plants amounted to 62 million dinars. If more than half is supposed to have been foreign-owned—according to accurate statistics from the 1920s—the direct investment of approximately 30 to 35 million dinars amounted to less than 3 per cent of the sum granted to Serbia by foreign capital in the form of government loans.

The activities of foreign capital were similar in Bulgaria. Here too, the most important area for capital inflow was the national debt. In 1887 the debt amounted to 26.4 million francs. Between 1888 and 1914 Bulgaria raised nine loans: one in London, one in Berlin, one in St. Petersburg, three in Paris, and three in Vienna. By 1900 government loans totaled 205.5 million francs, and by 1914 this amount increased more than fourfold, reaching 850 million francs.

Of these enormous amounts, granted on conditions as unfavorable as those described in connection with Serbian credits, 40 per cent went to cover the deficit in the state budget and to set up an army. Similar amounts were invested in railway construction and in the nationalization of railways. As mentioned before, the building of the Bulgarian sector of the Vienna-Constantinople line was started by a British syndicate with the cooperation of the Turkish government, to be continued in accordance with the agreement signed in 1883 by the Betriebsgesellschaft der Orientalischen Eisenbahnen backed by the Deutsche Bank. Investments of a noneconomic nature inflicted a heavy financial burden on Bulgaria. Since the acquired loans were primarily in investment fields which did not further economic growth, the domestic preconditions for repayment failed to materialize from an adequate increase in the national income. As in Serbia, so also in Bulgaria, the payment of interest swallowed up 30 per cent of the public revenue around the turn of the century.

Again like Serbia, owing to the swiftly increasing national debt and the unproductive utilization of the greater part of the credits, Bulgaria soon sank into a state of utter financial exhaustion as early as 1901. Commenting on the persistent recurrence of state bankruptcy in the Balkans, Feis remarked: "Every independent state can buy enough rope to hang itself if it is willing to pay the price."[2] The forms of solution were analogous to the bankruptcies. In 1902 Bulgaria obtained a large loan to consolidate the financial situation. The money came from a group of financiers under French control, with British participation, and in this case too the state revenues were seized as security of amortization. As a result of two more loans, raised in 1904 and 1907, international, particularly French, control grew stronger. These two loans were held mainly by the French. Whereas in the opening years of the century France thus became the all-powerful financial master of Bulgaria, with the loan of 1909 dominance passed to Austria, Great Britain, and Holland. Until 1912 Bulgaria was not granted any new French credit, but in that year a new loan was obtained through Russian mediation.

Thus, in Bulgaria the characteristic political and military motivation and utilization of loans again become evident. The role of economic investments was almost negligible. Until 1895 few foreign economic investments were made; between 1896 and 1905 altogether 15 million francs, and between 1906 and 1911 another 26.6 million, were invested in some fields of production. The capital of less than 42 million francs invested in private enterprises amounted to no more than 5 per cent of the several hundred millions of state loans.

These investments exerted hardly any influence on Bulgarian industry; until 1909, 13 big concerns were founded with a capital of 15 million francs. The conditions of a German-Austrian loan included the characteristic clause stipulating that 20 per cent of the credits were to be used for the purchase of German and Austrian industrial products. These minimal foreign investments were directed to benefit trade and the organization of a credit service. In the banking field, two were founded

[2] *Europe: The World's Banker,* p. 263.

by the French, one by Germans, and one by Austro-Hungarian groups of financiers.

Thus, it is beyond doubt that the nature of foreign capital outlay in Central Europe and in the Balkans differed considerably. Transactions in the Balkans exhibited strongly colonial traits, and the investments did little to lift the economy of these countries from an undeveloped, preindustrial level. There was no noticeable sign of the characteristic effect in Central Europe where economic mobility was greatly enhanced by foreign investments, leading to acceleration of the domestic accumulation of capital, so that at the beginning of the twentieth century home resources played a more important role in financing the economy than did foreign capital.

Notwithstanding these essential differences, the investment of foreign capital played a decisive part in East-Central Europe, exerting a direct influence on the start of economic modernization in certain countries from the last third of the nineteenth century, contributing to the development of the indispensable preconditions of this transformation in the Balkans, even to the beginnings of the process of modernization before World War I.

6 The Development of Manufacturing Industry and the Modernization of the Economy

The manifestations of progress in East-Central Europe investigated so far—the demographic developments of the nineteenth century, the agrarian transformation, the establishment of a banking system and infrastructure, and the state support of industry—provided the domestic preconditions for the revolutionary changes in industry. With the penetration of foreign capital, the rapid disintegration of traditional forms soon set in, and modern large-scale mechanized industry began to be established. In this sector the countries of East-Central Europe showed differences as pronounced as in the other branches of economic development.

Modern industrial transformation started first and proceeded most rapidly in Austria and Bohemia. Owing to relatively favorable conditions, industrialization here rose to a high level by the beginning of the present century. In the western provinces of the Hapsburg Monarchy manufacturing industry flourished in the eighteenth century. The mercantilist policy of Maria Theresa and Joseph II in support of industry encouraged the foundation of factories, mainly for budgetary reasons. Most of these industrial works, set up by the nobility—activities in which Francis of Lorraine, the consort of Maria Theresa, also took part—were concentrated in Bohemia. At the close of the eighteenth century factories were most numerous in the textile, glass, and mining industries. By the end of the century the number of bourgeois entrepreneurs among the founders steadily increased.

The earliest use of machines recorded in the Hapsburg Monarchy dates back to 1787 when Joseph Leitenberger installed a British, water-driven spinning frame in his textile factory. Not long after, the first large power-driven factory appeared. In 1801 the Englishman John Thornton set up at Pottendorf in Bohemia a mechanized cotton spinning mill. More than 18,000 spindles were in operation in 1805; by 1828 more than 47,000. By 1807, six other power-driven textile works had been established.

From about 1815 machines were introduced into other branches of the textile industry. The weaving mills were the next ones to be mechanized. The first mechanical linen-weaving works was founded in the vicinity of Vienna by Phillipe de Girard in 1816, and was put into operation the following year.

The use of machines in the machine-building industry occurred almost simultaneously with their use in the textile branches. In connection with the production of textile machinery several mechanized works were established, the first at Brünn in 1802. In 1815 an English mechanic undertook to construct the first steam engine in Moravia. As a momentous sign of revolutionized industry, coke was used in metallurgy for the first time in Bohemia at Darova, and in 1831 the first coke-heated furnace was built at Vitkovice, implying the use of the modern method of puddling. The first steam hammer was also installed there in the mid-1840s. As a result of technical innovations iron production increased between 1828 and 1850 from 73,000 tons to 154,000 tons. In the outskirts of Prague the first paper mill was equipped with machinery in 1826, and by the late 1830s three more power-driven paper mills were put into operation.

The appearance of machinery having created an industrial demand for coal, its production soared from 184,000 tons to 850,000 tons between 1830 and 1850. The mechanization of large-scale industry is illustrated most graphically by the spread of steam engines. After the installation of the first steam engine purchased in England in 1818, the number of such machines was slowly increased. The first steam engine produced in Austria was finished in 1825, but by 1830 no more than 11 steam engines were put into operation in the country. In the next decade another 30 were installed. With more vigorous growth in the forties, 903 steam engines were registered in 1852, totaling 12,114 horsepower; of these nearly 700 engines were produced in the country (with 8,800 horsepower).

Statistics from the year 1841, clearly reflecting the first stage in the progress of Austro-Bohemian large-scale industry, record that the value of production of these industries—together with that of the Lombard-Venetian Kingdom, which belonged to the Hapsburg Empire—amounted to 510.7 million florins. Of this figure 43.5 per cent derived from the textile industry; metallurgy and machine industry together contributed 11.1 per cent.

Austrian industrial production was carried on mainly in Bohemia and Moravia (34 per cent), Lombardy-Venice (27 per cent), and Lower Austria (16 per cent); Galicia supplied 7.5 per cent, while the share of the other provinces amounted to 15.5 per cent.

The next period of upswing in Austrian industry came about with the social transformation accomplished after the revolution of 1848. The 1860s, particularly, were marked by a spirit of initiative in the founding of new factories. The principal sphere of industrial development was the textile branch, which relied on extensive markets and was equipped to supply the requirements of the industrially less developed parts of the Monarchy, including Hungary with her 15 million inhabitants. In 1840, 35,000 spindles were in use in the Austrian-Bohemian textile industry and in 1850, 550,000. In 1880, despite the severe setback caused by the cotton crisis of the fifties and sixties (in 1865 only 400,000 spindles were operated), the number surpassed 1.6 million.

Machine industry also advanced appreciably. The first engine of Austrian make was produced at Wiener-Neustadt between 1843 and 1845. However, by 1870 the monthly output of engines was fifteen, a second factory having been built in Vienna in the meantime. Moreover, it was in this year that the thousandth engine produced in Austria was put into service. It was a historic event in the development of the iron industry when the first Bessemer converter was put into operation in 1863 at the old Schwarzenberg iron works. Through use of the Bessemer process, iron production rose tenfold in the next fifteen years. Coal production, estimated at 850,000 tons in 1850, leapt to 5.4 million tons by 1867, and to over 14.3 million tons by 1880.

Transformation followed inevitably in almost every branch of industry. Soda manufacture was started at Aussig in the late 1850s. Between 1850 and 1870 glassmaking was also completely transformed, chiefly by the new procedure of fusing and the use of Siemens Halske's rotary glass furnace (1867). Inventions followed one another in rapid succession, leading to fuel economies of 40 to 50 per cent. Typical of the transformation of minor branches between 1860 and 1870 was the establishment of leather factories, employing steam engines and machine tools. After 1873 leather production was drawn into the sphere of big industry.

The first serious economic crisis, in 1873, interrupted progress, and caused a sharp setback leading to prolonged stagnation in many branches. Even so, the average yearly growth of industrial production amounted to 4.1 per cent in the two decades from 1865 to 1885, far exceeding the yearly average increase of 2.25 per cent in the preceding twenty-five years (from 1841 to 1865). These figures indicate that in the period of initiative and enterprise in the 1860s the industrial development of Austria and Bohemia achieved an annual growth of 8 to 10 per cent.

In the first wave of industrialization ending in the 1870s, the use of machinery gained ground and modern big industry took shape. Table 6-1 presents this development in terms of the number of steam engines employed in industry and the value of industrial production.

The gross value of output was 2.4 billion crowns in 1880; the production of Austrian industry thus increased two and a half times between 1840 and 1880.

After the crisis-induced setback of the seventies and improvement in the eighties there arrived the true prosperity of the nineties. Austria

Table 6-1.   Austro-Bohemian Industry in 1880

	Engines (hp.)	No. of Workers (in thousands)	Net Production (value in million crowns)
Iron, metal, and machines	69,022	77.4	134.0
Textiles	63,918	204.4	333.8
Food (1890)	93,555	149.2	260.8
Chemicals	4,470	16.4	42.0
Building materials	8,151	51.7	67.8
Other branches (paper, leather, timber, printing, etc.)	57,763	78.7	84.1
Total	296,879	577.8	922.5

Source: *Statistik der österreichischen Industrie nach dem Strande vom Jahre 1880,* Vienna, 1884. The figures for the food industry are for the year 1890, as the records of 1880 contain no data on this branch, and the categories of manufacturing industry are not entirely accurate. The net production values are from the calculations in the manuscript of N. Gross, *Industrialization in Austria in the Nineteenth Century,* unpublished doctoral dissertation, University of California, Berkeley, 1966.

entered on a phase of economic maturity and reached a stage of sustained growth. From the closing decades of the nineteenth century until World War I the branches producing consumer goods continued to play a leading role in Austrian economic development. The textile industry expanded rapidly. In 1880 there were 1.6 million cotton spindles in operation; in 1902, 2.8 million; in 1907, 3.6 million; and by 1914, 4.9 million.

Cotton consumption per head in Austria was about 6.2 kg. in 1908-9, remaining far behind the British figure of 16 kg., approaching the German level (6.8 kg.) and Belgian (6.6 kg.), but exceeding the French (5.4 kg.) and Italian (4.9 kg.). The extensive markets offered by the Monarchy itself continued to play a role in the swift growth of the textile industry, one of the most advanced and internationally competitive branches of Austro-Bohemian industry. Many of the goods produced by Austrian and Bohemian factories were exported, the bulk of these exports (78.1 per cent of cotton and cotton goods, 62.4 per cent of wool and woollen articles, 56.1 per cent of silk goods, and 56.6 per cent of ready-made clothes) finding a market in Hungary as late as the early 1910s. Paper production was also noteworthy, the output of this branch having increased about fourfold from the 1880s, amounting to 5.7 per cent of the world's paper production. From the close of the nineteenth century food processing assumed particular importance. Sugar and beer production approximately doubled from 1890 to World War I. Many minor branches of food processing also developed and became important in the total production of the food industry.

Owing to limited sources of raw materials, heavy industry was substantially below the level of the Western European countries, nor was the rate of growth as rapid. The advance of heavy industry nevertheless was important in the expansion of industry as a whole. Hard coal production increased from 8.9 million tons in 1890 to 164 million tons by 1911, while brown coal production rose from 15.3 million tons to 25.6 million tons, crude iron production amounted to 320,000 tons in 1880, 1.0 million tons by 1900, and 1.75 million tons by 1913. Notwithstanding the progress achieved before the outbreak of World War I, crude iron production per head failed to reach 60 kg. in Austria at a time when it was 250 kg. in Germany and 206 kg. in Great Britain.

Among the levers of industrial advancement should be mentioned the new branches of industry—the chemical and electrical industry in the first place. In chemicals an important part was played by the refineries based on the oil fields of Galicia. Oil production of 57,000 tons in 1884 increased to 326,000 tons by 1900, and reached the peak output of 1.2 million tons in 1909, representing 5 per cent of world production.

The electrical industry was furthered on the one hand by the rapid growth of the generation of power and, on the other, by the development of the electrotechnical industry it called into existence. As regards power generation, the waterfalls of the Austrian Alps afforded a favorable source of energy for electric power plants. The first electric power plant was set up in 1886; by 1910 the total power supplied by Austrian electric plants was estimated to be about 370,000 kw. The electrotechnical industry developed through affiliation with foreign firms, chiefly German, but many Austrian firms were established with considerable domestic capital encouraged by several noteworthy Austrian inventions and the demand created by the electrification of railways. Though in volume of production the electrotechnical industry was not significant, its technical standard, concentration of capital, and competitiveness were on a high European level.

During the period of industrial progress and prosperity which began at the end of the nineteenth century and reached its zenith in the opening decade of the present century, a certain regional allocation of industry took place. A steadily increasing volume of Austrian industrial production was moved to Bohemia. This came about for several reasons. In metallurgy important branches of heavy industry were shifted to Bohemian regions endowed with coal and producing coke, replacing the earlier Austrian Alpine foundries heated with wood and charcoal. The change in the route of cotton imports and the access to American shipments now being sent on the Elbe River made textile production costs lower in Bohemia; this region benefited in general from its favorable location with regard to waterways and water carriage. With respect to the food processing industry, the broader agricultural base of Bohemia provided the foundation for sugar factories. The ascendancy of this region is apparent from the fact that in 1841, 34 per cent of the industry of the hereditary provinces was to be found in Bohemia (with Moravia), and by World War I Bohemia's share was 56 per cent and that of Austria proper only 30 per cent. The rest was distributed among Galicia and

Bukovina (9 per cent), and Dalmatia (under 5 per cent). Some 60 per cent of textile spindles were concentrated in Bohemia, over 90 per cent of sugar production, and 57 per cent of iron production. It was only in three branches that Austrian regions were superior to Bohemia: in machine production, in timber, and in the paper industry.

Thus the boom which started slowly in the eighties and gathered speed in the nineties multiplied the capital invested in Austrian industry (estimated at approximately 5 billion crowns before the war), the number of installed machines, the employed manpower, and the value of production, thereby raising industry's position in the national economy.

This dynamic development is borne out by the following figures on employment in Austrian industry:[1]

	Number of Employees	*Percentage Increase*
1890	845,946	100
1903	1,471,331	174
1913	2,304,799	272

Unfortunately reliable statistics on manpower, machines, and production are not available for the same years. To gauge advances we can only draw on statistics for 1902 concerning the performance of the machines applied and information about the prewar situation in industrial production.

According to the available data, the number of machines used in industry more than trebled between 1880 and 1902, and the total horsepower increased to 1.5 million by the turn of the century (Table 6-2).

Since data concerning the number of factories and manpower bear witness to an approximately 70 per cent increase from the turn of the century to World War I, the horsepower applied in Austrian manufacturing industry before the war may be supposed to have been around 2.5 million.

The increase in Austrian and Bohemian industrial production between 1880 and 1911 is estimated to have been 3.5 per cent yearly, as shown in Table 6-3.

---

[1] *Statistik des Jahres 1890,* Vienna, 1894, pp. 338–39; F. Hertz, *Die Produktionsgrundlagen der Osterreichischen Industrie vor und nach dem Krieg,* Vienna, 1917, p. 32.

Table 6-2. Horsepower of Machines
Applied in Austrian (Bohemian)
Manufacturing Industry in 1902

Mining and metallurgy	213,219
Iron goods and machines	277,308
Textiles	250,503
Food	313.480
Chemicals	45,966
Electric power generation	162,790
Other branches	208,507
Total	1,471,773

Source: Based on the Austrian industrial census
of 1902. Published in *Österreichisches Statistisches
Handbuch,* Vienna, 1904.

Table 6-3. Austrian and Bohemian
Industrial Production, 1880 and 1911

	1880	*1911*
Net production		
(in million crowns)	1,026	4,248
Production per capita		
at unchanged prices		
(in crowns)	59.17	162.8

Source: N. Gross, *Industrialization in Austria in
the Nineteenth Century,* unpublished doctoral
dissertation, University of California, Berkeley,
1966.

Table 6-4 shows the distribution in 1911 among the various branches
of production. Though the development of Austrian industry in the
fifteen years preceding World War I may be regarded as rapid, and may
seemed to have kept pace with that of other European countries,
Austria was in fact at a disadvantage. Austrian industry always lagged
behind that of her great rival, Germany, and behind that of the other
leading countries of Europe. In dealing with this question contemporary
literature emphasized the problems presented by raw material supplies
and the difficulties of transport.

There is no doubt that in this period the industrial development of a

Table 6-4.   Austrian and Bohemian Industrial
Production in 1911 *(value in million crowns)*

Branch	Net Production	Gross Production
Iron goods and machines	828.2	1,727.8
Textiles	1,035.2	2,361.6
Food	1,074.6	2,673.2
Chemicals	412.7	771.2
Building materials	324.0	561.8
Other branches	515.4	1,305.3
Total	4,190.1	9,400.9

Source: F. Fellner: "Das Volkseinkommen Österreichs und Ungarns," *Statistische Monatsschrift,* Vienna, 1916.

country was profoundly influenced by the proximity of coal and iron ore—the decisive raw materials of the transformation of industry. From the standpoint of costs, the iron ore in the Austrian provinces and the smaller quantities in Hungary, and the coal in Bohemia and Moravia, were not favorably distributed. On the whole, Austria did not belong to the countries richly endowed with raw materials, a fact which certainly influenced the trend of industrial development. It is also true that, compared with the other big powers, transport was more difficult for geographical reasons and, with new articles, involved a burden of heavy costs. Remoteness from the maritime trade routes considerably raised the costs of production, and even the use of river boats for shipping goods was more limited.

Above all, the relatively undeveloped state of the home market was the principal factor. In the western half of the Monarchy the process of urbanization was weaker than in the Western countries in general; there were few large towns except for the capital. The domestic market was also characterized by much lower accumulation of capital than, for instance, in Germany. The weak domestic market was a concomitant of the sluggish pace of urbanization, on the one hand, and of the backwardness of village markets and the persistence of primitive farming in rural districts accompanied by deplorably low purchasing power, on the other. For this reason mass production failed to materialize in the Austrian provinces. Moreover, modern industrial management, which had by that time evolved in industrial countries, was still lacking in this region, as reflected in the relatively small size of the manufacturing works.

The issue of domestic markets was further complicated by the multinational character of the country. The diverse requirements and consumption patterns, and particularly the different cultural levels of the various nationalities, limited the size of the market. The social backwardness of the Hapsburg Empire had economic consequences of its own. Wealth and rank still belonged to the landowners, to the aristocracy, while the accumulation of capital was severely restrained by the extravagance of these classes. Large sums were diverted by them for wasteful consumption which might otherwise have served to implement useful economic investments. The productivity of work was also lower than that attained in the Western countries. A comparison of some important indices of consumption (Table 6-5) reveals the marked superiority of one Western European country, Germany, to Austria.

In considering the relative backwardness of Austrian industry it is important to differentiate between the cis-Leithan parts of Austria and the rest of the provinces represented in the Reichsrath. These provinces, a conglomerate of areas conquered by the Hapsburgs at varied points in time and widely dissimilar in language and historical traditions, included the most advanced western and the most backward eastern types of economic development. Of the 28 million inhabitants of the so-called hereditary provinces, 11 million, or nearly 40 per cent, lived in Galicia,

Table 6-5.   Consumption per Head in
Germany and Austria in 1907 *(in kilograms)*

	Germany	Austria
Coal	2,196	740
Iron	145	45
Salt	22	15
Sugar	16.7	13.5
Paper	19.4	10.1
Petroleum	17.8	5.4

Source: Based on F. Hertz, *Die Productions-grundlagen der oesterreichischen Industrie vor und nach dem Kriege,* Vienna, 1917, p. 110, and national statistics.

Bukovina, and Dalmatia, but only 15 per cent of industry was in these parts. In the western half of the monarchy, in the Bohemian and Austrian provinces, both production and consumption were 30 to 40 per cent higher per head. In both character and structure they were therefore much closer to the Western pattern than suggested by the average figures referring to cis-Leithan regions.

The eastern parts of the Hapsburg, later the Austro-Hungarian, Monarchy followed strongly divergent paths of industrial development. Here industrialization began much later. Whereas the first half of the nineteenth century witnessed the emergence of large-scale industry and its first period of prosperity in Austro-Bohemia, in Hungary the scene was then dominated by disintegrating guilds. It was only Act 17 of 1840 which laid down the unrestricted right to found factories, supplemented by the parliamentary law of 1843–44, which conferred the right of civilian ownership outside the nobility. Statistics of 1841 show a substantial manufacturing industry in Austria, while a Hungarian statement of 1846 declares: "As regards our factories and other industrial works, their number may be put at maximum 453, including papermills, glassworks, and foundries."[2]

After the installation of the first steam engine in the cloth factory of Gács until the early forties there were in Hungary only one power-driven sugar factory, two provincial cloth and linen dyeing works, and two flour mills. Altogether nine steam engines were in operation in the country, using 100 horsepower, with 52 horsepower being applied in fields outside industry. In these years the use of coal as fuel was rare. The more important industrial establishments were the Rolling Mill Company of Pest established in 1838; about half a dozen sugar factories and approximately 100 ironworks put into operation in the 1830s chiefly by big landowners; machine shops at Buda and Pest in the 1840s; a few textile works, some in the capital and some on the estates of big landowners.

The period after the suppression of the revolution and the War of Independence of 1848–49 was an unpropitious time for the start of industrialization, with Hungary weighed down by absolutist oppression. After the union of Austrian and Hungarian customs areas in 1850–51, mechanized big industry began to take shape as a result of railway con-

[2] E. Fényes, *Magyarország Léirása* (The Description of Hungary), Pest, 1847.

struction initiated with Austrian capital. The most important stage of this slow advance was the building up of the sugar industry—as pointed out before in conjunction with the activities of foreign capital—realized by Austrian capital and entrepreneurs. It was in these years that coal mining started to develop. At the close of the decade and in the early 1870s the most important branch of Hungarian industry, flour milling, began to flourish and show rapid growth.

Until the year 1860 the appearance of machines may be said to have been only sporadic. Statistical evidence for 1863 reveals that no more than 480 steam engines were used in Hungary, totaling 8,134 horsepower. The steam engine park employed in the early sixties actually indicates the first steps of mechanization in a single field of industry: 308 out of the 480 steam engines were used in the food in-dustry. In the iron and metal industry, on the other hand, there were altogether 83 steam engines in operation; in machine industry 17; in the timber industry 29. There were whole branches of industry at the time (1863) where steam engines were still unknown. In others, they were being used very little: 6 in the textile industry, 2 in build-ing materials, 1 in the leather industry, and 7 in the paper industry.

After the 1860s the industrial revolution gathered strength. Indus-trial statistics of 1884 clearly demonstrate the first fruits. The years preceding the Austro-Hungarian Compromise, but especially those immediately following it, ushered in a period of lively initiative and energetic enterprise. In addition to the foundation of big banks and the construction of railway lines described earlier, basic industries were established. Big flour mills were built and rapidly put into opera-tion, chiefly in Budapest, by the owners of Hungarian commercial firms.

Hungarian flour milling—a counterpart of the Austrian-Bohemian textile industry—from the beginning supplied the extensive markets of the Monarchy, and other outlets for export. There was an ample and inexpensive supply of grain available. Because of their high tech-nical standards, Hungarian flour mills enjoyed priority on the world market in the middle and the second half of the nineteenth century. This was largely attributable to the Hungarian invention and mass production of the modern iron roller frame (by the Ganz Works). The grinding capacity of the large flour mills of Budapest which exported their produce increased more than fourfold between 1867 and 1870 (from 600,000 to 2,600,000 quintals). Their output (nearly 6 million quintals) expanded so rapidly that Budapest became the second center of flour milling in the world (after Minneapolis).

Thriving sugar factories, distilleries and breweries, iron manufacture, and a few branches of machine production also contributed to industrial growth. The production of rolling stock for the railways and the production of agricultural tools and machines assumed special importance. This brought considerable prosperity to mining and metallurgy. Coal production increased from 0.7 million to 1.63 million tons, iron production from 107,000 to 163,000 tons. Accompanying this was the rapid growth of Budapest, the capital of the country, which created a strong demand for building materials. The use of machines gained ground. Steam engines increased in number and in horsepower: from the 8,134 h.p. used in Hungarian industry in 1863 to 63,869 h.p. by 1884, or nearly eightfold.

However, the distribution of horsepower continued to be extremely disproportionate. Of the total, 36,646 h.p., or nearly 60 per cent, was to be found in the food industry. In the two decades between the registrations of 1863 and 1884 mechanization increased tenfold. The domination of machinery was realized in all but the small, local flour mills, which confined their activities to grinding the wheat of the peasants for their own consumption. In 1880, 17.5 million quintals of grain were ground in Hungary; 10 million quintals, i.e., 56.8 per cent, in steam mills. In the other leading branch of the food industry, sugar production, power-driven manufacture became virtually complete chiefly as a result of the equipment installed in the preceding period. The seventeen sugar-manufacturing concerns were mechanized according to the most modern technical standards of the age.

Apart from the food industry, the advance of the industrial revolution became most apparent in the iron and the metal industry. The 2,442 h.p. applied in 1863 rose to 14,844 h.p. by 1884, or sixfold. It was in these years that the technical achievements of the industrial revolution were introduced in metallurgy. Until 1867 Hungarian blast furnaces — except for the only modern metallurgic base of southern Transylvania — were heated with charcoal, and the blower system was based in most instances on water wheels. In the seventies coke was used as fuel in conjunction with the introduction of the Bessemer method. In Hungary the first Bessemer converter was put into operation in 1868, the second in 1875. Steel production began in 1869; the first open-hearth furnace was built in 1873. The old smelting works based on obsolete techniques were closed down one after another in these years. By the early eighties the number of active blast furnaces was reduced from 86 a decade earlier to 70, and the five large-scale works, equipped with modern techniques, produced 68 per cent of the country's crude iron output.

Thus the change-over actually took place in the existing iron and metal industry. It should be noted that in this branch the situation differed widely from that in the food processing industry where industrialization encompassed not only home consumption but also production for export. In the iron and metal industry, the introduction of machines was a slow process limited to a narrow field. In 1882 crude iron output per head scarcely exceeded 11 kg., while in Austria and Germany it had been more than 18 and 55 kg. respectively ten years before, and in Great Britain, 132 kg. a quarter of a century earlier. The additional machine stock of approximately 12,000 horsepower was scattered among various branches indicating that machinery had appeared but had not yet revolutionized production. In most branches of Hungarian industry the industrial revolution barely got started by the early 1880s.

The extensive technical revolution of industry took place around the turn of the century. As shown before, this process was closely related to the initiation of state support to industry, but still more to the active participation of foreign capital. As a result of investments by groups of Austrian financiers, several minor iron and coal mining firms were merged, and this amalgamation led to the floating of big companies by Hungarian standards. The founding of the Vasmü Társaság (Rima-murány-Salgótarján Ironworks Company), the Északmagyarországi Kőszénbánya Társaság (Coal-Mining Company of Northern Hungary), and later the Magyar Általános Kőszénbánya Társaság (Hungarian General Coal-Mining Company) accelerated the intensive development of mining, iron production, and metallurgy. From one million tons in 1880, brown coal production increased to 5.2 million tons by 1900, and to 8.9 million tons by 1913. Pig iron production rose from 140,000 tons in 1880 to 455,000 tons in 1900, and to 623,000 tons by 1913. Steel production, introduced in the meantime, increased from 364,000 tons in 1898 to the prewar peak of 800,000 tons.

The machine industry began to flourish in the late 1890s but was limited to the traditional production of railway rolling stock and agricultural machinery. The 161 per cent increase in horsepower promoted the growth of output in these two branches, more than doubling production in fifteen years.

Despite noteworthy progress in the traditional branches of heavy industry, the most important sphere of industrialization remained food processing. Here foreign capital undoubtedly played a relatively smaller role, but the fruits of domestic accumulation were concentrated in this sector. Flour milling retained its key position and represented a decisive factor in industrial advance, even though the rate of development slowed down after the turn of the century. Omitting the production of the small mills which ground the peasants' grain for their own consumption, the output of the milling industry was 1.6 million tons in 1898; by 1913, the volume having increased by 50 per cent, it reached 2.4 million tons. As in the preceding decades, constant growth was a concomitant of steady demand in foreign markets. Around the turn of the century Hungarian flour exports averaged 600,000 to 700,000 tons yearly, and in the prewar years they exceeded 800,000 tons. At the end of the nineteenth century about one-fifth of the exports were supplied to countries beyond the area of the customs union; after 1907, 97 to 98 per cent of Hungarian flour went to Austria and Bohemia.

Sugar production increased to 32,600 tons in 1880, soared to 198,000 tons by 1898–99, and to 591,000 tons by 1912–13. Hence, sugar production was a uniquely dynamic branch of Hungarian industrial development and, like flour milling, was among the few export industries. A considerable part of the output—at the turn of the century 173,000 tons and before the war 422,000 tons— was sold on foreign markets.

Brewing was also an important factor in the development of the food industry. Beer production was 427,000 hectolitres in 1880; by the close of the century it had increased to 1.1 million hectolitres, and to 1.3 million hectolitres before World War I.

At the end of the nineteenth century, and especially in the early twentieth, a few new branches also contributed to the acceleration of industrial development. Among these, strangely enough, was one of the oldest branches of modern industrial development, the textile industry. During the nineteenth century there had been scarcely any textile production in Hungary owing to the competition of the highly developed

Austrian and Bohemian textile factories within the Austro-Hungarian Monarchy. In the early years of the present century the textile industry got under way and in the period before World War I became the most rapidly advancing branch, along with sugar production. From 1870 to 1900, 77 textile factories were founded in the country; between 1900 and 1913 new textile works numbered 222. In the latter period the spindles used in the industry increased from 110,000 to 492,000, while the value of production rose fourfold.

Among the most dynamic branches were a few new industries born of the latest technical achievements, even though they were not of outstanding significance in total industrial production. Since the more advanced industrial countries lacked the advantage of several decades' experience in these new industries, the possibilities for competition were different from those in the traditional branches. One such field was the electrical industry; here, by the aid of several important inventions and patented processes of manufacture, the production of electric bulbs, electric motors, and electric locomotives could be developed for export. Another was the pharmacochemical-pharmaceutical industry, which came into being in the opening years of the present century.

The industrial boom that started in the mid-1880s with the growth of these branches and reached its peak at the beginning of the twentieth century attests to the peculiar course of the industrial revolution in Hungary. The widespread acceptance of machinery and the rise of large-scale mechanical industries are evident from contemporary statistics. In the period from 1884 to 1898, the first comprehensive collection of statistical evidence, horsepower increased from 63,869 to 262,070. By this time mechanical production dominated in almost every branch of industry. As a consequence large-scale industry gained superiority over small-scale industry in total industrial production. At the turn of the century 65 to 70 per cent of total industrial output came from factories working with machines.

The transformation which took place in the course of the industrial revolution was by no means terminated by these developments. It must be remembered that in the period until the turn of the century the use of machinery prevailed in a very narrow sector in manufacturing industry with a small productive capacity, which implied that until the turn of the century certain branches of industry were either lacking altogether or supplied only a slight part of the home requirement. For instance, in 1900 approximately 85 per cent of Hungarian textile consumption could be covered only by imports. Very heavy imports also prevailed in most branches of machines, in chemicals, and in others. Therefore, it would be inaccurate to speak about a truly revolutionized industry when only a few narrow branches were mechanized.

This industrializing process assumed wider proportions in the opening years of the present century and up to World War I. Between 1898 and 1913, particularly as a result of the wave of prosperity which made itself felt after 1906, Hungarian manufacturing industry spurted ahead. The number of factories increased from 2,747 to 5,521 and the number of employed workers from 302,000 to 563,000. In the factories horsepower rose from 307,000 to 930,000, more than threefold.

The data in Table 6-6 present a picture of industrial development from the close of the nineteenth century to the eve of World War I.

Of course, its rapid development did not mean that industry became the principal sector of the national economy, or that home industry dominated the domestic market even in the most decisive branches. Industrial products continued to be heavily imported. For example, the

Table 6-6.   Hungarian Industry, 1898 and 1913

Branch	Manpower (in thousands)		Horsepower of Engines (in thousand hp.)		Gross Production (value in million crowns)	
	1898	1913	1898	1913	1898	1913
Iron and machines	80.5	122.5	87.9	153.7	351.2	805.1
Textiles	17.3	57.3	12.9	56.9	73.9	242.0
Food	46.1	77.1	70.0	169.9	645.9	1,287.7
Chemicals	12.1	25.5	8.4	31.9	83.8	242.0
Building materials	31.6	35.8	15.8	66.0	51.3	136.6
Other branches	38.5	99.2	34.2	92.0	160.7	418.4
Total	226.1	417.4	230.2	570.4	1,366.8	3,131.8

Source: I. T. Berend and Gy. Ránki, Magyarország gyáripara 1900–1914 (The manufacturing industry of Hungary, 1900–1914), Budapest, 1955, p. 295.

textile industry, the most undeveloped branch which showed the speediest progress in the opening years of the century, trebling its output, could satisfy only about one-third of the domestic demand as late as the outbreak of World War I. Nevertheless, modern mechanized industry as a whole became an important economic factor.

This survey has thus far considered the Austro-Bohemian provinces and Hungary separately. From the aspect of industrialization, however, we must appraise the effects deriving from the unity of the Monarchy in dealing with the industrial development of East-Central Europe prior to World War I. These effects brought both advantages and disadvantages to the countries belonging to the Monarchy, leading to peculiar relations and creating an equally peculiar economic unity.

From the very beginning industrialization did not start within national boundaries, but in a special, broad, imperial integration. The extensive market offered by the 50 million people of the Empire created an economic situation where it was possible for the countries belonging to the Monarchy to omit the development of certain branches of industry and to concentrate their limited resources in a few sectors. As in the Austro-Bohemian textile industry and Hungarian flour milling, certain branches were favored with particularly good chances of development. This contributed to the emergence of a markedly one-sided industrial structure in the countries in question, with a striking weakness or negligible output of certain branches (for instance, textiles in Hungary).

Integration within the Monarchy brought advantages that were felt beyond industry, which also benefited. The common monetary system, the relatively small role of foreign trade outside the Monarchy, and the almost complete absence of problems involving foreign exchange facilitated the financing of the economy in less developed areas, provided for sources of cheap food and raw materials and for protected markets for the more advanced regions, thereby exerting mutually favorable effects on the countries belonging to the Monarchy. These arrangements had special advantages for Austria, the most industrialized country of the Monarchy. The common market, ensuring equal conditions to all parties formally, naturally favored the stronger in accordance with the inner laws of free competition. The situation of Austria grew all the more auspicious as it was only inside the Monarchy and in relation to countries of Eastern Europe that her development implied superiority; in equal competition with Western European firms she might have been less able to stand her ground. "The productive capacity of Austrian industry," said Neumann, one of the leading members of the Austrian Council of Industry at a session of that body on December 16, 1910, "depends on commanding access to extensive markets. Should the world market become inaccessible to us for reasons which I do not wish to discuss here, we certainly need at least the markets of the Austro-Hungarian Monarchy."[3]

At the same time Austria made it impossible for the less developed parts to avail themselves of artificial protection against the more highly industrialized partners, notably by tariffs, which from the 1870s and 1880s were applied all over Europe persistently and ever more extensively. In the common market, the less developed regions, therefore, were handicapped by the economic and industrial superiority of better developed parts, a condition which curbed their industrialization in many fields of fundamental importance. Moreover, when modern capitalist development was promoted, retarding forces were also mobilized which helped to preserve the elements of backwardness. Finally, this state of affairs elicited the Hungarian demands which culminated in the claim to an independent customs area and induced lengthy political skirmishing.

Despite these grave interior conflicts, the Monarchy could act as an economic unit in East-Central Europe and in Europe generally. Not only was it able to form a complex economic unit by including parts of varying economic levels and character and develop a multi-faceted economy, but it could also bring about the advancement of almost every branch of industry. In this respect the economy of the Monarchy resembled Europe as a whole. Before World War I Great Britain, Germany, and France produced 72 per cent of Europe's industrial output and played the leading role in almost every branch of industry: 93 per cent of European coal, 78 per cent of the steel, 80 per cent of the machines, and 74 per cent of the chemical products came from these countries, which also accounted for 73 per cent of cotton consumption. During the same period, in Belgium it was chiefly heavy industry, in Italy and Spain textiles, and in Sweden timber and steel, which represented a high level by international standards. The relative backwardness of the Monarchy was also apparent in the propinquity of undeveloped countries and provinces to the advanced regions.

[3] *Verwaltungsarchiv,* Vienna, Handelsministerium, 123–1911, 695.

While 15.6 per cent of the population of Europe lived in the Austro-Hungarian Monarchy, they produced only 6.3 per cent of Europe's industrial output. Yet the Monarchy ranked fourth in industrial output among the countries of Europe, after Great Britain (27 per cent), Germany (22 per cent), and France (13 per cent). However, this did not secure to the Monarchy any sort of "second place," since several other, relatively smaller, European countries approached its level of production.

On the eve of World War I the Monarchy was the third largest European coal producer with about 50 million tons—ahead of France—while in fuel value it occupied fifth place. In both crude iron (2.4 million tons) and steel (2.7 million tons) its output represented 5.8 per cent and 6.3 per cent respectively of the total production of Europe, fifth in order of magnitude. In number of spindles used in cotton spinning (4.9 million) the Monarchy was outstripped by Great Britain, Germany, Italy, and France.

The other big power of Eastern Europe, the Russian Empire—the study of which lies outside the scope of our present work—displayed many similarities to the eastern provinces of the Austro-Hungarian Monarchy in industrial development. In the first half of the nineteenth century only sporadic initial signs of modern mechanical large-scale industry appeared in Russia.

Until 1861, when the serfs were emancipated, only the preliminaries of the transformation existed, and even the years between 1861 and 1890 constituted only the initial period of the industrial revolution. In 1861 the number of industrial works may be put at 14,000 to 15,000, employing 850,000 workers. If the value of Russian industrial production in 1913 is designated as 100, in 1860 the index of output was 8, in 1890 only 27. In the late 1870s the total horsepower of the steam engines used in industry amounted to 115,000 and although the number of steam engines doubled by 1892 and horsepower increased threefold, the level was still extremely low. The first great strides were made in the 1890s, when the number of industrial enterprises rose by no more than 18.3 per cent, but factory workers increased by 66.5 per cent, while industrial production was doubled. The capacity of the steam engines in industry between 1890 and 1912 increased from 345,000 h.p. to 1.2 million h.p.

In the prewar years the rapid economic progress of Russia following the reforms of Stolypin—as in Hungary—led to such an expansion as to make mechanized large-scale industry an important economic factor.

Industrialization proceeded similarly in the Polish Kingdom. Mainly as a result of the emancipation of the peasantry in 1807 and the decrees issued between 1816 and 1823 providing privileges to foreign craftsmen and manufacturers, some animation characterized industry in the first half of the nineteenth century. The abolition of the customs frontier between Russia and Poland in 1850 and the simultaneous initiation of railway construction laid the foundations for the beginnings of industry. However, no noteworthy progress ensued until the mid-1870s. In 1877 some 8,349 factories employed in all 91,000 workers. It was at this time that industrialization began. By 1895 nearly 13,000 factories were in operation; their number was reduced by approximately 2,000 by 1910, but it was in these years that the era of large well-equipped mechanized factories set in. This is brought home by statistical evidence: while in the first period the number of factories increased by 50 per cent and manpower more than doubled (from 91,000 to 206,000), in the second, simultaneously with the fall in the number of factories, manpower again nearly doubled.

In the western parts of the Polish Kingdom, particularly in the environs of Lódź, Częstochowa, Dabrowa, and Sosnowiec as well as in Warsaw, it was chiefly textiles, food processing, and certain branches of heavy industry which throve. The leading industry, textiles, relied on the markets of the Russian Empire and exported three quarters of its output. It is still more remarkable and bears witness to the increased use of machinery that in the period between 1877 and 1895 the value of industrial output increased from 274 million francs to 739 million francs, and by 1910 to 2,279 million francs—about ninefold in hardly more than three decades.

The figures presented in Table 6-7 throw light on the prewar level of manufacturing industry in the Polish Kingdom.

The evidence of industrialization in the Austro-Hungarian Monarchy and in the Russian Empire poses the issue of whether the economic transformation and modernization which took place in the countries of East-Central Europe was sufficient to be considered a process of industrial revolution. In this connection reference is made to what has been said in the introduction—that we subscribe to the interpretation of industrial revolution which conceives of the process not merely as the technical transformation of single branches of industry but as the large-scale structural transformation of the whole national economy.

Table 6-7. Manufacturing Industry in Poland Before
World War I

	Manpower (in thousands)	Value of Products (in million francs)
Textiles	175.7	1,031.3
Food industry	42.5	409.9
Mining, metallurgy, iron, and machinery	107.7	451.8
Building materials	23.1	80.6
Chemicals	9.2	79.0
Other branches	42.8	226.6
Total	401.0	2,279.2

Source: E. Piltz, *Poland: Her People, History, Industries, Finance, Science, Literature, Art, and Social Development,* London, 1909, p. 160.

Judged by these standards, the facts presented furnish unequivocal proof that in East-Central Europe the impact of the changes that took place in the last third of the nineteenth century affected the whole economy and transformed all its branches. The reorganization of agriculture on a modern capitalistic basis advanced at a rapid rate while a system of modern banks and credit service was established. These years saw the rapid creation of modern transport, railway networks, and the infrastructure in general. In all of the countries under review modern, mechanized, large-scale industry appeared and the process of production assumed a cyclic rhythm though not in equal measure or on the same level. The whole economic and social position of these countries was transformed. From this time the national economy was influenced increasingly by industry, the dynamism of the economy in essence being determined by industrial development, while the changes within the various branches of the national economy—from agriculture to foreign trade— all came into correlation with industry, reflecting its effects. The changes that took place in social structure, urbanization, the development of the working classes, the emergence of the urban petty bourgeoisie—all the new elements brought into the society of these countries around the turn of the century—were inseparable from the growth and progress of industry.

Again, the western parts of the Austro-Hungarian Monarchy, strictly speaking the Austrian and Bohemian provinces, have to be dealt with separately. Though their development and maturity were influenced by their geographical situation and history and by being part of the East-Central European empire whose agrarian development differed from Western Europe's and though their retarded social transformation and other features resemble Eastern European conditions, these regions nevertheless display a quantitative lag relative to development in Continental Western Europe rather than a qualitative divergence. This interpretation is supported by developments that took place in the Austrian and Bohemian provinces almost simultaneously with those in Western Europe and also by their close approximation to the western level of development by the prewar years. The occupational distribution presented in Table 6-8 bears out this contention.

The occupational distribution of the working populations in these countries shows a similarity to the distribution of the national income in Austria by branches of production (Table 6-9). Thus, in the prewar years about one-third of the Austrian national income came from agriculture and 49 per cent from industry. Inasmuch as the average-reducing values of the undeveloped provinces belonging to Austria cannot be discriminated in the data referring to the national income (the average having been calculated with the inclusion of Galicia-Bukovina and Dalmatia where 79.9 and 85.2 per cent of the respective populations worked in agriculture), it becomes obvious that the economic level of the Austrian and Bohemian provinces reflected by occupational distribution corresponded to the average level of Continental Western Europe.

Table 6-8. Percentage Distribution of the Working Population of Germany, France, and Austro-Bohemia, by Occupation, 1906–1910

	Germany 1907	France 1906	Austrian Provinces 1910	Bohemian Provinces 1910
Agriculture	33.1	42.5	42.3	38.1
Mining and industry	37.4	30.0	25.0	34.5
Trade and communications	11.6	14.0	13.5	10.7
Other fields	17.9	13.5	19.2	16.7
Total	100.0	100.0	100.0	100.0

Source: Based on national statistics.

Table 6-9.   Austrian National Income,
1911–1913 *(in billion crowns)*

Agriculture	4.0
Mining and industry	6.1
Trade and communications	1.9
Net income from foreign investments	0.4
Total	12.4

Source: Based on F. Fellner, "Das Volkseinkommen Österreichs und Ungarns," *Statistische Monatsschrift,* Vienna, 1916.

The foreign trade of the western half of the Monarchy—though in this respect the Bohemian and Austrian parts are absolutely inseparable from the rest—suggests similar relations. When the foreign trade of the whole Monarchy is examined, the items show imports of finished goods to be 26.7 per cent and exports of finished goods 47.8 per cent, but these figures embrace non-Austrian imports of Hungary and Hungarian exports outside of Austria. In the foreign trade of the cis-Leithan provinces alone, including supplies to Hungary, 60 per cent of exports consisted of industrial products, 17 per cent of semi-finished goods, and 23 per cent of raw materials. (In exports to countries outside the customs union finished products amounted to no more than 52 per cent, while 73 per cent of supplies to Hungary consisted of industrial products.) Even the lowest estimates confirm the picture of a relatively highly developed industrial area, though foreign trade figures expose the relative backwardness of Austria's provinces compared with the most advanced industrial powers.

The Hungarian-Polish-Russian type of development cannot be identified with this model of advancement and maturity. The processes in operation there show essential differences. However, the fact of development cannot be doubted in these countries. In the economic transformation which took place under the impact of the industrial revolution starting in the last third of the nineteenth century, the rate of growth of the national income was accelerated at much the same pace as in Western Europe.

Between 1860 and 1913 in Russia—including the data on Poland which are not separately available—the yearly average increase in national income slightly exceeded 3 per cent. In roughly the same period in

Hungary it amounted to 3.7 per cent. These increases show clearly that in the period in question one group of Eastern European countries attained the dynamism characteristic of the age of industrial revolution. Various statistics that are available permit a comparison of the growth rate of East-Central Europe with that of Western Europe before and during the industrial revolution.

In the decades preceding the industrial revolution in Great Britain— between 1700 and 1780—according to the computations of S. Kuznets, the average yearly growth of the national income was around 0.5 per cent. In the same years, according to the work of W. Hoffmann, the average yearly increase in British industrial output was also 0.5 to 1 per cent. (In the two decades following the middle of the century, the yearly average increase of the national income in Germany was about 1.8 per cent.) The typically slow economic growth of the preceding years was strongly accelerated when industrial revolution got under way: in the century from 1780 to 1880 the yearly rate of growth in national income rose to 2.8 per cent and the yearly increase in industrial output exceeded 3 per cent.

Thus, the aforementioned increase in national income in Russia and Hungary from the last third of the nineteenth century to World War I shows rates of growth comparable to those prevailing in Western Europe during the industrial revolution rather than in the period preceding the process. Put more precisely, it was actually industrial development in the first place which lent modern economic dynamism to the national economy: the increase of industrial output was much more rapid than the growth of the national income. In Russia, while the yearly growth of the national income was 3 per cent, large-scale industrial output showed an average yearly increase of 5 per cent between 1860 and 1913 (between 1862 and 1882, 3.5 per cent; between 1882 and 1913, 5.72 per cent). For Hungary the corresponding figures were 3.2 per cent and 5.2 per cent respectively.

By the prewar period the economic and social structure was considerably transformed by the dynamism of development typical of the age of industrial revolution. The changes occurring in the distribution of employment and in the national income structure are the most revealing indicators of these processes. At the time of the reform of 1861 over 90 per cent of the population of Russia—again including the Polish Kingdom—earned their livelihood in agriculture. As a result of the industrialization that started in the last third of the century, at the census of 1897 the agrarian population was found to have been reduced to 78 per cent. For lack of information we are unable to gauge the consequences of accelerated progress after the turn of the century by the population distribution, but the tendencies become clear from the fact that between 1897 and 1913 the urban population increased from 16 million to 28 million, or from 12 per cent to 18 per cent of the total population. If the rate of growth of urban population is supposed to have been equal to the rate of increase of the industrial population (using a minimal estimate), before World War I only slightly more than 70 per cent of Russia's population was working in agriculture.

In Hungary, according to the first census, more than 75 per cent of the population were in farming in 1869. By the census of 1900, the agrarian population declined to 68 per cent and by 1910 to 64 per cent.

The picture presented by the occupational distribution of the population provides incontrovertible evidence that from the last third of the nineteenth century to World War I the social structure of these countries was essentially transformed. The 80 to 90 per cent preponderance of the agrarian population in the sixties was reduced to 60 to 70 per cent by the 1910s, and the previously insignificant industrial population became an increasingly important proportion. Supplementing this transformation was the structural change in the national income. According to estimates dealing with Hungary at the time of the Compromise of 1867, approximately 80 per cent of the national income was produced by agriculture. By the turn of the century the agricultural contribution sank to 64 per cent, by the prewar years to 62 per cent. During the same time the share of industry increased from 15 per cent to 25 per cent, then to 28 per cent.

Unfortunately no similar statistics are available for Russia; the earliest data are rather rough, subsequent estimates. According to these, in 1913 over half of the national income was produced by agriculture and about 28 per cent by industry. Unavoidable sources of error are suggested by these estimates since, from the distribution of the population, it seems certain that in prewar Russia a slightly larger part of the national income came from agriculture and a slightly smaller part from industry than in Hungary. This is confirmed by the fact that industrial output per head was about 15 per cent lower in Russia than in Hungary around the turn of the century.

It should also be noted that there was a much more rapid expansion of large-scale than of small-scale industry. By 1910 more than half of the total industrial manpower of Hungary worked in factories. About 75 per cent of the industrial output was produced by mechanized industry and only 25 per cent by small-scale industry. In the Polish Kingdom the ratio was similar around the turn of the century. Workers in small-scale industry numbered 140,000 in the mid-1890s, while 205,000 were employed in factories. However, the value of the products of small-scale industry amounted to 300-315 million francs, less than half of the 738 million francs produced by manufacturing industry. Prewar figures may have been closer to those in Hungary.

Available records provide adequate support for the statement that in Russia, Poland, and Hungary industry had become an important factor by the beginning of the present century, supplying about one quarter of the national income, contrasted with its insignificance in the 1860s when it accounted for one-tenth to one-seventh of the national income. Agriculture's share of the national income, on the other hand, declined from over three-fourths to about two-thirds.

The foreign trade of these countries also shows the level of development and the changes in economic structure. At the end of the nineteenth century, finished goods amounted to over 70 per cent of Hungarian imports. Imports of raw materials and semi-finished goods were extremely low: 20.6 per cent and 9.3 per cent respectively. By 1913 the proportion of finished articles imported had declined but still accounted for over 60 per cent of total imports, while the share of raw materials and semi-finished goods increased from less than 30 per cent to more than 38 per cent. These altered proportions alone shed light on the modernization of the economy. Moreover, as a result of industrialization, not only did the import of raw materials and semi-finished goods increase but the structure of finished goods imports also underwent a change. The items showing the most rapid increase on the import list were those produced by iron, metal, and machine industries. In relation to the 1882–91 figures, imports in this group of articles increased 92 per cent by the turn of the century, but from 1902 to 1911 the average growth was more than threefold—from 6.7 per cent to 12.6 per cent of the total imports of finished goods. The structure of exports showed little change. Slightly more than half of the total (in 1900, 54 per cent; in 1913, 52.2 per cent) consisted of agricultural raw materials, while finished goods remained between 37 and 38 per cent. Two-thirds of the finished goods exported derived from products of the food industry.

The undeveloped state of the processing and consumer goods industries is evidenced by the exportation of important raw materials of the timber, paper, leather, and textile industries and their importation in a processed, finished form (for example, timber exports in 1913 valued at 83 million crowns against imports of wooden articles having a value of 46 million crowns).

The structure of Russian foreign trade, though exhibiting similar tendencies, was at a slightly less developed level. On the export side, the dominant role of agricultural products was still more marked. Just before World War I nearly 74 per cent of exports were supplied by agriculture, while industrial raw materials and semi-finished goods accounted for over 13 per cent and finished industrial products for less than 13 per cent. The greater part of imported goods, about 60 per cent, were finished industrial articles—virtually corresponding with the Hungarian figure. Approximately 13 per cent of total imports consisted of machines and industrial equipment.

Notwithstanding the existing preponderance of agriculture, these data unmistakably confirm the advance of industry, the reduction of imports of finished industrial products accompanied by an increase in imports of machines. In exports hardly any role was played by other than agricultural products or their industrially processed forms. All this gives an unequivocal picture of the essential economic transformation which had taken place.

Unlike the Austrian-Bohemian or Russian-Polish-Hungarian type of East-Central European development, the processes which ran their course in the Balkan countries did not lead to a comparable transformation. Until the turn of the century Rumania, Bulgaria, and Serbia were unable to shake off the inertia typical of preindustrial economies. Their social and economic structure displayed the pattern characteristic of the level prior to industrial revolution. While thorough documentation is impossible owing to the incomplete statistical sources, the reliability of the available evidence is beyond doubt. The lack of dynamism and utter stagnation are fully revealed in Serbia by a comparison of 1836 records with the census of 1900. In 1836, 90 per cent of the population found a livelihood in farming, while the number of craftsmen was slightly more than 5 per cent. In 1900, after more than six decades, when the great transformation was well under way in many countries of East-Central Europe, 84 per cent of the population of Serbia still worked in agriculture, and the proportion of craftsmen was still under 7 per cent. Rumanian figures also demonstrate the absence of dynamism, for they disclose that from the 1860s to the turn of the century the urban population increased by only one-third.

Serbia's situation in the first decade of the twentieth century, with a vast preponderance of the population in agriculture and only 16,000 miners and factory workers by 1910, was largely duplicated in Bulgaria. According to the census of 1905 the agrarian population accounted for 82 per cent of the inhabitants, while the industrial population, including nearly 16,000 factory workers, was around 7 per cent.

The level of development was slightly more favorable in Rumania, chiefly owing to the onset of oil production. In 1910 only 10 per cent of the population earned their living as tradesmen, while about 25 per cent of the total production came from industry.

Modern industry appeared in the Balkan countries around the turn of the century. In the period prior to World War I this was an indisputably important step in development, even if the role of industry continued to be subordinate in the national economy as a whole.

Until the middle of the nineteenth century there were only a few works in Rumania which used machinery. According to statistics for 1863 there were 12,867 industrial workshops and factories employing altogether 28,500 workers. More than half of these (6,771) were flour mills, but only 117 of them operated a steam engine. After the emancipation of the serfs, industry started to advance slowly. At the time of the census of 1886 only 153 industrial works employed more than 25 workers, and only two branches of industry, flour milling and the sugar industry, rose above the level of handicraft workshops.

At the end of the nineteenth century the first, introductory steps of industrialization followed upon the favorable development of agriculture. Industrial transformation began chiefly in the flour milling and sugar industries. In 1902 only 625 large industrial works were recorded, with not quite 40,000 workers and engines totaling 45,000 horsepower. Over half of these were in the food industry. Of the 232.7 million lei of capital invested in Rumanian industry, nearly half was tied up in food processing. The other branches, perhaps with the exception of the timber industry, were virtually absent or had not yet started on the road to large-scale production.

At the beginning of the present century it was continuing agricultural prosperity but especially the exploitation of the oil fields with foreign capital which gave an impetus to industry. This stage went hand in hand with a wider use of machinery, greater coal consumption—coal production increasing in the period 1900–1915 from 100,000 to 300,000 tons— and the development of several branches into large-scale industry. A small amount of heavy industry was also established, but even by the early 1910s this branch could supply no more than 10 per cent of the very small domestic investment goods requirements. The use of electricity was initiated with the building of 34 minor electric power plants (of 40,000 kw.). The first stages of the textile industry were seen chiefly in the new works founded after 1906, leading to a 60 per cent increase in output by the outbreak of the war, especially in the spinneries. This output, however, covered only 12 per cent of home consumption.

The advance achieved in the early twentieth century and the level of development reached before World War I are illustrated in Table 6-10. The vigorous increase in manpower and horsepower in the opening years of the century bear witness to the start of the industrial revolution.

Table 6-10. Development of Rumanian Industry at the Beginning of the Twentieth Century

Branch	1902		1915	
	Manpower	*Horsepower*	*Manpower*	*Horsepower*
Food	9,810	18,990	7,607	42,111
Iron and machines	7,226	2,902	8,163	9,670
Chemicals	2,569	1,436	3,426	11,891
Timber	6,752	6,247	14,121	21,596
Textiles	2,346	1,745	6,678	9,082
Other branches	8,622	13,891	13,475	21,491
Total	37,325	45,211	53,470	115,841

Source: N. P. Arcadian, *Industrializarea României,* Bucharest, 1936, pp. 116, 121.

It may be added here that in the period in question the value of industrial output increased from 231.6 million lei to 547.1 million (i.e., by 136 per cent). The oil branch was the focus of prosperity. Though horsepower increased more than threefold in the iron, machine, and timber branches, and more than fivefold in the textile industry, it was nevertheless the eightfold increase in machinery in the chemical industry that was the most striking sign of growth. The central role of the oil industry becomes still more evident when we consider that of the total investment of 247.4 million lei in Rumanian industry in 1902, 31.5 million lei were invested in the chemical industry, but of the total investment of 636.5 million lei by 1915, investment in the chemical industry had soared to 403.6 million. It is not only the unprecedented rapidity of this increase (over thirteenfold) which is noteworthy but also the fact that nearly two-thirds of the total industrial capital was concentrated in the chemical branch before World War I.

As pointed out before, these were the years when Rumanian oil production developed with huge foreign investments. After the Steaua Română founded earlier with German capital and the Astra Română in which the Royal Dutch Shell held a financial interest, the most important were the Telega Oil Company, floated in 1900 with British and Belgian capital; the French enterprise Aquila Franco Română, established in 1904; the Creditul Petrolifer, a German undertaking; and the Romano-Americana, brought into existence by the Standard Oil Company. With the penetration of the largest international oil organizations production increased at an extremely rapid rate: from 297,500 tons in 1901 it grew to slightly more than 1,810,000 tons by 1914. With this output Rumania rose to fifth place among the major oil producers of the world. The bulk of the oil produced was exported in a crude state, but the above-mentioned companies also started to build oil refineries, investing 41 million lei before the war. For most refined products, however, Rumania was obliged to resort to imports.

Thus Rumania's industrial development at the beginning of the twentieth century differed markedly from industrialization in the countries of East-Central Europe. Advancement was induced by extraneous forces and was concentrated narrowly in crude oil exports. If the effects began to be felt in other fields of industry and in the national economy, they certainly did not penetrate strongly enough to bring about industrial revolution or the modernization of the economy.

In Bulgaria the late and feeble beginnings of industrial transformation do not go back further than the 1870s. The preceding decades saw only the incipient disintegration of handicraft industry associated with the introduction of modern transport and the appearance of foreign industrial products. The emigration of Turkish tradesmen was followed by a decline in the handicraft industry: in 1880, 25 per cent of tradesmen in Bulgaria were Turkish; by 1910, after the departure of approximately 200,000 Turkish tradesmen, the proportion sank to less than 12 per cent.

Before 1878 large-scale industry was represented by no more than a few factories: four woolen mills, one silk mill, one glassworks, two paper mills, a few flour mills and distilleries. In 1894, 500 industrial workshops and factories were active with 5,732 workers. Of these only 75 may be regarded as big plants, employing a total of 3,000 workers. Large concerns existed only in wool, flour-milling, breweries, and distilleries; the other branches stagnated at the level of small-scale industry.

Little progress was noticeable around the turn of the century. By 1909 the number of large works had increased more than threefold, but of the 266 plants, in which 66 million levas had been invested, large-scale industry was still represented in only two branches: food and textiles. Of the major firms 100 were active in food, 61 in textiles, so that 59.1 per cent of the total of invested capital was concentrated in these two branches of industry. In the other branches mechanized big industry, if any, was confined to a few foreign firms. Foreign capital, amounting to 21.4 per cent of the total investment, served to establish a few electric power plants, mining works, and chemical works. Foreign investments in large firms of these branches amounted to 95 per cent in electric power, 71 per cent in mining works, and 35 per cent in chemicals.

Thus, until the 1910s, large-scale industry did not gain much ground in Bulgaria. Of the exceedingly low industrial consumption, only about one-third was supplied by home production in the first decade of the twentieth century. Heavy industry was almost completely absent, and the machinery imported—valued at 151.2 million levas between 1882 and 1911—was not the type characteristic of industrialization. Of the imported machinery 17 per cent consisted of agricultural machines, 6 per cent of sewing and knitting machines—the typical instruments of small-scale industry—while the share of locomotives and steam engines was only 14 per cent.

Table 6-11.   Bulgarian Industrial Development, 1887–1911

	No. of Works	Invested Capital (in million levas)	Manpower	Horsepower	Value of Output (in million levas)
1887	36	—	—	—	—
1894	72	10.9	3,027	—	—
1900	103	19.3	4,716	8,970[a]	32.8[a]
1907	206	53.9	7,646	—	41.6
1909	266	66.0	12,942	17,677	78.3
1911	345	91.1	15,886	27,885	122.5

Sources: Based on G. Entscheff, *Die Industrie Bulgariens,* Leipzig, 1915, p. 123; and K. Popoff, *La Bulgarie Economique, 1879–1911,* Sofia, 1920, p. 329.

[a] Data from 1904.

The figures presented in Table 6-11, summarizing Bulgarian industrial development, show only rudimentary signs of an industrial revolution. Manpower of 15,000 and horsepower of 28,000 are figures that speak for themselves. It is nevertheless worthwhile to note the statistics for 1911—the year preceding the Balkan Wars—presented in Table 6-12.

Thus, before the war, mechanized big industry had made its appearance in only a few fields. The branches which were developing, food

Table 6-12.   Bulgarian Industry in 1911

Branch	Invested Capital (in million levas)	Manpower	Value of Output (in million levas)
Mining and metallurgy	11.5	4,176	11.1
Food	36.6	3,126	67.4
Textiles	15.9	4,267	21.4
Building materials	6.4	1,281	4.7
Chemicals	3.4	655	1.2
Others	17.3	2,381	16.7
Total	91.1	15,886	122.5

Source: L. Pasvolsky, *Bulgaria's Economic Position,* Washington, 1929, p. 27.

industry in particular, produced for export, as did the specialized tobacco industry in large measure.

The development of Serbian industry displayed the typical Balkan
pattern. The guilds had been formed only after the revolt of 1816. The
disintegration of the guilds began after the disappearance of the old
Turkish market and the penetration of mainly Austrian industrial products in the 1870s and 1880s as a result of modern commercial relations.
The first representative of manufacturing industry was a steam mill
founded in 1862, followed in the period until 1880 by the establishment
of several more steam mills, two power-driven sawmills, two distilleries,
a foundry, and a brick yard.

Owing to extremely poor domestic accumulation, the disinterest of
foreign capital, and the lack of markets, the Serbian economy was not
lifted out of its traditional backwardness until the 1880s. Beginning
slowly, a few new projects materialized. The first mechanized cloth
factory was founded with Austrian capital in 1880, a cotton mill with
German capital in 1891, and other woolen cloth factories and cotton
mills at the close of the decade.

In 1905 there were 153 flour mills, 14 steam sawmills, 9 distilleries,
and 93 factory-like works in other industries. The total capital invested
was 36 million dinars, and output was valued at 29 million dinars, of
which 16 million derived from flour mills and 2 million from breweries.
Thus, transformation into big industry had not even started in the food
branch; there was, for example, no sugar production until 1906, the
first factory founded in 1898 having been ruined in a short time. Sub-
sequently, new sugar factories were founded mainly with German
capital.

Although Serbia was very rich in timber and ore, apart from a few
steam sawmills there was no timber or mining industry and no processing of these raw materials. Metallurgy, paper, furniture, and machine
production had not yet been started.

In Serbia, too, it was only after the turn of the century that industrialization began to show a slow growth. Iron production started on a very
modest scale, coal production increased (from 1 million tons in 1898 to
3 million tons by 1913), as did the exploitation of nonferrous metals.

Such new branches as cement industry (1900: 162,500 quintals; 1910:
1,675,500 quintals), certain lines of chemical industry, and glassmaking

began to develop, while the textile and food industries continued to expand. In 1910, 470 factory-size works were in operation, half of them mills. Table 6-13 gives some idea of the scope in this period.

Thus the development of Serbian industry did not substantially differ from the Bulgarian pattern in character or level. Here, too, merely the beginnings are noticeable after the turn of the century. However, the relative advance in mining and metallurgy indicates that in Serbia industrial development was extrovert; and its relationship to foreign capital, intended as a source of raw materials by the investors, is still more obvious.

Meanwhile small-scale industry remained preponderant. In the years before World War I the total value of Bulgarian industrial output was estimated at between 440 and 500 million levas of which 120 million levas, or no more than one-fourth of total industrial output, was produced by manufacturing industry. In the same years, on the strength of records from 1911, fewer than one-third (46,000) of all industrial workers (142,000) were employed in big industry.

Therefore, in the Balkans not even the Russian-Polish-Hungarian variant of the East-Central European industrial revolution took place. Insignificant industrial production, generally marked by the preponderance of small-scale, handicraft industry, prevailed, together with the predominance of agriculture in the national economy. After the turn of the century the appearance of factories, the building of an infrastruc-

Table 6-13.   Serbian Industry in 1910

Branch	Invested Capital (in million dinars)	Horsepower	Manpower	Value of Output (in million dinars)
Mining, metallurgy	12.3	4,866	3,426	4.0
Iron and machinery	8.9	8,154	4,326	14.0
Food	24.8	6,987	3,874	41.8
Textiles	4.4	1,200	2,048	6.0
Building materials	4.0	1,175	1,221	2.4
Chemicals	2.7	473	333	2.1
Other branches	4.9	1,175	867	4.1
Total	62.0	24,030	16,095	74.4

Source: J. Kirkner, *Die Industrie und Industriepolitik Serbiens,* Halle, 1913, p. 159.

ture, and the establishment of a modern network of banks were the first beginnings of the industrial revolution.

All this was clearly discernible in the structure of foreign trade of the Balkan countries. For instance, in Rumania finished goods accounted for 75 per cent of imports while agricultural products made up 70 per cent of exports. No essential change came about until World War I, except for a slight increase in timber and oil exports. In Bulgaria in 1908, 60 per cent of imports consisted of three groups of articles—textiles and products of the iron and machine industries. Exports, on the other hand, consisted almost completely of agricultural products. It is typical of industrial backwardness that in the exports of Serbia at the close of the century even the share of products stemming from the food industry was only 5 per cent, while the rest was made up almost completely of crude agrarian produce.

The structure of foreign trade in the Balkans reflected the agrarian character of these countries and the almost complete absence of big industry. The growth, destination, and commodity structure of foreign trade in East-Central Europe are shown in Tables 6-14 to 6-18.

Notwithstanding the essential differences in industrial development and agrarian transformation, many similar features and tendencies may be found in the Russian-Hungarian-Polish variant and in the Balkans. The tardy development of industry started mostly with the cooperation of Western capital; the belated process of industrialization displayed a conspicuous one-sidedness, which, though varying widely in these countries, nevertheless was manifest in the relatively small role of the textile industry and the relatively dominating role of the food industry. All over Europe the branches producing the most important consumer goods made the most rapid progress. In both textiles and food processing, there were extensive markets, technical difficulties could be overcome more easily contributing to high profits, less capital was needed, and manpower could be recruited from the less skilled strata of labor, without the requirement of expensive training. The relative importance of textiles and food processing was decided in every country by economic factors. These included the nature of the available raw materials, the trends of demand in domestic and foreign markets, and, last but not least, the industrial level and structure of competing countries.

Table 6-14. Development of Foreign Trade in East-Central Europe, 1850–1913 (in million dollars: 1913 purchasing power)

Year	Exports					Imports				
	Austria	Hungary	Serbia	Rumania	Bulgaria	Austria	Hungary	Serbia	Rumania	Bulgaria
1850	50	30[a]	4.7	9.4	–	60	30[a]	2.5	5.6	–
1870	190	138	6.0	31.6	4.2[b]	207	134	5.6	14.2	6.4[b]
1890	309	212	9.2	55.0	14.2	244	194	7.6	72.4	16.9
1900	388	265	13.3	74.0[c]	10.8	339	222	10.8	58.2[c]	9.3
1913	800	381	23.4[d]	135.0	36.9[d]	864	415	23.1[d]	118.0	38.9[d]

Sources:

For Austria: *Aussenhandel und Zwischenverkehr der im Reichstrate vertretene Königreiche und Länder und der Länder der heiligen ungarischer Krone in Jahre 1913*, Vienna, 1914.

For Hungary: S. Konek, *Magyar Birodalom Statisztikai Kézikönyve* (Statistical Handbook of the Hungarian Empire), Budapest, 1875; *Külkereskedelmi Forgalmunk 1882–1913* (Foreign Trade of Hungary), Budapest, 1923.

For Serbia: I. Z. Nestorović, *Der Aussenhandel Serbiens*, Leipzig, 1913; *Statistika Spolasnie Trgovinie*, 1912, Belgrade, 1913.

For Rumania: M. Ströll, *Die Handelspolitik der Balkanstaaten Rumänien, Serbien und Bulgarien. Schriften des Vereines für Socialpolitik. Band III*. Leipzig, 1892; F. Schmatz, *Grossrumänien*, Gotha, 1921; *Commercial external al Rumaniei en 1910*, Bucharest, 1911.

For Bulgaria: W. K. Weiss-Bartenstein, *Bulgariens Volkswirtschaft und ihre Entwicklungsmöglichkeiten*, Berlin, 1918; M. Ströll, op. cit.; *Statistique du commercu du Rogaum Bulgarie avec les pays entrangers pendant l'anne 1910*, Sofia, 1911.

[a] 1847. [b] 1879. [c] 1901. [d] 1911.

Table 6-15. Destination of Foreign Trade in East-Central Europe, 1880–1913 (in per cent)

Austria

	Exports		Imports	
	1882	1913	1882	1913
Hungary	36	37	35	31
Germany	42	25	43	27
Balkan states	6	7	5	3

Hungary

	Exports		Imports	
	1882	1913	1882	1913
Austria	68.6	72.6	84.0	71.5
Germany	15.9	6.4	5.2	10.0
Balkan states	4.5	3.3	6.7	2.5

Rumania

	Exports		Imports	
	1876–1880	1906–1910	1876–1880	1906–1910
Austro-Hungarian Empire	38.1	10.0	51.5	24.6
Germany	0.3	7.8	8.9	33.9
France	12.9	6.4	8.9	5.3
England	26.0	10.0	17.1	15.3
Turkey	10.6	4.2	4.2	3.6
Belgium	–	28.0	–	9.2

Bulgaria

	Exports		Imports	
	1886	1906–1910	1886	1906–1910
Austro-Hungarian Empire	4.4	20.5	26.5	26.3
Germany	–	16.8	3.3	17.2
France	22.8	5.4	6.0	6.5
England	15.6	16.9	28.5	16.3
Turkey	37.9	14.1	17.5	13.1
Belgium	–	–	–	–

Serbia

	Exports		Imports	
	1879–1883	1906–1910	1879–1883	1906–1910
Austro-Hungarian Empire	86.0	28.9	91.0[a]	34.4
Germany	–	24.8	–	32.0
France	–	3.3	–	3.8
England	–	1.3	–	12.0
Turkey	5.4	14.8	3.6	5.4
Belgium	–	–	–	–

Source: See Table 6-14.
[a] With Bosnia.

Table 6-16.   Five Main Commodity Groups of East-
Central European Export in 1910 *(as per cent of
total value)*

	Hungary	Rumania	Serbia	Bulgaria
1. Cereals				
(total)	17.7	78.5	40.0	53.6
Wheat	4.6	53.0	12.7	25.0
Corn	3.2	11.5	21.7	18.0
2. Flour	12.5	1.5	3.4	9.0
3. Animals	20.1	1.0	11.0	5.6
4. Animal				
products	5.1	1.0	14.8	10.1
5. Fruits	2.5	1.0	17.1	2.0
1-5 total	57.9	83.0	87.3	80.3

Source: See Table 6-14.

At the time of the industrial revolution the textile industry played a
leading role in several countries—primarily in Great Britain and France
but also in Germany to a certain extent. However, only in Great Britain
did the textile industry have absolute preponderance; this followed from
the peculiar development of British agriculture, which afforded little
opportunity for the growth of the food industry while heavily promoting
the woolen industry, and even more from Great Britain's special function in the development of capitalism in the nineteenth century. As the
world's industrial workshop, from the very beginning Great Britain built
up her textile industry to meet world requirements. In France and
particularly in Germany the textile industry, while significant, was by no
means paramount.

In other countries of Western Europe, for instance in Belgium, Denmark, and Holland, the food branch already accounted for the largest
share of manufacturing output in the first period of industrial development. The more agrarian nature of their economies automatically created more favorable conditions for the food industry. In addition, these
countries were surrounded by big powers which had been industrialized
earlier (especially England), and thus offered an extensive and rapidly
growing market for agricultural products and processed foods. The textile industry of these small countries, on the other hand, faced strong
competition from neighboring big powers not only on foreign markets

Table 6-17. The Ten Main Wheat-
Exporting Countries and Their Share
of World Exports in 1910–1913

Country	Thousand Tons	Per Cent of World Exports
Russia	4,000	22.8
Argentina	2,400	13.7
Canada	2,200	12.6
Rumania	1,450	8.3
India	1,400	8.0
U.S.A.	1,400	8.0
Holland	1,300	7.4
Australia	1,200	6.8
Hungary	450	2.6
Bulgaria	120	0.7
World total	17,500	100.0

Source: Based on the publications of the Institut International d'Agriculture and the *Time Series of the World Economy,* Budapest, 1967.

but also at home. However, the food processing industry cannot be said to have been a determining factor in any Western European country. By the second half of the nineteenth century an important textile industry existed even in the smaller Western European countries though its share

Table 6-18. The Seven Main Flour-
Exporting Countries and Their Share of
World Exports in 1910–1913

Country	Thousand Tons	Per Cent of World Exports
U.S.A.	1,200	39.3
Hungary	725	23.7
Canada	350	11.4
Australia	135	4.4
Argentina	120	3.8
Russia	100	3.2
Rumania	90	2.9
World total	3,058	100.0

Source: See Table 6-17.

in total output of industry remained behind that of the food industry (see Table 6-19).

Certain branches of heavy industry were also important in the process of industrialization, particularly in countries where the steady progress of industrialization ensued in the middle of the nineteenth century. Light industry nevertheless retained its primacy to the end of the nineteenth century. The ratio of light to heavy industry was 2.3:1 in Germany in 1895; 1.7:1 in Belgium and 2.5:1 in Denmark in 1896; 2:1 in France in 1901.

Thus far the contribution of the leading branches in the industrial development of the nineteenth century has been discussed mainly in terms of their share in the total industrial output, that is, quantitatively. Their effect, however, was much too far-reaching to be reduced to simple ratios. Industrial output itself expresses more than a mere quantitative scale, and a branch of industry acquires particular importance for its dynamic growth and the influence it exerts on other fields of industry, on the rate of employment, on foreign trade, on the whole national economy. The industries in the Western countries were capable of furnishing a decisive impulse to the transformation of the whole of industry in the course of the industrial revolution.

By contrast, no such essential changes occurred in Eastern Europe and the Balkans. Here, the beginnings of manufacturing industry were accompanied by the leading role of the food branch. By the beginning of the twentiety century 44 per cent of the output of manufacturing

Table 6-19.   Share of the Textile and Food Branches in the Total Output of Industry, Late Nineteenth Century *(in per cent)*

	Great Britain 1871	France 1896	Germany 1895	Belgium 1896	Denmark 1897
Textiles	45	31	27	15	21
Food	7	13	19	34	25

Source: I. T. Berend and Gy. Ránki, *Das Niveau der Industrie Ungarns zu Beginn des 20. Jahrhunderts im Vergleich zu dem Europas: Studien zur Geschichte der Österreichisch-Ungarischen Monarchie,* Budapest, 1961.

industry in Hungary came from the food branch alone, while the share of the textile industry was only 5 per cent. As late as 1913 in Russia 26 per cent of the total output of industry was in food processing and only 22 per cent in textile, leather, and clothing industries. In Rumania in 1902 the corresponding figures were 55 and 10 per cent; in Bulgaria in 1910, 58 and 18 per cent respectively. In Serbia 55 per cent of the total output of manufacturing industry came from the food branch and only 8 per cent from textiles in 1910. This concentration limited the impact of advancing industry on other branches of the national economy; owing to the nature of its technology, the food industry exerted a milder influence on other sectors, and, needing comparatively less manpower, its transforming effect on society was much more modest than that of the textile or heavy industry branches.

In East-Central Europe, therefore, the process of industrialization reached the first stage during the last third of the nineteenth century and up to 1914. However, this process was peculiar not only on account of its long delay compared with Western Europe.

The industrial revolution was begun by and characterized by the dynamism of economic growth, the building up of infrastructure, and the transformation of the structure of the national economy. Understood in the widest sense of the term, as explained previously, and regarded as an integral part of the process of the development of capitalist structures, there is justification in placing the development which took place in East-Central Europe around the turn of the century in the category of industrial revolution. However, it would be wrong to equate the industrial revolutions of the West and of East-Central Europe, designating the latter simply as a later edition or copy of the former. Under its special conditions of development, East-Central Europe evolved a model of industrial revolution which differed qualitatively from that in the western half of the Continent.

We have drawn attention to the divergencies noted in numerous regions, to particular features of East-Central Europe such as the peculiar temporal correlations between industrialization and the revolutionizing of transport, the special structure of the branches of industry, the specific role of foreign capital in the advancement of the process. These factors not only explain the traits peculiar to the industrial revolution of East-Central Europe but by their joint effect unmistakably differentiate it from the model of industrial revolution in Western Europe. All the factors investigated so far acted in one direction: in the largest areas of East-Central Europe they produced a period of industrial revolution which began late, was carried out dissimilarly or in a contradictory manner, or was actually not pursued to its conclusion, terminating before it had been accomplished.

As a result of the industrial revolution in Western Europe a radical economic and social change took place. In a historically brief period traditional economy and society were suddenly transformed into a modern economy and society. In a few decades industry became a determining force and the largest branch of national economy not only through its dynamism and economic influence but also by its weight and direct role in the economy. The countries of Western Europe which went through the industrial revolution became industrial countries. By the middle or second third of the nineteenth century the Western countries of Europe had shed their earlier agrarian character. As mentioned before, in Great Britain the industrial population gained absolute numerical predominance; in Holland the agrarian population formed only 40 per cent of the total in 1849, while in France the share of agriculture in the production of the national income fell below 50 per cent.

In the countries of East-Central Europe the data from the beginning of our century clearly demonstrate the peculiar lag still existing in these parts several decades later. It was not only that the period of industrial revolution was still going on, but also that the industrial revolution did not bring about such changes or permeate the whole of industry as it did in the West. The countries of Eastern Europe remained agrarian countries. Authors like V. Jacunsky and R. Portal who have dealt with the subject have emphasized the partial, limited nature of the transformation in Russia, and have delineated industry as scattered islands in a sea of agrarianism.

The internal and external factors influencing economic growth did not produce the challenge that could generate a response of quick industrialization. As we have noted, the impetus in Eastern Europe came rather from the general conditions prevailing on the Continent than from the imperative of inner development. It was the steadily widening markets for agricultural products in the countries of Western Europe, where the industrial revolution had taken place and rapid industrialization was in progress, which gave a powerful impulse to the modernization of agriculture stagnating at a medievel level in Eastern Europe, and in this connection to building a modern infrastructure and establishing banks. The development of industry was started with the capital investments and loans of the industrialized West and raised to a certain level, but this young industry had to adjust itself throughout to the raw material requirements of creditors or foreign financiers, to the interests of transport and communications, and to the surviving agrarian character of the countries. Consequently, the inner economic structure of the countries of East-Central Europe changed but did not undergo a radical transformation; their international economic relations were not altered essentially; and they remained suppliers of agrarian products to the more industrialized West.

7 New Trends of Modern Capitalist Development Around the Turn of the Century

At the close of the nineteenth century, parallel with the economic growth, new phenomena began to appear in economic life, particularly in Germany which was in the vanguard of economic development. These affected only the forms of management at first but soon were felt in the whole economic structure. The first signs may be traced to the crisis of 1873 and the years of depression that followed when firms in a few branches of industry, having come up against sharp competition and unfavorable prices and market conditions, tried to improve the situation by concluding agreements. The forming of these cartels, or monopolistic combinations, on a national scale was assisted by the policy of protective tariffs introduced in the late 1870s, though this was not the primary cause of these new tendencies. Monopolistic trends were most widespread in the industrially advanced and dynamic countries. They were a consequence of capitalist maturity, appearing after a fairly long period of sustained growth and in highly concentrated branches or in those susceptible of high concentration. Monopolistic organizations were to be found in the economy of every Western European country, mostly in the form of cartels.

The other important new feature, referred to in contemporary literature as "finance capital," chiefly after Hilferding, was not so general or clear-cut. Finance capital denotes the process by which investment banks, whose principal activities formerly consisted of negotiating loans, gradually became the masters of the whole of economic life. Under their leadership industrial, commercial, and bank capital was amalgamated. The classic example of finance capital was Germany where the leading big banks, the so-called D Banks, became increasingly interrelated with the largest industrial concerns, and the key positions of economic life gradually came under their full control.

If these modern trends are regarded as the consequences of a period of sustained growth, to what degree can such tendencies be discovered in East-Central Europe where development had reached a much lower level, and what was their relation to internal progress as opposed to external influences? Again, the manifestations varied considerably from region to region. In the Monarchy, particularly in the western half comprising Austria and Bohemia, where economic development lagged only slightly behind the Western European countries, the first forms of monopoly organizations arose after the crisis of 1873, as in Germany. The early effects of protective tariffs and the relative weakness of the domestic market led, in 1878, to the formation of a cartel in the iron industry where limited resources and the large capital demanded by modern techniques and technology facilitated the emergence of monopolistic combination. At this time only the rail mills formed a cartel, which other branches of the industry joined in 1886.

According to early estimates, in 1880 four cartels were active in the cis-Leithan parts; in 1890, 18; and in 1900, 57. These 57 monopolistic organizations embraced the iron, chemical, and textile industries as well as building materials and various branches of the food industry. The primitive forms of cartels usually made arrangements for the marketing of certain products and for the fixing of uniform prices, or the division of markets, sometimes by regulating terms of sale. Only after the turn of the century did monopolistic arrangements encompass entire branches of industry and influence the whole economy. The number of cartels soared from 100 in 1905 to about 200 by 1912, extending to every field. Some of the combinations in iron, sugar, oil, cotton, spirits, cement, machines, electrical apparatus and appliances reached beyond the western half to the entire Monarchy. Because of the union of customs areas, actual monopolistic control could be secured only by agreements covering all the markets of the Monarchy; in Hungary, therefore, the formation of monopoly organizations was inseparable from their expansion in the Monarchy.

In the classical process of capitalist development, a period dominated by small-scale industry in the nineteenth century was followed by big industry, and this relatively longer historical stage led to the emergence of new monopolistic forms about the turn of the century. However, because the development of capitalism took place later in Hungary, as pointed out before, numerous processes were delayed and contorted.

This was true as well of other countries of East-Central Europe. Owing to her geographical situation Hungary maintained relatively close economic ties with the developed countries. As a part of the Austro-Hungarian Monarchy, Hungary experienced the economic processes occurring in the economically more advanced regions of the Monarchy, even though the domestic conditions of Hungary had not yet matured sufficiently. Hungary's less advanced stage of economic development was manifested in the smaller number of cartels—only 100 cartel agreements were concluded before the First World War. The first cartel was formed here too in the late seventies, but it was only after the turn of the century that the slow development of the eighties and nineties— when the majority of cartels were in a rather fluid state—was followed by the spread and consolidation of such combinations.

Of course, the formation of cartels in Hungary was influenced in many respects by the conditions prevailing in the Monarchy as a whole. In certain branches—where Hungarian industry appeared as a competitor on Austrian markets—the Austrians urged the formation of a common Austro-Hungarian organization embracing the whole territory of the Monarchy. In other spheres, where Hungarian products were not competitive, Austrian endeavors were in the opposite direction: Austrian manufacturers rejected every Hungarian proposal and were unwilling to form a common syndicate lest it weaken their influence on the Hungarian market. The Hungarian factories then either formed a union of their own or failed to do so when they had justifiable doubts about the efficacy of such an agreement. Thus, owing to the peculiar structure of the Monarchy and its multinational composition, separate Austrian and Hungarian cartels were also active, along with common combinations. Moreover, enhanced antagonism between nationalities led to the establishment of certain Bohemian combinations such as the syndicate of Czech banks formed in 1910.

Of the combinations in the Monarchy the most important were the iron, sugar, and oil cartels. The foundation of the iron cartel dates from the sharp competition which followed the crisis of 1873. This fight ended with the first agreement of its kind, concluded in 1878 by the leading Austrian-Bohemian ironworks, notably the Witkowitzer Eisenwerk, the Erzherzog Albrecht'sche Eisenwerke, the Teplitzer Eisenwerk, the Ternitzer Eisenwerk, the Prager Eisenindustriegesellschaft, the Hüttenberger Eisenwerkgesellschaft, and the Steyerische Eisenindustriegesell-schaft, bringing into existence the first rail cartel. The latter, marking out spheres of the market, served as the model for further agreements in the iron industry. After the partial agreements of the early 1880s, a comprehensive iron syndicate was organized in 1886, embracing almost all the branches of the iron industry. The signatory firms divided the market among themselves and fixed uniform prices.

An industrial combination similar to that formed by the Austrian factories was reached by the Hungarian ironworks in 1879, and signed in a more concrete form in 1886. This was followed by a combination of the respective rings of the Austrian and the Hungarian factories. According to the terms of this common cartel of 1897, the Hungarian market was allotted to the Hungarian factories, while the quota of Hungarian exports to Austria was laid down on a basis similar to that of Austrian exports to Hungary, providing mutually for the surplus re-quirements of the two countries.

In 1900 the common iron cartel found itself in a critical position be-cause a group of German financiers who owned a Hungarian ironworks (the Hernádvölgy Ironworks) began to compete with the cartel, but failed in the attempt. The shares of the company were bought by the largest Hungarian firm of the branch, the Rimamurány-Salgótarján Ironworks Company, which straightaway started to fight the Austrian factories for an increase in its production quota. This sharp competi-tion, pursued by means of undercutting (the Hungarian firm under-bidding bar-iron at the dumping price of 15.7 crowns instead of the current quotation of 20 crowns in its effort to gain a foothold on the Bohemian market), lead to the decartelizing of Austrian and Hungarian ironworks in 1900. However, after this episode in the opening year of the century, peace was restored in 1902, the quota of iron exports to Austria being raised by over 40 per cent—instead of the nearly three-fold increase originally demanded—and the cartel agreement was further consolidated.

Within the syndicate of ironworks those producing minor articles were classified into subgroups, and quotas were determined on the basis of the output in the three previous years. Simultaneously, the introduc-tion of new articles was prohibited. This successful agreement provoked heated debates in the Austro-Hungarian Monarchy in the 1910s. The price-raising effect of the iron cartel's activities exposed it to criticism for fleecing other branches of industry and to censure by the press as an obstacle to industrial development. Despite these attacks the iron cartel remained one of the strongest economic powers in the Monarchy until World War I.

The Austro-Hungarian sugar cartel was formed later than the iron cartel, in 1891. The brown sugar factories were the first to combine, followed by the refineries, and in 1897 the two combinations signed a cartel agreement. The signatory firms fixed the quotas of production and came to an understanding concerning prices. After the convention of Brussels the sugar cartel continued its activities with minor modifications, raising prices by about 50 per cent by 1910.

The activities of the Austro-Hungarian oil cartel also go back to the early nineties when the oil producers and then the refineries combined. After alternate decartelizing and reunion (1897, 1901) a more solid combination was finally formed in 1903 with the participation of thirty-two firms. It was on this basis that the crude oil producers floated the Petrolea Crude Oil Company, their exclusive common sales office, and the refineries bound themselves to purchase their requirement from the Petrolea Company alone. It was an important objective of this syndicate to broaden its foreign markets, and, above all, to conquer the German market. To realize this aim negotiations were begun with the Standard Oil Company.

These conversations having failed, the Austro-Hungarian Oil syndicate founded a joint export firm and tried to break into the German markets of the Standard Oil Company. The American trust accepted the challenge and retaliated without delay by founding the Vacuum Oil Company with 20 million crowns capital and three oil refineries within the Monarchy, one of them in Hungary. This sharp competition led to the breaking up of the oil syndicate in 1907. It was only the firm intervention of the Austrian government that saved the situation. First, the combination of crude oil producers was revived by the aid of substantial orders from the state; then contracts providing for preferential tariff rates and industrial tracks were repudiated.

At this point the Deutsche Bank intervened and offered to bring about cooperation among the major oil groups of Europe which could then face American competition successfully. In a letter dated June 5, 1910, the Deutsche Bank expressed the opinion that it would be a mistake on the part of the Austro-Hungarian oil syndicate to enter into negotiations with the Americans. Instead the Bank recommended collaboration with it, all the more so as it held considerable financial interests in the Russian and Rumanian oil industry. With close cooperation successful measures against the Standard Oil Company might wring from that company an agreement concerning spheres of market activities.

The German offer greatly contributed to completing the above-mentioned steps taken by the Austrian government, which had intended to open conversations with the Germans only after having cleared the situation. Finally, the refinery syndicate was revived in 1911.

Keen Europe-wide competition accelerated the formation of combinations in other branches of industry. In the new branch of electrotechnical industry Austrian and Hungarian firms appeared as members of international syndicates. For example, the Verkaufsstelle der Vereinigung Glühlampenfabrication (VVG), founded in 1903, counted German, Swedish, Italian, and Dutch, as well as the leading Austrian and Hungarian factories among its members. Besides the 22.6 per cent production quota of the A.E.G. and of the Siemens Works, the 11.3 per cent share of the Hungarian firm Egyesült Izzólámpa és Villamossági Gyár Rt. (United Incandescent Lamps and Electrical Company Ltd.) equaled that of the Philips Works. Of course, the electrical industry was not unique in this respect. In 1913 the sphere of activities of 18 international syndicates extended to the Austro-Hungarian Monarchy. Naturally the first to penetrate were those connected with German monopoly organizations since the inflow of German merchandise and capital was the strongest in the Monarchy in the period under review. Cartels were active in such fields as railway rolling stock, flour milling, brewing, mining, and brick making.

Though these monopolistic unions included syndicates and trust-like formations, the most widespread combination was unquestionably the cartel form. This may be explained not only by strong German influence and by the relatively less advanced economy of the Monarchy, but by the peculiar situation that in both Austria and Hungary bank capital was much more highly developed than industrial capital. In many instances the banks stood behind the foundation of industrial plants. Since large industrial firms were brought into existence with the cooperation of the banks, industry became increasingly dependent on the banks.

Often banks insisted upon the formation of cartels, taking it on themselves to organize cartel offices in certain branches. Moreover, the banks played a leading role in forming combinations by founding the Österreichische Kontrollbank in 1914. This institution was established by the big banks of Austria for the purpose of controlling cartels, managing the affairs of various syndicates, their central sales and supervision, and settling the sales and market quotas of the members. The foundation of this institution clearly shows the correlation between the big banks and the monopolies as well as the dominating position of the banks. In many cases these concerns could exercise the functions of vertical trusts, since formally independent enterprises active in various branches of industry but belonging to the same banks embodied a special form of concentration and cooperation and were able to avoid fluctuation of profits.

An investigation of the interrelations of Austrian bank and industrial capital has revealed the existence of four major groups around the banks of Vienna by the opening years of the twentieth century. The group headed by the Creditanstalt, backed, of course, by the financial power of the Rothschilds, and the group of the Wiener Bankverein were the most important, each with a serious industrial concern embracing almost every branch of economic life. However, the group led by the Anglo-Austrian Bank, the Länderbank, and the Unionbank, and that centered around the Bodencreditanstalt were also economically significant.

Some banks endeavored to extend their sphere of interest to all branches of industry; others strove to acquire influence over the most important major works within certain fields in order to gain control over the branch and its management. The Creditanstalt, the Wiener Bankverein, and the Niederösterreichische Escompte Gesellschaft held a capital interest of approximately 70 million crowns in mining, metallurgy, and the machine industry. Practically every big industrial firm was under the control of a bank (the Witkowitz Works, the Prager Eisenindustrie, and the Siegl Locomotive Works to the Creditanstalt; the Alpine Montan Gesellschaft to the Niederösterreichische Escompte Gesellschaft; the Böhmische Montan Gesellschaft to the Wiener Bankverein). Among the modern branches the Anglo-Austrian Bank and the Länderbank possessed strong influence in the electrical and chemical industries, while most of the big plants of the textile and food industries came under the control of the three largest banks or joined the combination headed by the Bodencreditanstalt.

According to certain statistics, the industrial concerns belonging to the nine big banks of Vienna controlled approximately two-thirds of the capital invested in Austrian industrial joint-stock companies on the eve of World War I. It must be added here that a Czech group of finance capital began to take shape around the Zivnostenská Bank of Prague.

In compliance with the aristocratic structure of Austrian society, the top group of Viennese *haute finance* comprised not only the heads of the big banks and industrial works but also members of the well-known families of the Austrian aristocracy bearing historic names. The boards of directors and of managing directors included the names of almost the whole Austrian aristocracy, revealing the close relations of the big estates with high finance.

The fundamental branches of industry in the Austro-Hungarian Monarchy were for the most part interwoven in cartel combinations, while the groups of banks organizing and directing monopolies were invariably found to be operating in the background.

It has been shown before that, because of Austrian and other foreign investments, Hungarian banks soon rose to a particularly high standard in relation to the domestic level of capitalist development, playing a primary role in economic life. This explains how trends similar to those in the modern capitalist development of Western Europe asserted themselves in the linking of industrial and bank monopolies and in the appearance of finance capital despite the relatively undeveloped state of the economy. Around 1900 and especially in the following years the big firms enjoying a monopolistic position in their industry entered into ever closer relations with the groups heading the banks.

The five big banks of Hungary—the General Hungarian Credit Bank, the Hungarian Commercial Bank of Pest, the Hungarian Discount and Exchange Bank, the First Hungarian Savings Bank of Pest, the Hungarian Bank and Commercial Company Ltd.—with their rapidly increasing network of branches and affiliations gained a position of control over the greater part of bank capital. By 1900 they controlled 47 per cent and by 1913 over 57 per cent of the total capital of credit banks. As a result of their central role in granting credit and their participation in the foundation of new industrial plants from the close of the nineteenth century, the leading financial groups acquired parcels of shares of increasing numbers of industrial companies, enhancing their power. At the turn of the century the big banks controlled no more than about 17 per cent of industrial firms, but before the outbreak of World War I the group of the Hungarian Commercial Bank of Pest controlled 59 industrial firms (with 243 million crowns of industrial capital) and the General Hungarian Credit Bank, 63 industrial firms (with 233 million crowns of capital). The five banks combined held control altogether of 225 industrial firms (with a share capital of 711 million crowns), representing 47 per cent of large Hungarian industries.

The powerful industrial banking groups providing finance capital were headed by rather narrow Hungarian concerns: the Hungarian Commercial Bank of Pest and its group directed by Leo Lánczy, Chorin and Manfred Weiss, and the Fellner family; the General Hungarian Credit Bank headed by the families Ullmann and Kornfeld. Of course, it would be impossible to give a true picture of Hungarian economic life and Hungarian society were we to separate the problems of finance capital from the remnants of feudalism still existing in the economic life, the state apparatus, and the ideology of the country. The landed estates, nearly 50 per cent of which were in the hands of the big landowners, and the strong political hegemony of the landowning class demanded a union between high finance and the large estates. So members of historic families filled a number of leading positions in the management of banks and industrial firms. For instance, in 1905 eighty-eight counts and sixty-four barons sat on the boards of directors and of supervision directors in various industrial works, railway companies, and banks, many of them on the board of more than one firm. Thus it was actually members of special groups of high finance and the aristocracy who became the leaders of economic life.

In his first work on national economy, *Hungarian Cartels,* published in Budapest in 1912, Jenö Varga, who was active in the Hungarian social democratic movement at the beginning of this century, appraised the situation: "It may be stated with good reason that the approximately fifty men who stand at the head of Hungarian big industry and the big banks own altogether 20 per cent of the total capital but draw half of the total net income."[1]

---

[1] J. Varga, *A magyar kartelek,* Budapest, 1912, p. 10.

Thus, after the turn of the century Hungary became the scene of all the new manifestations which were produced by modern capitalism throughout Europe. These phenomena were not sporadic occurrences but factors which gave the most adequate expression to the essence and form of development. However, since these new forms were restricted to certain spheres of the economy, relatively wide fields remained at a lower level of capitalist development, and to a certain degree these new forms were elements of superstructure on the old basis.

The manifestations of modern capitalist development which permeated Hungarian economy are inseparable from the circumstance that Hungary, as a part of the Austro-Hungarian Monarchy, responded also to the direct effects of Austrian advance before her domestic development reached a similar stage. It is nevertheless undeniable that the level of development attained in East-Central Europe around the turn of the century offered a firm basis for the activities of monopolies and finance capital. True, the advanced economic fields of industry and banking were really only islands in an ocean of backward agrarianism burdened by the weight of traditional farming. However, these islands represented a relatively high level of development.

The contradictory character of the economy of Eastern Europe is still more sharply distinguished in the Russian economy, which also produced monopolistic features of modern economic development. The rural stagnation which often preserved precapitalist conditions was compatible with the powerful monopoly organizations in full control of heavy industry and with the advanced forms of interrelated industrial and financial monopolies. Without going into an analysis of Russian development we should like to point out the significant aspects of the process.

In Russia the first industrial combination was formed in 1886 in a minor processing branch of the iron industry (manufacture of nails). In the next year a far more important agreement was reached by the sugar factories. In 1892 it was the firms of the oil industry which formed a syndicate. The true upswing in the formation of cartels came at the beginning of the present century. The two most powerful monopolies of Russian industry came into existence in these years—the Prodamet (1902) which controlled the iron and metal industry, and the Produgol (1904) which monopolized coal mining.

From the nineties here, too, the industrial monopolies were closely related to highly concentrated bank capital. In 1914 the largest industrial monopolies were backed by the seven biggest banks, which held over 52 per cent of the total bank capital. According to certain statistics the big banks controlled approximately 40 per cent of industry.

In the Balkan countries, which had hardly abandoned traditional economy and were only just reaching the introductory stage of the industrial revolution, monopolistic formations occurred more sporadically than in Hungary or Russia. Nor could these new formations in Rumania, Bulgaria, or the young state of Serbia be considered the result of domestic development and a sign of the maturity of capitalism. It may be said rather that these countries actually began to adapt themselves to the system of world economy around the turn of the century, and it was a recurring feature of this process of adjustment that latecomers promptly availed themselves of the economic and technological achievements, and even of the organizational forms, introduced by the first-comers.

The three countries are not on a par in respect to the appearance of the new formations. The relatively higher industrial development of Rumania but still more the circumstance that through her leading branch, the oil industry, Rumania was, in fact, directly connected with the world market, favored the establishment of monopolies. Furthermore, the petroleum industry was one of the most highly concentrated in the world, with important international concerns and trusts fighting for the possession of markets and sources of raw material. As pointed out before, the Rumanian oil industry was also under the control of big international syndicates. In Rumania concentration also showed progress—a familiar trait of industrial development in the case of late-comers. Around the turn of the century 60 per cent of the fixed capital of manufacturing industry was owned by 53 out of the 625 industrial plants (8.4 per cent). The first cartel was formed in 1895 in flour milling, followed soon after by combinations in several other branches of the food industry, including distilleries and sugar: later in paper, cement, and glass: and, last but not least, in the oil industry. The syndicate Distributia, which transacted the sale of oil within Rumania, was the most influential monopoly organization.

However, monopolies still did not leave their mark on the whole of industry and economic life. Full monopoly was encountered in only a few branches, for instance in mineral oil and sugar. The output of the branches which had not been monopolized was much higher, amounting to two-thirds of total industrial output according to certain statistics. Apart from a few branches of industry, no monopolies had materialized as yet in other spheres of economic life—in transport, foreign trade, or agriculture—which may again serve as a warning not to exaggerate their significance.

These new formations perhaps made themselves felt more strongly in financial life and in this connection in a certain interrelation of industrial and bank capital. Usually, this was the field of economic life where the control of foreign capital was the most extensive. In the development of the big banks after the turn of the century German capital or capital from the Monarchy dominated. The established Rumanian big banks mostly adopted business methods of the advanced capitalist countries, immediately demanding the formation of industrial concerns and taking an active part in the foundation of industrial enterprises or in their transformation into joint-stock companies. Besides the National Bank and the Agrarian Bank seven big banks ruled economic life. Most of them had been founded with foreign capital, which owned 61 per cent of the share capital and 83 per cent of the reserve fund. Of these seven big banks the Marmorosch Blank Company and the Banca de Credit acquired serious interest by 1913 in the textile industry as well as in a few other branches of industry. The Banca Românescă, founded a few years before the war, also soon turned its attention to industry. The majority of the big industrial works which were not under the direct control of foreign capital belonged to the Rumanian big banks. These close correlations of industrial and bank capital under the hegemony of banks thus came about also in Rumanian economic life in the years preceding World War I.

The first cartel organization was formed in Bulgaria in 1898. In that year the cloth manufacturers came to an agreement concerning the elimination of competition for state supplies and the fixing of quotas. Then the distilleries formed a combination, and so did a few other branches such as the tobacco industry and manufacturers of gunpowder. In gunpowder a factory which declined to join the cartel was purchased and closed down.

Yet there can be no doubt that in the Bulgarian economy monopolies may be regarded as still more ephemeral phenomena and there are hardly any available records on the formation of finance capital. The fact that in 1911 only 76 industrial and commercial joint-stock companies were active in the country with a total of 50 million levas of capital indicates that apart from a few big enterprises founded with foreign capital, domestic bank and industrial capital had scarcely started to cooperate, though bank capital was much stronger than industrial capital in Bulgaria, too.

In Serbia the appearance of monopolies and the industrial activities of the banks were equally sporadic.

On the whole, in the Balkan countries, forms typical of modern capitalism actually appeared. This may be ascribed not to the inevitable outcome of home development, though the protective tariffs had some effect in this sense, but to the gradual adaptation of these countries in their struggle to become links in the chain of world economy, to the important role of foreign (mostly finance) capital in the advancement of the economy, and to the uneven development of bank capital and industrial capital in the domestic economy.

Consequently, the new modern forms represented scattered manifestations of elements of superstructure on an extensive base of backward, poorly developed capitalist economy, as well as the essential tendency of advance, but not new conditions prevailing in the whole economy.

Part Two
Changes and
Stagnation in the
Twentieth Century:
1914–1949

8 The Consequences
of World War I:
Disintegration and Reconstruction

The rapid economic growth of the preceding decades was interrupted
in the summer of 1914. The process begun in the middle of the nineteenth century wherein traditional methods gradually gave way to
modern economic developments throughout the Continent, including
Eastern Europe, came to an end abruptly with the outbreak of World
War I. When the first military detachments left for the front imbued with
nationalistic fervor, it was thought that the war would be over by
autumn. None could foresee that after the armistice a profoundly different Europe and a radically transformed Eastern Europe would
emerge from the welter of fire and the torrents of blood. The first
modern mechanized war, waged over a long period, devastated much
of the Continent, particularly the eastern region. The fighting among
the German, Austro-Hungarian, and Russian troops on Polish territory
belonging to various empires, the engagements on the Balkan and Italian fronts, the campaigns which swept over Rumanian and Serbian
territory and the transient loss of independence in these countries, all
imposed a tremendous ordeal.

Equally significant was the exhaustion resulting from a long period
of modern warfare. At the beginning of the war the economic consequences of such warfare were utterly unknown. The countries involved
were totally unprepared for their effects as were the old schools of
political economy, which witnessed the new developments helplessly
without grasping their meaning. The conflicts that arose, while rooted
in the contradictions of the prewar political, social and economic systems, were deepened and intensified by the upheaval of war.

Although the countries of Central and Eastern Europe belonged to
opposing military blocs and consequently emerged from the war on the
side of the conquerors or on the side of the defeated, their situation in
1917 and 1918 was similar in respect to the severe disorganization of

their economies. There was a critical lack of fuel and raw materials and severe difficulties in supplying the population. Discontent was rife as a result of rationing and the extreme poverty of the masses. In some places this feeling was sharpened to the point of revolution; elsewhere it culminated in mass demonstrations and local outbreaks. But only in Russia did revolution produce a permanent radical change in the existing political, social, and economic structure. After World War I it was Soviet Russia alone that began building a new socio-economic system amidst sharp military attacks by the great powers, the repulsion of which induced economic blockade and complete political isolation.

As a consequence of these events the natural interaction existing between Russia and the East-Central European countries and the possibility of parallel economic progress ceased for a long time. In addition, foreign trade was reduced to a minimum. Hence, in our analysis of the economic development of the East-Central European countries during the interwar period, the economic history of the Soviet Union may be omitted, not only because the subject requires special study but also because there were no longer reciprocal economic effects. Notwithstanding her loss of contact with the world market, Russia developed, independently, whereas the other parts of Eastern Europe were closely dependent on capitalism and on the international market fluctuations.

Of course, there were revolutions and revolutionary movements in the Eastern European countries, all the more so as their socio-political problems were similar to those of Russia. But these revolutions either failed within a short time or facilitated the creation of a new national state rather than a new social and political order. Though the redrawing of maps and the tracing of new frontiers commenced during the war, their actual realization and their legal sanctioning would hardly have been brought about without the active aid of various mass movements. Power politics and the circumstances of economic growth were fundamentally altered for the peoples of East-Central Europe, on the one hand, by the disintegration of the Austro-Hungarian Monarchy and the emergence of the successor states—an independent Austria, an independent Hungary, and a newly created Czechoslovakia—and, on the other, by the annexation of important territory to several countries (Rumania and Serbia) and the rebirth of a new, independent Poland from the Russian, German, and Hapsburg empires.

Three independent states were formed within the borders of the former Austro-Hungarian Monarchy: the Austrian Republic, comprising the Austrian provinces alone; the Czechoslovak Republic, incorporating the former Bohemian and Moravian provinces as well as the northern Highlands of the former Hungarian Kingdom inhabited mostly by Slovaks; and the Hungarian Kingdom, reduced to less than one-third of its old territory. Of the former Austrian provinces Dalmatia, Slovenia, and the annexed Bosnia-Hercegovina came under the rule of the new Serbian-Croatian-Slovenian (later Yugoslav) Kingdom. Croatia, which had previously belonged to Hungary, as well as some southern regions (the so-called Vojvodina), and later some districts of Bulgaria were also integrated into Yugoslavia. The former Rumanian Kingdom was allotted a part of Bukovina from the Austrian provinces, Transylvania, and the border districts of the so-called Partium from Hungarian territory, and Bessarabia from Russia. The new Polish Kingdom consisted of parts of the Austro-Hungarian Monarchy, most of Galicia and Bukovina, its nucleus being the old territory regained from Germany and Russia. This comprehensive rearrangement, shown in Table 8–1, was rounded off by slight alterations in favor of Italy and Greece. These territorial changes alone make it evident that in the countries of East-Central Europe there could be no continuation of the prewar economies. A

Table 8-1.   The Countries of Southeastern Europe Before and After World War I

	Area (in square kilometers)		Population (in thousands)	
	1914	*1921*	*1914*	*1921*
Austro-Hungarian Monarchy	676,443[a]		51,390[a]	
Austria		85,533		6,536
Hungary		92,607		7,600
Czechoslovakia		140,394		13,613
Bulgaria	111,800	103,146	4,753	4,910
Rumania	137,903	304,244	7,516	17,594
Serbia	87,300		4,548	
Yugoslavia		248,987		12,017
Poland		388,279		27,184

Source: Based on national statistics.
[a] With Bosnia-Hercegovina.

radically new situation was created by the substitution of independent countries for powerful empires, by the disappearance of politico-economic units or by their substantial diminution or enlargement, and by the annexation of parts of different countries at varying levels of development to form new states. Adjustment to the new circumstances and integration into uniform economic entities alone would have required a long period of time, virtually a historical era, to achieve new paths of development and steady economic growth. This, circumstances did not allow. The postwar rearrangements took place when economies exhausted by the war had to face the grave problems presented by transition to a peacetime economy.

These complex problems, which had to be grappled with simultaneously, created utter economic chaos, oftentimes a situation of confusion and hopelessness which seemed to defy solution. Austria, Hungary, and Poland sustained the worst shocks. Economic exhaustion had been felt as far back as 1917 in the Austrian provinces of the former monarchy. In the summer of 1918 economic experts agreed that Austria was unable to cope with another wartime winter. Agricultural production was down to approximately 50 per cent of the prewar level; moreover, the Austrian provinces had not been self-supporting in agricultural products anyway and depended on imports, on Hungarian imports in the first place. However, Hungary was unable to send supplies, since she could not even take care of her own needs. Owing to lack of raw materials, production had to be reduced in many sectors, and in the industries which were of particular importance for the war effort— coal and iron production—output sank below the prewar level.

The young Austrian Republic, proclaimed in the autumn of 1918, was in a disastrous economic position. There was hardly any food in the country. As observed by K. Schuschnigg, rations of 10 to 15 decagrams of bread and flour per day were just enough to prevent starvation, but too little to live on. At the beginning of 1919 milk consumption was 7 per cent of the prewar figure in Vienna. Food relief provided at best for bare survival, and agricultural production in 1920 did not exceed 50 per cent of the prewar output.

Most of the railway lines ceased to operate for lack of coal. Blast furnaces could not be ignited. Industrial unemployment was estimated to have reached nearly 200,000 in the summer of 1919. A process of inflation had been started earlier by the exorbitant war expenditures of the Monarchy. By the end of 1918 the volume of war loans had caused depreciation of the crown to one-third of its former value. In 1919 the situation continued to deteriorate, Austria having been deprived of, and practically cut off from, the other parts of the Monarchy. The wartime economic decline worsened instead of improving; industrial output barely exceeded one-third of the 1913 level.

Hungary presented a substantially similar picture. Shortage of labor, the military requisitioning of horses, and the reduction of livestock caused a serious setback in agriculture, the outstanding economic sector. From 71 million quintals in 1913 production of grain fell to 42 million quintals by 1918, while output of maize declined from 48 million quintals to 24 million. A similar decline took place in industry. In branches of consumer goods, where raw materials and energy supplies were restricted in favor of war industry, a 60–70 per cent reduction of output was not uncommon. However, coal production, which was essential if military requirements were to be satisfied, also showed a rapid decline: by 1918 coal output was almost 33 per cent lower than in 1913 and iron and steel production fell to half of the prewar level.

By 1918 the nadir was reached: military requirements could no longer be satisfied, and the hinterland was subjected to the most severe hardships. Military expenditure consumed approximately 60 to 70 per cent of the wartime national income in 1918 and had to be covered in increasing measure by the issue of paper money. As in Austria inflation became rampant.

The transitory success of the revolutions was unable to overcome economic difficulties, and following the counterrevolution in the autumn of 1919 economic chaos worsened. The situation was aggravated by the activities of the occupation forces of the Rumanian army which had marched against the Hungarian Councils' Republic, causing considerable loss by dismantling and carrying off valuable machinery.

Finally, Hungarian agricultural production was around one-third of the prewar volume in 1919 and 50 to 60 per cent in 1920. In the autumn of 1919 industrial output amounted to only 15 to 20 per cent of peacetime production, but even in 1920 it rose no higher than 35 to 40 per cent of the peacetime level.

The difficulties of reborn Poland derived chiefly from the fact that the longest and most desperate battles of World War I had been fought there. A frontline battlefield for six years—unusual and unparalleled in World War I—this region was completely ravaged. Here it was not wartime exhaustion or weakness which induced the disorganization of production but devastation. Within the borders of the new Poland 1.8 million houses were gutted by fire or laid in ruins. The loss in communications can be gauged by the estimate that half of the railway bridges, station buildings, and workshops had been destroyed and almost the whole of the rolling stock had been taken away from the railways on former Russian territory.

The damage to agriculture was such that by the end of the war 4.5 million hectares of arable land lay fallow and about 2.4 million hectares of forests were ravaged; 2 million head of cattle, 1 million horses, and 1.5 million sheep had been destroyed.

Industry had also suffered severely in Polish territory: 4,259 electric engines and machines, over 3,800 machine tools, and various kinds of factory equipment weighing 98,000 tons were carried off. The losses sustained by industry reached the total value of 10 million gold francs.

In addition, complete financial confusion accompanied the creation of the new Polish Republic as a result of the juxtaposition of three different kinds of valid currency—the Russian ruble, the Austrian crown, and the German mark which were of dissimilar value—together with the so-called Polish mark. The uneven economic level of the regions that had formerly belonged to several different empires and the absence of any economic relations between these parts also raised serious problems. Before World War I the commerce of the various Polish districts with one another had amounted only to 7–8 per cent of their total trade, while about 85 per cent had been transacted with the occupying powers and 7–8 per cent with other countries. These circumstances explain the critical economic position of Poland.

The other countries of the region also suffered severe losses, damage, and setbacks in production. For example, Serbia, a one-sided agrarian country, having become a battlefield, showed grave economic decline as early as 1914–15. From the autumn of 1915 the military government of the Monarchy made serious efforts to promote Serbian agriculture for the purpose of producing goods for export, but it was only in 1917 that the prewar level was approached. Extortionist military demands on Yugoslav areas and adverse economic conditions caused a marked decline by 1919 in livestock breeding, which was the most important part of Yugoslav agriculture. The worst misfortune for the economy was the loss of about 500,000 horses, 1.7 million head of cattle, over 2.4 million pigs, 6.3 million sheep, and 1.2 million goats. This immense damage represented the loss of close to or more than half of the country's stock in pigs, sheep, and goats, over one-third of its horses, and more than one quarter of its cattle.

The Bohemian and Slovak areas forming Czechoslovakia, which came out of the war in a more favorable position than the other countries, could not avoid transient decline either. The wartime exhaustion and deterioration of the currency which marked the last days of the dying Monarchy in 1917–18 were also felt in Bohemian and Slovak areas. In the months following the foundation of the Czechoslovak Republic, at the close of 1918, industrial output amounted to only half of the prewar level, and by 1920 it rose no higher than 70 per cent. (Of the most important products steel stood at 78 per cent, iron at 72 per cent, cement at 85 per cent.) The firmly based strength of the Czechoslovak economy and the more favorable position of the victorious countries, however, opened avenues to easier and quicker recovery. By 1921, when Austria and Hungary were still in critical condition, Czechoslovak industry was producing 75 to 80 per cent of its prewar output and could therefore grapple more successfully with the depreciation of money.

In Bulgaria, agricultural production, the most important factor of decline, by 1918 was 57 per cent of the level before the Balkan War (1908–12 = 100), but by 1920 it already approached 80 per cent. Industrial output, which was actually of minor significance, also increased to 80 per cent, but only by 1921. The ravages of war in Rumania, aggravated by the activities and requisitioning of the occupying powers, led to the loss of 30 per cent of her agricultural equipment and a still larger part of her livestock, with the inevitable setback in agricultural productivity. In the prewar years 2.5 to 2.9 million tons of grain were exported; in 1919 only 0.9–1.7 million tons. In industry the principal decline was in oil production, from 1.9 million tons in 1912 to 0.9 million tons by 1919; output increased only to about 1.1 to 1.2 million tons in 1920 and 1921.

The situation which developed in various sectors of production in the postwar years, particularly the decline in agricultural productivity, nullified foreign trade possibilities in the (mostly agrarian) countries of the region. In Hungary, for example, all possibilities for foreign trade radically declined: in 1920 Hungary exported only 0.1 per cent of the wheat, 0.3 per cent of the flour, 2.1 per cent of the livestock, and 2.5 per cent of the meat exported before the war; in 1921 the respective figures were 7.4, 33, 20, and 78 per cent. Only the exports of wine and feathers equaled or exceeded prewar quantities. In fact, Hungarian agrarian exports in 1920 amounted to only 21 per cent of the prewar value (calculated on the basis of the new territory) and to 41 per cent in 1921.

This tremendous loss could certainly not have been recompensed by industrial exports owing to the economic structure of the country. In the existing situation this was even less feasible because industrial exports also diminished: in 1920 they barely exceeded 20 per cent of the prewar value, and rose no higher in 1921 than to around 57 per cent. A vicious circle set in to hinder the development of foreign trade: foreign currency and raw materials were needed to get the economy to function, to start industry, but these could have been provided only by the export of agricultural produce, which had become impracticable. The unwanted agrarian products might have been replaced by competitive industrial goods, but this would have made the import of raw materials indispensable.

On the whole this situation prevailed in the other agrarian countries of the Danube Valley. The inactivation of foreign trade in Rumania is evidenced by the decline of imports to less than one-third of the 1913 volume (from 1,374,100 tons to 413,900 tons), while exports shrank from the prewar volume of 4.6 million tons to 109,000 tons.

The value of Bulgarian exports, amounting to 184.6 million levas in 1911, fell to 44.7 million levas—less than one-fourth—by 1919. In 1920 exports increased only to 88.4 million levas, still under half of the prewar value. Imports in 1919 were one-third the prewar level and in 1920 one-half.

This inactivation of foreign trade produced a disastrous economic situation in most parts of East-Central Europe, for the war had left the economies of these countries closely dependent on foreign trade. This was chiefly a consequence of the disruption of old imperial units. Within the framework of the former Austro-Hungarian Monarchy the then existing territorial units had not faced the difficulties of foreign trade, for reasons previously explained: a considerable part of Austrian and Bohemian industrial goods found a ready market in the agrarian areas of the Monarchy, while the products of the agrarian regions, such as Hungarian corn and flour—in fact over 80 per cent of Hungarian exports—went to Austria and Bohemia. Thus foreign trade with countries outside the Monarchy played a relatively subordinate role in the multilateral economy realized inside the Monarchy itself.

In the new situation the successor states of the Monarchy, having broken away from the old economic unity, possessed a one-sided productive capacity. Thus, owing to the narrow national market, in Czechoslovakia and Austria industrial exports, and in Hungary agricultural exports, were a precondition for the functioning of the economy. Conversely, Czechoslovakia and Austria had to import agricultural products and many industrial raw materials, while Hungary had to import most industrial raw materials and investment goods. This dependence on foreign trade was true as well for the new Poland.

In the less developed Balkan countries, some of which were more richly endowed by nature, foreign trade was not of such vital importance as in the East-Central European countries. As noted previously, the preponderance of agriculture, the strong remnants of traditional economic conditions, had hardly allowed the countries of this region to rise from the circumstances of agricultural self-sufficiency. Nevertheless, when the significance of foreign trade in the Balkans is viewed in a dynamic, rather than a static, sense, we must conclude that although it may not have been of primary importance for the traditional functioning of the economy, it was all the more so for progress and development. In Rumania, Yugoslavia, and Bulgaria increased extroversion of structure and the will to promote exports actually followed from the very backwardness of the economy, exports offering the most important means of domestic accumulation of capital. With particularly narrow markets at home, it was in fact foreign markets that enhanced accumulation, which in turn formed the principal domestic source of investments serving development.

Thus, in reality, foreign trade was fundamental to advancement in all the countries of this region, and its inactivation jeopardized their means of existence and progress.

The problem of foreign trade raised the issue of the accumulation of capital in a new form. More capital was required to finance foreign trade, owing to the indispensable need for imports and the extremely reduced possibilities for exports. In the face of this higher demand the traditionally low accumulation of capital was further reduced because of a decline in production and the increasingly rapid depreciation of money. Domestic accumulation had been strikingly obvious in the case of Austria, which had formerly exported extensively and played a leading role in supplying capital to the less developed parts of the Monarchy. The inevitable concomitant of economic exhaustion and inflation, however, was the ruin of a considerable part of Austria's financial and monetary assets. By 1918 the volume of banknotes in circulation rose from the prewar 3 billion crowns to 42.6 billion crowns, exceeding 60 billion crowns by 1919, and approaching 200 billion by 1921. In 1922 currency circulation reached 4,405 billion crowns. The rapid depreciation of the Austrian crown is underscored by the equally precipitate decrease in the value of this swiftly growing volume of banknotes.

In 1914 the Austrian crown was on a par with the Swiss franc in value and rate of exchange. In October 1918, 100 Swiss francs were worth 227 Austrian crowns; that is to say, during the war the crown fell to about half its value in relation to the Swiss franc. However, by 1919, 100 Swiss francs were worth 2,950 Austrian crowns; by 1921, 10,471; and by 1922, 13,289. This rapid depreciation of the crown demolished a considerable part of the accumulated capital. Most investments were lost, domestic savings dwindled; from the prewar 31 crowns, the tax burden fell to 4 crowns per head, so that in 1919–20 the budget showed a deficit of 63 per cent, in 1920–21 a deficit of 58 per cent. An important field of accumulation of capital, the sum total of deposits at savings banks, was negligible: in 1913 the credit balance of the nine big banks of Vienna and that of the savings banks of the capital and the provinces had amounted to 2,213.4 million gold crowns, whereas in January 1923, deposits totaled only 8.7 million crowns, calculated on a par with gold. By the summer of 1925 the sum total of deposits had increased to only 11 per cent of the prewar level.

Inflation assumed still more excessive proportions in Hungary. By the end of the war money had lost about 60 per cent of its value. In the summer of 1919 the crown was worth about 15 per cent of its prewar value. In accordance with the peace treaty a separate Hungarian monetary system was introduced in March 1920, when the banknotes of the Austro-Hungarian Bank were stamped and the separate Hungarian crown was established. Thereafter depreciation accelerated. In August 1921 banknotes of 17.3 billion crowns nominal value were in circulation; by August 1922, the figure rose to 46.2 billion crowns; by the summer it reached 399.5 billion. Inflation culminated in the spring (May) of 1924. having reached 2,486.3 billion crowns. The value of the crown meanwhile sank to virtually zero. On a par with the Swiss franc before the war, 100 Swiss francs were equivalent to 227 crowns in October 1918, to 987 crowns in the summer of 1919, to 3,500 in the summer of 1920, and to over 19,000 in the summer of 1922. In the spring of 1924, 100 Swiss francs were worth around 1.8 million Hungarian crowns. Thus the earlier important sources of the accumulation of capital ran dry in Hungary too. Whereas before the war the sum total of deposits, debentures, and other bonds held by the banks amounted to 6.6 billion crowns, by December 1920, the total was 437 million crowns as a result of depreciation. On the evidence of their balance sheets, in 1921 the property status of the banks was only 8.1 per cent of the prewar level.

Of the successor states of the Austro-Hungarian Monarchy Czechoslovakia alone contrived to avoid the harmful consequences of grave and prolonged inflation. In Czechoslovakia the readjustment of currency was carried out very promptly. The separate Czechoslovak crown was established in 1919, when, in accordance with the decree issued on February 25, the Austrian banknotes were stamped and on April 10 the stamped banknotes were exchanged for banknotes for Czechoslovak crowns, the transaction being accompanied by a considerable levy on banknotes. In conjunction with this change-over, the value of the crown was to be restored to its prewar level, which was facilitated by the unique achievement of balancing the adverse budget as early as 1920. While endeavors at stabilization were not yet fully successful, inflation could be kept within bounds. In April 1919, 100 Czech crowns were equivalent to 34 Swiss francs, but in the summer months the value sank to 15 to 20 francs. In the first months of 1920 there was a further decline,

100 crowns being worth 5 Swiss francs. For two years after, stagnation and fluctuation may be observed around the level of 7 francs. There were months, as in the summer of 1920, when the value again rose to over 10 francs; the bedrock reached in the autumn of 1921 was not under 5 francs. This took place in circumstances when the depreciation of the Austrian crown, and still more of the Hungarian crown, was ceaseless and precipitate.

Finally, after a few years' fluctuation, from the beginning of 1922, efforts to stabilize the Czech crown were successful: by the middle of the year the value of 100 Czech crowns was again around 10 francs. In the second half of the year it reached about 16–17 francs, a level retained throughout 1923. Thus, one of the most characteristic processes of economic confusion and its most aggravating factor, inflation, reached no such proportions as it did in most of the other countries in East-Central Europe. This circumstance opened the road to economic recovery and development much earlier than elsewhere.

Czechoslovakia's position derived from the strength of her economy rather than from the status of a victorious country. A disproportionately large share of the former Monarchy's economic potential fell to the newly created country. Though the available statistics are not altogether in accord, they tend to agree that about 70 per cent of the industrial capacity of the Monarchy's western provinces was concentrated in the new Czechoslovakia, including 75 per cent of black-coal mining, 63 per cent of brown-coal mining, 60 per cent of the iron industry, 75 per cent of chemical works, 75 to 80 per cent of textile and building material industries, and actually over 90 per cent of the glass and sugar industries. Hence Czechoslovakia, with her 13.6 million inhabitants, hardly more than one quarter of the total population of the Monarchy, possessed a strong industry of Western European stature, capable of producing goods for export. Moreover, having sided with the victorious powers, she was given many opportunities for the rapid exploitation of this favorable position.

Rumania tackled her problems less successfully. The value of the gold leu fell to 3.6 paper lei by 1919; by 1921 to 17.2, by 1922 to 28.5, and in 1924, when inflation culminated, to 40.2. Notwithstanding the considerable measure of depreciation, the fall of the leu stopped at 2 per cent of the prewar value. Inflation was far from the level of Austrian or Hungarian depreciation; therefore, its detrimental consequences were also less destructive.

In Bulgaria, one of the defeated countries, the measure of inflation was slightly less severe than in Rumania. In 1915, 369.8 million levas were in circulation; by 1918 the sum total jumped to 2,248.6 million levas. From this time the money in circulation gradually increased at a relatively slow rate till 1924, when it reached 4,722 million levas. In the meantime the value of the leva continued to sink; whereas in 1915 it was roughly equivalent to the Swiss franc, in 1918, 100 francs were worth 166.5 levas, in 1924, 2,505 levas.

The most protracted and most paralyzing process of depreciation, however, took place in Poland. In 1920 the many kinds of currency valid after the establishment of the independent Polish state were replaced by the Polish mark of general validity whose value gradually declined, the process being accelerated by the war efforts of the country. In 1921 an attempt was made to curb inflation but the endeavor was doomed to failure. The currency in circulation amounted to 150,000 Polish marks in November 1918; to 5.3 million in December 1919; to 49.4 million in December 1920; to 229.5 million in December 1921. The irresistibility of the process of depreciation is illustrated by the fact that one year later the volume of banknotes in circulation attained the figure of 793.4 million, and the giddiest phase of inflation was yet to come. Records of money circulation in the years 1923 and 1924 provide revealing information. In December 1923 the volume of banknotes in circulation totaled 125,372 million marks; on April 30, 1924, the figure was 570,698 million.

In the meantime the rate of exchange of the dollar went from 8 marks in the autumn of 1918 to 2,922.5 marks by the end of 1921. By the spring of 1924 the Polish mark was practically worthless (9.3 million marks being equivalent to 1 dollar). It was only a few years later that efforts were renewed to stem this steadily increasing inflation. On January 11, 1924, the Sejm approved a scheme for the rehabilitation of finance, which provided for the introduction of a new currency on April 14, the zloty, planned to be of stable value. Though attempts were made to balance the budget by severe taxation, finally this second attempt also collapsed. Owing to the poor crop of 1925, to nonpayment of a part of the planned taxes, and especially to stabilization of the currency at too high a value, from the summer of 1925 a new depreciation of the zloty set in.

Domestic accumulation of capital and the portion available for utilization were also reduced by such indirect consequences of the war as the obligation to settle debts incurred during the war years, a burden to be borne chiefly by the victorious powers, and the payment of reparations incumbent on the conquered countries.

As regards the first category, the war debts of Yugoslavia and Rumania deserve special notice. During the war the Serbian government received loans amounting to 6.5 billion francs (16.4 billion dinars) from the victorious powers. The magnitude of this sum is indicated by the fact that the unsettled national debt inherited from the former Monarchy with the provinces of the latter annexed to Yugoslavia amounted to only 3.2 billion dinars of liability, and the postwar loans raised by Yugoslavia until the end of 1924—including the American loan of $15.2 million obtained in 1922, the French loan of 300 million francs for the purchase of materials, another American loan of $3 million, and a French credit of 150 million francs for the building of railways in September 1924—also approached only 2 billion dinars.

Rumania's war debt of 6 billion francs was not far behind the total of Yugoslavian loans.

Repayment of the amounts due to the creditors was a crippling burden for the indebted countries. Liabilities from the prewar years also weighed heavily on other countries of the region. Of the prewar Hungarian national debt 5.4 billion crowns was in the hands of foreign creditors. According to the peace treaty of Trianon, the refunding of 48 per cent, that is 2.34 billion crowns, devolved on postwar Hungary. Since two-thirds of the old loans were raised in crowns or marks, these debts were actually wiped out in the years of inflation. The liability which finally fell to Hungary amounted to 860 million crowns. In Hungary, as in the other conquered countries, it was the payment of reparations which inflicted the heavier burden. It was after the transitory occupation of some parts of the country that the sum of reparations was fixed. In compliance with the relevant clauses of the peace treaty, Hungary started to fulfill her obligations from September 1921 by supplying daily 800 tons of coal to Yugoslavia over a period of five years. In October 1923, the reparations committee passed a resolution imposing on Hungary the obligation to pay 200 million gold crowns in twenty years. For the first few years only minor installments were demanded. Therefore, until the year 1926 payments were effected only in the form of coal supplies to Yugoslavia.

Bulgaria was also compelled to pay reparations. As laid down in the peace treaty of Neuilly, Bulgaria was to pay 2.25 billion gold francs as reparation. The fulfillment of this obligation appeared to be impossible; therefore, the amount of reparation was modified in the protocol dated March 21, 1923, imposing on Bulgaria the payment of 550 million gold francs in sixty years, while 1.7 billion gold francs were to be remitted in installments within thirty years. However, the second item was regarded as settled, being covered by various claims of Bulgaria (costs of occupation, payments to Germany, etc.). Of the 550 million francs in reparations, altogether about 30 million was paid in installments by 1928. In accordance with the clauses of the above-mentioned protocol, 10 per cent was to be remitted in francs, while 90 per cent of the value was to be discharged in the form of goods.

As for Austria, the treaty of Saint-Germain laid down her obligation to pay reparations, but it did not fix the amount to be paid. Thus, in fact, postwar economy and consolidation were not burdened, but were nevertheless hindered, by reparations. Indeed, the obligation to pay reparations hung like the sword of Damocles over the economy of the defeated countries, threatening the balance of state finances and the budget, imposing to some degree psychological impediments to economic reconstruction, affecting the accumulation of capital, and preventing productive investments. On the whole, the countries of the region did not deliver considerable consignments of goods as reparation even where the obligation was precisely laid down. The political debates and innumerable economic talks continued for nearly a decade. The Sisyphean task of drawing up terms of payment and schedules thus did not actually impose too heavy a burden on the losers, or regroup essentially material goods in favor of the conquerors; rather, it kept the countries of East-Central Europe in perpetual uncertainty, served as a pretext for kindling a chauvinist-revanchist atmosphere, and became one of the handicaps to economic development in that era. Therefore, the fact that Czechoslovakia, in addition to advanced economic development, had to shoulder only a portion of the prewar debts of the Monarchy played an undeniably important part in her relatively favorable public finances. Though differing radically from Czechoslovakia in economic development, Poland was not weighed down by war debts either.

The postwar situation of the countries of East-Central Europe was rendered chaotic by many other factors. A series of inevitable alterations took place, ownership itself undergoing a change in various fields of economy. This kind of extensive transformation, even when it promoted development, contributed temporarily to a state of uncertainty and instability in an economy which was disorganized to begin with.

Among these developments two deserve special emphasis: the land reform which affected agriculture in nearly every country, and the steps in the rationalization of industry and credit service.

After World War I the countries of East-Central Europe were forced to correct the often glaring inequalities in the distribution of land. The governments of the Danubian countries were all influenced in this direction by the social contradictions intensified during the war and by the revolutionary spirit; by the victory of the Russian revolution and its impact on the neighboring countries; by the political education of the peasantry in the army and its widening political organization; by the growing peasant parties which sometimes acquired a majority and formed a government; and, last but not least, by the policy toward minorities.

Land reform constituted an integral part of the policy pursued by the governments of the new postwar states, often the first step in their program. In Yugoslavia the royal regent proclaimed agrarian reform, the abolition of feudal privileges, and the distribution of land in his first manifesto issued as early as the end of 1918. On February 25, 1919, the decree was published and its execution was begun. Here too, the above-mentioned political developments may be found among the motives for the reallotment of land. The peculiar features of the Yugoslav situation nevertheless deserve special attention.

In Yugoslavia the land reform was also intended to coordinate the agriculture of the areas forming the new nation which had previously belonged to other countries and had followed widely varying systems of agrarian development. The agriculture of old Serbia based on peasant smallholdings was incompatible with the large-estate system of Bosnia-Hercegovina stagnating under feudal conditions where the landlord's property was cultivated under the so-called kmet system, by peasant tenants. Nor was it compatible with the large-estate system of Hungarian type prevailing in Croatia and the Vojvodina, or with the feudal structure of landed property in Montenegro. Besides the establishment of a uniform agrarian structure, great political significance was attached to winning over the peasant masses in the areas making up Yugoslavia. Therefore, in the first wave of land reform, until the close of 1923, 262,000 hectares of land were expropriated from the large estates and distributed among nearly 211,000 families. In these years most of the repartitioned land was carved from the approximately 136,000 hectares expropriated in the Vojvodina, the 69,000 hectares in Croatia-Slavonia, and the 48,000 hectares in Macedonia.

Execution of the land reform, protracted and extended by the subsequent decrees of 1931 and 1933, was in progress during the whole interwar period. As a result every property of between 50 and 300 hectares was distributed with certain territorial variations. By 1934 altogether 1.6 million hectares of land had been reallotted to 535,600 families. More than half of the new holdings were distributed from the approximately 880,000 hectares expropriated for the purpose in Bosnia-Hercegovina. This phase was followed by the distribution of some 330,000 hectares in Macedonia and about 190,000 hectares in the Vojvodina. Altogether, 2.48 million hectares of land were repartitioned among 650,000 peasant families in the interwar period: 1.3 million hectares in Bosnia-Hercegovina, about 600,000 in Macedonia, 200,000 and 300,000 respectively in the Vojvodina and Croatia. This radical land reform abolished the system of big estates and established the domination of a peasant economy throughout the country. After the land reform, farms of over 50 hectares amounted to only 9.7 per cent of the total land area, a considerable part of which—one-third—was covered by forests.

Owing to agrarian overpopulation the Yugoslav land reform created grave contradictions. Since every family was to have its own land, and in areas of a feudal character land leased by peasants passed into the ownership of the tenants, the land was carved up into dwarf holdings. Thus in 1931, 671,000 owners of plots smaller than 2 hectares held 6.5 per cent of the land, which was to support 3.5 million people. The situation was not much more favorable in the category embracing dwarf holdings of 2 to 5 hectares (the average being 3.4 hectares): 676,000 holdings, or 21.5 per cent of the land, also had to maintain slightly more than 3.5 million people. It is evident from these figures that after the land reform in Yugoslavia agriculture posed exceedingly difficult economic and social problems.

In Rumania, in compliance with the earlier demands declared on December 1, 1918, at the assembly of Gyulafehérvár (Alba Julia), a new law of agrarian reform was passed as early as December 15, 1918, and was sanctioned and extended on July 17, 1921. In the new Rumania there was no great deviation in the agrarian structure among the various parts; with slight variations, the system of large estates predominated in the old Rumania, as well as the newly annexed Bessarabia and Transylvania. The intent to relieve profound socio-political contradictions, coupled with the attempt to supplant the non-Rumanian class of big landowners in the newly acquired provinces, nevertheless led to the execution of a rather radical land reform.

The land reform law fixed the upper limit of landed property at 100 to 500 hectares, depending on the area in question. The most radical upper limit of 100 hectares was enforced in Bessarabia (initially, any property over 50 hectares was to be distributed). The reform carried out in Transylvania was almost as radical, leaving only a few large properties of woodland untouched, since expropriation of land applied to arable fields in the first place. The precautionary clause of the land reform law providing for the confiscation of all land owned by non-Rumanian subjects or persons residing outside the borders of Rumania contributed to the dispossession and elimination of the class of foreign landowners (Hungarian, Russian, and others).

In the course of the land reform in Rumania 6.3 million hectares were finally expropriated, of which 3.8 million were allotted to nearly 1.4 million peasant families. The remaining stretches were kept partly to serve as state reserves (1.2 million hectares), partly to be let to settlers. The peasant recipients of land were obliged to pay down promptly 20 per cent of the value of the allotted land, 35 per cent was covered by the state, and the rest was to be remitted by the new holder in installments.

After the execution of the land reform the proportion of farms of 100 hectares was considerably reduced, to 27 per cent of all the landed property and only 14 per cent of the arable land. This produced a relatively narrow category of middle-sized farms. Peasant economy thus became preponderant as a result of the radical structural transformation of Rumanian agriculture.

Compared with the redistribution of land in Yugoslavia and Rumania, land reform was more moderate in Poland and in Czechoslovakia.

Poland, being made up of areas from countries with an agrarian structure favoring big landowners and landlords, was characterized by large estates and a landless peasantry. According to a register of 1921, holdings over 100 hectares accounted for only 0.6 per cent of all farms but for 43 per cent of the land. One-third of the agrarian population, 7.5 million peasants, had no land; another 50 per cent (11.4 million) were smallholders; and only 17 per cent possessed enough land for a livelihood.

The socio-political reasons mentioned in the introduction made it particularly important in Poland to eliminate glaring contradictions, but the power and conservatism of the landed classes permitted only slow and hesitant measures. The land reform law, passed on July 10, 1919, was enforced by a decree issued the following year. When political necessity became less pressing, after 1921, the execution of the reform slowed down so much that a new law had to be passed on December 28, 1925. A few years later, at the time of the crisis, execution was again frustrated, and it was only after 1935 that the parceling out of land was continued.

The law which served as the basis of this slow, protracted execution in itself set a rather radical upper limit on the size of landed property, putting it at 300 hectares on the territory of the old Polish Kingdom and between 60 and 180 hectares in the formerly German and Austrian parts of the country, obviously with the intention of a radical elimination of landowners of foreign nationality. The land reform law of 1925 laid down the rate of the reallotment of land, providing for the parceling out of 200,000 hectares a year in the next decade.

Finally a yearly average of 133,000 hectares of land was distributed in the interwar years among the peasantry. The 2.65 million hectares parceled out between 1919 and 1938 affected little more than 10 per cent of the 25 million hectares of arable land and perhaps one-third when the effects of other measures such as the increase in the ter-

ritory of previously existing peasant farms are taken into consideration. Only one quarter of the land belonging to large estates was expropriated, and about 20 per cent of the arable land was left in the
hands of the big landowners. The 2.65 million hectares of repartitioned land were carved up into 734,100 new peasant farms, while
859,000 peasant holdings were increased with the allotment of 5.4
million hectares of land.

The great majority of peasant farms in Poland were medium-sized
and smallholdings. Aside from the 20 per cent share of the big estates,
65 per cent of the arable land was in farms under 20 hectares, but
half of this land belonged to farmers with dwarf holdings of less than
5 hectares. Farms of 20 to 100 hectares made up only 10 per cent of
the total arable land, while stretches in common ownership amounted
to 5 per cent.

Owing to the moderate course followed in the execution of the
land reform in Poland, 1 million hectares of land falling legally under
dispossession were still untouched in 1939. So the land problem was
far from being solved, all the more so as the number of landless
peasants increased at a more rapid rate (because of the extraordinary
growth of the peasant population) than it could be reduced by the
long-drawn-out division of land into lots. During the interwar period
a yearly average of no more than 133,000 hectares was parceled out,
while the average yearly increase of the agrarian population reached
250,000.

The distribution of land became one of the first tasks of economic
reconstruction after the war in Czechoslovakia, too, though agrarian
problems were far less important here than in the other more agricultural countries. The union of the two parts of the country, the
Bohemian provinces and Slovakia, did not connect two contrasting
agricultural structures, since large estates were the predominant
agricultural type in both regions. However, while the large estates
formed strongly capitalist, highly developed agricultural units in the
western parts where, owing to high industrialization, the agrarian
problem had smaller economic and social significance, in Slovakia
the area of the large estates was more extensive and the land problem
more acute because of the landless peasants who could not find
industrial employment in the towns.

In general the land reform of 1919 and 1920 promised to be quite radical. According to its clauses all properties over 150 hectares of arable land and those with a total of 250 hectares were subject to expropriation for the purpose of reform. In justified cases dispossession could be raised to 500 hectares. Of course, heavy compensation was to be paid for the expropriated land, calculated on the basis of prewar prices. In addition to social and economic considerations, policy toward the national minorities also played a role in the land reform law, for the land taken from the Hungarian proprietors was disproportionately large, while the recipients of the newly allotted plots were mostly recruited from the soldiers of the Czech Legion. Moreover, a considerable part of the expropriated land was not parceled out at all. Indeed, the rate at which distribution was carried out cannot be regarded as radical, since the reform was to be executed in thirty years. It is indicative that until 1931, within approximately a decade, the area of the estates of over 100 hectares was actually reduced by no more than 300,000 hectares.

Thus, statistics of landed property from 1931 still show Czechoslovakia as a country of big estates, where 41 per cent of the land belonged to landowners with estates of over 100 hectares. In Slovakia the share of the big estates was still more preponderant, amounting to nearly 50 per cent. In the 1930s the practical realization of the reform advanced to a certain degree so that by 1937 about 1.3 million hectares of arable land were parceled out, approximately two-thirds serving the foundation of new units and one-third the completion of dwarf holdings of peasants. At all events, if arable land alone is considered, the large estates did not exceed one-sixth of the land in Czechoslovakia either.

In view of the land reforms of the neighboring countries, the problems raised by the unhealthy distribution of land could not be ignored in Hungary either, despite the rule of the strongly conservative political system which followed the suppression of the revolutionary movements. The issue could not be stalled for other reasons either: the victorious counterrevolution of 1919 itself strove to turn the peasantry against the Soviet Republic, which had omitted the distribution of land, by including among its slogans the promise of land reform. In 1919 and 1920 the peasantry, which possessed a relatively strong political influence—the Smallholders' Party having gained a majority at the elections of 1920—persistently urged the realization of land reform by new laws.

However, political life was dominated so strongly by the class of big landowners that the land reform law passed in 1920 could not be compared even to the most moderate of its counterparts in the neighboring countries. In the preamble of the bill it was declared that the aim was not to abolish the system of large estates, but to improve the distribution of landed property. Contrary to the other reforms, the law did not state the general maximal upper limit of landed property or declare the surplus to be liable to expropriation for the purpose of the reform. The number of peasants entitled to land was also strongly limited by various restrictions. The most moderate land reform of the era was thus formulated. In principle it claimed only 6 per cent of the arable land. Of the 700,000 hectares made available for the execution of the reform, in reality only half was cut off from large estates. Exactly 250,000 landless peasants were allotted not quite one hectare of land per head. Another approximately 100,000 hectares served public institutions donating medium-sized estates to ex-servicemen.

Of the expropriated stretches of land a certain part was utilized as building sites; the rest went to complete dwarf holdings of peasants. On the whole the reform did not produce any considerable change in the ownership of land in Hungary. The number of peasants with holdings which failed to provide a livelihood was at all events nearly doubled, but Hungary, almost alone in Europe, remained the home of a medieval system of large estates. On the evidence of statistics from 1935, 43.1 per cent of the land remained in the possession of the big landowners.

The smallest change in economic structure following World War I was registered in Bulgaria, which had been known as a country of peasant smallholders for some time. The agrarian government under Stanbolisky nevertheless decided to undertake a new distribution of land in 1921. The laws issued in 1921 and 1922 fixed the upper limit of private ownership of land at 30 hectares in general and at 50 hectares in the mountainous districts, and enacted the confiscation of the rest of the property against payment. This decree affected 6 per cent of the land of Bulgaria, allotting 133,000 hectares of new plots to 173,000 peasants. These new developments helped to strengthen the small-holder peasant character of the country. At the census of 1934 hardly any estate of over 100 hectares was found in private ownership, while the 1,000 farms over 50 hectares totaled 1.6 per cent of the arable land. (See Table 8-2.)

As a result of the postwar land reforms the division of land underwent a significant change in one place, a less significant change in others. In some countries the change came about at once—in the immediate postwar years; in others, only later. However, in general the distribution of land constituted an important element in the profound and extensive changes which followed the end of World War I.

Of the innumerable alterations and transformations which took place in the most varied fields of economy, giving rise to chaotic conditions, those closely affecting the ownership of capital deserve special mention, notably the situation produced by the confiscation of so-called alien property.

The principle approving the possibility of nationalization was laid down in the peace treaties of Versailles, Trianon, and Saint Germain (in clauses No. 297, 232 and 249, respectively, of the three treaties). On this legal basis Yugoslavia and Rumania began to make preparations as early as 1919 for the nationalization of firms which belonged to Austrian, Hungarian, and German capitalists. First they liquidated banks under foreign control, and where foreigners held a strong financial interest they tried to reduce the latter by stamping the shares. Moreover, foreign deposits were sequestered in 1921, to be released in 1924.

These measures hit Austria and Hungary in particular. It is enough to note that out of the 459 joint-stock companies with a total capital of 3,962 million crowns located in Vienna in 1918 the works or houses of 132 (with a capital of 1,168 million crowns) were active beyond the borders of Austria. The Hungarian big banks and industrial works had also set up an extensive network of branches and controlled interests in regions inhabited by national minorities, in Transylvania, Slovakia, Croatia, and other places.

Austrian and Hungarian capital was strongly affected by the announced nationalizations. The original owners naturally found

Table 8-2. Structure of the Ownership of Land in the Countries of East-Central Europe During the Interwar Period

	Hungary				Rumania				Yugoslavia	
	No. of Holdings	Per Cent	Land Area (in thousand hectares)	Per Cent	No. of Holdings	Per Cent	Land Area (in thousand hectares)	Per Cent	No. of Holdings	Per Cent
2 or 3 hectares	1,142,294	71.5	1,006	109	1,710,000	52.1	2,520	12.8	671,865	33.8
3 to 5 hectares	200,341	12.5	840	9.2	750,000	22.9	3,015	15.2	676,284	34.0
5 to 50 hectares	240,761	15.1	3,070	39.5	795,000	24.2	7,850	39.8	630,619	31.8
50 to 100 hectares	6,724	0.4	502	5.5	12,800	0.4	895	4.5	5,156	0.3
100 to 500 hectares	6,322	0.4	1,576	17.2	9,500	0.3	2,095	10.6	1,593	0.1
over 500 hectares	1,644	0.1	2,175	23.7	2,700	0.1	3,375	17.1	208	0
Total	1,597,646	100.0	9,169	100.0	3,280,000	100.0	19,750	100.0	1,985,725	100.0

	Yugoslavia (cont.)		Bulgaria				Czechoslovakia			
	Land Area (in thousand hectares)	Per Cent	No. of Holdings	Per Cent	Land Area (in thousand hectares)	Per Cent	No. of Holdings	Per Cent	Land Area (in thousand hectares)	Per Cent
2 or 3 hectares	694	6.5	239,412	27.0	233	5.3	422,716	26.3	212	1.6
3 to 5 hectares	2,288	21.5	319,688	36.1	1,000	24.7	704,023	43.8	1,869	13.9
5 to 50 hectares	6,642	62.4	325,203	36.8	2,986	68.4	464,264	29.0	5,535	41.2
50 to 100 hectares	338	3.2	561	0.1	69	1.6	7,302	0.4	505	3.7
100 to 500 hectares	294	2.8								
over 500 hectares	300	3.6					8,833	0.5	5,333	39.6
Total	10,646	100.0	884,869	100.0	4,368	100.0	1,607,138	100.0	13,455.3	100.0

Sources: Based on *Magyarország meżögazdaságának föbb üzemi adatai az 1935. évben.* Budapest, 1938; *Aspecte ale economiei Romanesti.* Ed. by N. Lupu-Kostaky. Bucharest, 1939; M. Mirković, *Ekonomska struktura Jugoslavija.* Belgrade, 1952; J. Moloff, *Die sozialekonomischen Struktur der bulgarischen Landwirtschaft,* Berlin, 1936; *Strucný hospodářský vývoj Československa do roku 1955.* Prague, 1969.

many means to protect themselves from nationalization. A widely used method was to transfer interests to partners who were immune to the regulations. Many French and Czechoslovak banks were willing to help their German and Austrian partners in this way. At the meeting of the board of directors of the Hungarian Coal Mines Company of Salgótarján, on November 18, 1919, with reference to the company's interests in Transylvanian mines under Rumanian supremacy, the chairman, Ferenc Chorin, declared: "It would be advantageous to let the company's ship sail under a foreign flag." He suggested a solution with the cooperation of a group of English financiers. The magnesite mines owned by the General Hungarian Credit Bank in Czechoslovakia were handed over to the French firm Schneider-Creusot. The shares of various Austrian and German groups in the Rumanian Marmarosch Bank were taken over by the Banque de Paris et des Pays Bas. The shares of the Banca Comerciala Romîna in Austrian hands were passed on to the Czechoslovak Živnostenska Bank.

With this rescue work the German, Austrian, and Hungarian owners contrived to place part of their former interests under protection or passed them on to their Western partners. Yet a considerable part of shares in banks and industrial works could not be protected against the aspirations of local capital which solicited nationalization. Of course, nationalization could proceed only by way of lengthy negotiations and haggling, and radical solutions were prevented from the very outset by the obligation to pay full indemnity. A considerable part of the interests held by the conquered countries found their way into the ownership of Rumanian, Yugoslav, and Czechoslovak groups of banks and industrial concerns.

In one of the four largest Rumanian banks, the Banca Generale Romina which had discharged the duties of the national bank during the German occupation, the former 60 per cent interest controlled by the Germans was reduced to 20 per cent. In the Rumanian oil industry the 6 per cent share owned by the country before the war was increased to 12 to 15 per cent by 1922 by supplanting groups of foreign financiers. A considerable part of its elaborate network of Transylvanian interests was sold by the Hungarian Commercial Bank of Pest (one of the two largest banks of Hungary) to a Rumanian group. The Bank of Marmorosch Blanc and the Banca Romanesca took over several industrial plants and the packets of their shares from Hungarian banks, for instance the Lugos Textile Industry Corp. and the Temesvár Kimmel Corp. The mines of Petrozsény, notwithstanding the remaining 80 per cent Hungarian interest, were placed under Rumanian management as the Petrosani Coal Mines. The Cement Factory of Torda and the Marta Motor-car Works also passed into Rumanian hands. The Anglo-Hungarian Bank sold all its banking interests in Transylvania and Slovakia, while Transylvanian branches and affiliations of the Commercial Bank of Pest were taken over by the Banque de Crédit Románe, to be united under the name of Transylvanian Bank and Savings Bank—a certain share being retained by the Hungarian bank.

In general the branches of Austrian banks were taken over by the big Czechoslovak banks; for instance, the branches of the Wiener Bankverein were taken over by the Všeobecná Ceska Banková Jednota, those of the Merkur by the Ceska Komerčni Banka, those of the Österreichische Länderbank by the Banka Pro Obchod a Průmysl.

The relatively moderate nationalization carried out in Yugoslavia consisted chiefly in handing over branches and a few affiliations, while some of the old concerns continued their activities under new names and the shares remained in the hands of the original owners.

A fairly long list could be drawn up of the prewar Austrian or Austro-Hungarian and Hungarian firms which changed hands chiefly in Rumania and Yugoslavia, and partly in Czechoslovakia as well. At all events, changes in the ownership of capital became an added factor of economic uncertainty and confusion, apart from their later postwar effects.

The many alterations which contributed to the development of the chaotic situation can, however, by no means be regarded as merely negative happenings hindering return to a normal economic life. Though factors of economic chaos, they also became forces of reconstruction and economic recovery, helping to overcome wartime exhaustion and disorganization while promoting adjustment to the prevailing new conditions. This was especially obvious in connection with the repartitioning of land, for in most countries the carving up of the big estates or their reduction in size and importance widened domestic markets and contributed to more intensive agrarian development.

From the aspect of reconstruction and readjustment, one of the principal elements of postwar economic confusion, inflation itself, became an important instrument of recovery. Though inflation certainly did not solve the grave problems produced in the countries of East-Central Europe by the lack of capital, by the inadequate accumulation of domestic capital, and by the interruption of connections with foreign capital, it helped to surmount difficulties for a short time. The rapid depreciation of the currency created a special inflation boom. Circulating capital and savings banks deposits for the most part became worthless, but simultaneously old debts became immaterial. "Flucht zum Sachwerke" took hold of the country, for investment expenditures were the only way not only to acquire wealth but also to save property and capital. Inflation, which subverted costs of production, reducing certain fixed expenses such as wages to near zero, rendered every investment rewarding and profitable, thus stimulating the spirit of enterprise.

The inflation boom was greatly promoted particularly in Hungary, where in its final stage the process assumed the vastest proportions, by the enormous banknote loans made available by the state and the big banks which could be paid back mostly without valorization. The cheap or free loans coming from the banks were for the greater part invested; machines were purchased, buildings were erected, stocks of raw materials were collected with worthless paper notes. The strong demand for goods produced by the flight of capital into merchandise created a favorable selling market; the banker-inflation of Vienna and Budapest, the rapid increase in the number of new firms, were signs of the contradictory manifestations which appeared in the economic life of the countries of East-Central Europe in the years of postwar impoverishment.

Speculation on the stock exchange assumed unprecedented proportions; part of the money fled into gold or foreign currency, but shares were also issued on a grand scale. The value of newly issued shares soared to thousands of millions, to 500,000 million crowns in Hungary alone. For the most part this implied only inflation of shares, but in some degree it formed the source from which to cover costs of renovation, purchases of gold, machines, etc. Therefore, this inflation also became a factor in the change-over to peacetime production.

In addition, inflation not only exerted an influence on the domestic market but also spurred exports. The advantages in foreign trade of countries with a weak currency are common knowledge, and so are its prohibitive effects on imports. Consequently, on the whole, inflation created a peculiar kind of prosperity in every country, accelerating the replacement of losses caused by the war, inducing the activation of new capacity in various sectors, as well as a rise of production to and sometimes over the prewar level.

In Austria the animating effect of inflation was seen in the increase in the number of factories from 6,283 to 7,414 between 1919 and 1922. During the same period the number of small-scale shops rose from 56,189 to 61,687, while the number of employed workers increased in these years by over 200,000, from 566,891 to 781,888. Of course, the boom created the liveliest demand for goods required for investments. Iron production, which was down to somewhere around one-sixth of the prewar level in 1920, began to pick up and rose to over 50 per cent by 1922, while steel output increased to over 80 per cent of the 1913 level.

In Hungary the number of workers employed in the steel and metal industries was raised by one-third, the number of those in machine industry by 25 per cent, as a result of the inflation boom. During the same time the output, more than doubling in one year, climbed to 70 per cent of the prewar level. Coal production reached the prewar level. The total manpower employed in manufacturing industry increased by 35 per cent as a result of inflation, and the growth of output may be estimated to have been of similar magnitude. At the peak of the inflation boom total industrial production was around 75 per cent of the prewar value.

In Yugoslavia the inflation-induced boom inspired feverish enterprise. In the four years 1918–22 more than 500 new factories were founded; the year 1922 alone witnessed the establishment of 157 new industrial works, a peak achievement. During the period of inflation the total growth of the volume of investments amounted to 25 per cent, while manpower increased by 38 per cent.

Though for a considerably briefer time, inflation made itself felt in a similar manner in Czechoslovakia. Here, investment was stimulated by production costs being masked by the high prices associated with inflation, leading to the rise of industrial output to the prewar level as early as 1921 according to available records. However, as in the economic life of the victorious Western powers, in 1921 a crisis of overproduction set in in Czechoslovakia, causing a decline of 15 to 20 per cent in production. Thus, though Czechoslovakia stood out among the countries of Eastern Europe on account of her well-ordered economic life, high employment and growth of output took place only in the late 1920s.

While the effect of the inflation boom on the economy varied as to time and extent, it contributed to forcing industrial output up to about 75 per cent of its prewar level in all the countries involved by the time the inflation had run its course. By 1922–23 the years of outright economic confusion were over, but none of the countries could by that time return to the status quo and resume normal growth. Not one of the countries in question could quite adjust itself to its new external conditions and domestic structure. These adaptations came about for the most part only in the late twenties in conjunction with stabilization, the readjustment of the accumulation of capital at home and in other countries, and the formulation of new concepts of economic policy.

9 Reconstruction and Its Inherent Contradictions

Amidst the economic confusion of the postwar years, several factors of chaos became elements of reconstruction. For countries which found themselves in a fundamentally new position economic recovery was unimaginable without a conscious economic policy of reconstruction supported by every other activity of the state. In each of the new independent countries the ruling classes and government circles wished to adapt economic policy to their own political aspirations and interests. It was nationalism in these small countries of East-Central Europe, expressed in their fight for independent political and economic existence, which became the dominant political trend and the shaper of economic policy.

Before World War I, besides the real political and economic grievances of the countries and provinces belonging to large empires, all the consequences of their underdeveloped state, the disadvantages experienced in the international division of labor, and the effects of economic weakness and helplessness were thought to be due to the partial or total lack of national independence. The panacea to heal these wounds seemed to be the achievement of national independence, the exclusion or elimination of more advanced partners, and the strongest possible national isolation.

The flare-up of nationalist passions fanned by the war, the disintegration of the old empires and the emergence of new states, the reinforced national aspirations intensified as a reaction to international proletarian movements and revolutions following the war provided a fertile field for the cultivation of economic nationalism. The actual conditions themselves helped to increase surface friction. Customs frontiers had grown 6,000 to 7,000 kilometers longer in Europe. Instead of the earlier 26 independent economic units there were 38, while the former 13 currencies were replaced by 27. All this took place mainly in East-Central Europe. On the territory of the Austro-Hungarian Monarchy alone, seven separate and independent customs areas came into existence.

In the period of economic confusion following World War I, one of the principal aims of the new states of East-Central Europe was to turn their independence to their advantage and to exploit the situation. In all the countries of the region this implied complete severance of former economic ties and the intention to go as far as practicable in establishing economic independence.

Formerly, the most extensive areas of East-Central Europe had been connected by close economic ties. This applied in the first place to the countries belonging to one empire, which formed a peculiar kind of economic union notwithstanding the inherent contradictions. It also applied to the relations between large empires and the neighboring small countries. Naturally, an important factor here was imperialist pressure and the economic superiority of the big powers, which not only made harmonious economic relations impossible but often led to sharp disagreements and tariff wars. These relations nevertheless derived from the natural economic interdependence and complementary role of neighboring countries.

Despite the shock of conflicts and clashes, an elaborate system of trade agreements had been concluded in East-Central Europe before the war. But the only advice, voiced occasionally from the victorious powers and the League of Nations, was a pious wish to straighten out and reinstate the ties broken off by the war. It was in vain that the supreme council of the allied powers pointed out the intolerability of the new conditions in its statement of March 1920, accentuating the need for friendly cooperation and unlimited exchange of goods among the new states. The Conference of Geneva held in the spring of 1922 also laid down the principle that the territorial changes brought about by the war should not be allowed to alter normal commercial conditions in any considerable degree.

Contrary to the principles agreed upon at conferences, historical reality produced far-reaching changes. It is true that no formal change took place immediately in the prewar customs policy. The newly created countries almost automatically took over the prewar imperial customs tariffs and put them into force at their own frontiers. Austria, Czechoslovakia, and Hungary applied the autonomous customs tariff of the Austro-Hungarian Monarchy valid since 1906, while Rumania and Yugoslavia extended the former Rumanian and Serbian customs systems to their newly acquired provinces. Of course, the prewar customs tariffs had been based on entirely different conditions and were intended to serve the interests of a widely divergent commercial policy, thus rendering them utterly unsuited for use in the new situation.

In 1919, however, the problem did not arise as to whether the old customs tariffs were suitable or not. The situation was turned upside down by the process of inflation in every country, as described in the preceding chapter. Under the impact of these events the earlier customs walls of most countries crumbled. For instance, the former rates of the Austro-Hungarian Monarchy were not paid as ad valorem duty, but fixed in amounts of crowns related to weight. After depreciation of the currency, tariffs which had exacted 10 to 20 per cent, and for a few articles as much as 30 to 40 per cent, of value before the war shrank to no more than a 1 to 4 per cent formal "protection." Thus customs tariffs became practically useless for regulating the exchange of goods, nor did they help to accomplish the desired aims of foreign trade and economic policy. The race between the depreciation of money and rates of duty which started after 1919 did not alter the situation either. The tariff bonus introduced because of the fall in the value of money and the subsequent surplus charges failed to prevent the shrinking of customs tariffs.

For instance, in Yugoslavia the rates payable amounted only to about two thirds of the former tariff level despite surplus charges. In Rumania no surplus charges were added at all.

It must be remarked here that no particular importance was attached to the efficacy of tariffs. While destroying the formerly protective support of tariffs, inflation simultaneously produced contrary results. Instead of the diminished customs tariffs, the depreciated money itself ensured the protection of national markets. Moreover, besides the well-known market-protecting effect of inflation, most of the countries in question availed themselves of radical regulatory wartime measures that were still valid. Between 1919 and 1923–24, and in some countries even longer, prohibition of imports and exports formed the principal means of control in foreign trade and economic policy. In a few countries such prohibitive measures were maintained or put into force almost directly after the war. In

Austria numerous articles were put on the valid list of prohibited imports, but, owing to the general lack of supplies in the country, rigid treatment of the issue was avoided, and customs houses were authorized to approve the import of many articles within the competence of their official function.

Prohibition of exports, on the other hand, applied only to raw materials and foods. In Czechoslovakia, it was chiefly the import of industrial products which was strictly limited until the middle of 1923. This strict prohibition was slightly relaxed for the first time in trade agreements with France and Austria. The prohibitive measures formally valid in Hungary from the time of the war were not applied between 1919 and 1921, and most articles were put on the approved list of imports. A new decree in July 1921 modified the free list of imports and considerably widened embargoes, particularly in the sphere of finished industrial products. The prohibition of imports was modified several times by October 1924, and further items were banned. In Yugoslavia embargo was kept in force until October 1923. Rumania introduced prohibition for the first time in July 1919, banning imports of luxury articles in particular; the applied measures remained essentially valid until 1924.

Hence, the countries of East-Central Europe did not engage in cooperation in commercial policy after the war, but chose isolation, mostly by means of direct interference by the state and prohibitive measures. This trend became stronger in the postwar years, mainly because of political incentives. It was by means of these radical steps that the new states hoped, among other benefits, for the development of economic unity or economic independence.

Consequently, the applied prohibitive measures were not of a transient character. True, methods typical of a war economy could not be treated as permanent weapons of economic policy; their function consisted mainly of tiding economies over the period until new customs tariffs could be drawn up and put into force. Therefore, the prohibitions of the early 1920s actually formed the prelude to new, independent customs tariffs. Economic consolidation, attained by the mid-twenties, the normalization of political and economic conditions, and, last but not least, the expiration of various prohibitive clauses in the peace treaties opened the door to introduction of new customs tariffs, which became the most important means of directing postwar economic policy.

The new Austrian customs tariff came into force on January 1, 1925, and so did the new Hungarian customs tariff in its complete form, following the partial measures of the preceding months. In Yugoslavia the new customs tariff was introduced in March 1925, in Czechoslovakia in 1926, in Rumania in June 1924, but in Rumania it was subjected to thorough reform and considerably raised in 1927. In Bulgaria the new customs tariff drawn up in 1922 was revised and given final form in 1924 after having been increased considerably.

Compared to the prewar tariffs, the new ones put into effect in the mid-twenties in East-Central Europe show two striking differences: a great increase in the number of items and much higher customs duties.

Rates often referring to several thousand items (in Hungary the new customs tariff contained rates for 2,244 articles) partly indicated the advancement of technology and the claim for increased specialization, but in themselves they were significant factors of increasing isolation. Extensive specialization was intended to prevent any other country from deriving on a preferential basis any advantages from the reduction of duties granted in trade agreements by the signatory parties.

In general the new customs tariffs were considerably higher than prewar duties had been. In Rumania, instead of the earlier, already high, 30 per cent, they provided protection of approximately 40 per cent. In Hungary the 20 per cent level formerly prevailing in the Monarchy was replaced by a customs tariff that averaged 30 per cent and as high as 50 per cent for finished industrial products imported in massive quantities. From the prewar level in Serbia of around 10 per cent, Yugoslav protective tariffs were raised to 20–26 per cent, but for industrial consumer goods they moved up to 70–170 per cent. Bulgarian rates of duty were increased by 100 to 300 per cent over the prewar level, and a prohibitive barrier was erected in every field where home industry was active.

Many national and international statistics are available as a basis for comparison of the average level of customs duties and customs tariffs. Of these the best known are the indices calculated by the

Economic and Financial Departments of the League of Nations, prepared for the Economic Conference of Geneva held in 1927. Although these statistics demonstrate the general upward tendency of customs tariffs, the data presented are largely inaccurate and the information they offer is more misleading than helpful. As a matter of fact, they include in the calculation of averages rates those fixed formally but not actually in force owing to lack of business in the goods in question (for instance, protective tariffs of agrarian countries which did not import any agricultural products). On the other hand, the data seem to disregard the effects of regulations apart from tariffs, for example, rules of animal hygiene, which importers of agricultural products liked to apply, and often did apply even more effectively than customs tariffs. (On the pretext of hygiene imports could be virtually banned at any time.) In many countries certain direct prohibitive measures were maintained as well when the customs tariff was put into force.

It is even less possible to define the scale of customs tariffs, for, concomitant with putting tariffs into force, governments made conscious efforts to introduce higher "fighting" tariffs. By this means they strove to break down the walls of ever more forbidding isolation in the case of another country. By increasing their own protective tariffs they hoped to compel their neighbors to accept a compromise. At the negotiation of trade agreements it really came then to extensive mutual concessions by the countries of East-Central Europe, granted partly to Western parties, partly to one another. Acting on the principle of highest preference, in general they considerably reduced the customs tariffs laid down by law.

The numerous trade agreements concluded between 1924 and 1927 thus practically normalized the economic relations of the countries in this region, but in reality the agreements did not bring about cooperation among the countries concerned nor did they halt the tendency toward isolation.

For one thing, they did not remain stationary for any length of time in the second half of the decade, and their changes often modified earlier concessions. For instance, on April 22, 1927, Austria repealed the three codicils signed by 1926 as supplements to the Austrian-Czechoslovak trade agreement of 1921, and the new codicil established more effective protection for many Austrian products. Earlier concessions concerning textiles, paper, and other goods were declared invalid. This led to another increase on the part of Czechoslovakia.

At the revision of the Austrian-Yugoslav agreement of 1925 in July 1928 rates were raised for fifty items by Austria, for seventy by Yugoslavia, and many earlier reductions and readjustments were repealed.

It should be noted that in these years the agrarian protectionism of the more advanced industrial countries became active. From 1925 Austria applied a sliding scale of tariffs to the import of cereals which had previously been exempt from customs, exacting the payment of 3 gold crowns as a supplementary duty on flour. Many prohibitions remained valid, barring the extension to other countries of the concessions granted to Italy in customs duties on wine and salami. The supplementary customs laws, the first issued in April 1926, the second in August of the same year, the third in November 1927, further increased agrarian protection. For example, rates of duty were raised by nearly 40 per cent on sugar, supplementary duty on flour by 66 per cent, tariffs on livestock and breeding-stock of cattle and pigs (of not more than 110 kg.) by 100 percent, on hog fat and bacon nearly threefold.

In Czechoslovakia efforts at agrarian isolation were strengthened in a similar manner, culminating in a considerable increase in the duty on corn, flour, livestock, and meat in 1930. Finally, the flour tariff was raised to 75–80 per cent of the value. These steps were supported by a new law regulating the grinding and mixing of flour. Not more than 25 per cent imported wheat or 5 per cent imported rye was to be used up at grinding.

Similarly, the agrarian countries of the Danube Valley sought to establish increasingly radical protection against industrial imports from Austria and Czechoslovakia. While an average tariff of 14 to 17 per cent was applied by Germany, 16 to 21 per cent by Italy, and 21 to 30 per cent by Czechoslovakia in trade with Austria, Hungary put into force a tariff of 30 to 40 per cent, Yugoslavia one of 27 to 41 per cent, and Poland one of 49 to 67 per cent, providing for maximal protection.

Isolation and entrenchment in the countries of East-Central Europe in defense of their own economies naturally meant protection against all foreign trading partners. In reality, however, this protection was most determined and strict against the neighboring countries and less so against those more remote. This followed from the prevailing situation. Since both agriculture and industry applied less advanced techniques and produced at higher costs in this region of Europe than in the more advanced countries, they were less able to compete on the world market. Hence, when apparently similar obstacles were put up at the Austrian or Czechoslovak frontier against all cereals and flour of foreign provenance, they proved to be much more difficult and insurmountable barriers to Hungarian than to American wheat, despite the higher cost of freight. When the import of machines was subjected to surcharge at the borders of the reinforced customs area of the Balkan countries, Austrian factories were hit harder than the British and Belgian.

Thus, self-protection invoked in the name of self-sufficiency inevitably pushed the countries of East-Central Europe much further away from one another than the countries of Eastern and Western Europe. It is characteristic that the foreign trade of Yugoslavia with the neighboring Balkan countries remained insignificant throughout the decade following the war, amounting only to 9 per cent of exports and 5 per cent of imports between 1926 and 1930. Although the Austro-Hungarian Monarchy with its share of two-thirds and three-fourths of Serbian foreign trade had been the most important trade connection before World War I, the total share of Hungary, Austria, and Czechoslovakia in imports from Yugoslavia sank to 41 per cent in 1929, in exports below 28 per cent.

Also, among the successor states of the Austro-Hungarian Monarchy which had earlier formed a united economic area, natural connections definitely ceased. The value of the goods supplied to Hungary from the Austrian and Czech parts of the Monarchy in 1913 diminished by 60 per cent by 1924—taking into account the postwar territorial changes. Whereas directly after the war—in the pattern of the old economic relations—nearly 52 per cent of Czechoslovak exports still went to the Danubian countries, by 1924 these exports were reduced to 37 per cent, by 1929 to 31 per cent. The situation was similar in Austria where more than 42 per cent of exports were still sent to the Danubian countries in 1922, but by 1929, only 34 per cent.

Simultaneously with the sharp decline in her exports to the Danubian countries Czechoslovakia imported more than half of her flour requirements from overseas and not from the neighboring agrarian countries by the late 1920s—a revealing fact about the reciprocity of these processes.

Austria also purchased approximately one-third of her wheat requirements from America while she was unable to sell the products of her machine industry in Eastern Europe, a region of agrarian character. Hungary and the Balkan countries bought French and English machine tools and equipment for textile factories on a considerable scale. The new Poland, with extensive districts which had formerly belonged to the Russian Empire and her former markets now mostly on Russian territory, transacted altogether 1.5 per cent of her foreign trade with the Soviet Union. In all the countries of the region, economic policy was marked by a consistent exclusion of the Soviet Union. As a result of this policy the trade of Czechoslovakia with the Soviet Union was kept at an equally low level, while the other countries practically broke off all relations with the USSR.

Notwithstanding the circumstance of proximity, natural opportunities, and historical traditions, trade among the countries of East-Central Europe shrank considerably. In the prewar years the Danubian countries, whether or not within the borders of the same empire, traded with one another to the extent of two-thirds to three-fourths of their total turnover. By 1929, exports having fallen to 35.9 per cent, imports to 30.9 per cent, their transactions amounted only to about one-third of the prewar level. Economic relations were shifted ever more decisively in the direction of Western Europe.

The national aspirations pervading economic policy, which weakened and interrupted traditional commercial relations, influenced not only foreign trade but also capital transactions and the role of foreign capital. The targets of an independent national economy naturally included also the demand that the leading positions in the economy, which previously had been occupied in most countries of East-Central Europe by groups of foreign financiers, should be acquired by the bourgeoisie of the country in question. In these parts of Europe the formerly weak financial and industrial circles, previously dependent on, and virtually at the mercy of, their stronger partners, strove to turn to their own advantage the chances for strengthening their

position afforded by independence and in some cases by the growth
of their territory. This activity could easily be converted to a general
national cause, under banners carrying attractive national slogans.
As the most typical and sharpest move in this respect Rumania issued
a new law for mining in 1925 according to clauses 32 and 33 of which
only Rumanian companies could obtain mining concessions, and the
interest controlled by foreign capital was limited to 40 per cent
of the shares. These paragraphs also applied to mining companies in
operation, which were obliged to comply with the decree and effect
the necessary changes within ten years.

However, where a nationalist economic policy was pursued in the
acquisition of capital and in investments, it soon came up against, and
was stopped by, the barriers of reality. In Rumania the new law was
repealed five years after its introduction and foreign capital was
granted opportunities equaling those open to domestic sources.
Finally, as will be pointed out later, in most countries the new laws
confined themselves to limiting the interests of subjects and firms of
the formerly alien countries.

The countries of this region nevertheless based their ideas of reconstruction on the cooperation of foreign capital instead of doing
without foreign capital in general.

The grave economic crisis of the first postwar years and the chaotic
conditions typical of the countries of East-Central Europe gave rise—
as shown in the preceding chapter—to certain factors inspiring a
search for alternatives in adapting to the new position, even to elements of recovery. However, the economic consolidation of these
countries, the reconstruction of economic power, could have proceeded only very slowly had they relied merely on home resources
and possibilities. Such slow advance was all the more unavoidable as
the countries in question not only had to overcome their wartime
exhaustion and wrestle with the tasks of a change-over to a peace
economy in an exceedingly complicated, new situation, within new
frontiers; they could draw only on domestic forces which had been
insufficient earlier, having served merely to supplement outside resources, and it was only in conjunction with these that they could
cover the requirements of economic development.

If foreign capital contributed in decisive measure to the industrial revolution and modern capitalist transformation of the Danubian countries, it is evident that in the very difficult postwar period reconstruction would have been long delayed without the aid of foreign capital.

From the aspect of economic reconstruction, in the East-Central European countries any changes in the general prosperity of the world economy therefore gained immense importance, and so did the political and economic aspirations of the big powers. This determined whether and to what extent they could avail themselves of the means put at their disposal by the economically advanced countries.

In the postwar years foreign capital was not forthcoming. This was due not only to the continuing political uncertainty in several of the countries involved and to former creditors having been rendered wary by revolutions, counterrevolutions, and warfare, but also to the grave political and economic circumstances in which the advanced capitalist powers found themselves. The revolutionary movements which flared up all over Europe, the bitter strikes and violent political crises between 1918 and 1921, did not spare the victorious big powers. They needed several years to master the situation, to stabilize their political position by economic consolidation.

This consolidation was realized in a relatively short time, so that between 1922 and 1924 a new boom was experienced, first in the United States, then in the victorious European countries. The reconstruction of Germany, started with American capital, and the extensive penetration of American capital into the European economy greatly contributed to the postwar prosperity of Europe. Europe's position underwent an essential change in the war years, for the enormous advance of the United States, which had grown into the strongest industrial and financial power, and the accelerated industrialization of other overseas countries broke up earlier commercial monopolies and created a new situation in foreign trade to which England, France, and the rest of the highly developed countries of Western Europe had to adapt themselves.

The postwar period witnessed the utilization of technical achievements, primarily the extensive application of electricity, and the introduction of modern techniques and methods of organization, including mass production. New branches were built up which could engage in exports, having modernized their manufacturing and altered their assortment of products. The prosperity of Europe in the twenties grew out of these changes.

In 1920 U.S. industrial output surpassed the prewar level by over 20 per cent, and England as well as Italy was not far behind. The temporary setback caused by the postwar crisis of overproduction in 1921–22 was followed by a considerable upswing of production between 1922 and 1924. However, England regained her 1920 level (i.e., roughly that of the prewar period) only by about 1924. France approached her prewar output in 1923, Belgium in 1924; in 1925 total European industrial output slightly exceeded that of 1913. In 1925 the United States already produced one and a half times as much as before the war.

The very fact that Western Europe had regained political and economic stability created entirely new conditions for East-Central Europe, particularly because stabilization went hand in hand with the strengthening of the new political attitude of the victorious big powers. Actually, the latter attached great importance to the economic and political stabilization of the countries of East-Central Europe in the interest of realizing their own political endeavors, especially after the victory of the Russian revolution, the failure of military intervention and the Civil War, and the stabilization of the Soviet system. Having overcome their own pressing postwar concerns and having given up the idea of crushing the Bolshevik revolution with arms, they turned their attention to the countries of East-Central Europe which were in the neighborhood of the Soviet Union, countries partly shaken by revolutionary movements and constituting in their instability a permanent danger of potential revolution. This political recognition, or more accurately, the economic and political consequences of this recognition, was first perceived and formulated most clearly by John M. Keynes:

The only safeguard against Revolution in Central Europe is indeed the fact that, even to the minds of men who are desperate, revolution offers no prospect of improvement whatever. There may, therefore, be ahead of us a long, silent process of semi-starvation, and of a gradual, steady lowering of the standards of life and comfort. The bankruptcy and decay of Europe, if we allow it to proceed, will affect everyone in the long run, but perhaps not in a way that is striking or immediate.[1]

Keynes proposed to counteract such developments by a program of promoting the recovery of Europe through international loans. "It will be very difficult for European production to get started again without a temporary measure of external assistance. I am therefore a supporter of an international loan." Loans were to be granted not only to former allies, but also to former adversaries.[2]

The views voiced by Keynes—together with the actual effect of his book on the formation of economic policy—were reflected a few years later in the policy of the big powers. Naturally this policy was also strongly motivated by individual ambitions to seize power, arising from the wish to profit from the situation produced in Europe by the defeat of Germany. Outstanding in this connection were the European aspirations of France, the country which had emerged from the war as the strongest continental power. Her role was enhanced by the creation of a zone of influence in East-Central Europe beyond Germany and the acquisition of German spheres of interest in the Balkans. Shifts of power of this kind induced England, always striving to maintain a balance of power in Europe, to support the recovery of Germany and to counterpoise in part the steps of France in Eastern and Southeastern Europe. Thus, in the postwar power system of European and world politics the line was taken that after a few years of postwar economic chaos old and new big powers appeared as creditors, and factors of European political and economic stabilization, in the economic reconstruction of the disordered countries of the Danube Valley. The starting point was to be financial stabilization.

One of the first links in the chain of events which brought about stabilization in East-Central Europe was the rehabilitation of Austrian finances on a sound basis. This was justified not only by the dimensions assumed by inflation but also by the particularly grave state of the economy, the problem of whether an independent Austria could exist

---

[1] J. M. Keynes, *The Economic Consequences of the Peace,* New York, 1921, p. 296.
[2] *Ibid.,* p. 283 and 287.

at all, and the consequent political dangers, not the least of which was the possibility of an Anschluss. Therefore, the possibility of a foreign loan was considered as early as the end of 1920, but at the time the project could not be realized. However, in 1921, the big powers concentrated in the League of Nations thought the time had come to intervene, and a financial delegation was dispatched to Austria. As a result of these steps the Protocol of Geneva, consisting of three parts, was signed on October 4, 1922.

The first part provided for the territorial integrity of Austria, her political, economic, and financial sovereignty. The second part ensured a loan of 650 million gold crowns, to be granted by the four signatory powers—Great Britain, France, Italy, and Czechoslovakia—for the purpose of ending the budget deficit within two years and of paying back the loans raised after 1919. In the third part of the Protocol the Austrian government undertook to introduce radical reforms when the reorganization of finances had been carried out, including appropriate reduction of the state apparatus and parliamentary approval of the necessary measures. Approval was to apply also to the appointment by the League of Nations of a control commission and a High Commissioner invested with powers to investigate the activities of the government in certain spheres. As security for the loan, Austria forfeited important revenues accruing from customs duties, the monopoly on tobacco, and, if necessary, from other sources. Thereupon, the Austrian government, having weathered the worst depths of the inflation of September, when one gold crown was equivalent to 17,000 paper crowns, stopped the issuance of uncovered banknotes at the end of 1922, having contrived to bring about some improvement in the value of the crown by means of deflation in October and November. In December the value of a gold crown rose to 14,500 paper crowns, and was stabilized at this level in 1923. The new currency, the gold schilling, was put into circulation on January 1, 1925; 1 gold crown was worth 1.44 schillings.

In the first postwar year Hungarian inflation did not keep pace with the depreciation of the Austrian crown. Though the economic situation cannot have been considerably better in Hungary than in Austria and adjustment to the new territorial demands took several years, the economic viability of the country—a point questioned by some parties for political reasons, by others from sincere anxiety—did not, and could not have, become an international political problem as with the Austrian Republic. Hence stabilization was not an issue of urgent international interest, either from the economic or from the political viewpoint. It was only in 1923 that it came within the sphere of interest of the League of Nations when the Hungarian government on the one hand to overcome inflation which had assumed dangerous proportions and, on the other, for international political reasons, thought it necessary, like Austria, to turn for financial help to the big powers, that is, to the League of Nations.

The control of inflation with external aid appeared to be a reasonable solution to the Hungarian government not only because an attempt at stabilization by raising a domestic loan in the form of property tax had failed in 1921 and another attempt seemed useless, but also because the Hungarian government intended to connect stabilization with the unsettled question of reparations. Exploratory talks with English financiers in the spring of 1923 ended with the English money market being willing to support the loan provided that the transaction was executed under the political auspices of the League of Nations, and as security the income of the state sequestrated for reparation payment was to be invalidated.

In April 1923, the government therefore asked for a short-term loan (of 40 to 50 million gold crowns) and a long-term loan (of 550 to 650 million gold crowns), requesting simultaneously the lifting of the sequestration of lien on reparations. A long diplomatic skirmish ensued in the course of which, supported by England, the Hungarian government contrived to persuade the reluctant French government and the countries of the Little Entente to consent to the suspension of lien and to allow the loan to be raised unencumbered by any obligation to pay reparations.

After these diplomatic preliminaries, in November 1923 the League of Nations sent to Hungary a delegation to study the economic situation, and at the same time a project was worked out in London for the loan to be granted to Hungary. This project caused some disappointment, because instead of the requested 650 million crowns it contemplated only 250 million crowns, and the time allowed for financial reorganization was to be two-and-a-half years. The delegation made certain recommendations concerning the conditions of the loan, stabilization of the currency, and the economic policy to be pursued. In the case of Hungary too, revenue from customs duty, from tobacco and salt *régie,* was to serve as collateral security for the loan. As in Austria, the League of Nations appointed a High Commissioner invested with the right to intervene in the financial management of Hungary.

Thus preparations for stabilization were started in the spring of 1924. The rain of nonvalorized credits was the first to be stopped. A few months of transition followed when loans had to be repaid at a certain rate of valorization (savings-bank crown). Inflation was still in full swing. The value of the crown continued to sink until May 1924, when it struck rock bottom at the level of 1 gold crown equal to 17,866 paper crowns. In July stabilization began and the ratio of the gold crown to the paper crown was fixed at 1:17,000. At the same time the new National Bank of Hungary was set up after the pattern of the western national banks and their relations to the government.

The loan of the League of Nations was issued on June 26, 1924. It was relatively easy to place the bonds at a low quotation price and high rate of interest, chiefly on the Royal Exchange (London) and also on the New York Exchange. Part of the amounts collected went into balancing the deficit, but by the end of 1924 it turned out that, together with the newly introduced taxes, the public revenue far surpassed expenditure. Therefore, the greater part of the loan was used for other purposes. Thus, stabilization was successfully carried out in Hungary, and in 1926 the introduction of the new currency (1 gold crown = 1.16 pengö) made this important step of economic reconstruction final.

In the region under review several other countries balanced their budget and stabilized their currency by the aid of loans from the League of Nations. Of special importance were the credits serving to stabilize the currency in Greece, Esthonia, and Danzig. Loans from the League of Nations played a role in Bulgaria too. In the twenties Bulgaria raised two loans: one in 1926 to cover the costs of population exchange; the other in 1928, expressly to stabilize her currency.

As pointed out before, inflation did not assume such excessive proportions in Bulgaria as in the other countries discussed so far. Preparations to curb inflation having been started as early as 1921, favorable progress was facilitated by the elimination of a deficit in the budget of 1921–22. In the summer of 1922 a decree was therefore issued, setting an upper limit to the amount of banknotes to be put into circulation. During the year 1923, only slow growth took place, not exceeding the permissible limit. The volume of currency did not exceed 3,000–4,000 million levas. However, the above measures did not insure stabilization, especially because the open question of reparations constituted a permanent factor of uncertainty. This was manifested by a series of sharp fluctuations in the value of money in 1923. To keep the rate of the leva on a firm basis, foreign exchange control was introduced in December 1923, and the new rates of exchange were fixed at the level of 1 dollar equal to 137 levas.

In the period between December 1923 and the close of 1928 this level was on the whole maintained. The budget could be balanced and minor deficits covered from home resources and by small loans—in particular, a loan of 3.3 million pounds sterling.

In these years the financial balance achieved was very precarious and the burden of reparations to be paid in increasing amounts beginning in 1930 involved particular dangers. According to the planned schedule, payments were first to be doubled, then tripled and quadrupled. Prompted by the wish to preserve Bulgaria's uncertain and threatened economy, experts suggested in 1926 that the League of Nations should interfere. The financial delegation appointed to study the situation elaborated the project and conditions of stabilization, as well as a regulation of the status of the National Bank of Bulgaria. The preparatory negotiation having been concluded, an agreement was signed providing for a major loan. Modernization of the banking system in connection with the loan was an important step. The old state bank was replaced by the National Bank of Bulgaria which—in accordance with the modern pattern followed in Europe—acted independently of the state apparatus, and the state refunded the loan of £ 1.5 million raised from the Bank. Another £ 650,000 went into consolidating the position of the Bulgarian Agricultural Bank and the Central Cooperative Bank of Bulgaria which took over the mortgage credit transactions of the National Bank.

Another important part of the loan from the League of Nations was to be applied to secure the complete stability of the budget, and 1.25 million was to be spent on the modernization of transport, first of all on railways and partly on roads and harbors.

Finally, the amount of the loan signed in March 1928 and approved on November 15—together with the further £ 500,000 granted to restore the damage caused by the severe earthquake of April in the same year—amounted to £ 5 million on which Bulgaria paid an interest of 7.5 per cent and pledged her customs revenue as security. The process of stabilization was thereby completed. Earlier restrictions were mostly lifted, and the leva, whose rate of exchange was not changed from the level of 1923, was restored to the gold standard.

Although Rumania belonged to the victorious powers, had suffered no loss of territory, and was untroubled by reparations, after 1919 a relatively gross inflation set in—the worst next to Austria's and Hungary's—as a result of war debts and the economic losses inflicted by the transient occupation of the country. State expenditure was increased because of the trebling of the territory and the number of inhabitants. Therefore the issue of uncovered banknotes became the principal concern of economic policy. The volume of currency in circulation was further enlarged by the exchange of non-Rumanian, chiefly Austro-Hungarian money—though the rate of this compulsory exchange was unfavorable for the population of the new provinces. The actual value of the Rumanian currency nevertheless sank rapidly until 1922.

By 1923 the depreciation of the leu was slightly slowed down, most probably owing to the Anglo-American loan of £ 37 million obtained in 1922. Even so, by 1924 the leu fell drastically, a Swiss franc being equivalent to 44.50 lei.

Having been granted a moratorium in the summer of 1922 by her foreign creditors, Rumania, which had been greatly strengthened by the acquisition of territory and economic resources, seized all the foreign credit balance and by 1925 contrived to realize the first stage of stabilization without any foreign loan. Resort to loans would in any case have been contrary to the prevailing nationalist economic policy based on the loudly proclaimed slogan "We should rely unaided on our own resources." In this phase an agreement was reached between the Ministry of Finance and the National Bank to cease gradually the issue of uncovered banknotes. Another agreement dealt with the banknotes issued previously and above all provided for the settlement of the national debt to the Bank, for which purpose a special fund was made available. Simultaneously, inflation was in fact stopped from May 25 and the value of the leu showed a slight rise.

Although there was no more inflation, the value of the leu continued to fluctuate; and soon after the improvement which followed inflation, in 1926, the Swiss franc was again around 50 lei. Around 1927 this rate of exchange was reduced, but final stabilization could be achieved here too only in the second stage, in 1929, when the rate of exchange of the Swiss franc was fixed at 34 lei. However, it was the $100 million loan raised by the new government which came into office in 1928, chiefly on the American money market, which played a decisive role in final stabilization, the new administration having abandoned nationalist economic policy. It was in fact the monopoly state fund, handling the revenue from all the state monopolies, except that from the match monopoly, which actually raised the loan. The monopoly of match-making had in fact been bought by the Swedish match trust, which had taken over $30 million of the $100 million loan. A part of the loan, $23 million, served to strengthen the position of the National Bank, making stabilization final, at least until the outbreak of the financial crisis of 1931.

It was by an equally slow process, unconnected with the League of Nations but with considerable foreign cooperation, that Polish finances were stabilized. In the chapter on inflation an account has been given of the series of attempts to stop the depreciation of the currency, of the efforts at stabilization in 1921 and 1924. The first attempt may indeed be regarded as half-hearted, much as in Hungary. However, the economic rehabilitation of 1924 was a determined effort to arrest any further depreciation of the Polish mark, which was falling to unprecedented depths (1 dollar equaling 9.3 million marks). In this instance the endeavor was to balance the budget by resort to home resources, chiefly through considerably increased taxes and severe discipline in their collection. With reliance on the correction of the adverse budget, the new currency, the zloty, which was planned to be stable, was introduced on April 14, 1924, in a value too high in relation to the dollar (5.18 zlotys being equivalent to 1 dollar). At the same time the National Bank of Poland was founded as a joint-stock company with a capital of 100 million zlotys. However, owing to inherent economic liability aggravated by the poor harvest of 1925, to stabilization at too high a value, to imbalance of the budget despite contrary expectations, to part of the taxes being irrecoverable, and to trends of deflation, the unsteady stabilization was again upset beginning in the summer of 1925, and depreciation of the zloty set in.

At this juncture the Polish government turned to the United States, whereupon a delegation of American experts, headed by Professor E. Kemmerer, was sent to Poland to work out a new project of stabilization. Their first step was to reorganize the exceedingly precarious financial and credit system of the country. The network of Polish banks was utterly incapable of financing the economy. It was suggested that a number of weak and immobile banks be liquidated and that the position of others be consolidated. Until that time the National Bank alone was able to grant substantial credits. Therefore, the delegation urged the foundation of several major banks in the form of joint-stock companies with a capital of 30 to 40 million zlotys. By transacting business in short-term loans they were intended to relieve the National Bank of this burden. Simultaneously with the regulation of the credit system the delegation advised gradual stabilization in three steps: first, actual stabilization, then its legal sanction, and finally change-over to the gold standard. This method of gradualness was justified by the failure of previous attempts.

Finally the loan of $72 million raised by the Polish government mostly in the United States contributed greatly to restoring a balanced budget, which was indispensable for the rehabilitation of finances. At this point the balance of foreign trade also became favorable, owing chiefly to the increase in coal exports as a result of the general coal strike of 1926 in England. In this way the depreciation of the zloty could finally be stopped in the autumn of 1926, and the currency was stabilized, 8.91 zlotys being worth 1 dollar at the new rate of exchange. It was only in October 1927 that the process was finished with the issuing of a stabilization law.

Stabilization with foreign cooperation became an important link in the chain of events which realized economic reconstruction in East-Central Europe. Reorganization of the budget and of financial affairs was intended not only to put an end to postwar economic chaos and inflation, involving both political and economic dangers, but also to create normal conditions for and to accelerate saving and investment.

There were, however, very serious obstacles to the achievement of this aim. In the period of rehabilitation measures of deflation were employed in every sector in order to protect the stability of the new currency. In most of the countries in this region prolonged inflation was followed by stages of deflation lasting a year or two. Though useful insofar as it helped to protect the currency, deflation produced side effects accompanied by severe stress. Its impact on prosperity will be dealt with later.

At all events, a financial policy of deflation was contrary to the desired acceleration of accumulation. It produced a general stringency in the money market and led to the flourishing of usury. For instance, in Hungary the most eligible bills were discounted in 1924 at the rate of 16 to 18 per cent, less eligible ones at 20 to 23 per cent. In the approximately two years following financial reorganization, up to 1926, loans were granted at an interest of 30 to 50 per cent, while provincial banks "either refused to grant credit or discounted bills for three months at the rate of 60 to 80 per cent interest." So stated the session held by the commission controlling the execution of the law of financial reorganization on April 22, 1925.

Of course, the situation was roughly similar in all the countries of East-Central Europe. This is evidenced convincingly by the fact that in 1923–24 the National Bank of Austria charged a discount rate of 15 per cent, while the interest on agricultural loans fluctuated between 25 and 45 per cent. In the mid-twenties, after stabilization of the currency in Yugoslavia, industrial and commercial firms which received the largest credits had to pay 16 to 24 per cent interest on bank loans. In the same years the official bank rate was 15 per cent yearly in Poland.

Such extremely costly credit—which rendered productive utilization virtually impossible—was a clear sign of a crippling lack of capital and funds, but it was by no means the consequence of deflation policy alone. Deflation only aggravated the existing shortage of capital and credit, deriving from inadequate accumulation. As a result, by the middle of the decade following the war the active capital to be found in the economy —as in Poland—reached only 20 to 25 per cent of the prewar level, and bank deposits amounted to 11 per cent of the prewar bank capital. The situation was similar in other countries of the region. On the evidence of detailed Hungarian statistics, one year after stabilization of the currency, bank deposits totaled no more than 15 to 20 per cent of the prewar amount. Adding together the balance of deposits, current accounts, bonds with fixed interest, the share capital and reserve funds of companies, as well as surplus items in the budget, in the prosperous late twenties following the stabilization, the average yearly accumulation reached 450 to 500 million pengös. In relation to the prewar territory of Hungary, this amounted to no more than approximately two-thirds of the prewar figure.

In the years after stabilization domestic accumulation thus advanced on a modest scale, remaining in general far below the prewar level. When we consider that in most of the countries in question the rate of accumulation had been very slow in the prewar years, and—as pointed out before—insufficient to finance the economy without aid, it becomes obvious that the financial reorganizations carried out in the mid-twenties could overcome economic confusion but were in themselves unable to solve the domestic problems of economic reconstruction or to create possibilities of home accumulation on a level required to achieve economic recovery. Therefore rehabilitation, instead of opening up a period of normal economic function, formed instead the introductory stage of a remarkably strong inflow of foreign capital, which became an essential source for the financing of economic reconstruction everywhere.

The highly significant changes which radically regrouped power relations in East-Central Europe after World War I did not leave the Western European economies unaffected. If the debtor countries of Eastern Europe depended much less than formerly on the money market of the creditor countries to ensure their economic development, the far-reaching postwar alteration in the position of the creditor countries cannot have been a factor of secondary importance either.

Before World War I the money market was ruled by the three principal creditor countries, notably by Great Britain, whose capital outlay was estimated at $18 billion, by France with loans totalling $8.7 billion, and Germany with $5.6 billion. At that time the United States was a debtor country. However, after the war Germany ceased to be an exporter of capital and was herself reduced to needing foreign capital, having lost the better part of her investments. During the war France became heavily indebted to the United States. Half of her outlay of capital had been lost, so she became a debtor country while remaining also a creditor in almost equal measure. Capital was still exported from France, but on a much smaller scale than before the war.

England retained her prewar status as a creditor, but the United States became the principal holder of debt claim and the strongest economic power in the world. The changes that came about in the world market undoubtedly exerted an influence on the economic life of all the countries which needed import of capital. Yet it was particularly in Eastern Europe that the new situation had to be faced, for the countries of this region had formerly imported capital primarily from Germany and France, that is to say, from countries which could not satisfy their capital requirements under the prevailing new conditions. The situation was aggravated by the circumstance noted previously that Austria, which had imported and exported capital about equally, was now herself reduced to the need for foreign capital.

Therefore, the countries of East-Central Europe could turn for their increased capital import requirements to two countries (England and the United States) which had formerly displayed little or no interest in the economic problems of this region. As a matter of fact England invested much larger amounts of capital in East-Central Europe in the twenties than in the years before World War I, and the same was true for the United States. The loans forthcoming from France were still considerable, yet the money market was far from having become more favorable.

After the stabilization of currencies the East-Central European countries could obtain plenty of credit, albeit at an exceedingly high interest — 7 per cent. (At this time safe government securities paid an interest of 3½ to 4 per cent.) The fact is that the Balkan countries could raise loans only at this same high interest in the prewar period; therefore the new terms of interest hit Austria and Hungary the hardest.

The stream of loans to the countries of East-Central Europe thus started after 1922 with the leading participation of the new creditor powers. After the very extensive credit granted by the League of Nations to stabilize her currency, Austria did not obtain any major long-term credit for quite a long time, but in financing the economy the inflow of foreign loans nevertheless played an important role. As mentioned before, the stabilization loan was substantial, actually approaching 1 billion schillings. Consequently, it served from the outset not only to carry out financial reorganization but also to develop economy and to make investments. Of the acquired loan, 63 per cent was used to balance the budget and the remaining 37 per cent provided the capital required by the state for investments. This sum, approximately 323 million schillings, became the source from which the electrification program of the railways was covered.

After 1927 a new need for credit arose for state investments as a result of which extensive transactions in loans again took place. In March 1930 a loan of 725 million schillings at the rate of 7 per cent mainly from English and American groups of financiers, to be transacted by the Bank für Internazionelle Zahlungsausgleich of Basle, was sanctioned by law. In June, when the first part of the loan was actually floated at a 91 per cent price, 394.8 million schillings were placed. Owing to the international financial crisis which broke out in the meantime, the floating of the second part, planned for the year 1932, never came to pass.

Between the two major state loans of 1922 and 1930 enormous sums nevertheless flowed into the country in the form of commodity credit and loans for the purchase of raw materials and machines, generally as short-term credits. The amount of the latter came to nearly 1.3 billion schillings, affording an important source for the operation and advancement of Austrian industry.

If the international aid of 800 million schillings received in 1920 and the national debt of over 1 billion from before the war are taken into consideration, in 1932 the national debt of Austria amounted to 4,251 million schillings, of which 2,575 million schillings were granted as long-term loans, 384 million schillings as loans to be repaid in a shorter time, and 1,287 million as short-term loans. Thus, at the time when the stream of credits made available in the twenties came to an end, more than one quarter of the total debt, and over half of the loans raised after the war, consisted of short-term credits.

The loan granted to Hungary for the purpose of stabilization amounted to only approximately 40 percent of that given to Austria to work out the rehabilitation of her finances. Since half of the loan was used to balance the budget and to pay off prewar debts, very little remained for the development of the economy and for investments by the state. A few months after the reorganization of finances, an emphatic statement appeared in a Hungarian economic journal: "As long as the terms of loans do not provide for the use of foreign capital in our economic life there can be no fundamental rehabilitation of agriculture. . . . The loan granted by the League of Nations is only the first step which should be followed by a whole series of further credit transactions."[3]

The next year "a whole series of further credit transactions" was actually initiated. In 1925 two long-term loans were signed. One was raised by forty-eight Hungarian towns in the value of $10 million; the other, a loan of $3 million, was granted by the New York firm Liessman & Co. for the reconstruction of the Rimamurány Ironworks, one of the largest of its kind in Hungary. In 1926 eight long-term credit transactions, in 1927 nine, and in 1928 fourteen were signed. Of these the most noteworthy was the loan of £ 2.25 million raised in 1926 by the Hungarian counties from the London Banks of N. M. Rothschild & Sons, Baring Brothers & Co., Ltd., and J. H. Schröder & Co. There was also the second loan of $6 million raised by the towns.

The Talbot loan of £ 3.3 million floated in May 1928 was utilized for the development of Hungarian electric energy production, the construction of long-distance transmission lines, and the electrification of the first railway line of not quite 200 kilometers. Finally, one of the biggest transactions of the decade was the so-called matchloan of the Svenska Tändstickes Aktiebolaget to the Hungarian government of $36 million for the purpose of settling the pecuniary consequences of the postwar land reform and of indemnifying the involved owners of large estates. In return a match monopoly was introduced and all the Hungarian match factories were handed over to the Swedish world trust. (The Swedish group bought the majority of the shares of the Szikra Hungarian Match Works possessing four match factories, and the other match factories purchased by the group were merged in this firm.)

Thus, between 1924 and 1931, Hungary raised long-term loans totaling 1,257 million pengös. However, as in Austria, these long-term loans formed only part of the inflowing capital, and short-term loans were more prominent in credits acquired by Hungary in the twenties. In the same years commercial credits and other medium- and short-term loans totaled 1,738 million pengös. Short- and medium-term loans thus amounted to 60 per cent of the acquired loans. In the national debt of 4,300 million pengös in the summer of 1931, as a result of prewar liabili-

[3] *Magyar Pénzügy,* November 5, 1924.

ties and interim payments, long-term loans totaled 45 per cent; other, mainly short-term loans, 55 per cent.

The stream of credits also poured into Yugoslavia, though that country made use of an international loan for the purpose of stabilization at a rather late date, in 1931. It was in 1922 that the first long-term loan of $100 million was granted, by the American firm of Blair & Co., at the rate of 8 per cent. However, instead of the originally announced amount, only a $15 million loan was realized, to be used mainly for the development of communications. In the next year the French government granted a loan of 300 million francs at the rate of 5 per cent, chiefly for the purchase of armament. In 1927 it was again the banking house of Blair & Co. which gave a credit of $30 million. (In this instance too, a much higher credit limit, one of $45 million, had been contemplated.) As in Hungary, a credit transaction was signed in 1928 with the Swedish match trust. In this case the Swedish firm acquired a match monopoly in Yugoslavia in return for a loan of $25 million at the rate of 6.25 per cent.

The last of the long-term credit operations was the international loan mentioned before in connection with stabilization of the currency, which was allowed to Yugoslavia in 1931 in the value of 1,015 million French francs.

In fact, from the mid-twenties until the financial crisis Yugoslavia raised long-term loans totaling 6,700 million dinars. Here too, the amount of short-term loans was remarkably high. It was only after stabilization of the currency in 1925 that such loans were granted, mostly in 1927 and 1928, when over 3,000 million dinars flowed into the country chiefly to finance surplus of imports. Therefore, in the period under review short-term loans may be estimated at approximately 4,000 to 5,000 million dinars.

In addition to the loans of 11,000 to 12,000 million dinars raised in the twenties, Yugoslavia, as pointed out before, was heavily burdened with prewar liabilities and especially with foreign war debts. The national debt of Yugoslavia thus totaled 32,800 million dinars (about $580 million) in 1932. That is to say, the loans raised in the twenties amounted only to approximately one-third of the total debt. From this, it followed that most of the national debt consisted of long-term credits and only about one-sixth of short-term loans.

Government loans played a relatively less important role in Rumania

—less important inasmuch as the ruling isolationist liberal party which had launched the slogan of self-reliance and self-sufficiency pursued an economic policy which did not favor new loans. Therefore, apart from the prewar debts inherited from the Monarchy and compensation to be paid for a few railway lines which added to liabilities without any credit operation, the Rumanian national debt was increased in the first place by the loan of $175 million raised in 1922. This loan, acquired chiefly from Anglo-American financial sources, was spent on converting the Rumanian treasury notes held in other countries into government stock to be repaid in forty years. The raising of a real government loan of $100 million in 1929 took place when the peasant party cabinet, having come into power, inaugurated a new economic policy. This was soon followed by a new loan of 1,300 million gold francs ($51 million). About one-sixth of this sum went into the foundation of a credit bank for the promotion of agricultural development and another 200 million francs was spent on productive agricultural investments. An additional 40 per cent was envisaged for the development of railways and roads, and only a relatively small part was used for the settlement of unfunded debts of the state and the state railways.

Until the financial crisis Rumania raised new long-term loans totaling around $320 million, an amount which placed her at the bottom of the list of debtors among the countries of East-Central Europe. (No data are available concerning the volume of Rumania's short-term loans, but these probably would not modify the picture very much.)

In Bulgaria the inflow of foreign capital as government loans in addition to the credits granted for the purpose of stabilizing the currency was not very considerable either. Though the conversion of old loans and the compensation to be paid by the state for certain railway lines may have actually increased the national debt from the aspect of the balance of payments, foreign capital in fact flowed mostly into private enterprise.

In the period between 1919 and 1926, 220,000 refugees settled within the new borders of Bulgaria. Of the government loans, the one raised in 1926 served chiefly for the settlement of the refugees. As in so many other instances, here too it was an Anglo-American group of financiers who allowed Bulgaria a credit of $15 million. The total government loans raised by Bulgaria were approximately $50 million. But if long-term prewar debts, reparations, and a few other obligations are taken into consideration, by the close of 1930 the Bulgarian national debt to foreign countries amounted to 22,000 million levas ($150 million), over 50 per cent of which derived from the postwar years. As regards additional short-term loans, they may be assumed to have totaled about 3,300 million levas by 1931, of which 1,900 million levas were credits from banks.

In Czechoslovakia, where the rate and volume of accumulation of capital, realized on a higher level of economic development, far exceeded progress in the other countries of East-Central Europe, much smaller importation of capital was needed in the late twenties to finance the economy. Foreign loans were raised by the government for the most part in the years directly after the war, for instance, one in England in 1922 of $50 million, which was used partly for investments, partly to pay back earlier supplies of food and floating debts. Another loan of $15 million was acquired in the same year by the city of Prague from Anglo-American banks to widen the electric network of the capital. In the second half of the twenties Czechoslovakia had a balanced budget, and additional requirements could be covered mainly by domestic loans.

It was only in the years of crisis that substantial foreign loans were called upon; thus, a credit of 60 million francs was allowed to Czechoslovakia on the Paris money market in 1931. The country was in the unique position that 75 to 80 per cent of her government loans were domestic loans, and only 20 to 25 per cent were raised abroad. On the whole this was a position contrary to that in which the other countries of East-Cental Europe found themselves. As regards other short-term and long-term loans, in the final analysis Czechoslovakia also belonged to the debtor countries by international standards, that is to say, to the countries which imported capital; but in the late twenties Czechoslovakia substantially reduced her foreign debts, chiefly by buying back shares and stocks to be found in other countries.

A survey of the volume of foreign capital lent to the countries of East-Central Europe in the twenties suggests that the total amount exceeded the prewar import of capital, in total sum and even more in yearly average. Therefore, it is justifiable to ask how far this capital inflow could become the starting point of a new phase of vigorous growth, inasmuch as the rapid economic development in this area from the end of the nineteenth century has been attributed mainly to the inductive influence

Table 9-1. Foreign Debts in East-Central
Europe, 1936

	Per Capita		
	National Debt (in dollars)	Foreign Loans	Total Debt (in million dollars)
Hungary	37	64	560
Austria	60	77	508
Czechoslovakia	80	34	480
Rumania	69	71	1,224
Yugoslavia	73	76	893

Source: Compiled from *Southeastern Europe: A Political and Economic Survey,* Royal Institute of International Affairs, London, 1939.

of foreign capital. A certain prosperity was unmistakably evident in all these countries in the second half of the 1920s, but the results were far from commensurate with the volume of foreign capital or with the heavy debts and grave burdens stemming from such involvements.

Why did the stream of foreign loans fail this time to exert a really stimulating influence? The difference between the two periods of prosperity—the full boom in the opening decade of the century and the moderate improvement experienced in the second half of the twenties— is clearly discernible. Moreover, it should be kept in mind that most of the loans were granted to the countries of East-Central Europe on exceedingly unfavorable terms. The low prices at which the loans were floated and sold brought an immediate profit of 11 to 12 per cent of the nominal value to the group of financiers who gave the credit. As a rule the rate of interest varied between 7 and 10 per cent. All this inflicted heavy burdens on the economy of the countries in question. Therefore, new loans were soon needed from which to pay the high rate of interest and the amounts due as amortization.

The serious financial consequences of the unfavorable terms made themselves felt all the more strongly as the amounts of the loans were much too high in relation to the capacity of the national economy and the means of utilization.

A study dealing with the subject in the 1930s accurately stated:

The foreign capital which was used for the reconstruction of Europe was very desirable and very necessary, but the amount which in the end was sent to this area was more than the debtors could hope to repay. . . . Capital invested in Europe was very largely used for "unproductive" purposes; it resulted in a rise in the standard of living in the borrowing countries but did not increase the efficiency of their export industries to an extent sufficient to enable most of them to meet the full service of payments on their indebtedness.[4]

Therefore the question may be put as to whether the loans were used for productive investments which, by promoting relatively rapid economic development, increased the national income by an amount greater than the burden of debt. As we have already observed, in most instances only a small part of the money was spent on productive schemes such as electrification or the development of transport and telecommunication. The greater part served to convert older debts, or to cover social investments or consumption—to say nothing of the funds swallowed up by corruption.

Accurate records on the utilization of the loans are available for Hungary. Only 20 per cent of the loans obtained were spent on productive investments. Another 15 per cent were invested in building projects, and in public health and education unconnected with production. Another 40 per cent served to repay debts and to amortize prewar debts. The portion of the loans used for consumption may be put at 25 per cent. Enlargement of the state apparatus and the army and the erection of luxury buildings were among the items for which loans were utilized. It is apparent, therefore, that the heavy burden of debts was by no means paralleled by improvement in the national economy. It was the drawbacks of close financial dependence which were felt most strongly. In this respect the example of Hungary is far from unique, for in the other countries detailed investigation would undoubtedly reveal comparable distortions. In fact, Rumanian and Yugoslav writers have come to a similar conclusion though without the support of accurate statistics.

Hence the financial policy of the West in the twenties and the peculiarly unfavorable economic utilization of the loans that were raised cannot be treated merely as an economic issue. Those writers who emphasize the obviously political aims of the postwar loans are correct. The arguments supporting this approach and even the wording may be drawn from so competent a source as Sir William Goode, who acted in

---

[4] *The Problem of International Investment: Report of the Royal Institute of International Affairs,* London, 1937, p. 279.

the 1920s as the financial adviser of the Hungarian government and as go-between for the government and the group of financiers in London. In one of his letters to the *Times* as early as October 12, 1925, Goode unequivocally stated that financial aid served primarily political aims in East-Central Europe. In his view food was the only firm foundation on which governments could base their power. For lack of this aid Austria and most likely several other countries would have gone the way Russia did.

Since the motives of the credit operations which increased steadily in the second half of the twenties were chiefly of a political nature and were intended to serve political objectives, these very extensive Western financial activities revealed no vivid interest in possible investments in the economies of the countries concerned. As mentioned before, the leading creditors and exporters of capital—the United States and England—had no strong interest in an economic position in East-Central Europe. For a long time it had been German and French capital which had extensive interests in banks and industrial works. After the war there remained little hope of German investments, nor was an amelioration of the French position very likely either.

It was the postwar hope of both French and German capital to improve their economic positions in East-Central Europe—France in order to broaden her political influence and to cement her leading role on the Continent; Germany, to find some consolation for the loss of her overseas possessions by gaining economic footholds in Eastern Europe with an eye to creating a firm basis for future conquests. Thus the postwar years witnessed the conception of far-reaching French and German projects. However, the German projects soon collapsed, again chiefly for political reasons, in part the opposing and counterbalancing steps by France and England.

As a result of Germany's defeat in the war, German capital lost the position it had acquired in earlier decades. About 60 per cent of German investments were confiscated by the victorious powers, and owing to the gross depreciation of the remaining part, the value of German investments sank to one-tenth of the prewar level. Notwithstanding the decline of the German economy and power, after the war groups of leading German financiers took steps to consolidate their shaken positions and particularly to widen their activities in East-Central Europe.

This endeavor led to the foundation of the Magyar-Német Bank (Hungarian-German Bank) in May 1920, backed by the Mannesmann group which had been forced to give up business in North Africa. From the preserved documents of the Dresdner Bank, this bank was apparently regarded as an advanced bridgehead, designed to safeguard the financial support of German industrial interests not only in Hungary but also in the Balkan countries. Simultaneously with the foundation of the bank in Hungary the Mannesmann group undertook to build up a network of interests in Czechoslovakia and Bulgaria.

In the meantime, Stinnes, the organizer of the Vereinigte Stahlwerke which reaped enormous benefits from the German inflation, in attempting to achieve domination of iron and coal production in Europe, strove to acquire the leading Austrian, Czechoslovak, and Hungarian metallurgic firms. However, the rapid purchase of all the shares of the Hungarian Rimamurány Ironworks Company on the market in the spring of 1922 led to the outbreak of a scandal and to the consequent failure of the scheme. Early in 1923 at the negotiations conducted by Stinnes in Hungary the outlines of new, far-reaching projects were put forward. An attempt was made to win positions in banks and industrial firms by smoothing the path of penetration to the markets of East-Central Europe, and steps were taken to initiate the search for bauxite in Hungary. The purchase of the Ferró Vas-és Érckereskedelmi Rt. (Ferro-Iron and Metal Commercial Company), the relations established with the Aluminum Érebánya és Ipari Rt. (Aluminium Mining and Industrial Company), the Anglo-Hungarian Bank acting as middleman, promoted the search for bauxite in Transdanubia and soon resulted in the exploitation of one of the most important bauxite mines in Europe. On the part of the Deutsche Bank the initiative was taken by buying up a few firms from private mine owners.

These German economic aspirations of the early twenties were soon frustrated. After the defeat sustained in the Ruhr conflict in 1923, German capital was compelled to withdraw and, except for a few firms, the new positions acquired after 1920 were relinquished. The Hungarian-German Bank was also dissolved.

As a result of French pressure primarily and of the political situation in Germany, plans for German economic expansion soon had to be abandoned. Such schemes constituted only brief episodes in the history of the postwar activity of capital.

The attempts undertaken by financial groups of victorious France, with firm and powerful Continental positions, had more lasting effects. The positions gained by capital before the war and maintained in the postwar period created a basis for financial operations. The French contrived to add a few more important interests to their earlier holdings. It was in these years, for instance, that the Austrian Länderbank was drawn into the concern of the Banque de Paris et des Pay Bas, and one-fifth of the shares of the biggest Hungarian bank, the General Hungarian Credit Bank, were bought by the financial group of Schneider-Creusot. The same French group bought the Rumanian Vulcan Machine Factory, Lt., with its branches in Brasov and Cluj. Other groups of French financiers purchased shares in other branches of Rumanian industry, securing a foothold in the oil industry as well.

In the oil industry the French had controlled an interest of only 5 per cent before the war; by 1931 they held 16 per cent. As a result of the economic positions acquired after the war, the interests controlled by French capital in other countries of this region increased considerably. For example, in Poland 24.4 per cent of the foreign capital invested in joint-stock companies was owned by French financiers on January 1, 1933, representing the largest group of foreign interests. In Bulgaria, France ranked second, with a 23.8 per cent share; Belguim controlled 33.6 per cent. In Yugoslavia, English and French investments were of similar magnitude; in Rumania, French capital occupied a position second to that of British capital.

It must be added here that the early postwar years offered opportunities which the leading groups of French financiers were eager to seize and profit from. The offer of the Schneider-Creusot group in April 1920 to the Hungarian government proposing to lease the Hungarian state railways and all the private railways under state management for ninety years is characteristic of this attitude. When it came to negotiations, the French laid claim to the coal mines supplying the railways, to the two big state-owned iron and machine works, the plants of the Machine Factory of the Hungarian State Railways at Diósgyör and Budapest. These maneuvers confirm the suspicion that it was not only the profit to be derived from the traditional methods of exporting capital which attracted French capitalists; political power and influence were grounded economically on the monopoly of communications and the essential fields of basic industries. The French projects were coun-

teracted and restrained in both Hungary and the other Danubian countries by political pressure on the part of England, ever anxious to maintain the balance of power on the Continent. The previously described
English activities on the money market were also motivated partly by
the wish to counterbalance French economic activity.

Italy, which had emerged from the war on the side of the victorious
powers, was also actuated by political interests. By taking advantage
of the incapacitation of her German rivals, she increased her influence
in East-Central Europe. For instance, the Banca Comerciala Italiana
of Milan strove to gain control of a considerable part of the Rumanian,
Yugoslav, and Hungarian timber industry. An international group
headed by Camillo Castiglioni, having bought the Fabank Rt. (Timber
Bank Company) holding thirty-two timber firms, chiefly in Transylvania
and Croatia, established the Foresta Company in Hungary and Rumania
as well as the OFA holding in Yugoslavia. The same Italian group
bought and united two formerly second-class banks, the Magyar
Fakereskedök Hitelintézete Rt. (Credit Bank of Hungarian Wood
Merchants) and the Hungarian National Bank, to found the Magyar-
Olasz Bank (Hungaro-Italian Bank) in 1920 and to raise it to the rank
of the Hungarian big banks. Italian capital was also active in the Polish
textile industry and in banking at Lodz.

The postwar activity of capital guided by the endeavor to win power
and influence in East-Central Europe took the form of alternating and
complementary German, French, and Italian ventures, but not much
ground was gained in these years by any of the countries in question.

The picture was not altered by the efforts of Austrian and Czechoslovak capitalists or by the exertions of some groups of Hungarian
financiers to maintain their interests, going so far as to make new investments. The activities of Austrian, Czechoslovak, and Hungarian
capitalists were, however, confined for the most part to the former
Monarchy.

In the economy of this region Anglo-American capital, in addition
to the big loans of the twenties, appeared also as a promoter and share-
holder. This was experienced chiefly in a few new branches of industry
(electrotechnical industry) in the East-Central European countries which
had international companies. The bulk of the newly issued shares of
one of the most important factories of the Hungarian electrotechnical

industry, the Ganz Works, was bought by General Electric; and the telephone factory section of the Hungarian Egyesült Izzólámpa es Villamossági Rt. (United Incandescent Lamps and Electrical Company, Ltd.) was made independent and developed with American capital under the name of Standard Villamossági Rt. (Standard Electrical Company, Ltd.). The trend of Anglo-American investments is clearly indicated by the English interests in the joint-stock company monopolizing Hungarian river navigation, and the foundation of the Anglo-Hungarian Bank by a group of financiers under the auspices of the Marconi Wireless Telegraph Co. Ltd. The rise of this bank was due in no small measure to the new investments of the British Overseas Bank.

In Rumania the English came to control Danube shipping, and in 1922 Vickers penetrated into the mining, metallurgy, and machine industry of southern Transylvania. An important indication of the influence gained by British capital was the fact that its share in the Rumanian oil industry increased from 6 per cent to 10 per cent. In Poland 13 per cent of the foreign bank capital was in English hands; and as a result of new American investments, concentrated chiefly in a few major oil and zinc mining companies, 22 per cent of the capital invested in Polish joint-stock companies was held by American financiers. Also in Yugoslav metal mining, Anglo-American groups were important. In Bulgaria, on the other hand, their role was negligible; in industry the larger American share remained under 3 per cent of the invested foreign capital.

In addition to extensive loans, lesser but still considerable amounts of active foreign capital greatly contributed to the financing of the economy in most countries of the region. After an interval of a few years following the war, the role of foreign capital thus regained significance in the twenties, providing as it did an important financial source complementing the domestic accumulation of capital in the countries of East-Central Europe.

At the present stage of investigations it is impossible to give an accurate quantitative picture of the role played by foreign capital. We are unable to demonstrate for each country the precise share of foreign capital in financing the economy. Some essential facts may be presented, however.

As regards the financing of the Hungarian economy, detailed data are available. According to our statistics, from stabilization of the currency until the outbreak of the economic crisis long- and short-term loans of 2,000 million pengös (approximately $400 million) and about 300 to 400 million pengös ($60 to $80 million) were invested directly in Hungary. During the same years domestic accumulation amounted to 2,400 million pengös—including savings banks and current account deposits, increase of share capital, various bonds, capital left over from self-financing in agriculture and industry, as well as budget surplus. Hence, between 1924 and 1929 home accumulation actually corresponded to the total foreign capital streaming into the country. Owing to the more modest amount of direct investment and the unproductive use of the bulk of the loans, foreign capital played a far from decisive role in investments. In the years under study 75 per cent of the capital invested in the Hungarian economy was of domestic origin and only 25 per cent came from foreign sources.

Though we lack accurate statistics for this whole period in Poland where economic conditions were less favorable than in Hungary, the statistics for 1929 published by the Polish Institute of Economic Research offer valuable information. According to these figures the capital accumulated at home amounted to 1,700 million zlotys while the imported foreign capital totaled 2,120 million zlotys. In other words, the ratio of domestic accumulation to foreign capital was exactly 40:60. Though these data refer only to the capital balance of one year, this ratio seems to be typical of the twenties. The share of foreign capital in Polish industry was also much larger than in Hungary, rising to 40 per cent of Polish industrial capital by the close of the decade. Moreover, these investments formed only one-fifth of the foreign capital invested in Poland. Another fifth was invested in banks and commercial firms, while 40 per cent was used for loans to the state and to public institutions.

In the Balkan countries domestic accumulation was at all times much lower than in the other countries of East-Central Europe. Therefore it would not be unrealistic to conclude that in the countries of Southeastern Europe foreign loans, though in smaller amount, came to a roughly similar or larger share in financing the economy of these countries. This assumption is supported by the fact that in the late twenties the interest of foreign capital in the national debt and share capital of the Balkan countries was remarkably high. In Rumania 89.2 per cent of government securities were placed abroad; in Yugoslavia 82.5 per cent of government securities and 44 per cent of the share capital were in the hands of foreign financiers. In Bulgaria 72.3 per cent of the national debt and 48 per cent of the share capital were owned by foreign groups.

In most countries of East-Central Europe foreign capital had a 50 to 70 per cent share in financing the economy during the postwar decades. Austria was no exception, though investment of active foreign capital earlier had not been extensive.

Thus the only exception was Czechoslovakia, which did not use large amounts of foreign capital and which had favorable conditions for home accumulation. In the twenties Czechoslovakia bought back considerable packets of shares and bonds on foreign markets: from 1925 to 1931 turnover in shares and securities showed a persistently passive balance implying that every year Czechoslovakia bought back on foreign markets more shares (chiefly shares of repatriated companies) than she sold there. During these seven years the outflowing capital was 3,900 million crowns ($150 to $160 million) more than the inflowing foreign capital. Therefore foreign capital did not play an essential role in the economy of independent Czechoslovakia.

Hence the countries of East-Central Europe failed to achieve their principal economic objective—to create their independent national economies. Moreover, at best they could only limit the competition of foreign goods, and they remained in strong need of foreign loans. This failure was manifested also by the inability to really accelerate economic development, to consolidate and improve the balance of economic life, to modify the internal structure appropriately in favor of more advanced sectors, of industry above all, notwithstanding extensive import of capital and heavy debts.

It is true that in the second half of the twenties the repercussions of the European boom were felt in East-Central Europe, and after the confusion of the immediate postwar period these years brought economic consolidation and prosperity. However, this prosperity of barely four or five years could not satisfy the needs of industrialization, as recognized by the governments of various countries. Though international conditions, foreign loans, and relatively good prices for agrarian products helped to accelerate development, they did not suffice to bring about economic growth of decisive force. What then were the factors which strongly hampered economic growth? Lack of capital and low domestic accumulation of capital, which were certainly not improved by inflation or by the period of deflation which followed in almost every country. Moreover, the distribution of land, so urgent from the social viewpoint but accompanied by a decline and stagnation of agricultural production, did not favor the accumulation of capital for the time being. Curiously enough, the retarding effect of agricultural production was most conspicuous in countries where—as in Hungary—agriculture became incapable of progress as long as the land reform failed to materialize and the system of big estates continued to prevail.

As a matter of fact, the difficulties stemming from the slow, inadequate domestic accumulation of capital could not be overcome by the importation of foreign capital because, as pointed out before, on the one hand a relatively small part was used for actually productive investments and, on the other, the burdens of interest and amortization were beyond the capacity of these countries. In this light the boom of the late twenties may be regarded as much weaker than the prosperity experienced in the first fifteen years of the twentieth century, and also when judged by the accumulation of capital.

There are, however, other factors which cannot be disregarded. In some countries the process of economic adaptation to new conditions was not yet concluded in the second half of the twenties, and the boom only restored the prewar level of production (Poland). Moreover, the nationalist conception of economic policy created new difficulties. Industrial production protected by high customs duty naturally weighed heavily on the home market. Therefore the boom for the most part produced only a relatively wider domestic market; but actual consumption, real wages, etc., usually remained below the prewar level, so the market did not exert a stimulating influence on production.

The contradiction deriving from a slackening of rational economic relations, speculation, disregard of production costs, and lack of cooperation was aggravated further by the low demand in the numerically small home market. Indeed, though the index figures of industrial development indicated considerable advance in some countries, this progress was by no means a characteristic feature of the entire national economy. New contradictions were created or sharpened between developing industry and stagnating agriculture, producing very strong social and political tension in the countries of fundamentally agrarian character.

In East-Central Europe economic advancement was, moreover, profoundly influenced by the fact that, except for Czechoslovakia, industrial progress did not keep pace with the changes of the technical preconditions of modern production. During the second part of the twenties in the developed countries the foundation of industrial growth was rationalization, which rested on the transformation of the methods of production and business organization and on the extensive application of new techniques. It was in the first postwar decade that electricity, mechanization, and novel forms of mass production were introduced in the industries of the developed countries. The first two were earlier inventions, but this was the time when their use became widespread. A few new inventions also contributed to these developments. The discovery that the quantity of coal required for the generation of current could be reduced by half created new possibilities for the industrial utilization of electricity, while the construction of high-voltage long-distance transmission lines greatly widened the radius within which electric energy could be used.

Concerning motorization, the first point to be considered is the impact of the widespread use of motorcars (and lorries) on industry. The quick and elastic acceptance of mechanization was promoted by the extensive use of electric engines. In addition to the important fact of modern works and business organization, technically it was these innovations which helped to build up mass production. Apart from the limited use of electric energy, at the time these new technical-technological processes hardly affected economic development and industrialization in East-Central Europe, where activities were concentrated on the development of branches (for instance, the textile industry) which had been leading sectors in the West as far back as the nineteenth century.

Although the export prices of agrarian products were not unfavorable in the twenties, agriculture did not fill the role of a dynamic sector as it had done around the turn of the century. The development of agriculture in the twenties only reached or surpassed slightly the prewar level. In Hungary value exceeded the prewar level by an average of 3 per cent between 1925 and 1929, and the situation was similar in the other countries. Methods for extensive production had long since been exhausted, while intensive production could not be developed for lack of capital. Therefore, productivity in general stagnated.

As regards the most important crops, production fell below the prewar level by 13 per cent in the Balkan countries, and by 2 per cent in Austria, Czechoslovakia, Hungary, and Poland (according to average figures of 1924 to 1928). The situation was more favorable in livestock, for in the Balkan countries there was a 10 to 20 per cent increase, owing chiefly to the supply of hogs. The other countries showed stagnation. Strangely enough, in this period real agricultural development, achieved in the spirit of a nationalist economic policy, could actually be observed in Austria, a country of strongly industrial character, whereas in the countries where the agrarian sector played a decisive role and determined the whole of economic growth stagnation and decline were evident.

Industrial development presented a more favorable picture. Most of the countries in question surpassed the prewar level of production by 1926, and by 1929 the industrial production index showed a rather steep rise compared to the early twenties. In 1929 it was only in Poland that industrial output remained below the prewar level. In contrast, the real output of industry (calculated in deflated prices) increased in rapidly advancing Czechoslovakia by 71.8 per cent, in Austria by 18 per cent, in Rumania by 37 per cent, and in Hungary by 12 per cent. The industrial output of Bulgaria and Yugoslavia may be supposed to have been about 40 per cent higher than the 1913 level.

Two conclusions may be drawn from these data. First, even in the three less developed Balkan countries, which showed a relatively rapid industrial advancement, the rate of growth remained far behind that of the prewar years. In Hungary, Austria, and Poland, the rate of development was even slower than the average European rate of growth; in 1929 average European industrial output exceeded the prewar level by 27 per cent. Thus, the economic development of the twenties failed to produce the dynamic advance which marked the economic progress of East-Central Europe in the opening years of the century. The process of industrial revolution, developed but not pursued to its conclusion in Hungary and Poland after the turn of the century, actually could not be finished in the twenties. In the Balkan countries the mere beginnings of industrialization showed up in the early 1900s, but the upswing of the twenties did not give any effective impetus for advancing much beyond the initial stage.

The second conclusion to be drawn from the economic development of the twenties refers to the position occupied by East-Central Europe in the world economy. The economic division of labor produced by the industrial revolution between the industrial West and the agricultural East, leading to a significant difference in the economic level of the two parts of Europe, displayed two important tendencies in the early years of the present century. It seemed, first, that the one-sided advantages of the division of labor were diminishing, that Western Europe was putting Eastern Europe on the same path of development; and secondly, that by modernizing their economy the countries which joined this development would be able to improve their production and reach a relatively high level. The developments of the twenties failed to strengthen either of these tendencies. On the one hand, even the enormous loans raised in the West were insufficient to develop the whole of the economy, and the old mechanism of the division of labor functioned much less efficiently. On the other hand, the development of the economies of Eastern Europe was inadequate to reduce the differences even relatively. With respect to capital, markets, and technology, Eastern Europe was more backward than formerly.

Thus the boom of the twenties may justly be regarded as a process of reconstruction. In fact, it brought no more than reconstruction, because it only helped to overcome the confusion caused by the wars and the new political and economic situation. The prewar level was restored, but this process of growth could not become continuous or systematic. There were altogether two or three years when the process of development continued undisturbed, but it was broken off all the more sharply when the achievements of reconstruction collapsed with the onset of the world economic crisis in 1929.

10 The Effect of the World Economic Crisis and the Policy of State Intervention

The period of international prosperity ended catastrophically with the Great Depression, signaled by a spectacular slump on the New York Stock Exchange in October 1929. Europe had barely recovered from its grave postwar condition only to receive one of the worst shocks in its history. The productive capacity of the leading powers during and after the war had greatly expanded while the effective demand for goods fell off drastically, causing a sharp decline in prices and industrial production. From the peak of prosperity in 1929, production had dropped by 46 per cent in the United States, 40 per cent in Germany, over 30 per cent in France, and about 16 per cent in the United Kingdom when the bottom was reached in 1932. The profound nature of the crisis is shown by the fact that in the most important items—in coal, crude iron, and steel—world production (apart from the Soviet Union) dropped 31 per cent, 65 per cent, and 61 per cent respectively. In contrast to the average 10 per cent decline in the industries turning out consumer goods, output of capital goods sank by nearly 40 per cent.

The result was extensive unemployment. The proportion of unemployed in the labor force was 22 per cent in England, nearly 44 per cent in Germany. In March 1933 the number of unemployed worldwide rose to 30 million, which, together with dependents, left about a hundred million people without a livelihood. During the exceedingly long crisis of approximately four years the effects of industrial overproduction were widespread. The market for agrarian products shrank as a result of industrial decline and mass unemployment, and an unparalleled collapse of prices was experienced in the early thirties. Thus the world market price of wheat dropped by over 50 per cent on the Liverpool Exchange. By 1934 world market quotations of corn hardly exceeded one-third of the pre-crisis level; meat prices sank to 40 per cent, while the price index of agricultural products was only slightly over one-third of the 1929 figure (37 per cent). This slump represented a crisis of unprecedented scope: up to 1937 the prices of agrarian products ranged between 37 and 54 per cent of the pre-crisis level.

Owing to the special nature of agriculture, the crisis reduced production only slightly, in some sectors not at all. In most of the large exporting countries the bulk of the unsold crops was destroyed: According to some estimates, in 1934 alone over a million truckloads of wheat, 267 thousand kg. of coffee, 250 million kg. of sugar, and 28 million kg. of meat.

The national income of the leading capitalist countries was reduced by one-tenth to one-third, France and England suffering minor losses, the United States and Germany heavier ones.

The crisis soon spread from severe price and production decline to credit transactions, foreign exchange and financial transactions between states. In addition to diminished production the usual methods of financing failed. Debtors were unable to pay back their bank loans; and the financial shocks sustained by certain national economies affected international financial and credit relations. It was, of course, impossible to mobilize large long-term loans, and short-term loans, serving partly to finance commerce, were also recalled with feverish haste. In the spring and summer of 1931 the whole financial and credit system became bankrupt, perhaps in the most spectacular manner in Germany, in June. The biggest banks of Europe, starting with the Creditanstalt of Vienna, failed. Between 1931 and 1933 the total of short-term loans sank by 56 per cent, underscoring the severity of the crisis in international financial relations.

The financial and credit crisis presented the most seriously shaken countries with painful dilemmas: the spectre of state bankruptcy, a complete loss of earlier sources of credit, bewildering radical measures, and currency reforms.

This ubiquitous depression exerted the most direct and most severe effects on the economic position of the East-Central European countries. In part this followed inevitably from the economic links between European and world markets, in part from the peculiar conditions prevailing in these countries. As explained before, in the postwar decade, besides nationalist economic policy, reconstruction could be based on two main factors: favorable prices for agrarian products on the world market and an ample supply of Western capital. After 1929 the most conspicuous feature of the economic crisis was the drop in agrarian prices, and beginning with 1931 credit relations broke off, the export of capital ceasing practically overnight. Thus the most important factors of prosperity in East-Central Europe not only disappeared, but became adverse forces, creating a particularly grave situation in the countries of this region.

Unlike the industrial crisis, the agrarian crisis did not reduce production. Neither the big estates of Hungary nor the peasant economy of the Balkans tried to adapt to poor demand by limiting production. Hence the area of cultivated land was not diminished in any of the countries, while any change in the harvest may be ascribed only to the fluctuations due to the weather. In the final analysis the agrarian crisis was manifested in the countries of Eastern Europe by three principal problems: (1) that presented by the loss of income caused by the fall in prices paid for agrarian products; (2) the gap between prices of agricultural and industrial products which upset relations between agrarian and industrial sectors while creating serious social tension, and (3) in connection with the narrowing of external markets a severe lack of stability in the balance of payments and of trade.

The steep fall in the price of agrarian products became disastrous in a few years. In 1932–33 the prices of most grains were between one-third and one-half of the 1929 prices. (See Table 10-1.)

As a result of the collapse of prices agricultural income decreased in

Table 10-1.   Price Index of Grains, East-Central Europe, 1930–1933
(1929 = 100)

	Hungary			Rumania			Bulgaria		Yugoslavia	
	Wheat	*Rye*	*Corn*	*Wheat*	*Rye*	*Corn*	*Wheat*	*Corn*	*Wheat*	*Corn*
1930	87	63	59	63	50	46	47	51	55	31
1931	72	87	63	39	52	34	45	46	57	29
1932	77	85	59	54	53	30	34	37	67	29
1933	62	50	32	63	33	26	34	25	44	26

Sources: Based on *Magyar Gazdaságkutató Intézet évi helyzetjelentései* (Yearly Reports of the Hungarian Economic Research Institute); *Statistisches Handbuch der Weltwirtschaft,* Berlin, 1937; N. Vuco, *Agrarna kriza u Jugoslaviji, 1930–1934,* Belgrade, 1968.

the years of crisis by 57.6 per cent in Rumania, 51.8 per cent in Bulgaria, 58.8 per cent in Poland, 35.8 per cent in Hungary. The fall of prices and diminished profits plunged agriculture into a serious predicament, all the more so as the interest—what is more, high interest—and amortization to be paid on loans raised in the twenties had mostly been calculated on the basis of the more favorable financial conditions of the late twenties. In the new situation these obligations were an unbearable burden.

By 1930 Bulgaria had an accumulation of 6 billion levas of bank debts and 2.5 billion levas of unpaid taxes which could not be met when the debt amounted to 10 per cent of the yearly income from agriculture. By 1934 the value of these debts was equivalent to 25 per cent of the income derived from agriculture.

The agrarian obligations which the debtors were unable to meet during the years of crisis amounted to 35 billion lei in Rumania, and 2.3 billion dinars in Yugoslavia. In Hungary in 1928 debts amounted to 78 per cent of the income from agriculture, in 1933 to 133 per cent. In 1929 interest and amortization totaled 9 per cent of the income, by 1933 the total rose to 25 per cent. Debts were relatively heavier among the peasant smallholders, and the situation of this class became disastrous. The existing difficulties were increased by additional factors. Notwithstanding the industrial crisis, the fall in the prices of industrial products was less radical; therefore, the gap between prices of agricultural products and prices of industrial products became steadily wider. Such disparity was not a feature peculiar to East-Central Europe but corresponded to the trend of the world market. The world market price level witnessed a fall of 50 per cent in industrial products, of 58 per cent in foodstuffs, of 60 per cent in raw materials. Hence, it may be stated that the gap between the prices of agricultural and industrial products occurred also under Western conditions, even in Czechoslovakia and Austria, though it did not exceed 10 to 15 per cent in general. However, in industrial countries the consequences of this disparity were not so destructive because it remained relatively insignificant, and also because, for big importers of agrarian products, the strong decline in their prices caused less trouble at home while yielding advantages in foreign trade.

By contrast, in agrarian countries this disparity tended to aggravate the consequences of the crisis, the gap between the prices of agricultural and industrial products—on the basis of 1929—being 30 per cent in Rumania, 33 per cent in Yugoslavia, and 38 per cent in Hungary. Within the general reduction of income there was a sharp disproportion between industrial and agrarian incomes. In Bulgaria in 1929, 80 per cent of the agrarian population earned 60 per cent of the total income; by 1934, 78 per cent earned 50 per cent of the total. For the most part changes on a similar scale came about in urban and rural incomes in other agrarian countries as well.

The impact of these processes on economic and social conditions—above all on industry and agriculture or, more accurately, on the contrast between towns and villages—led to severely strained relations. It was only by energetic state intervention that the government was somehow able to sustain the masses of peasant farmers who were on the verge of complete bankruptcy and collapse.

In Yugoslavia efforts were made to rescue agriculture first by a bankruptcy law, by several consecutive moratoria granting more favorable terms of payment, and finally, in 1935, by canceling part of the debt in proportion to the property.

Rumania first resorted to granting state credits and rehabilitating heavily encumbered farms in an attempt to master the grave situation. However, these and other supportive measures failed, and in 1932 here too the rehabilitation of agricultural finances became inevitable. It was carried out in the form of canceling 50 per cent of agrarian liabilities by an exchange for bonds of 50 per cent value.

In Hungary sale by auction was prohibited. Then, after the reduction of high rates of interest, in 1933 a comprehensive decree was issued providing for the protection of farmers. All the farms encumbered to fifteenfold of the net income as fixed in the land register (for purposes of taxation) came under protection. Both interest and amortization were considerably reduced, partly covered by the state itself. In some cases the payment of mortgage was suspended.

These measures helped to relieve the extremely sharp social contradictions. Although the number of ruined farmers ran to tens of thousands in the country, complete collapse was prevented. However, agricultural indebtedness prevailed and living standards were deplorably low. The problems and significance of the agrarian crisis in the countries of Eastern Europe cannot be confined to aspects of the home market and differences between domestic sectors. It was agriculture which had developed into the most advanced export branch, playing a decisive role in the balance of foreign trade and payments.

During the world economic crisis there began a veritable cutthroat competition for the agrarian markets of Europe. Most of the importing countries strove to increase their own production in order to curtail imports. Home production increased by 34.4 per cent in 1932–34 over 1923–27. Czechoslovakia, which was one of the most important importers in East-Central Europe, purchased 2 million crowns worth of grain in 1928, but only 400,000 crowns in 1932.

Owing to ever keener competition and growing tendencies toward self-sufficiency, the countries of this area had to overcome increasing difficulties in selling their agrarian surplus in other countries. In Rumania exports of livestock sank to 55 per cent from the 1929 level, exports of wheat to 45 per cent. Exports of cattle fell by 59 per cent in Yugoslavia, by 73 per cent in Rumania, by 86 per cent in Bulgaria, by 89.1 per cent in Poland.

The drop in export prices was particularly grave, leading as it did to an incomparably worse decline in the income deriving from exports than in volume of goods exported. Rumanian exports of cereals afford an illustration. In 1929 Rumania exported 1.7 million tons of cereals valued at 8,954 million lei. In 1930 and 1931, 3.2 to 3.4 million tons of cereals had to be supplied for the same amount of money. In 1933, when the volume of exports hardly exceeded the level of 1929, the returns for exports shrank to 3,262 million lei; in 1934, when prices touched bedrock, 1,003 million tons of cereals brought in no more than 2,381 million lei. Compared to conditions in 1929, the 42 per cent fall in the export of cereals in 1934 thus reduced the receipts by 73 per cent.

A similar process took place in Hungary. Calculated at 1929 prices, the value of Hungarian agricultural exports declined in 1934 by 27 per cent from the pre-crisis level. At the same time receipts showed a disproportionately steeper decline owing to the fall of prices. Agrarian exports calculated at current prices showed a drop of 60 per cent between 1929 and 1934.

Thus, owing to the joint effect of limited markets and falling prices, the former position of most countries of East-Central Europe in foreign trade was wrecked. The value of exports shrank disastrously, as can be seen in Table 10-2.

Thus in the years of crisis the export incomes of the countries of East-Central Europe fell by one-third—to roughly 40 per cent of the preceding level of prosperity. This had very grave economic consequences. First to be affected was the balance of foreign trade. Reduced income from exports made it impossible to keep up the former level of imports. Owing to the crisis-induced narrowing of home markets, import requirements were reduced anyway, but by no means in the measure demanded by the actual decline. Most of the countries under review, their natural endowments being one-sided, were badly in need of imports of raw materials. Moreover, owing to their previously developed structure, they could not do without large imports of industrial consumer goods and investment goods.

In the years of crisis the possibility of imports, formerly based on agrarian exports, was seriously reduced. It may be added that this reduction—considerable in itself—came to exceed the measure dictated by the diminution in the value of exports. Import capacity of the agrarian countries was further reduced by the widening on an international scale of the gap between agricultural and industrial prices in agrarian and industrial countries. For instance, between 1930 and 1933 Hungary could buy on the average 15 to 20 per cent less of foreign goods for the value of equal quantities of her export articles than between 1925 and 1927. The situation was similar in other countries relying on agrarian exports. In the industrial countries, particularly where foreign trade was marked by import of agrarian goods and raw materials and export of fin-

Table 10-2.   East-Central European Export Indices During the Depression *(in current prices: 1929 = 100)*

Year	Rumania	Hungary	Yugoslavia	Poland	Bulgaria
1930	75	88	86	86	96
1931	50	55	60	52	92
1932	44	32	39	38	53
1933	42	38	42	34	44
1934	42	39	50	34	41

Source: Based on miscellaneous national statistics.

ished industrial products, the change of prices during the years of crisis was favorable. In England import prices fell to 43 per cent of the 1929 level, export prices to only 54 per cent. In Germany the corresponding figures were 45 and 65.

Of the countries in the region in question it was Czechoslovakia and Austria alone that profited from the shift in prices through the larger reduction of import than of export prices. The prices of Czechoslovak and Austrian imports were 48 and 49 per cent of the 1929 level, while their export prices were 65 and 57 per cent. The reverse happened in the other countries of the area, as we have noted for Hungary. The extent to which import expenditures shrank can be seen in Table 10-3.

These effects came into closest contact with the *industrial* manifestations of the crisis. Since imports had consisted chiefly of finished industrial goods, the reduction of imports indicates a narrowing of the domestic market. On the other hand, the control of industrial imports was intended to relieve the industrial crisis at home. As a matter of fact, the economic position of agrarian-industrial and agrarian countries of East-Central Europe was determined primarily by the agrarian crisis. Though their industrial production was in the main subordinate to their agrarian production and the domestic consumption of industrial goods, the involvement of industry in the crisis nevertheless exerted a profound influence on their economic position and further progress.

In the Balkan countries industrial overproduction could not, of course, assume really large proportions, capacity being relatively insignificant, and reduced consumption being easily counterbalanced in numerous fields by the restriction of imports. Considerable industrial

Table 10-3. East-Central European Import Indices During the Depression *(in current prices: 1929 = 100)*

Year	Rumania	Hungary	Yugoslavia	Poland	Bulgaria
1930	71	77	92	68	55
1931	53	51	63	47	56
1932	40	31	38	27	42
1933	39	29	38	26	24
1934	43	32	47	25	24

Source: Based on miscellaneous national statistics.

overproduction and cutting down of production nevertheless ensued in Rumania in a few typical spheres of industrial investment. The production of cement factories and sawmills fell by 40 to 50 per cent, that of iron goods by more than one-third, that of coal by 37 per cent. However, production of most industrial consumer goods declined only moderately. In paper the drop was 10 to 17 per cent while in cotton goods, except for the year 1932 which saw a fall of 25 per cent owing to the poor crop, there was a rise of 10 to 25 per cent. In the leather industry, too, production increased. Decline in the already low production of the processing industry was, however, strongly counterbalanced by the increase of oil production, which increased more than one-and-a-half times by 1932, and was nearly double the pre-crisis level in 1933. The higher output of oil was intended to make up for the losses due to the failure of agrarian export. Therefore, the Rumanian oil exports increased more than did production, from 2,881,000 tons in 1929 to 6,547,000 tons. (The income from exports nevertheless decreased, amounting to 7,200 million lei instead of 9,600 million lei collected in 1929.) So, on the whole, there was only a moderate 11 per cent decline in Rumanian industrial production compared with peak values before the crisis, but it was only in 1932 that production failed to reach the 1929 level, while in the other years it was similar or slightly higher.

The industrial situation exhibited many similarities in Yugoslavia and Bulgaria. In Yugoslavia the 25 per cent fall in coal production and the transient suspension of iron ore exploitation brought only a moderate drop in the output of mining products. As a result of progress in the exploitation of nonferrous metals, the total production of the mines sank only by 10 per cent from the output in the pre-crisis years. At the time of the worst decline, in 1931-32, the total output of Yugoslav industry was 17 per cent below the pre-crisis level. According to available documentary evidence, between 1928 and 1933 employment increased by 10 per cent, while the total value of industrial investments also increased by approximately 10 per cent. Hence, as in Rumania, the adverse effects of the great economic crisis made themselves felt moderately and for a short time in Yugoslav industry.

The agrarian-industrial countries of the region, Hungary and Poland, were shaken much more profoundly by the crisis. In these countries industry, which played a more prominent part in the national economy, was overtaken by a lasting, serious crisis. The total production of the branches hit hardest by the Hungarian industrial crisis, notably the industries turning out capital equipment, the iron and metal industry, the building material industry, machine factories, declined by 1932 to 52 per cent of the pre-crisis level. (Machine production dropped to 45 per cent of the 1929 level, crude iron production to 10 per cent, and iron ore exploitation to 20 per cent.)

In the consumer goods industries the situation was a peculiar one. As in the Balkan countries, production of textiles, leather, and paper showed only a temporary fluctuation, but even in the years of crisis production increased, surpassing the 1929 level by 10 per cent in 1933. On the other hand, the weighty food industry, having lost its previously existing foreign markets, was much the worse for the crisis, and its output fell by about 20 per cent.

Since the chemical industry and the generation of electric power were not affected by the crisis, the average decline of industrial production in Hungary was 24 per cent, which in itself was grave. It exceeded the Balkan setback but was less than that of the industrial countries. All these events were accompanied by mass unemployment. By 1932 the number of employed workers was reduced by 30 per cent, and complete unemployment deprived 200,000 workers of a livelihood.

The industrial crisis was of long duration, beginning in the autumn of 1929 and affecting industrial production even after the bottom was reached in 1932. It took several years to climb back to the pre-crisis level. This was achieved only in 1936, when industrial production finally surpassed the 1929 output by 3 per cent.

Very similar processes took place in Poland. Here the production of capital equipment was hit hardest, with a fall of 43.4 per cent from the pre-crisis peak to the nadir in 1932. The Polish crisis was intensified by the particularly unfavorable situation of coal on the international market, for coal was an important branch of the Polish economy and export trade. Under the impact of this change Polish coal production sank from 46.2 million tons before the crisis to 27.3 million tons by 1933, a drop of over 40 per cent. The situation of iron ore mining was still worse: in 1932 it reached only 11 per cent of the pre-crisis output, crude iron and steel production only 37.3 per cent.

The general, more moderate, decline of the consumer goods industries may be observed here too, particularly in the paper and leather branches.

On the whole the crisis of Polish industry was extremely severe, more so than the Hungarian crisis, as demonstrated by the fall of new investments to one-third of the pre-crisis level, while the total of industrial output was reduced by 37 per cent. The serious consequences of the crisis are illustrated by the extraordinary increase of industrial unemployment. Whereas in 1929 the number of industrial workers was 766,900, in 1933 only 458,900 were employed; in other words, employment was reduced by 40 per cent.

In Poland too the industrial crisis lasted a long time, production approaching the pre-crisis level only in 1936 (94.3 per cent), and surpassing that level by 10.7 per cent in 1937.

The worst consequences of the crisis were observable in the industrial countries of East-Central Europe—in Austria and Czechoslovakia. In Austria the industrial crisis was especially acute. The economy was exceedingly unstable and industry strongly dependent on exports. Therefore the severe imbalance produced by the world crisis caused shock and bewilderment. Among the leading branches of Austrian industry the situation was the most critical in heavy industry and in machine works, the sectors which suffered the heaviest setback all over Europe. Iron ore production fell from 19.3 million quintals to 3.1 million quintals. The manufacture of pig iron practically came to a standstill; pig iron production plummeted from 437,000 tons to 87,000 tons. Steel production sank to one-third in the crisis years.

The branches of heavy industry declined everywhere, but in Austria light industry also soon found itself in an extremely critical position. These branches relied mainly on foreign markets. In their effort to avoid the crisis, the countries importing industrial goods promptly barred the purchase of supplies so that many branches of Austrian light industry lost their customers. Compared with East-Central Europe the fall of production in Austria was of much larger proportion. In cotton yarn output fell by approximately 25 per cent, from 23 million tons to 17 million tons; in paper production by around 15 per cent, from 229,000 tons to 201,000 tons.

The runover of capital equipment and semi-finished articles diminished by over 40 per cent, that of consumer goods by 20 to 25 per cent.

Table 10-4. National and Foreign Debts of the East-Central
European Countries in 1930

	Hungary	Austria	Czechoslovakia	Yugoslavia	Rumania
			(in million dollars)		
National debt	28	42	965	111	88
Foreign debt	755	485	410	855	1,050
Yearly interest	30	26	16	25	35
Foreign debt			*(in dollars)*		
per capita	65	77	34	66	75
National income					
per capita	116	160	171	93	107

Source: Based on the reports of the national banks of the related countries and
Southeastern Europe: A Political and Economic Survey, Royal Institute of International Affairs, London, 1939.

Owing to the vital importance of foreign trade, Austrian industrial output dropped 9 per cent from the 1929 level by 1930, 31 per cent by 1931, 40 per cent by 1932—the low point. At the worst stage of the crisis industrial unemployment (192,000 before the crisis) was more than double, rising to 406,000, or about 25 per cent of total manpower.

The depth of the crisis in Austria can be gauged by its unusually long duration, for no true solution was found even by the close of the decade. In 1936, when most countries had regained the former level of production, Austrian industry still turned out 20 per cent less than in 1929, and as late as the beginning of 1937, 13 per cent less. The pre-crisis volume was reached only in the spring of 1937. Accordingly, improvement of unemployment was also slow. In 1937 the figure was still only 321,000, about 20 per cent of total industrial manpower.

Similar processes took place in Czechoslovak industry. Here too the general decline of heavy industry and the setback caused by the absence of new investments were accompanied by a severe crisis of industries producing consumer goods for export, particularly in the textile and glass branches.

Thus hard coal production declined from 16.5 million tons to 10.5 million (35 per cent); brown coal, from 22.6 million tons to 15.1 million (approximately 33 per cent); coke production, 60 per cent. In pig iron and steel alike, the output sank by 65 per cent during the crisis. In the worst year of the crisis, 1932, Czechoslovak metal industry produced 60 per cent less than in 1929. The fall in motorcar production from 17,000 a year in 1930 to 9,000 by 1934 reveals the conditions in the machine-building industry.

The various branches of light industry experienced an equally acute crisis: textile and glass production sank by 36 and 52 per cent respectively.

The production of Czechoslovak industry at the nadir showed a 40 per cent fall from the 1929 level, bringing on extensive unemployment. In 1929 altogether 50,000 unemployed were recorded; by 1932 their number grew to 738,000, over one-third of the total industrial manpower. Early in 1933, 75 per cent of the glass workers were unemployed.

The acute agricultural and industrial conditions were aggravated in every country of the region by the financial and credit crisis in the summer of 1931 as a result of overproduction. Notwithstanding the increasingly severe industrial and agrarian crisis of 1929 and 1930, international financial and credit relations had continued undisturbed for a time, owing to the willingness of creditors on several occasions to grant new short or moderately long-term loans to support the solvency and producing ability of their debtors. However, by 1931 financial relations also became confused in the atmosphere of deepening depression. The solvency of the debtor countries laboring under adverse conditions grew more questionable, while the creditors, afraid of losing their money, declined to advance further loans. The export of capital by the two biggest creditors sank from $1,356 million in 1930 to $300 million by 1931, and to $30 million by 1932.

The unavailability of new loans created a grave situation in the debtor countries, most of which had accumulated such enormous debts that the yearly amortization and interest could be paid only by raising new loans. In the late twenties in most of the countries of East-Central Europe the amount of yearly amortization was larger than the amount of the new loans. For instance in Hungary in 1929 the total interest and amortization to be paid in the year exceeded by 16 per cent the amount of the new loans, and half of the new credits were used to pay off old debts. The consequences of the denial of new loans assumed a particularly dramatic form in Germany. Having to pay her old debts as well as considerable reparations, Germany was unable to fulfill her obligations.

When the financial breakdown of the country became apparent in the spring of 1931, so many creditors recalled their capital that the gold and foreign currency reserves of the Bank of Germany were almost entirely exhausted. The big German banks were on the verge of bankruptcy. Emergency measures became inevitable, and on July 13, 1931, the government decreed the closing of all banks for two days.

The failure of German finances and banks exerted a direct influence on the banks and credit system of Austria. The collapse of the Austrian credit system, badly weakened after the war, actually started in 1929 with the bankruptcy of the Bodencreditanstalt which had accumulated too many large long-term loans. At the time it was saved from ruin by the Creditanstalt. The grave shocks of the next year, however, did not spare the Creditanstalt either, so that the balance sheet published in May 1931 showed a loss of 400 million schillings. The public declaration of bankruptcy by the Creditanstalt, which played a central role, shook the whole financial system of Austria. The National Bank made efforts to save the situation and to finance the economy by discounting bills. In May 1931 the bills held by the National Bank increased in a single month from 69.5 million schillings to 451 million schillings. Since foreign exchange and gold were also used simultaneously for payments and reserves diminished during May by over 100 million schillings, the cover of the schilling rapidly fell from 83.5 per cent at the beginning of the month to 57.1 per cent by its end. In subsequent months foreign exchange and gold flowed out of the country at a rapidly increasing rate, the total exceeding 500 million schillings by the beginning of October. During 1931 loans amounting to over 500 million schillings were withdrawn from Austria. This ushered in the collapse of not only one bank but the whole financial system.

The financial network being international in nature, there were immediate repercussions from one country to another. The failure of the Creditanstalt of Vienna and the Austrian House of the Rothschilds at once involved the Rothschild concern in Budapest, the General Hungarian Credit Bank. With a prompt loan of 40 million pengös in the spring of 1931 the Hungarian government helped the bank over its immediate difficulties.

However, the rescue of the biggest Austrian and the most important Hungarian banks from ruin did not surmount the ever more difficult problems presented by the unfolding financial crisis. Further loans were called in, the significance of which becomes evident in surveying the financial situation and foreign debts of the countries of East-Central Europe on the threshold of financial crisis.

From the spring and summer of 1931, after the German and Austrian bankruptcies, foreign creditors promptly recalled all redeemable loans. Between May 1 and July 13 the National Bank of Hungary paid out 200 million pengös ($40 million) in gold and foreign currency, which exceeded the value of gold and foreign exchange held at the end of April. Payment was made possible by the Bank for International Settlements and the big European banks to which the National Bank of Hungary turned for help, issuing treasury notes in the value of £5 million at the same time. Poland paid off short-term loans of 933 million zlotys (around $115 million) in 1930 and 1931.

Austria paid off 1,000 million schillings (nearly $110 million) of mostly short-term loans in 1931, so gold and foreign exchange reserves diminished rapidly: from the original 930 million schillings to 318 million in 1931 and to 114 million by July 1932. The gold reserve sank from 84 per cent to 25 per cent.

In Czechoslovakia approximately $60 million worth of short-term loans were recalled in 1931. Frozen foreign assets amounted to approximately the same sum.

Short-term loans amounting to 1,800 million lei were withdrawn from Rumania in 1931, and the National Bank of Rumania lost gold and foreign exchange valued at about $20 million. Consequently, gold and foreign exchange reserves dropped from about $40 million in 1929 to $1.5 million by 1933. The gold and foreign exchange reserve of the Rumanian leu fell from 52 per cent to 37 per cent.

In the same months credits of 1,500 million dinars (about $30 million) were recalled from Yugoslavia. In 1932 the larger items of state expenditure were the amounts to be paid as amortization. These were responsible for 35 per cent of the total expenditure in Bulgaria, for 27 per cent in Rumania, for 21 per cent in Yugoslavia.

At the same time the network of banks also sustained serious losses. Between 1930 and 1934 total deposits shrank to half in Yugoslavia (from 10,300 million dinars to 5,400 million) driving more than half of the banks (representing 48 per cent of the total of bank share capital) into bankruptcy. The crisis of Bulgarian banks is obvious from the failure of the Banque de Sofia and the merger of several banks.

Among the countries under review Czechoslovakia was the only exception. Unlike the other countries of East-Central Europe, she did not become a debtor in the decade following World War I, but even paid off earlier debts gradually and bought back part of the shares and loans held by foreign owners. Moreover, Czechoslovakia herself granted credit extensively, chiefly in trade by supplying goods on credit. Consequently, the effect of the financial crisis was not the same there as in other East-Central European countries. It did not bring financial ruin or a critical state of insolvency. The freezing of assets abroad and the adverse balance of foreign trade naturally involved severe losses and rendered it necessary to balance the budget by strict and radical measures. However, these steps usually remained within the traditional limits. Expenditures were severely curtailed, taxes and other revenues (customs duty) were increased, and substantial support of industrial exports (with 600 million crowns a year) was accompanied by strong protection and stimulation of agricultural production. Nevertheless, Czechoslovakia too finally found herself in a position where problems of foreign trade could be coped with only by devaluation of the currency after the Western pattern. In 1934 the crown was devalued by 16 per cent.

In virtually all of East-Central Europe financial failure was almost complete. Its repercussions were felt in nearly every country of the region and affected every sector of the economy. While the Great Depression dealt a heavy blow to the economies of the leading powers, these Eastern European countries were particularly hard hit. Mostly agrarian or agrarian-industrial, they were not only shaken and depleted but attacked at their very core. Already in debt, they were faced with bankruptcy in a state of international insolvency. Suddenly they were deprived of the foreign loans which had until then been vital in financing their industry.

In the Danube countries an entirely new economic situation arose, the problems of which defied any solution by the usual methods. In the summer of 1931 only prompt and radical measures could prevent complete economic collapse. After the closing of the banks in Germany in July 1931, the countries of East-Central Europe adopted the German method in quick succession or simultaneously, and energetic intervention by the state was practiced in various forms.

In the hours following the announcement of the closing of all banks in Germany on July 13, the Hungarian government held a night meeting and decided to close the banks for three days from July 14. When they reopened their doors on the 17th, a series of emergency decrees had been put into force to control the situation. In vain did holders of deposits storm the banks. From the morning of July 17 only 5 per cent of deposits in savings banks or on current accounts were paid out, a maximum of 1,000 pengös. The simultaneous introduction of control over the use of foreign exchange on the German model was, however, still more important. Free exchange of the national currency for foreign currency ceased, and payment in foreign currency could be effected only with a permit from the National Bank. The policy of controlled foreign exchange not only created a new situation in money circulation but also brought essential changes in foreign trade. After its introduction all export and import deals depended on the permit of the National Bank; all foreign trade thus came under state control, with the possibility of further regulatory measures.

To complement the effects of controlled foreign exchange policy the Hungarian government unilaterally suspended the payment of foreign debts and prohibited such payments by private debtors. This situation was legalized in November 1931 by the National Committee on Foreign Loans set up in the meantime. As a result of negotiations with foreign creditors, agreements were signed, fixing existing credits. From December 22, 1931, payments of interest were also stopped and a complete transfer moratorium was put into force. From this time Hungarian debtors (the state and private parties alike) paid amortization in pengös to the Fund of Foreign Creditors set up alongside the National Bank, and payment in foreign exchange was effected only at the end of 1933 when the transfer moratorium was lifted.

In accordance with controlled foreign exchange policy creditors could use their accumulated assets only in Hungary, in pengös. The significance of this step is accentuated by the fact that the interest and amortization of the total debt in 1931 amounted to 300 million pengös, approaching the total value of exports in that year. Notwithstanding the agreement of 1937 which slightly lightened the burden of amortization, in the course of the 1930s an average of 50 million pengös was paid off yearly. By these exceptional measures enormous amounts of capital were thus retained in the country, bringing stability to the balance of payments, of foreign trade, and to the budget.

These regulations were not mere coercive provisions enforced during the worst years of the crisis. They remained valid—with minor amendments discussion of which is outside the scope of the present work—until World War II and became the basis of a much more comprehensive system of regulations in wartime. Also, the field of intervention was extended.

Beginning in 1932–33 the other most important step was the introduction of the bonus system. This coincided with the devaluation of currency in many countries all over the world in the last period of the crisis and in subsequent years. Besides consolidating the currencies shaken during these years, devaluation became an important weapon in the competition for wider markets. Obviously, such a weapon was needed not only by the big powers but also by the more disrupted economies of East-Central Europe. In those countries, however, devaluation involved numerous hazards. The extensive wave of devaluation automatically destroyed part of the capital invested by creditor countries abroad. Loans granted in English pounds, U.S. dollars, and French francs were reduced in direct proportion to devaluation. For instance, one-third of Hungary's debts were wiped out. In this situation devaluation of the national currency would have harmfully counterbalanced the effect of the devaluation carried out by the creditors. Therefore, following the example of Germany, several countries of East-Central Europe abstained from devaluation. However, they were unwilling to give up the advantages of enhanced competitiveness in foreign trade deriving from devaluation. The solution lay in the so-called bonus system. In Hungary, for example, a larger sum was paid in pengös than the official rate of exchange when the exporter received the pengö value of certain foreign currencies.

Until 1935 there was no uniform bonus system for each foreign currency; the amount of the bonus varied according to certain articles and markets. In general the bonus corresponded to about a 20 to 40 per cent devaluation of the pengö. However, after 1935 the exceedingly intricate and extensive system—with approximately five hundred kinds of bonus

—was modified and simplified. A uniform bonus key was fixed for the various currencies—the highest bonus, about 50 per cent, being paid on currency of countries where the use of foreign exchange was not controlled. The advantages of this devaluation in the form of a bonus system were to reduce imports and increase exports, rendering the balance of foreign trade more favorable. In its means and methods the control of foreign exchange policy was largely similar in the other countries of East-Central Europe.

From the autumn of 1931 to the beginning of 1932 Austrian control of foreign exchange was very strict, and every deal of over 1,000 schillings could be transacted on a foreign market only through the National Bank. However, since the benefit from financial control failed to fulfill expectations, control was slightly relaxed early in 1932. A special system of so-called private compensation was introduced for the principal export goods, the activities of the National Bank being confined to fixing the bonus. By the end of 1932 the most important clauses of foreign exchange control were canceled, and in 1934 the gold value of the schilling was regulated, implying the official admission of an approximately 22 per cent devaluation.

Controlled foreign exchange policy was introduced also in Czechoslovakia, but it did not reach the stage of suspending the payment of foreign debts. The National Bank of Czechoslovakia endeavored to balance internal and international price levels by a policy of deflation and devaluated the crown to obtain an active balance of foreign trade.

Similar measures were taken in Yugoslavia and Rumania, bringing about an average devaluation of 38 per cent in Rumania and 28 per cent in Yugoslavia where the change in the value of the dinar was legalized in 1937. In both countries control was accompanied by covert prices and bonuses. A transfer moratorium was declared in Rumania in December 1932, and a transitory agreement being signed, amortization was suspended until March 31, 1933. The moratorium was prolonged by a new agreement until March 31, 1935, and by another until the end of 1936.

Yugoslavia concluded a "Stillhalte" agreement concerning short-term loans and suspended amortization of her French loan for one year.

Bulgaria in 1932 paid off 50 per cent, and in 1933, 40 per cent, of her obligations. However, in the following years she reduced payments to 25 per cent.

Thus, under pressure, similar systems of state intervention were devised in the countries of the region. A noteworthy difference has been observed in Poland alone. The governments, following a conservative economic policy, did not take any restrictive measures during the crisis or after it, but maintained the gold standard of the zloty and paid amortization when it was due. The sums transferred from Poland to other countries from the beginning of the crisis to the end of 1935 as profit, amortization, interest, etc., amounted to 4.8 million zloty (nearly $500 million). Consequently, the gold and foreign exchange reserves of the National Bank of Poland sank to one-third of the 1929 level. The disastrous postwar inflation and the rapid collapse of the first financial stabilization had rendered Polish economists particularly wary and strengthened their insistence on a policy of deflation and on preserving the value of the national currency even during the crisis. (In the early thirties, for instance, the discount rate fell on the world market in general from about 5 per cent to 2–4 per cent. In Poland it remained over 7 per cent until 1932.)

However, in the spring of 1936 the financial crisis became so acute that the policy of noninterference could not be continued any longer. Therefore, the Polish government came to an agreement with its creditors, suspended the transfer of interest, and adopted foreign exchange control. State control became extensive, and penetrated to every sector of the economy. Besides measures to protect the peasantry and support agriculture, which were typical of agrarian countries, efforts at planning were also discernible. The focus of these endeavors was the energetic and modern industrialization of the so-called Central Industrial Area, the triangle including Warsaw-Krakow-Lwow. The possibility of intervention was greatly facilitated by the circumstance that a considerable part of the Polish economy was owned by the state, and more active intervention took the form of strengthening the state-owned sector. By the close of the 1930s the Polish state ran about 100 industrial enterprises, including all the armaments factories, 80 per cent of the chemical industry, 40 per cent of the iron industry, and 50 per cent of other metal industries. The total air transport, 95 per cent of merchant shipping, and 93 per cent of the railways were state property, and the nucleus of the network of Polish banks was formed by state-owned banks.

These new forms of state intervention appeared also in foreign trade and the control of production. However, they were much too generally applied to be treated as typically Polish developments.

Although having some efficacy, these various forms of intervention proved inadequate to overcome the existing economic confusion. Better protection of markets and increased stimulation of exports were indispensable to correct the catastrophic balance of foreign trade and payments.

Successive and increasingly severe customs duties, introduced in virtually every part of the world, were intended to serve these aims. In 1933 Czechoslovakia, Poland, and Hungary raised their customs tariffs. In Czechoslovakia the wheat tariff was trebled. Between 1930 and 1934 in Austria the wheat tariff was doubled and other agrarian tariffs were similarly raised.

Traditional steps to derive advantages from high customs tariffs, however, were gradually abandoned. Instead, efficient protection of home industrial products was achieved by the Hungarian government, not primarily by increasing customs on industrial goods but by prohibiting the importation of certain articles. By the beginning of 1933 the importation of almost every kind of foreign finished goods was prohibited and could be obtained only by a special permit. According to available statistics, by barring the import of finished industrial goods the government contrived to improve the domestic market for Hungarian industry. While the Hungarian market for factory products shrank by 38 per cent by 1932, the domestic sales of the Hungarian manufacturing industry were reduced only by 26 per cent.

The reestablishment or extension of the embargo was, of course, applied in other countries of the region as well. It was in these years that the system of import quotas was introduced as a new method in foreign trade. In some countries the overall import of certain goods was set, and the producing countries were then allotted their respective shares.

With certain exceptions, the import quotas of Bulgaria were around 50 per cent of the level before the crisis.

In Austria and Czechoslovakia import quotas, fixed mainly for agrarian products, were upheld even for countries where Austrian and Czechoslovak assets had been frozen.

Foreign trade based on quotas fixed by the state was monopolized in most countries and partly left in the hands of organizations in which the state held a financial interest or to which it gave support. In Yugoslavia grain trade was monopolized from 1930 on by Prizad, founded with state support. In the same year a Directorate for the Purchase of Grain was set up in Bulgaria to control home prices by intervening purchases and to monopolize foreign trade. State organizations were created in Rumania and Poland for the sale of grain, while in Hungary, besides a system of government subsidies for promoting exports and influencing home sales, monopolies were developed with state support to sell and export various kinds of goods.

The transformation which became apparent in the methods of economic activity as a result of intervention by the state was much wider in scope than described above. Varying methods of subsidizing export, control of the production of certain agrarian goods, and particularly the growth of certain industrial plants, were all introduced. Without discussing the ramifications of these measures, we would conclude by drawing attention to another process due to the crisis, namely, the widespread acceptance of clearing in the foreign trade relations of the countries of East-Central Europe. The severe lack of foreign exchange during and long after the crisis rendered previous methods of foreign trade impossible in many respects. Controlled foreign exchange made it urgent to find new ways to promote the transaction of business in the countries of the region. This aim was served by agreements to settle accounts by clearing. From the early 1930s such agreements were signed by a growing number of countries. Foreign trade turnover being based on reciprocal exchange of goods of approximately equal value, the use of foreign exchange was restricted to payment of the balances where liabilities arose.

The idea of clearing, suggested by the difficulties of effecting international payments and by lack of foreign exchange, was put before the conference of national banks at Prague in 1931 by Dr. Reisch, president of the National Bank of Austria. The starting-point was to be to open adequate cumulative accounts at the national banks. That is to say, the first steps were to be mainly of a technical nature. However, clearing was to bring about a shift from the system of multilateral commerce in the direction of bilateral agreements in international trade, for within the framework of bilateral agreements the exports of one country to another were for the most part determined by its imports from that other country. Moreover, soon all accounts were settled by clearing.

Trade between the countries of Southeastern Europe, as well as their

Table 10-5.   Per Cent of Foreign
Trade Settled by Clearing in Southeastern
European Countries, 1938
*(including all special variants of
clearing)*

	Import	Export
Bulgaria	86.7	88.0
Hungary	85.9	83.0
Rumania	82.5	72.9
Yugoslavia	76.4	79.5

Source: H. S. Ellis, *Exchange Control in
Central Europe,* Cambridge, 1941.

turnover with Germany and Italy, was before long settled by clearing. Yugoslavia signed her first clearing agreement with Austria in January 1932; with Germany in May 1934. In the second half of the 1930s, 73 to 75 per cent of Yugoslav foreign trade was transacted on the basis of clearing agreements. Austria concluded clearing agreements also with Switzerland, Hungary, Italy, and Bulgaria. An important role in the widening adoption of the clearing system was played by Germany, which signed clearing agreements with all countries of East-Central Europe in 1932. Hungary lost no time in regrouping her foreign trade toward the countries accepting settlement by clearing. In 1935 more than 63 per cent of her foreign trade was pursued within the framework of clearing agreements.

All these changes of methods, the transformation of commercial policy after the world wide crisis, were closely connected with German expansion, with the *Lebensraum* policy of Hitler's Germany which exerted a most powerful influence on the whole political and economic history of the countries of East-Central Europe.

11 German Economic Expansion: Grossraumwirtschaft in East-Central Europe

Among the momentous changes of the thirties, the new situation created by the ascendancy of Hitler and the rise of Nazism in Germany was of crucial importance to East-Central Europe. The transformation of the German economy beginning in January 1933, designed to bring the world under Nazi domination, was coupled with a new orientation in economic relations with the countries to the east and southeast of Germany. The Nazi ideas, intensively carried out, had a strong influence on the economic position of these countries.

The unlimited power of the Nazi party in Germany made it possible to begin a rapid economic reorganization and a switch to a war economy. After the measures for creating new jobs for workers had been introduced by the Nazis in 1933, partly in connection with military preparations, the rearmament of Germany on a large scale was started by Hitler in the summer of 1934. In accordance with the requirements of modern warfare, the rearmament program was not restricted to the manufacture of arms but affected the whole of economic life: industry, agriculture, finance, and foreign trade. The readjustment of production to a war footing implied a stronger intervention by the state in economic life than had ever before been experienced. In fact, it was in Hitler's Germany that a war economy in peacetime through state intervention was first introduced.

State intervention, which created an enormous boom for German monopoly capital, was concentrated chiefly in three spheres beginning in mid-1934—direct and indirect huge military orders to industry; achieving economic autarky; and a very energetic control of foreign trade and the turnover of international payments. The activities in the last two spheres embraced the principal steps of so-called economic rearmament. The policy of economic self-sufficiency was applied methodically with the objective of rendering Germany independent of sources of raw materials out of reach in case of war. The strict control of foreign trade and the turnover of payments advanced the policy of autarky, and also helped to solve the exceedingly difficult balance-of-payments problems.

Without strict state control of foreign trade autarky could not have been carried out, for it called for the reduction of imports and considerable changes in the area of foreign trade activities. By the spring of 1934 the balance of payments situation had reached its most critical stage. An extra burden had been imposed by the policy of state investment and by devaluation of the currency in England and the United States, the two most powerful trading countries of the world. Moreover, for the first time in many years the turnover of foreign trade showed a debit: in the second quarter of 1934 the deficit in the balance of trade was over 160 million marks.

Schacht's "Neuer Plan," conceived in September 1934 to overcome the difficulties of economic armament and of foreign trade simultaneously, was to support Nazi preparations for the war from the aspects of international economic relations. The Plan, insuring complete control of foreign trade and international payments, rested on the following principles. The quantity of imports was to be severely limited and its total volume fixed by the Nazi government authorities as required by the changeover to a war economy. In a breakaway from former commercial policy, foreign trade was to be conducted with most parties on the basis of bilateral trade and financial agreements. The fundamental principle laid down in the "Neuer Plan" was that Germany was to buy from states which did not stipulate payment in foreign exchange but accepted German goods instead. This modification of import policy was to be accompanied by the regulation of exports, the furtherance of barter transactions, and veiled awards of premiums on exports.

The "Neuer Plan" was suitable for the support of the Nazi economic program. The restriction of imports in certain sectors led to an increase in the manufacture of articles of strategic importance at home. At the same time available means were utilized with the strictest thrift for the purchase of raw material and foodstuffs of military importance which could not be obtained in satisfactory quantities in Germany, in order that domestic resources might be mobilized and exploited to the maximum in the service of rearmament and preparations for war. Through bilateral trade agreements and payment with German products Schacht's economic policy solved the problem of foreign exchange, which was the primary precondition of a war economy. Expenditure in foreign currency being cut to the utmost, the available foreign exchange could be spent on buying military raw materials which could not be secured by any other means.

The system introduced by the Neuer Plan automatically turned the foreign trade of Nazi Germany toward Central Europe and the Balkans, for it seemed feasible to use these countries as the main base of foreign raw materials for the development of the German war economy. Indeed, the German economy was badly isolated by its new commercial policy, adherence to which was ensured by strict control, since neither the Western European nor the overseas countries approved of bilateral trade and of payment in goods, terms on which they declined to transact business.

On the other hand, the economic policy devised for Hitler by Schacht was very well suited to intensify economic relations with East-Central Europe. These countries had played an important role in German economic policy at an earlier date, and the acquisition of their markets had figured in the plans of some significant German concerns in the 1920s. In the Neuer Plan these regions were regarded as an organic complement of the German war economy.

What were the factors which induced Nazi economic policy to rely on these countries? First of all, most of them were agrarian countries in economic straits, afflicted with the problem of how to market their agrarian products. There could be no doubt—as shown by the experiences of earlier years—that they would welcome any proposal which would promote the sale of their products. The preconditions were also present, because the Danubian countries had accepted the principle of bilateral trade proclaimed by the Germans. When one considers that these countries, being debtors, suffered most from the financial crisis along with Germany, and that, being unable to cope with their foreign currency problems, they were the first to introduce a controlled foreign exchange policy, it is understandable that bilateral trade and barter seemed to promise considerable advantages.

The Danube countries disposed of their surplus food and raw materials—Yugoslav cereals and nonferrous metals; Rumanian maize and oil; Hungarian meat, lard, cereals, and bauxite; Bulgarian tobacco—

which the German war economy needed in the period of rearmament and would need still more later. These countries were near Germany, they could be reached by land, and when war came there was no fear of sources being cut off by a sea blockade. Therefore the Danube countries could be regarded by Nazi Germany as safe reserves economically and strategically.

The realization of Nazi ideas in connection with the countries in question was forwarded by the status of Germany. As a great power, she could use pressure to bend them to her wishes. At this juncture only Hungary was on Hitler's side, but Germany could expect to gain influence over the other small economically and politically weak countries, in part by establishing economic relations.

Thus the new economic policy initiated by the Neuer Plan served the German goal of world domination not only by promoting preparations for war but also by chaining East-Central Europe to the German economy, by incorporating the region in the German *Grossraumwirtschaft*. German government circles left no doubt that the Neuer Plan served this aim. In 1934 a high government official, Hans Ernst Posse, wrote: "Since the readjustment of the interior German economic space, the most important task of national socialist government in the year, had been accomplished according to plans, it was time to consider it as the most essential task of economic policy to fit German economy in the 'Grossraumwirtschaft' which was taking shape."[1]

The new trend of Nazi economic policy was developed into a uniform system from mid-1934, but its elements and ideas had permeated German foreign trade policy somewhat earlier. Signs of relaxation in the rigid attitude of agrarian isolation toward the countries of East-Central Europe had become noticeable in the autumn of 1933. At this time heads of the department of economic policy in the Ministry of Foreign Affairs indicated that they were willing to promote the export of Hungarian agricultural products with the aid of a system providing for certain veiled premiums. The head of the Hungarian Commercial Delegation in conversations in Berlin, in a confidential account, reported that Waldeck, the senior official dealing with Hungarian affairs in the economic policy department, let him know: "Now is the time to strike

[1] "Möglichkeiten der Grossraumwirtschaft," an article published in *Die nationale Wirtschaft*, vol. 2.

the German iron because it is hot, and matters have reached a stage where we can carry our point with the German government, even on issues which have been out of the question so far."

In November 1933 a mixed German-Hungarian commission was set up, and at the end of the month preliminary talks were begun.

As a result of the expansive economic policy of the Nazis and the political situation which had taken shape by the end of 1933, German-Hungarian commercial negotiations carried on in January and February 1934 led to the signing of an agreement.

Competent German government authorities formulated their decision in January 1934: "It is the intention of Germany"—the statement says—"to link Hungarian economy closely and inseparably to the German economy by the agreement to be concluded and by increasing the exchange of goods."[2] This decision was of fundamental significance and implied a departure from earlier principles governing foreign trade. No contract was signed providing for an open reduction of customs tariffs because the same advantages might have been claimed by other countries, but a new form of drawback made it possible for Germany to import Hungarian agrarian commodities. High customs tariffs for farm products were upheld and Hungary alone was granted import concessions, inasmuch as part of the customs duty was to be repaid by Germany. A government fund of 15 million marks was to be made available for the purpose. On February 21 the agreement was signed and was put into force as of April 1 as the second codicil to the trade agreement of 1931.

In clauses No. 1 and 2 of the second codicil the German government undertook to promote Hungarian exports by barter transactions and settlement of accounts through clearing. The Hungarian government was to take into consideration German interests in imports. The realization of these clauses meant that for the first time since World War I a German-Hungarian agreement was reached which provided for the possibility of substantial Hungarian agrarian exports to Germany. The German government undertook to buy 50,000 tons of wheat in 1934, 75,000 tons of corn fodder (barley and maize), 6,000 heads of beef cattle, 3,000 tons of pork, 1,500 tons of bacon, and 3,000 tons of lard. More-

---

[2] Deutsches Zentral Archiv. Potsdam, Ausswertiges Amt. abt. II, 41,288.

over, the Germans were to purchase considerable quantities of pulse, seeds, butter, eggs, etc.

The second codicil of 1934, however, not only provided for quotas for Hungarian agriculture, but, abandoning the practice of earlier trade agreements, the system of quotas was supplemented by a system of re-payment in accordance with the principles laid down in January. From these repayments the Hungarian government could spend 22 million pengös a year on subsidizing agrarian exports to Germany. Under such conditions the subsidized articles not only became competitive on the German market, but the big Hungarian estates could sell their products at more favorable prices than in the world market. The state paid out on exports to Germany subsidies of 4.2 to 5.5 pengös per quintal on wheat, 4 on maize, 27 on beef cattle, 56 on bacon, 74 on lard. The yearly total amounted to 6.5 million pengös in cereals, 2 million in oilseeds, 8.5 mil-lion in bacon and lard, 5 million in other products.

In return for these German concessions the Hungarian government moderated or repealed measures preventing the importation of German industrial products. First of all, the reduction of duties laid down in the agreement of 1931 was put into full force by the agreement of 1934. It applied to paper goods, textiles, metal ware, machines, and many kinds of consumer goods, with reductions running as high as 20 to 30 per cent. Still more important was the repeal of embargoes and the granting of quotas on many articles for which no import licence had been given since 1931. Quotas were fixed for the import of yarn, cotton materials, shoes, machines, etc.

The new trade agreement of February 1934 was complemented by a new financial agreement according to which German importers were to pay for Hungarian goods in marks in the account of the National Bank of Hungary at the Reichsbank. The Reichsbank entered the received payments on separate accounts opened for the various kinds of Hungari-an goods. German exporters were paid for their supplies to Hungary from these amounts.

Settlement by clearing was continued in an unchanged form, 93 per cent of the countervalue of Hungarian exports being retained to cover German supplies, and the remaining 10 per cent being put on the so-called *conto ordinario* at the free disposal of the National Bank of Hun-gary. As specified in the agreement, this 10 per cent was to be used not for settling accounts but for the purchase of goods to be had only for foreign exchange. The new agreement divided the *conto ordinario* into two parts, the so-called "unbeschränkte freie Quote," limited to the fixed amount of 2 million marks, for which the National Bank of Hungary was entitled to buy foreign exchange to be used at will for any purpose. The rest of the 10 per cent on the *conto ordinario* accumulated as "beschränkte freie Quote." These amounts could be used for buying German raw materials not specified in the trade agreement or transit goods whose purchase could be effected only with convertible foreign exchange.

The increase produced by the agreement of February 1934 in the turnover of Hungarian-German trade surpassed all expectations. Hungarian agrarian exports soared, increasing, for instance, in lard and bacon over twentyfold, in beef cattle over sevenfold, in wool over sixfold, in pulse over fourfold, in butter threefold. Total Hungarian exports more than doubled from 1933 to 1934, and their value rose by 46 million pengös, approaching 90 million pengös.

Whereas the increase in the value of Hungarian exports far exceeded all expectations, imports of German industrial products remained far behind. The value of imports increased by no more than 2 million pengös over the preceding years, hardly surpassing 63 million pengös.

As demonstrated by these figures, not only did Hungarian exports to Germany increase considerably in 1934, but this was the first time since World War I that the yearly balance of Hungarian-German trade showed noteworthy Hungarian surpluses. The share of Germany in Hungarian exports soared from 11.2 per cent in 1933 to 22.2 per cent in 1934.

Their new economic policy, including the new Hungarian-German economic agreement of 1934, was claimed by German government circles to be a proof of the interdependence of Germany and the small countries of Southeastern Europe. They endeavored to make their policy appear as a "generous friendly concession" offered to the small countries in their difficult economic situation. The views of Nazi politicians and the whole of German economic literature were effectively propagandized. They were formulated, for instance, by Ernst Wagemann, president of the German Institute of Economic Research. In his book entitled *Der neue Balkan* he wrote about the countries in difficult circumstances: "Who else but Germany could have lent a helping hand?" by her aid; Germany "drew the countries of Southeastern Europe into the train of tempestuous advancement." The viewpoint proclaimed by the Germans was put still more crudely: "Germany was the only industrial country which was ready to support the agrarian countries of Southeastern Europe by generously giving preference to their products and multiplying their import."[3]

There can be no doubt that the aim of the agreement of 1934 was to lay the foundations of aggressive German political aspirations. This, however, by no means implies that the Nazi government failed to connect this step with safeguarding and promoting its economic interests. The Nazis intended to achieve more distant political objectives by exploiting the resources of the countries of Southeastern Europe maximally and making them serve the policy of German rearmament.

As regards admission to the German market, we have mentioned the exceedingly unfavorable commercial and financial position of Germany, which rendered it impossible to cover her agrarian requirements with supplies from overseas countries as formerly. The products of those countries were certainly much cheaper, but payments had to be made in most instances in foreign exchange of which Germany possessed limited sums, and those at her disposal had to be reserved for the purchase of raw materials of strategic importance. Hence Germany was gradually compelled to buy her food requirements in countries willing to settle accounts by bilateral clearing and export their goods in exchange for German industrial products. From this it follows that the willingness of the Nazi government to buy the surplus of Hungarian agrarian goods as laid down in the agreement of 1934 was inspired not by economic concession but by the primary interests of the German economy.

This fact throws a different light on the price problem. Whereas in the twenties prices had played a decisive part in German purchases, under the Nazi government price problems were relegated to the background and those presented by foreign exchange came to the fore. For the German economy buying cheap was less of an advantage than barter, which could be transacted without foreign exchange. This was laid down as a principle of economic policy. From the economic point of view the purchase of agrarian products at higher prices in the coun-

---

[3] Hermann Gross, *Die wirtschaftliche Bedeutung Südosteuropas für das Deutsche Reich,* Stuttgart-Berlin, 1938, p. 18.

tries of Southeastern Europe was the most advantageous for Germany in the existing situation, because the expenditure of foreign exchange could be avoided.

For a proper perspective the source of the premiums serving to cover the prices which were higher than the world-market level cannot be disregarded. It is known from the clauses of the agreement that the German government undertook to pay 22 million pengös as export premium. However, in reality the payment of this amount did not impose any burden on the German economy, for the Nazi government skillfully connected the premiums to be paid on Hungarian agrarian exports with German assets frozen in Hungary. In 1934 the German government created the necessary financial basis for premiums on Hungarian agrarian exports from the approximately 60 million pengös of frozen German assets. German capitalists were pleased to have the government buy their apparently worthless outstanding debts for cash, even if they got 25 per cent less than the nominal value.

In fact the German government spent 17 million marks on the purchase of frozen German assets, but the whole of the sum went to German firms which possessed assets in Hungary. Therefore, the money remained in the country. Moreover, this expenditure, which cannot be regarded as a true loss when estimated on the scale of the national economy, was made good, for the turnover of foreign trade increased by the premium on exports brought in approximately 10 million marks more in customs duty. Furthermore, taking into consideration that against the value of imported agricultural goods Germany exported industrial products to Hungary without any subsidy at higher prices than they would have fetched on the world market, it becomes clear that the German government did not make any sacrifice when it signed the codicil of the trade agreement of 1934.

The trade agreement with Hungary concluded in February 1934, the first of its kind, was soon followed by similar agreements with the other countries of East-Central Europe. Thus the German-Hungarian commercial treaty, the first step in the practical realization of Nazi *Grossraumwirtschaft,* was the prototype of agreements intended to serve the new order.

Apart from the applied means, the success of German penetration depended also on the strength of the opposite party's situation—whether the country in question had products for which there was demand on other markets, and whether and how far it was capable of adjusting its prices to the new situation. Consequently, German economic penetration was much stronger in the weaker countries. (It must be remarked here that the intensity of economic relations was also influenced by the aims of foreign policy.)

Germany's share in Bulgarian foreign trade had been considerable before the crisis and continued to increase while the crisis lasted. In the German-Bulgarian trade agreement of February 1933 the Germans granted significant reduction of tariffs to the Bulgarians, and in return demanded greater specialization of Bulgarian agriculture to meet the demands of the German market. It was chiefly larger supplies of industrial plants, fodder, and certain animal products that they wished to have, a request that could be easily satisfied since Bulgarian exports had never been concentrated on cereals. In a few years the products in question were cultivated on a steadily growing area, and Germany bought everything with her overvalued currency. Thus Germany's share in Bulgarian exports rose from 29.4 per cent to 43.1 per cent; its share in Bulgarian imports from 23.2 per cent to 54 per cent.

Rumania and Yugoslavia were in a stronger position because their economic resources were richer and more varied than those of Bulgaria. To begin with, Rumania had oil, which was always one of the most important items on her list of exports. Moreover, owing to the possibility of sea transport, exports of corn to Western Europe were more practicable than in the case of Hungary.

During the crisis the products which Rumania usually sold in German markets were badly hit by German import restrictions. Therefore, the share of German foreign trade was reduced nearly one-third. The pre-crisis level was reached again only in 1937 as a consequence of the agreement of 1935. Here too, the Germans urged the cultivation of new kinds of agricultural products such as oilseeds and soya beans, with some success.

The position of Yugoslavia was strengthened by her nonferrous metals, but these products gave less firm support than did Rumanian oil. Yugoslav foreign trade with Germany, rather insignificant earlier (8.5 per cent), showed a slight increase in the early thirties owing to various commercial favors and higher prices. After the agreement of 1934 German purchases, stimulated in the case of nonferrous metals by rearmament, steadily increased, reaching a balance of 500 million dinars higher than the clearing limit, the settlement of which surplus seemed to be most practicable by means of larger German imports. Overvaluation of the mark and clearing agreements were the most helpful ways of acquiring a hold over the commerce of the Southeastern European countries while isolating them ever more effectively from the world market.

Officially Germany did not devaluate her currency and insisted on retaining the old gold standard in relation to the currencies of the countries of Southeastern Europe in the settlement of accounts by clearing. Since the purchasing power of the mark had considerably deteriorated during the crisis, this implied overvaluation of the mark and devaluation of the other currencies.

The economic leaders of Germany were fully aware of the economic consequences of the overvalued mark for the countries of Southeastern Europe. Schacht, the president of the National Bank, clearly expressed their view: ". . . the foreign countries concerned would under any circumstances prefer to sell their goods for so-called convertible currency instead of marks. If they nevertheless sell on the German market it is because they are as good as compelled to do so; and if they are, they have to and will adjust their prices to German instructions."[4]

Germany demanded the maintenance of the original clauses in the case of Bulgaria, Hungary, and Rumania, but in reality it was Bulgaria alone that acted on them (1 mark = 33 levas), while the other countries endeavored to take into consideration the depreciation of the mark, notwithstanding German disapproval. For instance, Hungary gave an 18 per cent premium on the mark, which still meant an overvaluation.

The Rumanians wished to bring about a realistic valuation of the mark by insisting on free commerce up to a certain point. They succeeded partly, but free trade had to be abandoned because of German pressure in 1936. By this time a certain depreciation of the mark had been officially recognized.

Yugoslav clearing arrangements were also based on the official rate of exchange, but soon German liabilities ran so high that the National

[4] National Archives, Department of Economic Policy, Ministry of Foreign Affairs, German file no. 642. Confidential report of the Hungarian Legation of Berlin, dated June 15, 1933.

Bank of Yugoslavia was compelled to introduce private clearing, which meant that importers could buy the assets of exporters with cheques presentable for clearing. This brought an approximately 25 per cent fall in the rate of the mark.

On the whole, the mark was nevertheless overvalued, which had its inevitable influence on the foreign trade of the East-Central European countries. Theoretically, it seems that a lower rate of the mark would have been more advantageous to Germany in striving to cope with an import surplus, since overvaluation acted as a premium in the case of imports, as an inhibitor when it came to exports. However, as pointed out before, Germany was not averse to having surplus imports from countries with whom accounts were settled by clearing.

This artificial rate of the mark made it easier for exporters to Germany to get higher prices in their national currency than they could have obtained had the rate been normal. Moreover, in many instances the Germans paid prices which were well above the international level to strengthen their relations with the countries of East-Central Europe. At the same time, owing to her clearing arrangements, and to her power and political influence, Germany had no fear that her exports would actually be reduced because of overvaluation of the mark. Although German export prices which had been below the British before the crisis surpassed them by 10 to 20 per cent in the thirties, the Danube countries mostly bought the proposed quantities of German export goods, since clearing afforded ways and means for restoring balance.

The Germans thought it even a momentary advantage for a considerable difference to exist temporarily between export and import levels. There is documentary evidence to confirm that their foreign trade showed a debit balance in every relation.

That Germany in her new situation had to increase her trade with the countries of Southeastern Europe which were amenable to clearing arrangements and that these countries were to be drawn on as sources of raw material at a growing rate do not in themselves explain the debit balance. The less so because before 1933 a noteworthy surplus in the balance of trade was attained in transactions with the same countries. Increasing imports of food and raw materials might have been covered by larger exports of industrial products. But it came about differently.

By the end of 1934 it became clear that considerable German liabilities had accumulated on clearing accounts, rising to 14-15 million pengös at times in the case of Hungary. "This accumulation of marks," it was stated, "may be ascribed to the forced purchases of the Germans on our markets.[5]

From the beginning of 1935 to the autumn of that year German debts were slightly reduced, to under 9 million pengös in September, increasing again as a result of large supplies of livestock and meat. From 1931 to 1936, that is in three years, German debts not settled by supplies of goods reached 46 million pengös.

Her considerably increased imports from the countries of Southeastern Europe were not covered by German exports. At the end of 1936 German debts on clearing accounts amounted to 463 million marks, deriving for the most part from the countries of Southeastern Europe. The German debts stemming from arrears in the supply of goods in the twenties were shifted from the West to Eastern and Southeastern Europe.

The leaders of Nazi economic policy discussed the debit balance of their trade with the countries of Southeastern Europe on several occasions and reiterated in public statements, as did, for instance, Hjalmar Schacht in a speech at Leipzig in 1935: "The German government has no intention to increase German arrears in the supply of goods; we shall do our best to pay off these debts by exports as soon as possible." However, in reality—notwithstanding these high-sounding statements—it was untrue that the Germans wanted to balance their agrarian imports from the countries of Southeastern Europe by exports of their industrial products. As a matter of fact these German arrears in the supply of goods played a definite and important role in financing German rearmament.

Under the Nazi economic policy the financing of rearmament was not confined to domestic resources in the thirties. In addition to the powerful increase of the output of heavy industry and the limitation of home consumption, an important role was played by the acceleration of the accumulation of German capital at the cost of other countries. The Nazi government applied the method of refusing to pay any amortization or interest on huge loans raised by former administrations and of striving

[5] National Archives, Department of Economic Policy, Ministry of Foreign Affairs, German file no. 642, 1-3A., 16-23 report on talks of the joint commission on Oct. 3, 1934.

to take advantage of the opposite party in commerce. The conscious accumulation of German arrears in the supply of goods was closely connected with the latter endeavors. In the thirties Germany was simply unable to obtain any foreign loan, although she was badly in need of import of capital to finance her high-speed preparations for war. Under such circumstances the idea of accumulating arrears in the supply of goods was suggested as the only feasible though peculiar way of importing capital.

Before 1933 German trade showed an active balance. In the same period the balance of payments of the country showed a deficit owing to reparations, withdrawal of capital, etc. After 1934 the situation changed as execution of the Neuer Plan got under way. The demands of rearmament led to a debit balance in foreign trade. This and the deficit of other financial obligations could be covered only by arrears in goods on clearing accounts, which actually provided short-term credits. This was all the more favorable for Germany as such a move implied a form of veiled credit unencumbered by interest. The latter momentum was closely connected with the wish of the Nazi economic leaders to conceal by hook or by crook the true character of the German arrears in the supply of goods. What really did happen was that the economically less developed countries of Southeastern Europe which had suffered grievously from the crisis helped Nazi rearmament with their own resources in the form of short-term credits, while Nazi propaganda claimed that they were receiving generous support from Germany.

By the time World War II was imminent, Nazi economic policy had contrived to bring all the countries of East-Central Europe under German influence. The objective of making these countries into a base of food and raw materials for the German economy, more accurately for the German war economy, and to prepare thereby their adjustment to German *Grossraumwirtschaft* had practically been achieved. German economic policy succeeded in systematically increasing foreign trade with the countries of Southeastern Europe.

In 1937 total German foreign trade amounted to only 40 per cent of the 1929 value, but trade with Southeastern Europe reached the 1929 level (Table 11-1). Trade with this region far exceeded the 1929 volume when the fall in prices is taken into account. These figures alone afford

Table 11-1. German Foreign Trade with
Southeastern Europe,* 1929–1938

Year	Export		Import	
	Million marks	*Per cent*	*Million marks*	*Per cent*
1929	585.0	4.3	516.1	3.8
1933	154.3	2.8	138.5	4.7
1934	170.6	3.9	248.2	5.6
1935	252.6	5.9	319.1	7.7
1936	374.9	7.4	386.9	9.2
1937	555.7	9.4	574.0	10.5
1938	553.3	10.4	536.0	9.9

*Bulgaria, Hungary, Yugoslavia, and Rumania.
Source: Based on *Statistischen Jahrbüchern des Deutsches Reiches,* 1929–1938.

insight into the territorial regrouping of German foreign trade as a result of Nazi economic policy.

As shown in Table 11-2, German foreign trade with Southeastern Europe increased markedly after Hitler came to power, demonstrating the policy of integration into the German economic *Lebensraum* achieved in this area.

The percentage increase in Southeastern Europe's trade with Ger-

Table 11-2. Territorial Regrouping of German Foreign Trade, 1929–1937

Region or Country	*Per Cent of German Imports*				*Per Cent of German Exports*			
	1929	*1932*	*1935*	*1937*	*1929*	*1932*	*1935*	*1937*
Southeastern Europe	4.3	3.5	5.9	9.4	3.8	5.0	7.7	10.5
Near East	1.4	1.3	3.4	3.6	1.4	2.5	3.8	9.0
Latin America	7.3	4.1	9.1	11.0	11.4	9.6	13.1	15.5
Northern Europe	10.2	9.4	11.4	10.2	7.3	6.4	9.9	12.1
Western Europe	26.2	31.9	26.1	22.6	15.7	15.1	14.1	12.6
Great Britain	9.7	7.8	8.8	7.3	6.4	5.5	6.2	5.7
U.S.A.	7.4	4.9	4.0	3.5	13.3	12.7	5.8	5.2
Other countries	33.5	37.1	31.3	32.4	40.7	43.2	39.4	43.6

Source: Vierteljahrshefte zur Wirtschaftsforschung des Institut für Konjunkturforschung 1939–40, Heft 1, 75, 77.

many does not disclose its rapidly growing role in supplying to the German economy food and several raw materials of strategic importance. Table 11-3 gives this specific information. Imports of all essential agrarian products and of several raw materials indispensable for the war economy greatly increased. If this trade was important for Germany, it was still more so for these small exporting countries. Germany thus assumed a decisive role in the foreign trade of Southeastern Europe.

The greatly increased role of Germany in the foreign trade of Southeastern Europe clearly shows the success of Nazi economic policy in divorcing the economy of these countries from the world market and chaining it to the German market. By 1937 Germany had not only regained through foreign trade her position lost after World War I, but had also acquired a much stronger economic influence over the countries of the region than she possessed formerly (Table 11-4).

As in other instances, an essential difference existed in the case of Czechoslovakia and Austria. The dissimilar economic structure of these countries was less suitable for applying the methods of Nazi *Grossraumwirtschaft*. There were no possibilities of economic penetration by buying their agrarian surplus and there was little opportunity to establish commercial relations with these industrialized countries of the Danube Valley, except for the purchase of a few industrial raw materials and primary products. This was also due to the different political situation which in the thirties strengthened the tendency of estrangement rather than of rapprochement in economic relations between Germany on the one hand and Austria and Czechoslovakia on the other. Whereas in the late twenties Austria had sent 27-28 per cent of her exports to Germany and received 17-21 per cent of her imports from Germany, by 1933 these figures fell to 16 and 20 per cent, by 1937 to 15 and 16 per cent, respectively. This trend was still stronger in Czechoslovakia. German exports fell from 23-25 per cent in the twenties to 20 per cent (1933), then to 15 per cent (1937), while imports from Germany sank from 21-24 per cent to 20 per cent by 1933, and to 15 per cent by 1937.

Hitler's Germany adopted other methods for the subjugation of these countries. Open pressure and military blackmail to the point of revolutionary attempts to overthrow the regime, economic blockade, prohibition of German tourism which was of economic importance to Aus-

Table 11-3. The Share of Southeastern Europe in
German Imports, 1929 and 1937 *(in per cent)*

Commodity	1929	1937
Wheat	2.4	36.9
Barley	37.4	80.5
Corn	6.8	32.9
Eggs	17.3	24.3
Fruit	24.5	35.0
Meat	7.0	35.0
Cattle	9.6	18.8
Pigs	0.0	21.0
Lard, bacon	0.1	31.0
Tobacco	47.8	61.3
Timber	24.5	35.0
Bauxite	37.2	62.1
Ores	2.9	28.9

Source: A. Basch, *The Danube Basin and the German Economic Sphere,* London, 1944, p. 181.

tria, limitation of foreign trade, and capturing former Austrian markets, all were weapons by which Austria was driven to the brink of economic ruin.

In Hitler's plans Austria and Czechoslovakia were not envisaged as zones of influence to be fitted into the pattern of German *Grossraumwirtschaft* but as areas to be annexed. The first steps in Nazi aggression, methodically prepared in the thirties, culminated in 1938-39 with the

Table 11-4. The Role of Germany in the Foreign
Trade of the Countries of Southeastern Europe,
1929–1937

Country	Exports to Germany as Per Cent of Total			Imports from Germany as Per Cent of Total		
	1929	1933	1937	1929	1933	1937
Bulgaria	29.9	36.0	43.1	22.2	38.2	54.8
Hungary	11.7	11.2	24.1	20.0	19.6	26.2
Rumania	27.6	16.6	19.2	24.1	18.6	28.9
Yugoslavia	8.5	13.9	21.7	15.6	13.2	32.4

Sources: Based on miscellaneous national statistics and *Statistisches Handbuch der Weltwirtschaft,* Berlin, 1937; A. Basch, *The Danube Basin and the German Economic Sphere,* London, 1944, p. 192.

Anschluss, the Munich Agreement, and the tragic series of events which crushed Czechoslovak independence. The year 1938 and the spring of 1939 actually opened a new chapter in the history of German aggression. This was due in no small measure to the strengthening of Germany's position in Europe and in East-Central Europe by the annexation of Austria and Czechoslovakia.

By 1939 the Danube countries were fettered by economic ties to Germany. The commercial relations had systematically increased during the thirties and were rapidly reinforced at the end of the decade, leading to the preponderance of Germany in the foreign trade of the region.

After the Anschluss and the occupation of Czechoslovakia German economic hegemony was strengthened not only by rapidly growing foreign trade but by dominating positions acquired in industry and banking through seizure of considerable Austrian and Czechoslovak interests stemming partly from the time of the Austro-Hungarian Monarchy, partly from later periods. In the case of Hungary the acquisitions by groups of German capitalists amounted to 125 million pengös, about 13 to 14 per cent of the total capital of 900 million pengös invested in mining and industry (representing, however, 50 per cent of all foreign investments in Hungary). Germany thus became the power which controlled the largest financial interest in Hungary, holding more than half of the foreign share capital (25 per cent) invested in Hungarian industry.

In Yugoslavia German capital had been insignificant earlier, but by 1937-39 it had a direct part in the financing of several Yugoslav firms

Table 11-5.   The Role of Germany in the Foreign
Trade of the Countries of Southeastern Europe,
1937 and 1939

	Exports to Germany as Per Cent of Total		Imports from Germany as Per Cent of Total	
Country	1937	1939	1937	1939
Bulgaria	43.1	71.1	54.8	69.5
Hungary	24.1	52.4	26.2	52.5
Rumania	19.2	43.1	28.9	56.1
Yugoslavia	21.7	45.9	32.4	53.2

Source: Based on national statistics.

(naturally in the exploitation of mines). The incorporation of Austrian and Czechoslovak interests was still more important. Austrian capital had widely ramifying investments in the Yugoslav economy in the form of shares and loans, while Czech capital controlled interests in the textile industry primarily. In 1939 investments amassed by Germany soared to 800 million dinars ($15 million), amounting to approximately 10 per cent of all foreign investments.

In prewar Bulgaria German capitalists had owned 5.2 per cent of all foreign investments; this ownership increased to 13.4 per cent when the Germans took possession of Austrian and Czech concerns, reaching third place after Belgian and Swiss holdings. Besides banks, German control grew strong in the developing heavy industry.

After the Anschluss and the Munich Agreement Germany launched a powerful drive to enhance her economic influence in the region. At this stage not only quantitative demands were raised. Besides laying down the final rate of exchange and fixing prices at a still more satisfactory level for themselves, the Germans conceived a scheme for the complete economic reorganization of the whole area in accordance with German demands.

These new German endeavors, expounded by the minister of economy, Funk, were concentrated on concluding long-term agreements by which Nazi Germany intended to gain full and permanent control over the greater part of foreign trade. It was also suggested that Germany should take over and reexport the remaining surplus products of these countries. True, this project was rejected by all the countries of East-Central Europe, even by Bulgaria which was economically the most closely dependent on Germany, but the Germans nevertheless again contrived to extort significant concessions in the new trade agreements.

Rumania revalued the mark, raised the rate of exchange, and undertook to keep her exports to Germany above the total of her former exports to Germany, Czechoslovakia, and Austria, and to increase the proportion of oil within the total. A new agreement, drawn up in the spring of 1939, was concluded in the spirit of complete economic subservience. Germany acquired virtually full monopoly of foreign trade, while the adjustment of Rumanian agriculture to German demands was confirmed officially. Joint German-Rumanian firms were founded to exploit Rumanian mineral treasures. In addition, free scope was assured to the activities of German capital and enterprise in Rumania, above all in approved branches regarded as national industry the further development of which was deemed desirable. Both to Rumania and to Yugoslavia Germany held out the hope of loans for investment and rearmament. In reality it was poorly carried out by war materials confiscated in Czechoslovakia.

New trade talks were started with Hungary in February 1939. The German attitude was characterized by the head of the Hungarian delegation in his report to the minister of foreign affairs as follows. "In general the tendency became obvious that Hungary was to be degraded to the level of a raw material base."[6] This tendency was formulated most graphically in the memorandum addressed by the Germans to the Hungarian government on the subject of Hungarian economic policy. The first part deals with Hungarian agriculture. Here the German attitude is stated clearly: ". . . Hungarian agriculture will have to adjust itself more efficiently to the requirements of the German market." This meant that Hungarian farming was expected to increase production mainly in the articles needed by the Germans (oilseeds, wheat, lard, fodder). The second part goes into issues of industry under the descriptive title "The Adjustment of Hungarian Industrial Production to the Exports Required by Germany." In this part of the memorandum the principles are laid down which the Germans wished to see followed in the development of German-Hungarian economic relations, emphasizing the view that in Hungary the development of agriculture and food industry alone was expedient. The memorandum categorically demanded the abrogation of customs duties on Hungarian imports and the cessation of all tax and credit allowances to Hungarian factories.

The new trade agreements signed in 1939 were concluded in the spirit of undisguised German dictatorship and unconditional hegemony. They were introductory to the process which was fully realized during the war when Nazi Germany virtually swallowed up the economy of East-Central Europe, degrading the countries of the region to the level of sectors of her own war economy.

---

[6] National Archives, Department of Economic Policy of the Ministry of Foreign Affairs, 1939, Res. 30.

12 Economic Growth and Structural Changes in the Interwar Period

From the survey of the interwar years in the preceding chapter, the two decades after World War I clearly emerge as very unfavorable for the countries of East-Central Europe. The economic chaos which followed the war, the period of severe inflation and delayed reconstruction, the Great Depression of the thirties, limited the effects of the boom to a few years. The prosperity of the late twenties, appearing mainly in the years 1926–28, and the upturn from 1936 to 1938 remained behind previous peaks.

Owing to the general effects of world economic conditions and to traits peculiar to the region, the rhythm of economic growth in East-Central Europe in the two interwar decades failed to equal the dynamism before World War I. Instead of the approximately 3 to 4 per cent yearly increase in national income before World War I the rate of growth sank to 1 to 2 per cent. In Hungary the growth in national income was about 1 per cent in the twenties calculated from the 1913 level (in the 1920 territory). Using 1924 as a base, the rate of growth was over 2 per cent, but the 1924 level was far below that of 1913. Much the same is true for the other countries. In general the prewar national income was reached in 1926–27. The growth was about 10 to 15 per cent everywhere until the outbreak of the crisis. The level of 1938, on the other hand, exceeded that of 1929 by about 15 to 20 per cent (except for Czechoslovakia).

Thus, apart from Bulgaria where the growth rate varied around 3 per cent, it did not exceed 1.5 per cent in any of the other countries, while the rise in the national income per head remained under 1 per cent in countries with high birthrates—Poland, Yugoslavia, and Rumania. In many respects the modernization of industry begun in the nineteenth century came to a standstill and failed to reach the desired stage of development. Instead of the dynamism so characteristic of all economic sectors before World War I, several important sectors showed complete stagnation and in others growth was weak and partial, appearing in certain branches but without providing a basis for general socio-economic advancement. Compared with the prewar level of development, progress was slowed down so much as to produce only minor structural modifications but no radical changes.

As mentioned before, the generally slow economic growth was closely connected with the almost complete absence of dynamism noticeable in important fields of the economy. One of the central factors of rapid growth from the middle of the nineteenth century, particularly from the last third, vigorous activity in railway building and, in general, the development of the infrastructure, practically came to a halt or showed very moderate advance. In these years the development of railways and of the traditional branches of communication in general made hardly any headway in the countries of East-Central Europe. The cessation of railway building in itself is not contrary to the demands of modern transport, since railway building and the growth of traditional branches of communication showed a tendency to stagnation in these decades everywhere. However, in countries on a higher level of development, the rapid advancement of modern means of transport was associated with the stagnation of traditional ones. The dynamic branches of transport and communications accomplished the building of a network of public roads and highways, and introduced the use of motorcars and regular air services. In many countries the steady expansion of the infrastructure was still accompanied by the execution of extensive housing programs.

The considerable activity in railway building before World War I in the countries of East-Central Europe was not continued in the interwar years. Unlike the Western countries, stagnation set in at a stage where the density of the railway network was far from the Western European standard. It was only in the most advanced countries of the region, in the Austro-Hungarian Monarchy, that 5 to 6 km. lines per 100 square km. approached the level of Western Europe, while the other countries, with 1 to 3 km. per 100 square km. showed a lag of several decades at the beginning of the present century. After territorial readjustments the railway situation improved slightly in Yugoslavia and Rumania, but the level was still low and very moderate new construction failed to raise it to the European standard.

According to estimates of the Polish ministry of transport, the unevenness in the railway network among the various Polish districts could have been raised to a uniform level by the building of new lines of about 6,000 km. Yet, between 1918 and 1938 lines of only 2,500 km. were constructed, increasing the total length of the Polish railways only to 18,300 km. by 1938. At this stage the railway network averaged 58 km. per 1,000 inhabitants, that is to say, about half of that in Western Europe. In Yugoslavia nearly 1,400 km. of railway lines were built in the interwar period. In Hungary practically no new lines were constructed. Rumanian and Bulgarian railways were in an undeveloped state: approximately 12,000 and 2,700 km. of railway lines, respectively, or 48 and 42 km. per 100,000 inhabitants in the 1930s.

Before World War II the length of railways was 3 to 4 km. per 100 square km. in the Balkan countries, less than half that in the countries of Western Europe at the turn of the century. Stagnation at this undeveloped level set in at the time because more modern branches of transport and communication took over.

The United States was the first major country to show a rapid increase in the number of motorcars and trucks. Before World War II there were 205 motorcars per thousand inhabitants. In Great Britain and France the figure was 43.4 and 49.2 per thousand, respectively, and in the other Western European countries 10 to 24 per thousand. However, in the most advanced of the countries under review, in Czechoslovakia, there were only 8.2 motorcars per thousand inhabitants, while the respective figures were 2.3 in Hungary, 1.5 in Rumania, and 0.7 in Poland. These very small percentages referred mainly to passenger cars, while modern transport by lorries was in a rudimentary stage. The total Czechoslovak, Hungarian, Polish, Yugoslav, Rumanian and Bulgarian figures show 0.56 lorries, tractors, and buses per thousand inhabitants in 1938.

The retarded development of modern transport which prevailed all over Europe in the interwar period is illustrated most graphically by the motorization indicator, which gives the number of motor vehicles in relation to the area and the population of the country. In 1938 the motorization indicator was 5.7 in fourteen countries of Europe, whereas in Czechoslovakia it was only 1.8, in Hungary 0.5, in Poland, Yugoslavia, and Rumania 0.3.

The primitive stage of modern telecommunication is shown by the total index of telephone, radio, and other telecommunication instruments along with the density of the railway network. It reveals that of the Danube countries Austria alone was on a Western European level; Czechoslovakia and Hungary were between 50 and 75 per cent of Western Europe's, while the Balkan states were under 50 per cent.

Cement consumption per head, as a direct and comprehensive index of house building and the construction of roads, throws light on the general level of infrastructure development. (However, in Eastern Europe cement consumption per head is a much less adequate indicator of boom in investments, because traditional building materials were not superseded by cement so extensively as in the West.) In Bulgaria, Rumania, Yugoslavia, and Czechoslovakia cement consumption increased slightly in the thirties over the twenties, but in Hungary and Austria it diminished. Even so, average consumption ranged between 15 and 25 kg. per head, except for Czechoslovakia and Austria, where it reached 60 to 70 kg., still far behind the 100 kg. per head in the Western countries.

A pattern similar to that in the development of communication may be observed in agriculture. If the rapid building of infrastructure was one factor in the advance which began at the close of the last century, the other principal event undoubtedly was the rapid development of agriculture on a capitalist basis. From the last third of the nineteenth century agriculture was rapidly modernized and production was doubled in most countries. The postwar situation and radically changed market conditions caused a severe setback which was hardly overcome when the world economic crisis dealt another blow. In the second half of the thirties there was again some improvement, as a result of which all the countries of the region surpassed the prewar level in varying degrees. In the countries of East-Central Europe—particularly in the typical agrarian countries—stagnation was more noticeable, and any rise in the total agrarian index may be ascribed to the agricultural growth of Austria and Czechoslovakia, both of them industrial countries. Livestock breeding shows a slightly, but not essentially, more favorable picture.

This insignificant growth itself defined the place and function of agriculture in the economic development of the interwar period. All the more so as growth, if any, came about mostly in the years after the crisis when larger production could contribute slightly to counterbal-

Table 12-1. Index of East-Central European Production of Principal Agrarian Products, 1924–1929 and 1934–1938 *(1909–1913 = 100)*

	1924–29	1934–38
Group 1		
(Austria, Czecho-		
slovakia, Hungary,		
Poland)	98	117
Group 2		
(Rumania, Bulgaria,		
Yugoslavia, Greece)	87	116

Source: I. Svennilson, *Growth and Stagnation in the European Economy*, Geneva, 1954, p. 248.

Table 12-2. Index of East-Central European Stocks of Cattle and Pigs, 1928 and 1934–1938 *(1913 = 100)*

	1928	1934–38
Group 1		
cattle	115	115
pigs	93	125
Group 2		
cattle	124	125
pigs	137	151

Source: I. Svennilson, *Growth and Stagnation in the European Economy,* Geneva, 1954, pp. 248–49.

ancing the loss of income from the steep fall of prices. This being the case, no branch of agriculture could perform its prewar function in the accumulation of capital.

It is worthwhile to look more closely at the factors which were responsible for changing agriculture—the leading sector of national economy in the countries of East-Central Europe—into the bottleneck of economic advancement. Structure of ownership, availability of capital, productivity, and the agrarian population, as well as market problems, must be considered as the decisive factors determining advancement and stagnation.

As regards structure of ownership, the postwar land reforms have been briefly described in the chapter on the twenties, which pointed out their inadequacy and deficiencies. There can be no doubt that, apart from Hungary, in most countries the old agrarian structure was strongly modified by the land reform, making it more just and proportionate.

However, in Poland and Hungary conservation of the large estates (in both countries about 45 per cent of the land remained in the hands of the big landowners) and the parallel landlessness of a considerable part of the agrarian population created fundamental problems. In the Balkan countries, owing to the inability of the peasant smallholders to procure a livelihood and to the permanent fear of pauperization, the situation was marked by official measures often contrary to rational economy, issued for the purpose of preventing pauperization.

In East-Central Europe contemporary estimates denoted holdings of 5 to 15 hectares as reasonably sound, so-called family farms which did not sell or hire labor but produced by intensive work enough for subsistence as well as for the market. This kind of farm was far from the dynamic economic development required to ensure accumulation of capital, but in the Balkan countries the great majority of the smallholder peasants possessed still smaller plots of land. In Yugoslavia over 75 per cent, in Bulgaria 60 per cent, of the farms were under 5 hectares, and the situation was similar in Rumania with a larger number of big estates and in Hungary with the strongest, most pervading remnants of feudal landownership. Singly, these smallholder peasants were unable to farm their land profitably, to make adequate investments and produce bigger crops. All this was coupled with the dismemberment of the property. (As a rule, a property consisted of 13 parcels of land.) In Poland 47 per cent of peasant farms also consisted of narrow strips of land.

In these countries, with an almost purely peasant population, the big problem of how to increase crops was presented by these disconnected tiny plots. In the countries with big estates, on the other hand, it was the magnitude of the property and the requisite capital which sharply conflicted and proved to be restraining forces, hindering the growth of agricultural production, while dwarf holdings, unable to support their owners, occurred here too among the peasantry. Thus, in the interwar period in East-Central Europe agriculture had to struggle against two evils, the Scylla of unprofitable tiny plots and the Charybdis of oppressive big estates which swallowed up everything. The problems caused by the division of land naturally became more acute after the crisis, because the question was in close correlation with other factors hampering advancement, mainly the problem of obtaining the requisite capital.

The acquisition of agricultural loans was sharply limited in the early twenties by lack of capital and severe financial difficulties. By the second half of the decade the situation improved, the financing of agriculture being made possible partly by the slow accumulation of capital at home but still more by substantial foreign credits. In the countries where the big estates dominated, most of the loans made available to agriculture, particularly large credits, went to the big landowners. In Rumania, where agriculture received no share of foreign loans, the big banks of

Bucharest allowed credits to owners of large landed property only where investment was safeguarded by satisfactory security. Rural organizations of credit service operated with state support, but cooperative banks did not dispose of enough capital to play an essential role in providing peasant farmers with funds.

In Hungary foreign loans were raised in the twenties partly in the form of debentures, while the big banks of Budapest were also liberal in lending on mortgage. If not all, at least the greater part, of these loans were granted to the big landowners, but neither on the large estates nor on peasant farms were actual investments in proportion to the credits obtained. As a matter of fact most of the big landowners did not use these credits for investments. Of the long-term foreign loans raised by Hungary approximately 300 million pengös ($60 million) went to agriculture. According to contemporary statistics, 50 per cent served to cover the purchase of land, consumption goods, and luxury items; therefore the money was not used as productive capital. Of the acquired loans approximately 33 per cent was spent on building, which may be regarded as partly productive utilization. Altogether 10 per cent was tied up in productive investments actually serving to increase working efficiency. Under such conditions certain improvements in machinery resulted, for in a few years several thousand tractors and motorized threshing machines were put into operation, and fertilizers began to be used. The big estates were nevertheless short of capital, and the general difficulties which hindered the accumulation of capital became sharply apparent.

In the countries with big estates the landed class were certainly in a more favorable position to raise capital than the peasantry, but in the peasant countries of the Balkans there was a more severe lack of capital than, for instance, in Hungary. Agriculture was given hardly any share in foreign loans, domestic accumulation of capital was lower, and the banks whose sphere of activities was not confined to agricultural credits mostly refrained from lending on mortgage.

Rural cooperative credit service was relatively better organized in Bulgaria, but these loans were intended to bring relief in unexpected difficulties or occasionally to tide peasants over when they lacked working capital rather than to be used as capital for investment. In Yugoslavia loans to finance agriculture remained unavailable even in years of prosperity though a system was devised to solve the problem. The fact that local banks exacted 20 to 50 per cent yearly interest on loans indicates the lack of normal credit. Most of these loans were granted for brief periods. Altogether, 26 per cent of agricultural credits were long-term, while 45 per cent of the agricultural mortgage loans to be used for development consisted of credits from private parties or merchants at usurious interest. This explains why the debts of peasants had for the most part nothing to do with the modernization and advancement of production. Of the loans raised by peasants with farms of 20 to 50 hectares, 50 per cent was spent on buying land, 25 per cent to pay off debts, 9 per cent to contruct buildings, and only 8 per cent went into improving production.

The debts of peasants with smaller holdings differ insofar as nearly one-third of the loans were spent on food, and a lesser part on buying land. A larger portion of credits were diverted to the construction of buildings, but the amounts expended on improving production were not greater here either.

In the thirties agricultural credit conditions badly deteriorated. In the countries where the bulk of credit derived from foreign loans and was related to the mortgage activities of the big banks there was a change for the worse. In the thirties merchant usury reminiscent of credit operations in the Middle Ages was not accompanied by sudden foreclosure of debts, but lack of capital became more acute and the terms of loans still more unfavorable.

Thus, in the interwar period both the large estates and the peasant farms ran into heavy debts in East-Central Europe without modernizing agriculture or improving techniques and production adequately. In 1932 in Hungary debts amounted to 36 per cent of the value of big estates, to 40 per cent of the value of peasant holdings. Calculated in terms of gross income this meant that even on the basis of the relatively favorable prices of 1929, debts rose to 78 per cent of the yearly income of Hungarian agriculture. This proportion was much higher by the thirties. In Yugoslavia debts amounted to 80–90 percent of the agricultural income.

These huge sums of money were, however, either squandered in an "aristocratic" manner or spent on purchasing land. With the peasant farmers considerable amounts were simply spent on buying bread and bacon from the grocer or at best on building a house. Thus agrarian credit service and the modernization of agriculture by the aid of loans present a very unfavorable picture.

All this was inseparably connected with the stagnation of agrarian productivity in the interwar period. The development of agrotechniques and the mechanization of agriculture made hardly any progress in these years and the grave setbacks of the thirties reduced to nought the accomplishments of the more favorable late twenties. For instance in Hungary, the number of tractors failed to reach the prewar peak of 7,000. In the thirties there was one tractor per 829 hectares in Hungary, one per 8,400 hectares in Poland, and the situation in the Balkan countries was similar. In Rumania with 2,000 tractors, there was one per 4,600 hectares; in Yugoslavia with an equal number of tractors there was one per more than 3,400 hectares. In Bulgaria 2,800 tractors were in operation, one per roughly 1,500 hectares. By contrast, in England and Sweden the figure was one per 135 hectares, in Italy one per less than 400 hectares. The extremely slow progress of mechanization in other spheres is indicated by the fact that in Hungary the prewar mechanization of threshing was followed by only minimal mechanization of other kinds of work. In the thirties there was one harvester per 1,000 hectares. Considering the areas sown with cereals, this provided for the use of reaping machines in 15 per cent of the grainfields.

There was still hardly any agrarian mechanization in Bulgaria. In 1936, in addition to 254,000 iron ploughs, 450,000 wooden ones were also in use—an example of the persistence of medieval techniques. Altogether, 100 sowing machines were to be found in the country, while the less than 4,000 threshing machines could only do half of the threshing. Reaping was mostly done in the traditional manner with sickles. In Yugoslavia the number of iron ploughs was more than double the number of wooden ones, but one-third of the ploughs in use consisted of some 300,000 wooden ones.

The use of fertilizers remained on such a primitive level that it may be said to have made hardly any progress. The quantity of fertilizers used nevertheless increased considerably—fourfold in the postwar decade in Hungary, for example. However, in the next decade the use of fertilizers declined by two-thirds. In Yugoslavia it trebled in 1929, and was reduced by half in the thirties. The extraordinary backward-

Table 12-3   Fertilizer Use in
European Agriculture, 1936–
1938

	Kilograms per Hectare (pure nutritive material)
Holland	311
Belgium	125
Germany	100
Hungary	2
Yugoslavia	1
Bulgaria	1.8
Rumania	0.2

Source: Based on International Yearbook of Agricultural Statistics.

ness in the use of fertilizers is shown in Table 12-3. Consequently, there could be no essential change in productivity.

In the interwar years crop averages were still around the levels attained at the beginning of the century. This is clearly demonstrated in Table 12-4, though distortions caused in this respect by territorial

Table 12-4.   Crop Production in East-Central Europe, 1903–1912 and
1934–1938 *(in quintals per hectare)*

	Wheat		Rye		Corn		Potatoes		Sugar-Beets	
Country	*(1)*	*(2)*	*(1)*	*(2)*	*(1)*	*(2)*	*(1)*	*(2)*	*(1)*	*(2)*
Austria	14	17	14	15	15	26	83	137	242	260
Czechoslovakia[a]	15	17	15	16	5	21	91	135	260	290
Hungary	13	14	12	11	18	20	80	73	254	210
Bulgaria	11	13	8	10	13	12	38	61	129	160
Yugoslavia[b]	9	11	8	8	13	18	41	62	195	190
Rumania	11	10	9	9	13	10	75	77	205	150
Poland	12	15	11	13	11	14	103	138	243	270

Sources: Based on I. Svennilson, *Growth and Stagnation in the European Economy,*
Geneva, 1954, p. 251; S. Zagoroff, J. Végh and A. Blimovich, *The Agricultural Economy
of the Danubian Countries, 1935–1945,* Stanford, 1955, p. 127, N. Spulber; *The State and
Economic Development in Eastern Europe,* New York, 1966, p. 84.
(1) = yearly average for 1903–12.
(2) = yearly average for 1934–38.
[a] 1901–10 Bohemian territories.
[b] 1909–14 Serbia.

Table 12-5. Index of European
Production per Hectare of Seven
Chief Crops Between 1931 and
1935

Europe	100
Czechoslovakia	112.5
Austria	113.4
Bulgaria	74.3
Hungary	85.2
Rumania	63.0
Yugoslavia	69.2

Source: W. Moore, *Economic Demog-
graphy of Eastern and Southeastern Europe,* Geneva, 1945, p. 193.

changes cannot be disregarded. With the exception of Czechoslovakia
and Austria, the countries of the area lagged behind the European average in crop production in the early 1930s (Table 12-5).

Small crops and low productivity were of all the greater consequence
as they exerted an adverse influence on the profitability of agriculture
as well as on its capacity to accumulate capital. Moreover, the numerically large agrarian population tended to render the problem of low
productivity more acute. In most of East-Central Europe the population was very dense for countries of agrarian character. This very density of population exerted a permanent pressure on the labor market,
for rural districts concealed a large surplus of agrarian manpower. In
value of agricultural production per agrarian head in the early 1930s
the countries of the region were exceedingly backward in productivity.
With the European average equal to 100, only Austria (134) and Czechoslovakia (105) exceeded this: the index was 78 for Hungary, 48 for Rumania, 47 for Bulgaria, and only 38 for Yugoslavia.

Masses of the rural population could not find any employment, agricultural laborers were out of work the greater part of the year (in Hungary working days totaled an average of 105 per year). The members of
families owning land were not occupied the entire year either. According to certain statistics, out of the total agrarian population of East-
Central Europe (Czechoslovakia, Hungary, Poland, Yugoslavia, Rumania, Bulgaria) numbering approximately 60 million, about 25 per cent

were unemployed. The low productivity is shown by statistics comparing the actual agrarian population which would have been required had productivity equaled the average European level. Czechoslovakia would have needed 5 per cent more (while Slovakia had an excess of 39 per cent, Sub-Carpathia 58 per cent). Hungary would have had a surplus of 22 per cent, Rumania of 51 per cent, Bulgaria of 53 per cent, Yugoslavia of 61 per cent. This manpower might have found employment in industry or in various services. According to these statistics, in the whole area there was a 50 per cent excess of labor in 1930.

Lack of capital and low productivity together with agrarian over-population formed a vicious circle which could have been broken only by some radical change in market conditions. However, in the interwar period there was no sign of such a radical change in Europe. Owing to agrarian overpopulation and relatively weak industrialization, the domestic markets did not show any development. They were unable to absorb in any considerable measure the surplus of agrarian products or rural population. Foreign markets did not expand either. In the absence of Russian competition theoretically the countries of East-Central Europe might have enlarged their exports, but overseas countries were quick to fill the void.

In reality even in the thirties agrarian exports in most countries of Eastern Europe (at least in the most valuable cereals) remained 20 to 25 per cent below the level attained before World War I. (This was partly due to the small increase in cereal consumption in Europe of only 3 per cent between 1910 and 1938.) Between 1909 and 1913 the wheat exports of the Danube countries amounted to 13 per cent of world exports. In the twenties the figure was only 4 per cent, and in the late thirties it was still no higher than 8 per cent. Hence the traditional branches did not ensure any noteworthy opportunity for developing markets.

The situation on foreign markets was more favorable for the vegetable and animal products raised by intensive farming. A slow transformation in this direction was certainly discernible in the Danube countries. Noteworthy advance in growing fruit and chickens in Hungary, tobacco and garden produce in Bulgaria, and oilseeds in Rumania are typical of the thirties. At this time livestock breeding also became more prominent. However, a radical transformation which might have lifted agriculture out of its stagnation could not come about because the capital required for the change was unavailable. There were not adequate domestic markets or increased consumption, nor was there any strong migration to secondary and tertiary branches or any consequent growth in the rate of accumulation.

This combination of problems determined the position of agriculture and made it the weakest point in the national economies of East-Central Europe both economically and socially. In this respect economic development and the advance of industrialization were deprived of the basis which might have been offered by agrarian expansion.

Thus in the interwar period the principal sectors of the economy were marked by slackening and stagnation in the countries of East-Central Europe. In the absence of general economic dynamism industry became the chief factor of growth. This was promoted by the achievement of national independence and the subsequent introduction of industrial isolation, by industry-advancing nationalist economic policy flowing from the political aspirations of the Danube countries. The efforts to strengthen independence through economic self-sufficiency have been dealt with in connection with the postwar years. Except for Austria and Czechoslovakia where such endeavors were realized on the widest scale in agriculture, the development of industry became the focus of economic policy in the countries of Eastern Europe and the Balkans. The weight of industry having been slight in these countries and imports of finished goods considerable, it was not difficult to attain industrial progress by the development of certain inactive branches of industry in the spirit of independence.

At the same time the circumstances described also exerted a contrary, restraining effect on industrialization. Amidst the general stagnation of the economy industry certainly became prominent as the most dynamic branch, but the stagnant environment checked its advance, by limiting markets. Protective tariffs did give an impetus to industrialization by restricting the import of finished goods from other countries, but earlier financial relations having been broken off, the capital required by the new demands of modern technical development could be obtained only in part during the brief period of roughly five years from 1924 to 1929. Therefore, in the new situation the growth of industrial production took place under conditions which were in many respects more unfavorable than previously, and the rate of development failed to equal that of the years before World War I.

Moderate industrial growth is shown by the output of Hungarian manufacturing industry in the interwar period (Table 12-6). Though the growth of output was larger in Hungarian manufacturing industry than in other branches of the economy, the slowing down of the rate of development is nevertheless striking. Unlike the average yearly growth of over 5 per cent in the last third of the nineteenth century and the beginning of the twentieth, in the decades under review the average yearly growth remained under 1.5 per cent.

In some of the countries in question the rate of industrial growth was still more unfavorable than in Hungary. Though they were at different levels of development and the sources of their economic troubles were dissimilar in many respects, Austria and Poland both suffered the hardships of readjustment during the whole interwar period. Austrian heavy industry and certain consumer industries having become oversized, the shrinking of business due to the loss of markets which had formerly been within the borders of the Monarchy could only be counterbalanced by the advancement of some branches connected with the transformation of the structure of industry.

As a result of these changes Austrian industry did not develop very much in the interwar period. In 1929 production was 18 per cent higher than before World War I, but in 1937 it reached only 83 per cent of the 1929 value, implying that before World War II the output of Austrian industry was similar to that preceding World War I. As a whole, therefore, the period was one of stagnation. So it can be seen that in the interwar period the Austrian economy had to grapple with permanent massive unemployment, economic confusion, and depression.

In Poland the decline of production due to the disparate economic levels of the districts, as well as to the ravages of war and to setbacks in branches which had formerly relied on supplies to Russian markets, particularly in textiles and certain branches of machinery, could be made good only by the war industry set up during the boom of the thirties, by the chemical industry, and by certain new branches of the food industry. In the long run the volume of industrial production nevertheless showed only a moderate increase, verging on stagnation (Table 12-7).

The industrial development of the Balkan countries presents a different picture and a more favorable one as regards the rate of growth. By the aid of isolation and a better foothold on the home market, ear-

Table 12-6. Index of Manufacturing Output in Hungary, 1921–1938 *(1913 = 100*)*

Year	Index
1921	51
1929	112
1932	84
1938	128

*Within the territorial boundaries of 1920.

Source: I. T. Berend and Gy. Ránki, *The Development of Manufacturing Industry in Hungary, 1900-1944*, Budapest, 1960, p. 86.

Table 12-7. Index of Industrial Output in Poland, 1921–1938 *(1913 = 100*)*

Year	Index
1921	47
1929	86
1932	52
1938	105

*Within the territorial boundaries of 1920.

Sources: I. Svennilson, *Growth and Stagnation in the European Economy*, Geneva, 1954, p. 305; *Concise Statistical Yearbook of Poland, 1939–1941*, p. 67.

lier nonexistent or poorly producing branches of consumer goods were developed successfully. The grave crises of the thirties in the sale of agrarian products and the difficulties of acquiring foreign exchange gave a new impetus to efforts aimed at achieving industrial self-sufficiency. Finally, industrial production, having started from a very low level, nearly doubled in a relatively brief time.

In the more advanced countries vigorous development generally took place in the atmosphere of industrial prosperity following World War I, and after the depression very moderate progress ensued in the second half of the thirties. Hence it is noteworthy that in most of the countries industrial development assumed a more rapid rate in the thirties. In Western Europe the increase of industrial output was less than 13 per cent from 1928 to 1937, while in the countries of East-Central Europe it was over 37 per cent. (This was due partly to the economic crisis having been much more serious in the West than in the East; in the West the index of production was 72.3, in the East 86.6 at the worst stage in 1932.)

Thus, the rate of industrial growth in the interwar period resulted on the one hand from enhanced protection of the domestic market and other forced measures introduced after the crisis and on the other from the narrowing international markets of the exporting industrial countries of Western Europe. The latter process—accompanied by the shrinking of home markets in the thirties—was also noticeable in Austria where the progress of the twenties was brought to nought by the

Table 12-8.   Index of Growth in Output
of Manufacturing Industry, 1929–1938
(1913 = 100*)

Year	Rumania	Yugoslavia	Bulgaria
1929	137	140	179
1932	113	116	195
1938	180	190	245

*Within the territorial boundaries of 1920.
Source: Calculated on the basis of data in the
following books: V. Axenciuc, "La place occupée
par la Roumanie dans la division mondiale capi-
taliste á la veille de la seconde guerre mondiale,"
Revue Roumaine d'Histoire, 1966, no. 4; M.
Kukoleca, *Industrija Jugoslavije, 1918–1933,* Bel-
grade, 1940; M. Mirković, *Ekonomska struktura
Jugoslavije,* Belgrade, 1952; A. Gerschenkron,
Economic Backwardness in Historical Perspective,
Cambridge, 1962.

setbacks of the thirties. The development of Czechoslovak industry
showed a similar tendency. The considerable prosperity of Western
Europe in the decade after World War I spread to Czechoslovakia upon
extension of her home markets and the introduction of new branches of
production. By 1929 the output of industry exceeded the level of 1913
by 40 per cent. However, the improvement that followed the crisis on
the whole only made up for the setbacks: in 1938 Czechoslovak industry
produced 97 per cent of the output of 1929.

In the interwar period the generally moderate rate of advance in industrial output was associated with a regrouping of essential branches
in the countries of East-Central Europe. Some branches showed considerable decline while others multiplied their output, resulting in overall stagnation or growth. For instance, the slow growth of Hungarian industrial production derived from extreme shifts occurring when the
output of the formerly important food industry sank to three-fourths of
the prewar level while the production of the weakest sector, the textile
industry, rose fourfold. Reversal of growth rates between the food and
textile industries, with development slowed down in the former and accelerated in the latter, was in general characteristic of the Balkan coun-

Table 12-9.   The Structure of Industry in East-Central Europe,
1913–1938 *(in per cent)*

	Hungary		Poland		Rumania		Yugoslavia		Bulgaria	
Branch	*1913*	*1938*	*1913*	*1938*	*1922*	*1938*	*1913*	*1938*	*1913*	*1938*
Iron, metal,										
and machines	25.8	28.7	20	20	12	17.4	20	17	6	6
Chemicals	7.7	9.1	3.6	8	22.1	21.4	3	8	4	2
Textiles,										
leather, and										
clothing	11	21.3	44	26	19.7	26.1	9	26	24	22
Food	41.2	28.8	18	31	27.4	22.6	59	27	58	43

Sources: Based on national statistics; *Industrial Statistics,* OEEC Statistical Bulletins,
Paris, 1955; I. T. Berend and G. Ránki, *The Hungarian Manufacturing Industry: Its Place
in Europe, 1900–1938,* Etudes Historiques, Budapest, 1960.

tries as well. Table 12-9 points up some of these changes. It shows trends
of development rather than an accurate distribution of the various
branches. In the case of Hungary statistics have been calculated with-
.out regard to territorial changes. For Rumania comparison was based on
data from 1922. For Poland and Yugoslavia the comparisons are inaccurate because the prewar figures refer to the Polish Kingdom and to
Serbia. Nor has exact analysis for each branch been possible, for in
certain instances the production values of mining and metallurgy could
not be separated from those of the iron, metal, and machine industries.
Moreover, the heading "textile, leather, and clothing industries" sometimes refers only to the textile industry; sometimes to the whole of light
industry.

The figures reflecting the structural changes of manufacturing industry reveal that in the interwar period in the countries of East-Central
Europe textile and other branches of light industry considerably advanced (with the exception of Poland), rising to one-fifth or one-fourth
of total production. Food industries generally declined in a considerable
measure. In the meantime the share of the processing branches of heavy
industry stagnated or increased very moderately.

In estimating these principal trends it should, of course, be noted that
in the countries involved earlier blatant disproportions were being balanced by these developments. Even so, the transformation of industrial

structure in East-Central Europe produced trends which were contrary to the modern demands of technical developments as compared with the processes taking place in Western Europe. In these Western countries the interwar period witnessed the continuation of the processes begun around the turn of the century and led to an ample flow of capital into heavy industry and to the increasing strength of this sector in relation to other branches of industry. The share of textile and other light industries considerably diminished.

Although comparison is rendered more difficult because data from the early years of the century were not calculated on the same basis as statistics from 1938, and regrouping within branches must lead to considerable inaccuracy, the following data nevertheless present the trend of development.

The share of British heavy industry in the total output of manufacturing industry increased from 32 per cent in 1913 to 49.5 per cent by 1938. During the same period the share of German heavy industry rose from 45 per cent to 58.5 per cent. From 1900 to 1938 the share of heavy industry in France increased from 25 per cent to 46.6 per cent; in Belgium from 29 per cent in 1898 to 55.8 per cent in 1938. Swedish heavy industry increased from 34 per cent of the total output in 1913 to 47.3 per cent by 1938; in the four decades from the turn of the century the share of heavy industry rose from 19 per cent (in 1897) to 36.4 per cent. In Holland where the share of heavy industry was not more than 20 per cent in 1920, it increased to around 50 per cent of the total manufacturing production by 1938. In Italy heavy industry supplied 54 per cent of total industrial production, in Norway 47.8 per cent.

On the other hand, the textile industry became much less significant. Its share in the total output of British manufacturing industry fell from 26 per cent in the prewar years to 8 per cent on the eve of World War II. In Germany it declined from 19 per cent to 7 per cent; in France from 37 per cent at the turn of the century to less than 13 per cent by 1938; in Holland from 16 per cent in 1920 to 9.3 per cent by 1938.

Therefore, the modification of the one-sidedness of industrial structure in the first decades of the twentieth century in the countries of East-Central Europe, altering the excessively large share of the food industry and the disproportionately small share of other branches of light industry, reflects a tendency contrary to the structural changes which ensued in Western Europe. Textiles and other branches of light industry advanced rapidly in East-Central Europe when their importance was diminishing in developed industrial countries. But at the same time there was no precipitate advance in the processing branches of heavy industry as seen in the West. Yet the whole course of industrial developmemt in the interwar period and the domestic distribution of the production of manufacturing industry in the developed industrial countries clearly show that before World War II heavy industry was the most decisive indicator of industrial level, particularly the development of machine industry and the magnitude of its share in total industrial production. This lag in the development of heavy industry considerably increased in the period under review. The undeveloped state of machine industry deserves special attention. In contrast to the 20 per cent of that branch in total industry in Western Europe, in Hungary it was 10 per cent of total production, in Yugoslavia not even 1 per cent. In the Balkan countries, the industrially most undeveloped region of Europe, heavy industry was limited to branches of exploitation or primary processing, while there was no machine industry at all.

In appraising the results of industrial development in the interwar period we can attempt to determine the level achieved before the outbreak of World War II and the position occupied by the East-Central European countries. The share per country in the total population and in the industrial production of Europe is shown in Table 12-10.

Before World War II—and in general in the period of modern capitalism—*approximately two-thirds of European industrial output was produced by the three big powers*. Except for France the share of these countries in industrial production was more than double their share in the population. Notwithstanding their advanced industry the small countries could supply only a negligible part of total European production, yet the share of Belgium, Sweden, and Switzerland was larger than the share of their population. Near this group stood Czechoslovakia and Austria, which accounted about equally for production and population. Judged by the same criteria Hungary showed a lag of nearly 60 per cent, and underdevelopment was still worse in Poland and the Balkan countries.

The above picture may be supplemented by one showing value of industrial production in the countries of Eastern and Western Europe

Table 12-10.   Percentage Distribution of
Population and Industrial Production in
Europe, by Country, 1938

	Population	Industrial Production
Great Britain	11.7	23.7
Germany	16.8	32.1
France	10.2	11.2
Belgium	2.1	2.9
Switzerland	1.0	1.4
Sweden	1.5	2.7
Czechoslovakia	3.7	3.1
Austria	1.7	1.4
Hungary	2.2	0.9
Poland	8.5	2.5
Bulgaria	1.5	0.2
Rumania	4.8	0.8

Source: Industrialization and Foreign Trade, Geneva,
1945, pp. 13 and 26.

(Table 12-11). The East-Central European countries exhibit the most
striking backwardness in industrial production per head. The Austrian
and Czechoslovak figures were two-thirds of the average of fifteen Western countries. Hungarian industrial production per head was only 43
per cent of the Western average, or slightly below that of 1913 (43.8
per cent). Poland was about one-third, Rumania one-sixth. On the other
hand, in several less developed European countries—Italy, Finland,
etc.—the average level considerably increased.

The moderate rate of industrial development and its low level were inadequate to transform the underdeveloped economic structure of the
countries of East-Central Europe. In the interwar period industrial and
in general nonagrarian populations increased markedly. Between 1920
and 1940 there was an average increase of 33 per cent in the nonagrarian
population of Europe. During the same period the increase was over
100 per cent in Rumania, Bulgaria, and Yugoslavia, nearly 100 per cent
in Poland, and more than 50 per cent in Hungary. In the occupational
distribution of the population, however, there was hardly any or only
slight change. In 1910 and in 1939, 80 per cent of the active population

Table 12-11.   Industrial Production in European
Countries, 1938

Country	Value of Industrial Production (in million dollars)	Industrial Production per Capita (in dollars)
Great Britain	$6,696	140
Germany	9,066	132
France	3,155	76
Belgium	830	96
Sweden	771	122
Holland	665	77
Austria	400	59
Czechoslovakia	875	57
Hungary	241	26
Poland	711	21
Rumania	234	12

Source: I. Svennilson, *Growth and Stagnation in the European Economy,* Geneva, 1954, p. 306.

worked in agriculture in Rumania. A quite insignificant, less than 2 per cent, decline came about between 1910 and 1940 in Bulgaria in the 80 per cent agrarian population. In Yugoslavia the 79 per cent figure of 1920 fell only to 76 per cent. Polish and Hungarian records indicate a slightly more marked change and more modern distribution in the ratio of active population. Between 1920 and 1940 the agrarian population was reduced from 72 per cent to 65 per cent in Poland, from 56 to 51 per cent in Hungary.

Thus no major change ensued in the socio-economic structure. Industrial development did not bring about any essential change in the relative level or in the position of the countries of this area. The distribution of the population in European countries of varying type of development is illustrated in Table 12-12.

The peculiar demographic development of Eastern Europe helped to preserve its underdeveloped level. The increase in the industrial labor force, though not insignificant, was insufficient to absorb the rapid growth of population; therefore, in most countries it could not afford an outlet for the surplus agrarian population. Whereas in Europe

Table 12-12.   Percentage Distribution of European Population by
Occupation, 1930

Country	Agriculture	Industry and Mining	Trade and Communications	Other Branches
Highly developed industrial countries				
Great Britain	7	37	23	33
Germany	29	40	19	12
France	36	34	17	13
Belgium	17	48	21	14
Switzerland	21	45	19	15
Sweden	36	32	18	14
Czechoslovakia	28	42	14	16
Austria	32	34	18	14
Holland	21	38	23	18
Agrarian-industrial countries				
Spain	56	21	8	5
Portugal	51	19	9	21
Poland	65	17	8	10
Hungary	51	23	8	18
Agrarian countries				
Bulgaria	80	8	4	8
Yugoslavia	79	11	4	8
Rumania	78	7	5	10

Source: Industrialization and Foreign Trade, Geneva, 1945, p. 26.

the population showed a nearly 20 per cent growth between 1920 and
1940, in most of East-Central Europe the increase was much higher: in
Yugoslavia 35 per cent, in Bulgaria 32 per cent, in Rumania 30 per cent,
in Poland 27 per cent. In Hungary alone the increase corresponded to
the general European growth.

In the interwar period population growth was the most rapid in the
Balkan countries. This resulted largely from the death rate having been
considerably reduced, from about 20 to 15 per 1,000. Moreover, owing
to a smaller degree of urbanization and conservation of the rural way
of life, the birthrate continued to be much higher—around 30 per 1,000
—than in the industrialized countries.

This population growth, far exceeding the European average, was not
moderated by any outlet. Before World War I the countries of Eastern

Europe ranked foremost in emigration, but after the war mass emigration was stopped by American restrictions. In the interwar period altogether 400,000 people emigrated from East-Central Europe to America. Only a negligible number left Hungary, and it was perhaps Yugoslavia alone among the countries of the region from which there was mass emigration — 200,000 to 250,000, when repatriations are deducted.

As a result of these factors the countries of East-Central Europe by the outbreak of World War II failed to reach the stage of development where the number and proportion of the agrarian population were reduced. In some countries slight improvement may be noted in the proportion of the agrarian population, but its numerical increase continued.

From these statistics it becomes obvious that population distribution by occupation does not afford an accurate picture of the structural changes in the economy of the countries in question, for it shows less change than actually took place. The picture is more complete when distribution of national income for the various countries is shown. This index is all the more important for — unlike distribution per population — it throws light on the differences in technical level and productivity among the various branches (Table 12-13).

Table 12-13. Percentage Distribution of National Income by Economic Sector, 1920 and 1938

Country	Agriculture		Industry		Other Branches	
	(1)	*(2)*	*(1)*	*(2)*	*(1)*	*(2)*
Austria	24.8	35.0	47.0	43.0	28.2	22.0
Czechoslovakia	33	23.2	50.8	53.2	16.2	23.6
Hungary	41.8	36.5	29.8	35.7	28.4	27.8
Poland	—	39.0	—	32.2	—	28.8
Rumania	60.2	53.2	24.2	28.4	15.6	18.4
Yugoslavia	58.0	53.6	20.9	22.1	21.1	24.3
Bulgaria	71.4	63.3	5.6	18.3	13.0	18.4

Sources: See the relevant parts of the Bibliographical Summary for chapter 12.

(1) = 1920. For Austria, Czechoslovakia (Bohemia only), and Hungary, 1913 data calculated on territorial boundaries as of 1920.

(2) = 1938.

Thus the modernization of the economy through the growth of industry made considerable headway in East-Central Europe during the interwar period. On the eve of World War II the Balkan countries actually approached the level of development and the structure of the Hungarian and Polish economies a quarter of a century earlier, in the opening decades of the century. In Hungary and Poland the respective shares of agriculture and industry in total production displayed a tendency toward equalization, indicating the development of a typical agrarian-industrial structure. Austria and Czechoslovakia, on the other hand, presented the traits of industrialized economic structure after the pattern of Western Europe.

As a matter of fact, in 1938 the share of industry in the national income amounted to 60–70 per cent in the highly industrialized countries of Europe (Great Britain, Sweden, Germany, Switzerland, Belgium), and in other strongly industrialized countries it reached or exceeded 50 per cent (France, Holland, Denmark, Norway, Austria, Czechoslovakia, Italy). Hungary, Poland, and Finland, on the other hand, showed moderate development, inasmuch as 30 to 40 per cent of the national income came from industry. The picture is still less favorable in the Balkan countries where the share of industry was only around 20 to 25 per cent.

These figures also reveal that the sharp differences in the level of development did not lessen; the historical underdevelopment of East-

Table 12-14. Structure of Foreign Trade in East-Central Europe, 1938 *(in per cent)*

	Hungary		Poland		Rumania		Yugoslavia		Bulgaria	
	Exp.	*Imp.*	*Exp.*	*Imp.*	*Exp.*	*Imp.*	*Exp.*	*Imp.*	*Exp.*	*Imp.*
Industrial products	13.0	30.2	6.4	28.4	1.9	68.3	0.8	44.8	2.0	68.0
Raw or semi-finished products	31.7	61.5	65.1	54.1	64.3	27.3	49.5	50.1	66.6	31.5
Food and livestock	55.3	8.3	28.5	17.5	33.8	4.5	49.7	5.1	31.4	0.5

Source: N. Spulber, *The Economics of Communist Eastern Europe,* New York, 1957, p. 8.

Central Europe persisted. This is unmistakably manifested in the position occupied by these countries in the structure of foreign trade. Prior to World War II they still supplied food and bought finished industrial goods. There was little change from conditions in the opening years of the century. Whereas the import of finished industrial goods ranged between 30 and 70 per cent, export of such goods amounted to no more than 1 to 13 per cent. Moreover, 30 to 55 per cent of exports consisted of food and livestock, raw materials and semifinished goods making up half to two-thirds of the consignments from most countries.

Of course, the structure of Austrian and Czechoslovak foreign trade was very different. Characterized by the preponderance of industrial exports (in the case of Czechoslovakia 72 per cent) against large imports of raw materials and semifinished products (Czechoslovakia 58 per cent) and considerable imports of industrial products (30 per cent), it exhibited traits typical of industrialized countries.

The historical underdevelopment of the East-Central European countries and its persistence are also illustrated by a comparison of national income per head in Europe. The income per head was lower in every country of East-Central Europe than the $200 per head average national income for the twenty-four European countries. Compared with the

Table 12-15. National Income
per Capita in Europe, 1937

Great Britain	$440
Sweden	400
Germany	340
Belgium	330
Holland	306
France	265
Austria	190
Czechoslovakia	170
Hungary	120
Poland	100
Rumania	81
Yugoslavia	80
Bulgaria	75

Source: *Economic Survey of Europe,
1948,* Geneva, 1949.

European average even Austria (by 5 per cent) and Czechoslovakia (by 15 per cent) stayed a little bit behind. These levels were at most about half of the national income per head in the most advanced Western countries.

In Hungary and Poland national income per head was about half of the European level, and only one-fourth to one-fifth of that in the most highly developed European countries.

Evidently the exceedingly slow and clumsy modernization of economic life was insufficient to produce radical change in the economies of Eastern Europe, but it sufficed to deepen the contradictions which had become apparent at the beginning of the century. These contradictions were manifested in a certain degree by the contrasts between rural districts and towns, between agriculture and the more modern branches of economy.

Although capitalist transformation progressed rapidly or had already taken place, the villages and agriculture characterized by large feudal estates and peasant smallholders pursuing small-scale farming continued to represent traditional society as opposed to the towns, which were the home and the symbol of industry, commerce, and powerful banks. The superiority of mobile capital over real estate increased in this period as a result not only of actual development but also of economic policy, international financial difficulties, etc. In countries of still strongly agrarian character mobile capital was in a certain degree separated from, and in opposition to, the agrarian population. Owing to its organization, access to credit, relation to prices and positions of power, this mobile capital could rule the whole of economic life and gain ascendancy over the traditional agrarian sector.

The international market and credit conditions as well as prices only strengthened this tendency, which was further intensified by the general acceptance of the most modern forms of capitalism in big industry and financial life—introduced partly before World War I—while agrarian sectors and small-scale industry retained much of their traditional character. After the turn of the century, at least in the Balkan countries, modern forms of capitalism made their first appearance, but in the interwar period they became general in industry and financial life. It was particularly the formation of cartels to control industry which made headway. In almost every branch where noteworthy development was achieved in the interwar period a dominant position was acquired by a few large firms, naturally with the support of foreign capital.

Though nearly 4,000 manufacturing firms were active in Rumania around 1938, about two-thirds of the capital was controlled by only one hundred companies belonging to various branches. The situation was similar in Hungary where 43 per cent of the manpower and 52 per cent of the machine equipment were used by 100 out of the 3,000 factories. Advancing concentration certainly created a basis for monopoly. However, it would be one-sided to view monopolization as a mechanical consequence of the process of concentration. The widespread appearance of cartels in the interwar period was in every respect connected with the international aspects of the development of banks and industry. These monopolies were organized as part of the international monopolization processes, most of them having been set up to protect the market from domestic and foreign competition in the first place.

However, this defensive attitude swung over to one diametrically opposed where agriculture and consumers were concerned. Being safeguards of high profits, the monopoly organizations acted as the chief ransomers of the peasantry and the working classes through industrial and agrarian prices, through prices and wages, as well as through interest and income in the case of bank monopolies. Owing to the general absence of prosperity, industrial development could be financed only in part from the increase in the national income. A part of the income from agriculture and consumption was realized by the monopoly organizations, to be used in no small measure as a source from which industry was developed through self-financing. For instance, in Rumania in 1937 — when as a result of the anti-cartel atmosphere a law was introduced to restrict cartel activity, as in the other countries of East-Central Europe — the new law in reality did not provide for any noteworthy step except for the registration of the cartels. There were 94 cartel organizations uniting about 1,600 firms (1,203 of them in the chemical industry). These 94 organizations represented 50 per cent of the invested capital, 53 per cent of the machinery, and 23 per cent of the production value. (In the twenties only thirty cartels had been active.)

Though officially they were called cartels, in fact many of these organizations brought into being a higher form of monopoly. About 43 organizations, in addition to agreements for the protection of prices and the distribution of markets and/or production, set up a common body to arrange sales, acting as a syndicate. In certain branches, for example in iron and metal, in coal mining and timber, one or two big companies acquired unlimited influence and monopolized the home market. Since these were mostly key industries, monopolization also affected the position of nonmonopolized sectors, particularly the consumer branches.

In Hungary the situation was almost identical. Before the outbreak of World War I there were about 100 cartels, but by the late twenties their number may be estimated to have risen to 150 to 180. In 1931, 256 cartels were registered after the new cartel law had come into force, and by 1938 as many as 357 were kept on record. They controlled 41 per cent of total industrial production, including 95.9 per cent of the iron and metal industries, 83 per cent of stone and clay, and 100 per cent of coal mining.

In Poland there were 11 cartels in 1919. In 1929 there were already 100 which controlled 40 per cent of production. By 1936 their number increased to 266. Here too, the coal, iron, timber, and oil cartels were the strongest and the sugar cartel was equally active. The Polish cartels were members of several international institutions—for the control of timber and coal export, for the distribution of iron and steel markets in East-Central Europe, etc. In Yugoslavia the number of cartels grew from 30 in the twenties to 80 in the thirties, to control 25 per cent of investments. In Bulgaria numerous cartels were founded in the thirties which in reality acted as syndicates (with a common organization to effect sales). However, these cartels cannot be estimated to have controlled more than 20 to 30 per cent of industrial production. (Of course, in this respect Austria and Czechoslovakia were in the forefront. In these countries monopolies were not only strong, but they also cooperated intensively in the activities of international monopoly organizations.)

On the whole it may be stated that the spread of cartels and their rise to power were considerably promoted by the protective tariffs of the twenties, by the special obstacles of export and import trade, as well as by lack of capital. Though equally strong propaganda was carried on in the press against cartels in Hungary, Rumania, Yugoslavia, and Poland, and it was not difficult to prove the disparity between cartel prices and free prices or the role of the cartels in the gap between the prices of agrarian and industrial products, actually no effective measures were taken against them. Cartel laws were put into force in every country (Hungary, 1931; Poland, 1933; Rumania, 1937), but they provided only for compulsory registration and some state control. Of course, cartels might have been dissolved or their prices declared illegal, but such measures were rarely taken, and if so mostly in the case of insignificant cartels. The late thirties were marked instead by attempts of the state to interfere in branches overtaken by crisis and to break down competition by making cartel agreements obligatory.

As far back as before World War I, in accordance with the traditional line of industrial development, monopoly organizations were backed either by foreign capital which—though in a diminishing degree and not equally in every country—was still of outstanding importance in national economy, particularly in financial life and in industry, or by domestic bank capital. The banks of the Balkan countries and those of the former Monarchy were much less dependent on the banks of Vienna, yet their role and their financial policy did not undergo any essential change. Especially in the twenties they had a more or less indirect share in every noteworthy new enterprise and in enlarging firms.

As regards Austria, the gradual reduction of the oversized banks of Vienna in the twenties and their crisis in the early thirties did not bring any decisive change in the relations of industry and the banks or in the rule of high finance. In Czechoslovakia the situation was similar. In countries on a higher plane of economic development the decisive role of the banks in the economy was still more conspicuous and an important trait of the situation. The principal new element was that in independent Czechoslovakia a dominant influence was acquired by the big capitalists of Prague, first of all by the Živnostenska Banka which controlled 40 to 50 per cent of the total bank capital.

The Zivnostenska Banka controlled interests in every important branch of export, including the sugar, iron, steel, and machine industries, in distilleries and in the Skoda Works and numerous other large firms.

There was no change in the character of the relations between the banks and industry in Hungary either. The credit monopoly enjoyed by a few big banks of Budapest in the Hungarian economy before World War I was evidently strengthened by progress in the process of concentration, by the independence of the country, and by the weaker position of the Vienna banks. This monopoly was not affected by the Anglo-American loans of the twenties, since most of these credits reached Hungary through banks which pocketed a large share of the profit. The central position of certain groups of financiers close to these big banks was further emphasized by this credit monopoly, and so was their control over the whole of economic life, including agriculture, indirectly, and other sectors of the economy. Of the capital of the 426 banks of the country, 72 per cent was controlled by the nine leading banks, directly or through their affiliations; 60 per cent of the share capital of industrial companies was held by leading bank groups. The Hungarian General Credit Bank and the Hungarian Commercial Bank of Pest controlled over 50 per cent of Hungarian industry along with its heavy industry concerns.

In Yugoslavia the Croat financial system was superior to the financial means of the old Serbian Kingdom as regards capital, etc. Therefore Zagreb became the financial center of the new state after the war. As late as 1929, 47 per cent of the bank capital was in Zagreb. The Yugoslav banks gained strong influence over industrial firms through credits on current account. These credits moved around 50 per cent of the assets of banks and constituted the most important form of control in sugar, cement, and paper industries. In other cases establishment of banks and increase of capital stock were the decisive steps which established the control of the banks. For instance, between 1919 and 1924 the Bank of Jugoslavia participated in the foundation of 27 firms and in increase of capital stock in 47 companies. The First Croat Savings Bank exercised direct control over 30 industrial firms.

In Rumania a strong concentration of banks took place in the thirties as a result of which the leading role of the five big banks (Banca Romineasca, Banca de Credit Româna, Banca Comerciala Româna, Banca Comerciala Italiana si Româna, and Societatea Bancaru Româna) became still more clear-cut. By 1939 they controlled more than 50 per cent of all bank capital.

Three of the Rumanian banks—the Credit Româna, the Marmorosch Bank, and the Banka Commercial Româna—had extensive industrial concerns, the first chiefly in the timber, textile, and vegetable-oil branches, the third in machine and food industries. The leading big banks con-

trolled altogether 47 per cent of the share capital of industrial companies. Their participation in iron and metal industry (67 per cent)
and in the building industry (60 per cent) was still stronger.

Also in Bulgaria a few leading big banks became a dominating force
in economic life by 1929, when 30 per cent of capital was controlled by
seven big banks. Here, too, literature on economic history has shed light
on the close relations between the major industrial firms and the big
banks, though as a consequence of the undeveloped economy the centralization process was less advanced.

In Poland as a result of concentration the six banks came to control
about 50 per cent of the share capital. Owing to the strong indirect
role of the state, the share capital of the industrial firms controlled by
the banks may be put at approximately one-third of the invested capital.

The economic monopolization of the countries of the region and the
intertwining of industrial and bank capital were practically inseparable
from the activity of foreign capital. Before World War I the interests
controlled by foreign capital in the economies of these countries had
played a decisive role. The transformations following the war created a
situation where domestic capital gained ground so that import of capital,
which grew more buoyant in the mid-twenties, assumed the form of
loans, while direct investments of capital and industrial foundations
remained within modest limits. Earlier and newly acquired economic
positions were still of consequence, continuing to carry weight in the
most important banks and industrial firms and promoting the development of relations between bank interests and domestic as well as international monopolies.

As pointed out in connection with processes which occurred after
World War I, foreign capital continued to play a significant role even in
the most advanced countries of the region. In fact Czechoslovakia was
an exporter of capital, her capital turnover showing a credit balance
between 1925 and 1937, except for the three years of the crisis. Czechoslovakia had considerable foreign investments, about 12 per cent of
Yugoslavian and 5 per cent of Bulgarian foreign investments and interests in Hungary and Rumania.

Notwithstanding the purchase of shares in the interwar period, in 1935
foreign capital still held industrial shares in the value of 1,500 million
crowns, short- and long-term loans of approximately 2,500 million

crowns, and government bonds of 8,000 million crowns. In Czechoslovakia one-fifth of the total share capital may be estimated to have been
under foreign control. Most of these shares were held by French groups
of financiers, particularly in metallurgy and heavy industry, but British
and German interests were also considerable.

In the moderately advanced countries of East-Central Europe foreign
capital played a much more significant part. In the Hungarian economy,
as pointed out before, the capitalist forces prevailing before World War
I lost many of their positions in the interwar period and groups of Hungarian financiers grew much stronger. New inflow of capital came in the
form of loans. However, despite noteworthy reduction, there were still
important economic positions in foreign possession on the eve of World
War II. Of the four big banks, it was the leading Hungarian General
Credit Bank which deserves special mention on account of the 20 per
cent control by French and Austrian financial groups respectively. Of
the second-line banks it was the Hungaro-Italian Bank and the Anglo-
Hungarian Bank. The take-over of industrial firms by Hungarian capital
in the twenties and the purchase of considerable packets of shares from
Austrian owners were continued in the thirties, even with a new impetus
after the failure of the Creditanstalt-Bankverein. Yet in 1938, 24 per
cent of the shares of Hungarian industrial firms were still held by
foreigners, half of them by German capitalists.

The Polish economy was still more strongly pervaded by foreign influence. In the late thirties slightly more than 40 per cent of the total
share capital of joint-stock companies was in the hands of foreign financiers. They held several key positions. In mining and metallurgy 26
firms working with foreign capital held 71 per cent of the total capital;
in the oil industry 17 firms held nearly 87 per cent; in the electrical
industry 18 firms 55 per cent; and in the chemical industry 59 firms 60
per cent. Approximately 30 per cent of the capital sunk in communications and 46 per cent of the capital used for electric power plants, gas
production, and hydroelectric power plants were foreign investments.

The largest proportion of foreign capital (27 per cent) invested in
Polish joint-stock companies before World War II belonged to French
financiers. Groups of U.S. financiers occupied the second place (19 per
cent); the next in order of magnitude were the Germans with their 14
per cent (in 1931 it was already 25 per cent) and the Belgians with 13 per
cent.

In the economies of the Balkan countries foreign capital still played a decisive role despite reductions in a few cases. For instance in Rumania the interest controlled by Rumanian businessmen considerably increased in the oil industry which had been owned almost completely by foreign financiers before World War I. Of the capital invested in the oil industry 77 per cent—which amounted to 40 to 50 per cent of the total capital invested in industry—nevertheless came from foreign sources (20 per cent from Great Britain, 20 per cent from Anglo-Dutch financiers, 23 per cent from French-Belgian groups). Despite a slight reduction, considerable foreign capital was still invested in metallurgy, in the cellulose and paper industry, rising to 60 per cent in textiles, cement, and building materials.

Of the 7,444 million dinars total capital of all Yugoslav joint-stock companies, about 3,280 million dinars, i.e., 44 per cent, was owned by financiers in 1937. In sectors of vital importance the ratio was 69 per cent in mining, 83 per cent in the generation of electric power, and 70 per cent in the chemical industry. About 40 per cent of the capital invested in communications and 33 per cent of that in insurance companies came from groups of foreign financiers.

French groups occupied the first place in Yugoslavia, owning 25 per cent of industrial investments; British capital controlled an interest of 17 per cent; Americans held 15 per cent; Germans 11 per cent; Italians 10 per cent.

In Bulgaria, where foreign capital had been unable to acquire any important positions owing to the undeveloped state of industry and poor sources of raw materials, 26 per cent of the industrial share capital was in foreign hands in 1921. By 1938 this was reduced to 18 per cent. However, certain foreign groups of financiers controlled considerable interests in Bulgarian banks.

Thus, in the interwar period the processes of modern capitalist development of East-Central Europe were still strongly influenced by the firm position of foreign capital. In fact, the share of foreign capital did show a tendency to diminish and sank below the level it held before World War I. However, with its control of one-fifth to three-fourths in industry, mining, and communications, it nevertheless retained a strong influence on the economic structure of the countries on the threshold of World War II.

In sum, the slackening economic growth of the interwar decades was unable to produce any decisive change in the economic structure of the countries of East-Central Europe. As regards such aspects as agrarian-industrial character, modernization of industry, domestic accumulation and dependence on foreign capital, the structure of foreign trade, and level of national income, at best a slight shift or partial progress took place without any change in the fundamental structure of the economy. The dynamism to be noted in the opening years of the century slowed down; economic changes were not accompanied by any essential social transformation. On the contrary, whereas early in the century economic growth was associated with a rise in the living standard, in the interwar period it did not in general bring any actual increase of income to the population. In such circumstances, contradictions only grew more profound and more acute instead of being resolved. From political, economic, and social aspects, East-Central Europe became an area struggling with permanent crisis and fraught with inner contradictions in a tense, explosive atmosphere where everything called for change.

13 *In the System of the German War Economy*

The methodical endeavors whereby Hitler tried to extend Germany's *Lebensraum* to include the whole territory of East-Central Europe reached the stage of realization from 1938 and the outbreak of World War II. After the Anschluss, the dismemberment of Czechoslovakia and the annexation of the Bohemian provinces, the most highly developed countries of the region were integrated into the Third Reich. They were fully incorporated politically and economically. It was under the impact of these events and as a consequence of her increasing military potential and political power that Germany's influence grew rapidly in this part of Europe. Forcible political and economic pressure could be exerted on several unoccupied countries, in order to use them as satellites. This hold was strengthened, particularly after the outbreak of World War II and the attack against the Soviet Union.

Recalcitrant countries could now be compelled by military power to surrender and become part of the zone under German rule. Whereas the Anschluss and the dismemberment of Czechoslovakia were events of a specific date, the development of a network of satellites cannot be connected to any definite point of time. Here we have to deal with lengthy processes. The subjugation of countries at the beginning of the war or of those attacked later can again be connected with definite points of time, but the organization of these countries to fit into the German war machine cannot be pinpointed. German wartime *Grossraumwirtschaft,* which welded the steadily expanding Nazi empire, the conquered territory under military rule, and the network of obsequious satellites into a coherent unit may be conceived of from 1938 on as a part of the German war economy, as a system built up continuously.

The economic history of the countries of East-Central Europe during World War II is therefore connected with the history of the German war economy in varying ways. All the countries under review became a part of it in some form. Though the fate of every country, from Austria to Bulgaria and from Poland to Yugoslavia, was similar in the main, different military and political developments influenced the economic situation and the nature of the relationship to Germany. In this respect the countries of the region may be divided into three groups. Austria and the Czechoslovak provinces annexed by Germany belong to the first group. The satellites—Hungary, Rumania, and Bulgaria—may be put in the second; formally, these countries remained independent and occupation by Germany came later, in some instances only at the end of the war. Finally, the countries invaded and conquered by the German army—Poland and Yugoslovia—made up a separate group, for fighting continued almost throughout the whole time of the war on their territory.

As concerns the first group, adjustment to the German war economy rested primarily on a number of common traits. The annexation of both Austria and Czechoslovakia took place in peacetime, before the outbreak of World War II. Though not in equal measure, both were regarded as organic parts of the Reich; both had highly developed industrial economies, and were not intended to play the role of food and raw material suppliers as was expected of most of Southeastern Europe. German economic policy was aimed at integrating Austria and Czechoslovakia completely so as to make their industrial capacity part of the German war economy not only from the standpoint of production and finances but also of ownership, in order that accumulated capital, gold and foreign exchange reserves might be utilized to finance the German war machine. These common fundamental features were not modified by the differences in the legal status of the two countries, Austria having been made into a province of the Third Reich under the name of "Alpen und Donau Reichsgau," while the Czech-Moravian Protectorate was allowed to retain a certain formal autonomy as part of the Greater German Empire.

In the starting points of economic policy there were also deviations. In the case of Austria adjustment to the German war economy brought great prosperity for a few years after a period of economic crises and slumps. However, on Czech territory this "adjustment" did not bring even temporarily any considerable economic upswing. There were, furthermore, differences in the treatment of the population and of manpower. The German people of Austria were absorbed and classified as German Herrenvolk, while the Czechs were treated as "inferior Slavs."

Austria and the Czech provinces were very important in the German war economy. After the annexation the Germans took possession of the gold and foreign exchange reserves of the National Bank of Austria, amounting to 400 million schillings, as well as clearing assets worth 200 million schillings. The packets of shares appropriated by the Germans from the Austrian and Czech banks, which strengthened their economic position in Southeastern Europe, have been mentioned before. The valuable raw materials found in the two countries—notably Austrian timber, oil, and magnesite, and Czech coal—but above all their considerable industrial capacity and war material production—iron and steel industry, machine factories, vehicle industries and armament factories—considerably increased the German industrial potential.

After the annexation, immense industrial and banking interests of Central European significance were integrated into the German economy. The entry of the German troops was only the first step, soon followed by further equally harsh measures. After the Anschluss the dispossession of Jewish property, the systematic penetration and integration of big German concerns, the rapid expansion of existing German interests, helped to put the greater part of the Austrian economy into the hands of German capital. The leading banks of Vienna were fitted into the system of German banks. After a merger with several smaller banks the Creditanstalt-Bankverein became the concern of the Deutsche Bank, the Länder-Bank that of the Dresdner Bank. The affiliation of Austrian firms with German institutions was promoted by merging numerous small enterprises, granting loans, signing licenses for the use of patents, etc. By the end of the war approximately 200 Austrian firms had passed into German ownership, embracing almost two-thirds of the capital of the joint-stock companies, the whole of the oil industry and the electrical industry, a considerable part of the chemical industry, and the iron and metal branch.

In Czech territory more direct forms of expropriation were instituted. After the confiscation of Jewish property—valued at approximately 600 million crowns—a wide range of methods were applied to extort the signing of so-called Treuhand agreements, which implied the "leasing" of leading Czech firms to German concerns. The drastic methods of expansion practiced by the Göring concern were particularly flagrant. In a short time this company grabbed eight big firms with 150,000 workers, including the Witkowicz Ironworks, the Skoda Works, the Poldina

Foundries, and other giant industrial plants. The Tatra Motorcar Factory fell into the hands of the Dresdner Bank, and so did the Czech Discount Bank. The Mannesmann concern got hold of the Railway Company of Prague and numerous industrial works of Ostrava. In the long run the Germans laid hands on about half of the industrial share capital of the Protectorate, including 90 to 100 per cent of the coal mining, cement, paper, and oil industries, as well as a minimum of 25 to 33 per cent of most other branches of industry.

Austrian-Czech industry, thus controlled predominantly by Germany, was then reorganized to become an integral part of the German war machine. With the familiar methods of the German Nazi war economy, a highly centralized system of extensive state intervention was set up, the discussion of which lies outside the scope of the present work. By the control of finances, orders, and material management, the Austrian and Czech economies were soon shaped into an organic part of the Nazi war economy and ran a typical course of development, in the war pattern.

From the year 1938 an enormous boom developed within the framework of the war economy in Austria, which had formerly been incapable of economic recovery. In 1937, 320,000 unemployed were recorded; in two years their number fell to 250,000. The building of huge industrial plants was begun, partly in an effort to create organic economic relations with German parts. Added to strategic defensive requirements, this consideration lent a strong impetus to the development of war industry in Upper Austria (besides the existing industrial centers of Vienna and Lower Austria which had employed 65 per cent of industrial and commercial manpower in 1934). In Linz a large harbor was built, and as a result of wider possibilities of transport three major plants of heavy industry were established in the town—coke works, steel works, and a nitrogen factory. The dimensions of the metallurgic base at Linz were such that originally it was planned for the production of 2 million tons of crude iron, with steel works and rolling mills. In the war years it was ultimately constructed to have 50 to 70 per cent capacity, to produce 500,000 tons of iron and 120,000 tons of steel. Chemical works for the production of 60 to 70 tons of synthetic material were also built in Linz and put into operation in 1942. Large aluminium works were set up at Ranshofen, the planned 60,000 tons output of which amounted at the time to 10 per cent of the world's total production. In 1943 the factory already produced 40,000 tons of aluminium. With the establishment of many new plants, including the newly established oil industry, and the further development of existing factories, the branches of Austrian industry which possessed strategic importance advanced rapidly. For instance, between 1937 and 1943 iron ore and crude iron production increased by 67 and 149 per cent respectively. From 33,000 tons before the war oil production soared to 1.2 million tons.

In the absence of comprehensive statistics, revealing information may be derived from the representative records containing the data of 1,678 major industrial works which in March 1945 employed manpower averaging 239 for every 100 employed in 1934. In iron, steel, and machine industries the figure was 482, in mining, 234. However, in the textile industry it was 85, in the paper industry 102, in the food industry 107.

A similar tendency is exhibited by the development of Czech industry. Between 1939 and 1943 coal production increased more than one-third, in black coal 31 per cent, in brown coal 43 per cent; steel output rose 11 per cent, production of electric current 44 per cent. The powerful advance of war industry is illustrated by the two to threefold increase in manpower employed in the largest works of war industry and in metallurgic works.

Simultaneously with the increase of raw material production and the output of heavy industry and because of the typically one-sided pressure of the war effort, a gradual decline ensued in the consumer industries. Even the incomplete Austrian records clearly indicate the tendency: paper industry, which until 1941 slightly exceeded the 1927 level, sank to the prewar level after 1941. Production of cotton yarn, on the other hand, fell to half of the prewar output by 1941. In 1944 the workers employed in the textile industry numbered only 40 per cent of the prewar manpower. In the leather industry the figure was 80 per cent. Even the production of the most important foodstuffs diminished; for instance, the output of the breweries fell by 15 per cent, that of the sugar factories by 5 per cent.

Consequently, the level of war production showed a relatively moderate rise. Calculated at unchanged prices the peak of increase in the industrial output of the Czech-Moravian Protectorate during the war was 18 per cent over the prewar level, while the decline of agriculture was quite considerable, clearly demonstrated by milk production diminishing to half and a significant fall in the volume of animal products.

In Austria, simultaneously with industrial advance there was a serious agricultural decline. Wheat output sank from 4 million quintals in 1937 to below 3 million by 1944; rye, from 4.8 million quintals to 2.3 million; potato crops to less than half (from 36.1 million quintals to 17.5 million). At the same time stocks of pigs were reduced by 1.2 million, poultry by nearly 4 million (to 1.7 and 5.3 million respectively).

A different type of war economy was evolved by the allies of Germany in Southeastern Europe—in Hungary, Rumania, Bulgaria, and Slovakia, a puppet state created by Germany in 1939. In these countries the elements of formal political independence and a home policy not controlled directly by Germans were, on the whole, allowed to survive, though only under the strong influence of German pressure. (German troops were, of course, stationed in Slovakia from the foundation of the state, in Rumania from the autumn of 1940, in Bulgaria from the spring of 1941; but these units did not interfere directly in daily life, and the occupation of Hungary did not take place until the spring of 1944.)

However, the outbreak of World War II coincided with the initiation of the open economic offensive which served to turn these countries into political allies of Germany and economically into organic parts of the German *Grossraumwirtschaft.* From the signing of the Munich Agreement Germany regarded East-Central Europe as exclusively her own domain of interest, but after the success of the Blitzkrieg in the West her position became so strong that her slightly disguised economic ambitions could be formulated quite frankly. No longer the expression of theoretical wishes, these soon became realized and applied. The German point of view was put forward in several articles in the spring of 1941 in the semi-official paper *Berliner Börsenzeitung.* It was explained that the countries of Southeastern Europe would have to "adapt themselves to their natural endowments" and that "industrialization was contrary to the agricultural character" of these states.

Simultaneously with political revision the countries of South-eastern Europe will have to adapt themselves to the requirements of continental Grossraumwirtschaft. Their agricultural production will be determined by the needs of the rest of the continent, the principal products are to be cereals and oil-seeds; in addition industrial plants are to be operated and in this connection an agricultural industry may be developed. . . . The production of raw materials is to be completed by local processing into semi-finished goods and the utilization of waterpower (oil, ores, light ores).

In his confidential report to the Hungarian Ministry of Foreign Affairs the Hungarian *chargé d'affaires* summed up German conceptions concerning industry in the countries of Southeastern Europe as endeavoring to accomplish three targets. In the development of agricultural branches of industry the objective was "controlled co-operation," implying complete adjustment to the requirements of the German market. Other existing branches of industry were to be brought under German control. Finally, the establishment of industrial firms inconvenient for the Germans was to be prevented by every means.[1]

As regards the first two points, namely the maximal development of agricultural and raw material production to serve the interests of the German war effort, the planned policy was carried out consistently to the end of the war, yet it brought only partial results.

In Hungary, Rumania, and Bulgaria during the war agriculture was unable to come up to the expectations of the Germans. As a result of carefully elaborated trade agreements from 1934 on surplus produce which seemed considerable in the thirties and, according to German experts, could be counted on to increase would all be taken to Germany. But in the war years export could be increased in only a few items. The volume of agrarian products exported to Germany fell far behind German expectations.

As a matter of fact the domestic problems of agriculture in the countries of Southeastern Europe became apparent in a particularly acute form during the war. It soon became evident that the enormous surplus available during and after the depression of 1929–33 originated from extraordinarily low consumption. The low yields and low level of productivity involved the fundamental problem: increased crops by enhanced productivity could hardly be achieved for lack of machines and the requisite capital. For the same reasons there were no possibilities for replacing labor promptly when large numbers were called away. At certain periods this caused difficulties even in traditional production

[1] Hungarian National Archives, Department of Economic Policy of the Ministry of Foreign Affairs. Res. 466-1941.

such as wheat, etc., while the rapid development of the more labor-intensive branches demanded by the Germans was severely hampered.

So agricultural crops could not be increased. On the contrary, in most products there was a reduction. Moreover, none of the countries had any surplus to dispose of, for domestic requirements rose considerably as a result of industrialization associated with war production, the progress of urbanization, and still more because of the food supplies for the army.

At the beginning the true state of affairs was concealed by the bumper crop of 1938 in Hungary and an equally rich harvest in Rumania in 1939. In the first years of the war agrarian exports to Germany considerably increased from every country, and it seemed that manpower which left agriculture for industry or was called up for military service could be replaced by large imports of agricultural machinery from Germany. For instance, thousands of tractors, harvesters, and other agricultural machinery were delivered to Rumania in a few years. However, the missing manpower was replaced only in part, and the yield did not increase. The use of fertilizers, disastrously low in the thirties, ceased completely during the war, and the livestock having decreased in number, the amount of natural manure also decreased.

To extend cultivation to new agricultural areas was out of the question. In fact, the area of cultivated land became slightly smaller in many parts. Under such conditions crops remained far below the prewar level, except for an exceptional year now and then. When the averages of the second half of the thirties are compared to the wartime figures, a 20–30 per cent fall is registered in the agricultural crops of the countries of Southeastern Europe. This fall was due in the first place to smaller output of grains.

This generally negative picture was partly counterbalanced by larger crops in a few special branches of production, above all in oilseeds, on the more extensive cultivation of which the Germans strongly insisted. However, here too the enlargement of sown areas and increased surplus for export were actually realized in the thirties and in the first stage of the war rather than in the later years. In Bulgaria, where German production requirements were complied with most obsequiously in the thirties, sunflower seed crops reached the peak in 1937; in 1939 and 1940

Table 13-1.   Output of Principal Grains
in Hungary, Rumania, and Bulgaria,
1934–1938 and 1940–1942 *(in thousand
quintals)*

	1934–38	1940–42
Hungary[a]		
Wheat	22,196	18,025
Rye	6,976	5,566
Corn	23,061	18,763
Barley	6,079	5,550
Rumania[b]		
Wheat	25,963	14,059
Rye	1,229	449
Corn	39,028	30,950
Barley	5,503	4,108
Bulgaria		
Wheat	16,588	11,047
Rye	1,995	1,269
Corn	7,632	7,697
Barley	2,987	1,982

Sources: Based on national statistics and S. Zagoroff, J. Vegh and A. Blimovich, *The Agricultural
Economy of the Danubian Countries, 1935–1945,*
Stanford, 1955, p. 127.
[a]Territory as of 1938.
[b]Territory as of 1940.

they diminished by 10 per cent; in 1941 production increased again, but
in 1942–43 production was only about 50 per cent of the 1937 level.

The situation was similar in other oilseeds except for soya beans the
production of which rose steeply until 1941, and thereafter rapidly decreased. The cultivation of other industrial plants followed the same pattern. The growing of vegetables and fruit fell off, as did the production
of tobacco, one of the most important items on Germany's import list,
after a more than threefold increase of tobacco exports between 1937
and 1943.

In Rumania the sown area of industrial plants and fodder increased
from 7.4 to 11.6 per cent between 1940 and 1943. Beans and peas were
cultivated on a considerably larger scale, but in the decisive articles,
oilseeds and industrial plants, production failed to reach the 1939 level.

In Hungary also it was only in sunflower seeds and soya beans that production increased considerably.

Owing to the approximately 25 per cent lower production and much larger home consumption, none of the countries in question could satisfy the demands of the Germans. Moreover, the inadequacy of imports from the German viewpoint and their excessive expectations for the producing countries jeopardized provision of domestic needs and created an inner social tension and permanent conflicts between Germany and her satellites.

Contradictions arose not only in the growing of plants. It was in Hungary alone that livestock increased in the first stage of the war, but this surplus was used up at home, since the areas acquired during the war were for the most part unable to cover their own needs. The surplus of agricultural products won by the annexation of the rich agrarian district of Bácska after the campaign against Yugoslavia was to be supplied to the Germans as long as the war lasted. In Bulgaria and Rumania the supply of livestock did not increase. On the contrary, between 1941 and 1944 it was reduced by 15–25 per cent. Therefore exports to Germany had to be stopped in the last stage of the war. Exports of animal and dairy products also remained far behind the prewar figures.

In many respects Germany's endeavors to use its allies as suppliers of raw materials were more successful. Rumania and Hungary particularly possessed a few industrial raw materials of basic importance for the war economy, on the supply of which Germany relied. The most significant items were bauxite in Hungary and oil in Rumania, but Rumanian timber and nonferrous metals and Hungarian oil and manganese were also essential for the German war economy. The Germans therefore urged the increase of their production by every means and were even willing to promote it by substantial investments. In addition to the industrial raw materials from Hungary and Rumania, the enhanced production of iron and manganese ore and timber in the puppet state of Slovakia and the iron ore from Bulgaria were also very important.

Hungarian bauxite, held to be the second largest source of supply in Europe, played a significant role in German aircraft manufacture and other branches of the war industry from the thirties. The bulk of the rapidly increasing production, amounting to half a million tons in 1938, was processed in Germany. During the war exploitation was approximately doubled, reaching 1 million tons in 1943, of which 90 per cent (900,000 tons) was taken to Germany. It was in the interest of the German war effort that Hungarian oil production, initiated with American capital before the war, was developed so forcibly. From 42,000 tons in 1938 Hungarian crude oil output increased to 842,000 tons in 1943, of which 458,000 tons were sent to Germany in the form of mineral oil. The Germans furthermore acquired various licences investing them with the right to prospect for oil in any part of Hungary.

Hungarian manganese ore production was also doubled, rising from 50,000 tons to 100,000 tons. The quantity supplied to Germany was about 60 per cent of this output.

As regards agricultural products and raw materials, German wishes did not undergo any change throughout the war, since the immediate interests of the German war economy fully coincided with the division of labor the Nazis intended to realize in the new Europe. However, in industry immediate interests soon came into conflict with long-term conceptions. As mentioned before, the Germans were strictly against every kind of processing industry (heavy or light); they alluded to such works as unnecessary, as glasshouse industry, and sentenced them openly to a reduced scale. This hostility to industry applied chiefly to Hungary which, unlike the agrarian countries of Southeastern Europe, already possessed an agrarian-industrial character in the thirties, with a relatively strong industry. German efforts in 1939–40 to reduce and ruin Hungarian industry—through indirect political pressure and increasing competition—actually led to differences between the two governments. However, from the second half of 1941, after Germany had launched war against the Soviet Union, this antagonism underwent first a slow, than a more marked, modification. The ceaselessly growing requirements of the war called for an unprecedented increase of German war material production. Therefore, the industrial potential of the satellites was to be utilized instead of being cut down. Moreover, the day-by-day heavier attacks of the Western powers induced the German High Command to encourage the war industries of the satellite countries, which were not exposed to bombing at the time. Thus, in 1941, conversations were started on two issues: first, the existing war industry was to be made to supply war material to Germany; secondly, new units were to be set up with German help to build up capacity—mostly in the branches whose development had been impeded earlier by every means—and in which 70 per cent of the output was to be reserved for Germany.[2]

No accurate comprehensive records are available concerning the total value of the war material manufactured for the Germans, but it is a fact that 30 to 80 per cent of the largest Hungarian armaments factories worked for the German war machine. Estimates put the supplies sent to Germany at about 60 per cent.

Work done for hire was another important form whereby Hungarian war industry was made to supply the German army. At first this served the aim of obtaining light armament and ammunition, produced partly according to German plans and patents. The credit granted by the Hungarian government for work done on the basis of hire was 130 million pengös in 1941, 580 million pengös in 1942, and as high as 825 million pengös in the spring of 1944.

Within this system of work for hire a peculiar position was occupied by the common program of aircraft construction. An agreement was reached in 1941 concerning the so-called Messerschmidt project. The idea was that Hungarian aircraft industry should be built up by uniting the two largest Hungarian aircraft factories, and should produce 50 ME 109 and 50 ME 210 airplanes monthly, as well as 700 Daimler Benz aircraft engines. As a result of enormous investments valued at about 3,000 million pengös, mass production was in fact started at the close of 1943, and until the summer of 1944, when most of the premises and workshops were destroyed by American bombers, about 600 ME 109 fighter planes, 100 ME 210 fighter-bombers, and nearly 1,000 aircraft engines were produced.

The wartime advancement of the Hungarian aluminium industry was partly connected with the scheme of common aircraft production. "The Germans who had for many years fought against the establishment of an aluminium factory in Hungary, have now swung over to the contrary extreme," stated the Hungarian minister of industry.[3] It was indeed on German initiative that the Danube Alumina Factory was founded in 1942 with the target of constructing an alumina factory of 60,000 tons together with an aluminium factory.

---

[2] Hungarian National Archives. Weiss Manfred Munitions Works, 85, August 25, 1941.
[3] Hungarian National Archives. Parliamentary Committees, Nov. 4, 1941.

German encouragement to develop certain branches of war industry contributed to the process which from 1938 brought on a boom. It was furthered by the development of the Hungarian army, with its large demand for industrial requirements, and by considerable investments in this connection. A plan of investments was worked out in Hungary in 1938 which produced extensive prosperity in 1939 and 1940 in practically every branch of industry. In 1940 the output of Hungarian manufacturing industry was 32 per cent higher than two years before, indicating that the war boom induced larger growth in two years than was achieved in the twenty years of the interwar period.

From 1941 this general prosperity came to a halt. Typical signs of the war economy began to appear. The rapid growth of the war material branches of heavy industry was followed by a rather sudden decline of branches supplying consumer goods, owing to lack of raw material and manpower. The advance of heavy industry continued at a rapid pace; according to the statistics, output increased by 50 per cent in the iron and metal industry and by over 150 per cent in machine industry. Eighty-five per cent of the new manpower employed in Hungarian manufacturing industry found jobs in these two branches. On the other hand, production sank 25 to 30 per cent in textiles, leather, and paper, and there was also a decline in the foodstuff industry. At the wartime peak of 1943 Hungarian industrial production was 38 per cent higher than before the war.

The share of heavy industry in total industrial production increased from 44 to 51 per cent, while light industry and food industries showed a corresponding fall. The role of industry grew much more important in the national economy during the war. It was the first time that the share of the agrarian population sank below 50 per cent, and it was the first time that industry produced a larger part of the national income than did agriculture. Even if the war did not bring about a fundamental change in the social and economic underdevelopment of Hungary, there can be no doubt that the promotion of industry strengthened Hungary's position in relation to the other countries of Southeastern Europe.

The agreement concluded with Rumania in 1939, by which the Germans contrived to secure huge supplies of oil and cereals, was definitely drawn up to further the realization of the German program devised for the countries of Southeastern Europe, demanding the halt of industrialization. This objective was formulated in the paragraph providing for "co-operation in the field of industry."

Thus during the first stage of the war, here too emphasis was placed on the production of food and raw materials. German financial groups established a number of firms which concentrated on increasing the export of these articles. The oil agreement signed in the spring of 1940 stipulated that Rumanian oil consignments be delivered at the prewar price. The agreement of December 4, 1940, again served to increase the volume of exports in agrarian and forestry products. In the years 1940–41 over 60 per cent of Rumanian oil went to Germany, while the Germans clamored for still larger supplies. From 1940 to August 1944 altogether 10.3 million tons of oil were delivered to Germany besides the approximately 1 million tons estimated to have been used up by the German army in Rumania.

The exploitation of agriculture went so far as to necessitate rationing, as in Hungary, and there were periods when stricter measures had to be introduced in order to ensure exports, for Rumania supplied to Germany 1.4 million tons of cereals between 1940 and 1944. Some agreements stipulated that only the quantities left over when German requirements had been satisfied might be diverted to cover the needs of the population.

Timber was also an important raw material supplied by Rumania. About half a million tons of timber and articles of wood went to Germany during the war.

These consignments involved the plunder of the Rumanian economy in several forms. At first, the Germans fulfilled their obligations and delivered the goods they sold to the Rumanians as countervalue. But Rumanian oil was invoiced at the prewar price, even though the prices of German commodities kept rising. (During the war Rumanian export prices increased by 123 per cent, German prices by 614 per cent.) Certain Rumanian economists estimate the loss to Rumania at $95 million.

In Bulgaria wartime prosperity was less apparent owing to the undeveloped state of industry and the weak role of heavy industry. Here the Germans had fewer chances to make the country's industry serve their war machine. The only branch where output could be considerably increased during wartime was the food industry. It was only before Bulgaria entered the war that the chemical industry showed a slight advance. Most other branches of heavy industry stagnated, while light industry produced 30 to 40 per cent less in 1943 than before the war. (Thus, if 1939 is used as a base, Bulgarian industry reached its maximum with 118 in 1941, but in 1942 and 1943 production sank to 113 and 110, respectively.) During the war the economic and social consequences of industrialization were relatively less significant in Bulgaria than in Hungary or Rumania.

In Slovakia the war boom brought considerable prosperity, partly by release from Czech competition, partly by the development of certain branches to produce enough for exports to Germany. In 1943 the output of Slovak industry was 63 per cent higher than in 1937, with a 50 per cent increase in the manpower employed. In this period the output of the chemical industry rose more than threefold, that of the leather industry nearly threefold.

Thus the typical industrial effects of the one-sided war boom were felt in the countries of Southeastern Europe, particularly after 1941. However, under the conditions prevailing in these undeveloped industries of small output, the branches developed as complements of German war industry were really units of war production intentionally decentralized as a result of bombing, rather than the outcome of industrialization affecting and connected with the whole of the economy.

The effects of the general boom were counteracted not only by the sharp structural disproportions described above but also by the grave economic consequences of the open plunder suffered by the economies of the satellites in subordination to the German war machine. A considerable part of the supplies of food and raw materials, followed soon after by industrial products, was delivered to Germany without the exporting countries receiving the countervalue. The Germans did not even take the trouble to dissemble in connection with the debts accumulating in the war years as they did in the thirties when their liabilities mounted on clearing accounts. In Germany's altered position the Nazi minister of finances simply declared in the case of Hungary: "The bulk of Hungarian supplies has to be actually regarded as contribution to our common war, the countervalue of which is to be passed to account.[4]

The value of unpaid supplies increased dramatically, especially after

[4] Hungarian National Archives, Department of Economic Policy of the Ministry of Foreign Affairs, Material of the Hungarian-German economic negotiations in 1942.

1941. For instance, in Hungary German debts amounted to not more than 140 million marks in 1941, but in 1942 the figure was already 500 million marks and in 1943, 1,000 million marks. In 1944, another 1,500 million marks of debt accumulated, including the costs of the German occupation. The debts run up by Germany in Bulgaria were similar. In 1941 Germany owed Bulgaria 210 million marks; in 1942 the total was 380 million marks; by the close of 1943 it jumped to 680 million marks. The costs of maintaining the German troops stationed in Bulgaria during the whole time of the war cost about 250 million marks. Debts to Slovakia accumulated between 1939 and 1944—including the value of transport by rail and maintenance of the German troops— amounted to 1,000 million marks.

The magnitude of German debts is illustrated by the fact that in Hungary—with assets similar to those of the other countries in the area— they amounted to one quarter of the total war expenditure, imposing a burden which greatly contributed to inflation. The unpaid German orders had to be settled in the countries concerned by the treasury; this could be done only by issuing a large number of uncovered bank-notes. In Hungary 40 per cent of such issues was made necessary by the German debts. Thus the decisive factor in the war-induced depreciation of money was the ruthless plunder of these countries by the Germans.

The measure of integration into the German war economy is apparent from the fact that the sales and purchases of Hungary, Rumania, and Yugoslavia were transacted almost exclusively with Germany—75–80 per cent—in the war years.

The enormous demands on the satellite countries and their linking to the German war economy called for effects the realization of which could be counted on only by the aid of the strongest state intervention. A comprehensive wartime system of state intervention was therefore put into force in these countries, particularly from 1941 on.

The most important new forms of intervention were connected with the above-mentioned German orders and with the approximately equally large orders of the Hungarian army. Together these huge orders utilized the greater part of agrarian, mining, and industrial production; that is to say, producing enterprises in the war years worked for the most part upon orders from the state. Inevitably, the financing of the economy gradually also passed into the hands of the state. Year by year a larger part of the national income was used up through the budget. For instance, in Hungary the budget utilized 33 per cent of the national income in 1938–39; by 1944, 71 per cent. During the same period the amount of war expenditure jumped from 12 per cent of the total national income to 44 per cent, including the German debt.

The activities of the state extended to the rationing of food and industrial products, to organizing the compulsory delivery of a fixed quota of surplus agricultural produce and livestock to the state at fixed prices, and to the system of distribution of raw materials and energy. These measures were completed by the introduction of a system of price regulation. Practically every kind of fuel and raw material, and important investment and consumer goods, could change hands only through distribution by the state at prices fixed and controlled by the state. Naturally this strong centralization was accompanied by the establishment of adequate state institutions, supply centers and price control offices, by the appointment of commissioners in various fields, by the organization and function of central state offices and secretariats.

It is virtually impossible to give a comprehensive picture of the wartime economic situation in Poland and Yugoslavia, the countries classified into the third group. With the loss of their national independence these countries not only ceased to exist as political units, but their economic unity did not survive either, not even in the form permitted in the Czech-Moravian Protectorate. Actually, one part of Yugoslavia was occupied by the Germans, another by Italy. Still another part of the country was annexed by Hungary and a further stretch by Bulgaria, while Croatia was set up as an "independent" German puppet state.

The western districts of Poland were annexed by the Third Reich as a German province. Western Ukraine and Western Byelorussia, the eastern parts of former Poland, came under the rule of the Soviet Union in 1939, and were occupied by the Germans in 1941 after their invasion. Only the Polish province embracing the central region and kept under German occupation retained vestiges of a separate administrative unit. Hence it is obvious that no uniform Polish or Yugoslav economy existed once the Germans entered. The situation was further complicated by guerrilla warfare with clashes between regular armies, changing these countries into battlefields for the whole time of the war, particularly in the last stage.

In Polish and Yugoslav territory under German occupation, the German army, after it had marched in, first acted on the principle that the economy should be completely crushed. Thus in October 1939 in Poland the occupation army was instructed by Göring that independent Polish economic life was unnecessary. Every important factory was to be demolished; the machinery and, where possible, power stations were to be dismantled and taken away; essential lines of communication were to be disrupted. The removal of telephone and telegraph transmission lines was also planned, and so was the destruction of railways, apart from a few single-track lines.

However, the program of the Nazis soon changed. The occupied country was still regarded as booty and no independent economy was tolerated, but instead of annihilating existing economic resources the Nazis wished to exploit them to the utmost to serve the aims of the Third Reich. Göring's four-year-plan-of-war preparations were accordingly extended to occupied Poland and, in agreement with the principles laid down by Hans Frank, the highest Nazi expert, efforts were to be concentrated on increasing agricultural production and on fully exploiting sources of raw material and forwarding the material to Germany. In the endeavor to increase the production of certain strategically important raw materials even considerable investments were made. This happened in the case of Polish coal mines, Croatian oil production, and Yugoslav nonferrous metal mines, particularly at Bor.

In most areas German demands were satisfied not so much from the increase of production, but by reducing the population to the level of starvation and by closing down works the products of which were unnecessary for the German war machine. The statistics on the requisitioning of grains present a picture of merciless sacking. The Germans collected and sent mostly to Germany 370,000 tons of grains in 1940, 700,000 tons in 1941, 1.2 million tons in 1942, and 1.5 million tons in 1943. The same was done with meat, lard, potatoes, and other foodstuffs.

No accurate and comprehensive records are available concerning supplies of manufactured goods, but looting was practiced inexorably in industrial spheres of the economy. The output of Polish mining and industry increased only in the branches producing raw materials. For instance, coal production increased between 1939 and 1943 from 38 million to 57 million tons. Apart from a few raw materials, increase of production was less characteristic of Polish industry than were dismantling and decline due to prohibitions on delivering supplies. In numerous branches of industry output was down to 20 to 30 per cent of the prewar level, and according to some statistics the production of Polish mining and industry reached at best 60 per cent of the prewar figure.

However, German economic policy was not content to plunder and subdue. Besides carrying off food from the starving population and divesting the country of raw materials, masses of Polish and Yugoslav workers were deported for forced labor to the war factories of the Reich. During the war years until the summer of 1943, from the central province of Poland alone 1.28 million persons were taken to Germany for forced labor, and another 600,000 to 700,000 Polish prisoners of war were put to work in the Reich. There were further impracticable Nazi plans to increase the number of Polish forced laborers to 4 million. The subjugation, dismemberment, and ravaging of these countries presented the worst traits of colonization.

In Yugoslavia, where, owing to dismemberment and to ceaseless guerrilla warfare, efforts to create some sort of organized war economy was still less successful, the export of food and raw materials was most important for the Germans. According to certain estimates, the occupying armies carried off 10 million tons of food during the four years of occupation. As regards raw materials, the Germans strove to increase the volume of timber from Croatia (there is documentary evidence of 40 per cent of the forests having been cleared). Furthermore, they urged raising the production of some newly discovered oil fields and in the Serbian districts the production of nonferrous metals. To achieve this, the Nazis even went so far as to make some investments.

Thus in some of the countries of East-Central Europe, linked to the German war economy by force, economic processes took place typical of one-sided wartime prosperity; others suffered the consequences of being plundered in varying degree for the good of the Third Reich. Though there were great differences in the war years between the advancement of Austrian and Czech industry in the service of the German war machine, the peculiar one-sided prosperity in Hungary and Rumania consistently accompanied by efforts to rob these countries, and the complete looting and destruction of the economies of Poland and Yugoslavia, by the end of the war these differences began to fade in many respects. Severe exploitation, but still more the military operations of 1944–45 which rendered these countries battlefields, left them economically exhausted.

By the end of World War II most countries of East-Central Europe were severely damaged. Not only were the majority of plants established during the war destroyed but a significant part of the prewar capacity too.

The measure of devastation caused by the war was unequal. Poland, Yugoslavia, and Hungary were hit hardest, the former two by the chain of events previously outlined, Hungary by the six months of heavy fighting on her territory.

Yugoslavia lost over 10 per cent of her population of 1941 — 1.7 million people. The destruction of half of the railway lines meant the ruin of the national economy. Tracks of over 6,000 km., more than half of the total network, were damaged or completely wrecked. Half of the engines operated in 1940 and more than half of the other rolling stock were destroyed and half of the repair workshops were also put out of action. The unparalleled devastation of communications and telecommunication is illustrated by the complete ruin of almost the entire stock of motorcars and 40 per cent of peasant carts, the loss of half of Yugoslavia's deep-sea vessels and two-thirds of her river boats and coasting ships, and the destruction of 45 per cent of telephone and telegraph networks. Besides the ruin of infrastructure, one-sixth of the buildings which had existed before the war were gutted, destroyed, or badly damaged. The war inflicted equally heavy losses on agriculture: 40 to 50 per cent of agricultural machines and equipment were destroyed, and 60 per cent of the horses, 53 per cent of the cattle, and half of the sheep, goats, and poultry stocks perished.

Industrial production also declined seriously owing to the dismantling of machinery and the destruction of factories and stocks of material. The steel industry was completely paralyzed by the ruin of the extremely important installations in the two steel works of Slovenia and Bosnia. In the textile industries, which had advanced considerably in the interwar period, cotton mills lost 40 per cent, wool-spinneries 20 per cent, of their capacity (spindles and looms). Iron ore production declined to 30 per cent of the prewar level. Though there were differences between various branches, total industrial production was down to 30 to 35 per cent of the 1939 level.

The losses sustained by Poland were equally heavy: 40 per cent of railway lines, 70 per cent of railway buildings and installations, and 70 per cent of the major railway bridges lay in ruins. Housing was exceptionally hard hit: 85 per cent of the houses of Warsaw were devastated in the war; 15 per cent of agricultural buildings were destroyed. The most serious blow to agriculture was the loss of livestock: 60 per cent of cattle, 75 per cent of horses, 80 per cent of swine. The Germans also mowed down 25 per cent of the forests.

Industrial damage was particularly grave. On the evidence of certain statistics, the loss of industry amounted to $11,500 million, exceeding one-tenth of the total national wealth. However, calculated for the prewar area of the country the damage of industry does not present a truthful picture, since the sphere of economy affected the most by the altered borders of postwar Poland was industry. In the former eastern districts (Western Ukraine) industry was weak, while the new western areas of Poland were highly industrialized. In fact, 20 per cent of the industrial capacity of the latter was dismantled and removed or destroyed; yet with the remaining plants the industry of postwar Poland was still stronger than that of prewar Poland had been, notwithstanding the heavy losses during the war. In 1945 the number of big factories exceeded the prewar figure by 42 per cent, mechanical power exceeded the prewar level by 150,000 h.p.

Like Poland and Yugoslavia, it was in communications that Hungary suffered the most grievous losses: 40 per cent of her railway tracks and half her engines were destroyed (another 25 per cent were damaged and became unfit for service). The fleet of river boats was lost completely. The explosion of all the large river bridges and many of the minor ones caused a heavy loss, about 36 per cent of the total length of bridges. Half of the national wealth invested in communications was annihilated.

In the list of losses sustained by agriculture the worst calamity was the destruction of 44 per cent of the stock of cattle, 56 per cent of the horses, 79 per cent of the pigs, and 80 per cent of the sheep.

Industry also suffered considerable devastation, with 50 per cent of its buildings and equipment damaged and 33 per cent of engines and 75 per cent of machine tools lost. After the war the production of industry fell to 25 to 30 per cent of the prewar level, the situation being aggravated by lack of materials and stock.

To this picture of economic disaster should be added the fact that about 4 per cent of the houses of Budapest were destroyed and another 23 per cent badly damaged.

The Austrian war losses, though less than the ruin brought to the above-mentioned countries, were nevertheless serious in their impact on the whole of the economy. The damage done by bombing and especially by the military operations in the eastern provinces had been estimated at approximately 38,000 million schillings, a considerable part deriving from the ruin of houses (in Vienna alone 37,000 apartments became uninhabitable) and of networks of communication. In industry a loss of 46,000 machines was registered and the building material industry alone forfeited 40 per cent of its peacetime capacity.

Losses due to the war were less heavy in Czechoslovakia (particularly in the Bohemian provinces), and still less in Rumania and Bulgaria. Besides the oilfields, a target of bombers, it was the network of communications and livestock which sustained damage in Rumania, and the situation was similar in Bulgaria.

Thus, most of the countries of East-Central Europe suffered extremely heavy losses in the war. In Yugoslavia, Poland, and Hungary—

Table 13-2.   Devastation Caused by World War II in East-Central European Countries

	Damage, at 1938 Prices (in million dollars)	As Per Cent of National Income of 1938
Poland	20,000	350
Czechoslovakia	4,200	115
Hungary	4,330	194
Rumania	683	29
Bulgaria	420	33
Yugoslavia	10,497	374

Source: J. Marczewski: *Planification et croissance économique des démocraties populaires,* Paris, 1956, p. 121.

and Austria did not fare much better—the damage amounted to about twice to four times the national income of the last year of peace. With due regard to the disparate and often inaccurate appraisals, these tremendous losses involved the ruin of about one-third of the national wealth. The countries of the other group sustained lighter damage, the loss amounting to approximately one year's national income in Czechoslovakia, and to one-third of the yearly national income in Rumania and Bulgaria. However, by the end of the war the economy was exhausted, stocks ran out, the physical condition of the population deteriorated, the producing apparatus was worn out, creating a critical situation almost everywhere.

The victory of the Allied powers in World War II, the complete defeat of Nazi Germany, found the countries of East-Central Europe in an extremely grave economic position. However, they were liberated from the oppressive expansion of the Third Reich, as well as from the rule of conservative Nazi systems serving Hitler and quisling governments, which collapsed. By the aid of the systems set up after the armistice and the peace treaties, the way was cleared for new social forces, and radically new possibilities arose for the economies of the countries of the region.

14 *Postwar Reconstruction*

The military defeat and collapse of Nazi Germany and the liberation of the East European countries from the German occupation meant not only the end of the war and the bitter years of occupation; it became a starting point for major political and social changes. The radically altered relations among the internal forces, the leading role of left-wing and revolutionary forces in the resistance movements, the discrediting or failure of the old governmental systems, the completely different international situation, the predominant role of the Soviet Union in driving out the Germans and smashing the Hitler regime, and Russia's changed role in world politics made impossible a return to the prewar conditions in these countries. While most of the East-Central European governments were of conservative, autocratic, Fascist character before the war, the power had now been grasped by a coalition of democratic, bourgeois, left-wing, and worker parties, previously in opposition to interwar regimes. Earlier, it was not possible for the Communist parties to have a voice in the activity of the government, since most of them had been compelled to operate illegally. Now the Communists became an important force in the new governments and acquired key positions.

By the very end of the war democratization was started together with the introduction of long-delayed social legislation. A real social revolution was developed by liberalizing the formerly oppressed forces of social progress. The first years following the war were characterized by emerging revolutionary processes. The Communist parties stepped to the forefront. They enjoyed the direct support of the Soviet Union, which became a decisive power in the former German satellite countries, and had direct political and military control through the Allied Control Commission and the Soviet Army. These parties, representing a dynamic force with a program for rapid solution of the difficult social, political, and economic questions that could not be solved heretofore, obtained a more and more important mass influence, and gradually became the holders of political power.

The conclusion of this process, which in most of the countries of the area was performed without uprisings and civil wars, was the political take-over by the Communist parties and the establishment of a political system, the dictatorship of the proletariat, during 1947–48. Thus, the short transition period provided a revolutionary transformation from capitalism to socialism and created radically new political, social, and economic conditions for the postwar progress of the East European countries.

As the first most important step of their socio-economic transformation, the East-Central European countries carried out land reforms in accordance with the differences in land tenure. This was a basic requirement because of the economic and social structure in the countries of the area—described in the previous chapters—which was characterized by the persistence of large estates and the landlessness of the peasants, conditions that still prevailed despite the reforms introduced in most of the countries after World War I. At the same time, the land reforms had a primary political aim of winning the sympathy of the broad masses of peasantry and facilitating unified action and cooperation between the Communist and peasant parties. The latter had different tendencies but represented an important political force. Consequently, among the chief demands in the programs of the left-wing party coalitions, established at the end of the war, were land reform plans, as formulated in the program of the Polish National Liberation Committee at Lublin on July 22, 1944, the program of the Czechoslovak Government of the National Front at Kosice, or the program of the Hungarian Front of Independency at Szeged in December 1944. The land reforms carried out during 1944–45 were naturally most extensive in those countries where the largest estates remained. According to a law issued in Hungary on March 18, 1945 by the Provisional Government, estates of more than 57 hectares owned by landlords and peasant-owned properties of more than 114 hectares were, with few exceptions, redistributed. By confiscation of the lands of Nazis and war criminals and by formal redemption of the rest of the land, the new state obtained 3.3 million hectares, of which 1.9 million were distributed among 642,000 peasant families. The remaining undistributed territories, mostly forests, formed the basis of the foundation of large state-owned farms. The Hungarian land reform, expropriating more than one-third of the whole territory and distributing about one-fourth, was the most radical land reform following World War II.

Similar radicalism characterized the land reform in Poland. By an order issued on September 6, 1944, all land owned by Germans, war criminals, and traitors was confiscated, and in addition all holdings over 100 hectares were ordered without redemption. On the 13.8 million hectares of confiscated land, 788,000 new farms were established, providing land for 216,000 landless families and giving additional parcels of land to 572,000 peasant families. Most of the new farms, 483,000 estates with an average of 8.3 hectares, were established on former German territories.

The Polish land reform was also connected with important territorial and population changes after the war; the Polish population from West Byelorussia and West Ukrainia were transferred to the new western territories from which the German population had been removed. The Polish land reform involved the expropriation of about half of the country's territory and the redistribution of more than one-fifth of it.

Although the land reform in Czechoslovakia lagged behind the measures introduced in Hungary and Poland, it brought comprehensive structural changes. According to the law issued on June 21, 1945, all the enemy-owned (German and Hungarian) land was expropriated, together with the 1.8 million hectares of arable land and 1.3 million hectares of forest, accounting for one-third of the Czech-Moravian territories and more than one-tenth of Slovakian territories. Through the confiscation, 122,000 families received land, totaling 1.04 million hectares.

As a revision of the land reform, issued after World War I, a supplementary article was enacted in July 1947, according to which the upper limit of holdings was 150 hectares in general. This made another land reform possible, distributing an additional 700,000–800,000 hectares of land. The upper limit of estates was readjusted to 50 hectares in March 1948, which meant the release of another 700,000 hectares. Altogether, the three arrangements involved 4.5 million hectares. They gave 350,000 landless peasant families 1.7 million hectares of land and established the basis of important state-owned forests and farms on an area of about 2.5 million hectares. As a result of the reform 14 per cent of the lands were distributed. But this relatively important change included not only the transformation of the large estates. The large estates

were not so important even before World War II, and the ratio of estates over the limit of 50 hectares did not change substantially. The
change was reflected rather in the structure of landownership, which
meant first the extension of state-owned lands. Secondly, as a consequence of the policy toward the national minorities, the German and
Hungarian peasants were replaced by Czech and Slovak peasant landowners.

The extent of land reform carried out in the Balkan countries was
much less significant. Here, as a result either of the previously existing
peasant landownership (Yugoslavia, Bulgaria) or of the redistribution
of lands after World War I, most of the territories were owned by peasants (Rumania). The land reforms after World War II carried out only
minor changes to supplement the smaller estates and to provide lands
for new landless groups. In Rumania, according to the law issued on
March 22, 1945, 8 per cent of the cultivated lands were redistributed.
The appropriation of the lands of Germans and war criminals and of the
estates over the 50 hectare limit formed the basis for redistribution. This
provided 1.1 million hectares of land to 680,000 claimants, averaging
1.2 hectares. In Yugoslavia, according to the law issued August 29, 1945,
5 per cent of all cultivated land was distributed. Besides the confiscation of the enemy's lands, the leveling of the estates was helped by setting a maximum size for the farms; that is, 25–35 hectares for arable
land and 45 hectares for all the estates. Thereby, more than 1.5 million
hectares were taken over by the state, from which 797,000 hectares were
distributed among 316,000 families. Among the new owners, however,
only 71,000 were landless formerly, so the average of 2.5 hectares per
capita of distributed land served mostly as a supplement. On half of
the confiscated territories state farms were established.

The smallest land reform was carried out in Bulgaria, where only 2
per cent of the cultivated land was expropriated and about 1.5 per cent
was distributed. Besides the 120,000 hectares appropriated from the
church, an additional 45,000 hectares were taken away from 5,000 estates during the reforms. Most of the lands obtained were utilized to
supplement the farms of 120,000 families.

Through these changes the structure of land tenure in the East-Central
European countries, which was very different in the previous historical

periods, became almost identical and reflected the rule of small peasant farms. These changes in land distribution by size of estates, before and after World War II, are shown in the accompanying table.

The distribution of land already reflected the anti-capitalist endeavors of the Communists, socialists, and other left-wing forces participating in the governments. Besides the confiscation of lands owned by capitalist enterprises (in Hungary about 0.5 million hectares), there was also the important reduction of rich peasant estates. The anti-capitalist tendencies were connected with the increasing role of the state farms, and their significant expansion. These trends, however, had not come into full operation under the influence of the internal and international situation, but were already operating on a large scale through the action against enemy property and restrictions on the wealthiest strata of the population.

Table 14.1 Percentage Distribution of Land in East-Central European Countries by Size of Estates Before and After Land Reforms

Country	Size of Estates in Hectares				
	0–2	*2–5*	*5–50*	*50–100*	*100–*
Czechoslovakia					
before reforms	7.8	14.3	61.9	16.0	
after reforms	7.9	17.9	74.2		
Poland					
before reforms					
after reforms	6.0	21.5	72.5		
Hungary					
before reforms	10.9	9.2	33.5	5.5	40.9
after reforms	23.1	27.3	49.6		
Rumania					
before reforms	12.8	15.2	39.8	4.5	27.7
after reforms	57.7		39.3	3.0	
Bulgaria					
before reforms	5.3	24.7	68.4	1.6	
after reforms	6.7	30.9	62.4		
Yugoslavia					
before reforms	6.5	21.5	62.4	3.2	6.4
after reforms	7.6	28.3	64.1		

Source: Based on national statistics.

Among the postwar political demands the confiscation of capital of the enemy or collaborators, the limitation of the biggest monopolies, and the nationalization of some basic industries became important even from the first on the initiative of the Communist and workers' parties, with the almost total approval of the anti-Fascist forces. These measures were carried out in the countries of the area in the months immediately after the war.

The most extensive limitations on capital were imposed in Yugoslavia, Poland, and Czechoslovakia. The property of the citizens of Axis countries and of collaborators was very soon nationalized in all three countries, followed during 1945–46 by the nationalization of several important branches of industry and the economy.

An order was issued as early as the end of 1944 on the confiscation of enemy and collaborator property in Yugoslavia. The constitution adopted in January 1946 declared in principle that all the minerals, natural resources, and means of transportation are public properties. This was followed by the December law, according to which all the industries of national importance were nationalized. Owing to the broad range of definition, mines, power stations, and iron and metal works were almost completely nationalized, while chemicals and the building material industries were for the most part nationalized. As a result of these measures, 82 per cent of Yugoslav industry became state property in 1945–46.

Similarly in Poland. As one of the first steps, enemy property was nationalized. This was soon followed, in January 1946, by new radical measures, according to which all factories employing more than 50 workers in important industries were nationalized. As a result, most of the industrial sector, employing 84 per cent of the industrial workers, became nationalized.

State ownership started relatively early in Czechoslovakia, too. The industrial sector was regulated by a series of orders, and the types of enterprises to be nationalized were defined either by national interest or by their size in the different branches. Those employing from 150–500 workers were to be nationalized. These orders alone increased the state sector in industry to about 57 per cent. The extent of nationalization differed according to industrial branch; 100 per cent of mining was nationalized; 70 per cent of chemicals, 50 per cent of textiles, 20 per cent of wood processing, but only 3 per cent of the printing industry. The situation that had developed by the end of 1945 did not change essentially up to 1948.

In Hungary, Rumania, and Bulgaria, the situation was different. Nationalization could not have been carried out after the war in these countries, either because of the political power relations or because of their international status and possibilities. The new balance of power, however, soon made possible a broader restriction of capital. The serious losses of the war, and the economic chaos and exhaustion following the war, made strong intervention by the state inevitable. In Hungary in the early postwar years (1945–46), 75 per cent of incomes in the manufacturing industries came from state sources, as was stated in the spring of 1946 by the Gazdasági Fötanács (Chief Economic Council), the main state managing organization. More than 90 per cent of the output of mining, iron, metal and machine industry was produced by state orders—for reconstruction and war compensation. The textile industry could sell only 30 per cent of its output free. The formerly omnipotent big banks also lost their independence of action, since the value of their deposits depreciated in the inflation following the war. Their role in this situation was limited to transferring the uncovered paper money, issued by the state, to the money market: 90 per cent of the assets of the joint-stock banks originated from the National Bank, even at the end of 1945, and about 76 per cent in 1946.

The lack of fuel and raw materials and the shortage of food and consumer goods gave rise to the need for state distribution and rationing, providing further impetus to the economic activity of the state.

These forms of intervention represented not merely temporary measures in the months following the war. State intervention could not be eased even in the period of gradual economic recovery; in fact, just the opposite was true in many fields. The preservation and even extension of state intervention was inevitable between 1946 and 1948 in order to curb inflation and preserve the stability of money. The stabilization carried out in Hungary in August 1946, based strictly on internal sources, could only be maintained on the basis of a strict deflationary monetary policy, totally centralized price regulation and control, and a strong tax policy, which served to balance the state budget.

These regulations created a system where the traditional free market and price fluctuations determined by supply and demand were squeezed into the narrow limits of regulations carried out from above. The state acquired an extraordinary influence over the economy, maintaining a strong restriction on private capital which established in the changed political-social situation a peculiar state capitalist economy.

Most industrial enterprises became increasingly unprofitable owing to the general money shortage, credit control, the fixed price level, and the big state burdens. "The officially fixed paper prices have not covered the production costs now and since," stated the report of Hungary's biggest paper factory. "As a consequence the firm has worked with a continuous deficit. This loss takes about 20% of the gross turnover." At the general assembly of the National Federation of Hungarian Manufacturers in June 1947 the Chairman, Paul Fellner, complained, "Growing burdens are imposed on the shaky, weak shoulders of industrial firms, partly by the government, partly by the given situation. These, and the extremely grave taxes, represent such a serious load, which on the surface is expressed in the industrial prices but in this respect the industry is only a collector for the treasury. According to our calculations 35–65% of the industrial price level is an expenditure of that nature."[1]

In fact, more and more state tax and credit debts were accumulated by the enterprises, and they became more dependent on the state. The different government regulations and the activities of the so-called factory communities, with the rights of broad control and intervention imposed a strict restriction on capital and was a preparation for capital expropriation.

Many steps had been taken toward partial nationalization in Hungary between 1945 and 1947, characteristic of the regulations under state capitalism. According to the program of the Front of Independence in December 1944, a law was issued on the national control of coal mines. (Coal mines were nationalized in the summer of 1946.) As a consequence, 22 per cent of the factory workers and miners were already employed in state enterprises. Some of the large iron and machine factories had been state property from the end of the nineteenth century. The four biggest factories in heavy industry had been controlled by the

[1] Két Beszéd (Two Speeches), Budapest, 1947, pp. 6–7.

state, though formally only during the period of compensational deliveries. Later, the electric power stations were nationalized. At the end of 1946 more than 45 per cent of industrial workers were in the state sector. The next steps in gradual nationalization were accomplished during the summer and fall of 1947. This time the ten biggest banks were nationalized, which not only resulted in complete state monopoly of the credit system but linked a further important part of the industry to the state sector (with 58 per cent of the workers).

Although the clearest form of state control was realized in Hungary, a basically similar policy was carried out in the other countries of the area. The process started later and developed in less resolved forms in Rumania and Bulgaria.

In Rumania state control was connected with financial stabilization, by nationalizing the National Bank in December 1946; and at the same time it was realized in the field of credit regulations. After the middle of 1947, however, state intervention expanded broadly. The reorganization of the ministry of industry and trade, centralization of different bureaus dealing with the direction of the economy, and the fact that they were placed under Communist leadership, with the ministerial nomination of G. Georghiu-Dej, introduced complete state control. Enterprises were included in the framework of the Officiale Industriale, organized according to industrial sectors and controlled by the state; decision making thus was handed over to the state.

To complete these measures, and as a result of the political changes taking place in 1947–48, the dictatorship of the proletariat was introduced, the coalition government liquidated, and the restrictions of state capitalism were given up and replaced by radical nationalizations. A law on the nationalization of industry was issued in Bulgaria, on December 24, 1947, immediately increasing the proportion of the state sector from 6 per cent to 85 per cent. In Hungary the nationalization of factories employing more than 100 workers was declared on March 25, 1948, increasing the state sector to 83 per cent, on the basis of the number of workers. A very radical law on June 11, 1948, with flexible criteria, nationalized 85 per cent of the industry in Rumania.

The political changes completed the nationalization in all the countries. The factories employing more than 50 workers were ordered to be nationalized in Czechoslovakia at that time. The nationalization was even extended to smaller factories with local importance in Yugoslavia. The limit of private enterprise was fixed at 10 workers employed in Hungary, but in some areas—for instance, the printing industry—there was 100 per cent nationalization.

The liquidation of private enterprise was extended to all sectors of the economy, and state control was completed in the fields of foreign trade and also in domestic wholesale trade. At the same time the building up of the network of the state-owned internal retail trade was started. The existing private foreign trade businesses, which were still important everywhere in 1945–48, were completely liquidated. (Before 1948, two-thirds of the imports and about half of the exports were in private hands in Czechoslovakia, and 60 per cent of the entire foreign trade in Hungary.) The nationalization of the internal wholesale trade was also carried out in most of the countries during 1948–49 (Czechoslovakia, Hungary, Rumania). This had already been accomplished in Yugoslavia during 1945–46, and these processes had also taken place earlier in Bulgaria, during 1946–47.

The revolutionary transformation and the very extensive state intervention created basically favorable conditions for postwar reconstruction. The socio-economic changes created new sources of reconstruction; a maximum concentration of forces and consciousness. The possibility of central regulation was realized through the introduction of planned economies.

The state sector strengthened by partial or extensive nationalization and state regulation and control of economic activities led to the formation of a multisectoral economy and the introduction of central planning. The first economic plans were elaborated, or came into force, during 1947, at almost the same time in the various countries. In January the first five-year plan of Yugoslavia started with a Soviet-type program of industrialization. At the same time a three-year plan was started in Poland, the central aim of which was to create the economic unity of the new Polish state. The Czechoslovak two-year plan, which also started in January 1947, emphasized in addition to reconstruction targets, the start of industrialization in Slovakia. At the center of the Bulgarian two-year plan, started in April 1947, and also of the Hungarian three-year plan, which came into force in August, was reconstruction and a schedule for reaching the prewar production level. Only Rumania did not elaborate reconstruction plans in this period.

The East European countries completed their peculiar state capitalist system with planning, based on comprehensively controlled market relations. In these years planning was extended only to the main sectors of the economy, and was concentrated on the largest investments in order to liquidate bottlenecks caused by war damage and to secure fast returns and high productivity. Dynamic progress in the central sectors, it was hoped, would push forward the economy as a whole. All the plans contained elements promoting some structural changes that would put industry and the output of investment goods in the forefront.

The introduction of planned economies helped to solve the extremely difficult problems of financing. The reconstruction involved grave economic burdens because the East-Central European countries, especially Poland, Yugoslavia, and Hungary, suffered very serious war damage. As mentioned before, they lost from one-third to 40 per cent of their national wealth. Reconstruction expenditures had to come from an output and national income one-fourth to one-fifth lower than the prewar level. In the past these countries had relied heavily on massive foreign sources to solve their much more modest investment problems. After 1945, however, there were scarcely any possibilities of utilizing foreign sources. The only exception was UNRRA, which provided substantial aid to Yugoslavia and Poland. According to the agreement of March 24, 1945, Yugoslavia received aid amounting to $3.7 billion up to June 1947, the end of deliveries. Most of the shipments were of raw materials and food. During 1945–46, 60 per cent of the grain and 100 per cent of the fats needed in the country were covered by UNRRA deliveries, which also provided the total supply of medicines. The assistance was also important for the communication and transport system, replacing a part of the rolling stock that had been destroyed. The value of the deliveries amounted to about 50–60 per cent of all imports in 1934–38.

Poland also received important UNRRA aid during 1945–46, amounting to $481 million. Shipments valued at $92 million were delivered in 1945, and $306 million worth in 1946. In 1946, 11 per cent of all the marketed goods were delivered through the aid program. The most important item was food (over $300 million), textile goods, and medicines; but animals, equipment, and machinery, of which $76 million went for reconstruction of agriculture and $95 million for industry, played a marginal role.

UNRRA assistance received by Czechoslovakia, amounting to $261 million in the form of industrial, transport, and other equipment and goods, was also very important.

The UNRRA program, however, was meaningless in the other countries of the area—in the former German satellites. Only $4 million worth of food and medicine were approved in January 1946 for Hungary, for instance. This modest help was equal to only one-fourth of all Hungarian imports in 1946.

The available external sources could be extended by only very limited credit possibilities. Most of these were also at the disposal of those countries that took part in the anti-Hitler coalition. Poland, for instance, received $40 million in American credit from the Export-Import Bank in April 1946 for the purchase of transport and mining equipment, and another $30 million for purchasing equipment from the U.S. military stocks in Europe. In the early postwar years $150 million credit was granted to Czechoslovakia from the United States, England, and Canada.

The loan-raising possibilities for the other countries did not even reach this modest figure. In the summer of 1946 the representatives of the Hungarian General Credit Bank, for instance, were told by Anthony Rothschild in response to their loan request that there would have to be a delay in granting credits for Hungary.[2] Besides the smaller export credits received through commercial contracts early in 1947 under a decision by the U.S. government, Hungary received a loan of $15 million to purchase equipment from the European stock of the American Army. (Some 500 steam engines and a number of trucks helped the reconstruction of transportation.)

Although the U.S. government announced that it had doubled the credit limit for purchasing goods in February 1947, the disbursement of the credit was stopped at the beginning of June.

During 1945 and 1948 only smaller loans, mostly for purchasing goods, had been granted to the East-Central European countries, with the

[2] Hungarian National Archives, Creditbank. 239 ch. October 7, 1946.

exception of the UNRRA aid provided to Yugoslavia. Their former creditors generally refused to grant newer loans. This was partly the consequence of the special economic situation—that some of the former creditors had not even had capital surpluses immediately after the war— and partly because further credits depended on the settlement of their prewar debts. Most of the East European countries were strongly indebted to the Western countries in 1945, as a consequence of freezing payments in the 1930s. Hungary, for instance, had an outstanding debt of 2.8 billion pengös, which was more than $500 million on September 30, 1945. Most of the creditor countries were reluctant even to conclude agreements until the debtor countries undertook to gradually service at least part of their debts through commodity deliveries. The main reason for the rejection, however, was evidently not economic but political, and was connected with the uncertain status of East Europe; the Western great powers at that time by no means wanted to grant significant credits. The hope of the Hungarian government of receiving Western credits of about $450 million, which was semi-officially announced by the Communist undersecretary of state for finances, Istvan Antos, in April 1946, was not realized. The more firmly formulated Polish request for credit which was presented to the World Bank by the Polish government was also rejected at the beginning of 1947.

The Western attitude toward granting larger credits changed substantially in 1947, undoubtedly in connection with political aims. The Marshall plan was introduced; but because of increasing cold-war tension the Soviet Union rejected participation as did the Czechoslovak and Polish governments, altering their former position. After the radical political changes and the growing international tension, there was no further possibility of getting credits from the former creditors. On the one hand, the Western countries did not want to offer any help; on the other hand, the socialist countries did not request it principally for political reasons. The Polish three-year plan, which based 15–20 per cent of its financing on foreign sources, and the Hungarian three-year plan, one variant of which was based on foreign investments amounting to 13–18 per cent, had to depend on internal sources alone. This was not changed by the fact that the Soviet Union provided some credit to the East European countries from 1947 on, following the smaller loans in 1945 of food and raw material deliveries. Yugoslavia, Poland, and

Rumania in 1947, and Czechoslovakia and Bulgaria in 1948, received credits of $10–$15 million for purchasing raw materials. Poland and Czechoslovakia received credits also in foreign currency from the Soviet Union. The total amount of these credits up to 1948–49 was $90 million, of which the foreign currency credit for Poland and Czechoslovakia totaled $51 million.

The modest credit-granting by the Soviet Union after the war—with the exception of the foreign currency loans—was mostly connected with foreign trade; it materialized in export credits ($25 million in food, $15 million in transportation equipment). Although the Soviet credits were clearly connected with political developments, they were at the same time inseparable from the new foreign trade orientation of the East European countries after the war. With the temporary or permanent loss of their traditional trade partners, the extreme isolation and unavailability of deliveries in the critical postwar months, trade with the Soviet Union was the only possibility for most East European countries, to establish the necessary international economic relations and to serve as a basis for the reconstruction. The share of the Soviet Union in the imports of many East European countries in 1945 was 80–90 per cent of the supplies of raw materials (cotton, iron, ores, grain, etc.), delivered mainly in the first months. It is true that this share decreased after the partial restoration of traditional trade relations, but it was still about one-fifth of the total Hungarian, Polish, and Czechoslovak foreign trade in 1948. In Rumania the Soviet share approached one-fourth, in Bulgaria one-half, of the total.

Taking into account the growing volume of foreign trade, it is evident that export and import among the Eastern European countries increased to one-third to three-fourths of their total trade in the period of reconstruction as compared with the prewar proportion of one-tenth to one-sixth.

The Soviet credits hardly exceeded the category of commercial credits, and though they contributed to the reconstruction of foreign trade in East Europe, essentially Soviet credits did not ease the problems of finance. The East European countries had to solve the difficult tasks of reconstruction basically from their own sources.

The burdens of financing reconstruction were especially grave in countries where the internal accumulation in the prewar years was traditionally low and where the countries also suffered heavy war damages. The case of the former satellites seemed practically hopeless. Not only did they have to rely on their own resources but at the same time they had to fulfill their obligations to pay compensation for the war damages. This was true for Hungary and Rumania. The 12th paragraph of the armistice agreement, concluded between the Allied Powers and Hungary in January 1945, declared that Hungary was obliged to compensate for its part of the damages caused during the occupation of Soviet, Czechoslovak, and Yugoslav territories. The sum to be paid was $200 million to the Soviet Union, $70 million to Yugoslavia and $30 million to Czechoslovakia in six years, mostly in the form of goods. It would not have been hard to pay this sum in normal circumstances, but the ruined economy and the needs of reconstruction required the greatest efforts and sacrifices. The value of delivered goods was based on 1938 world market prices, increased by 10–15 per cent. However, the real burdens were higher than the nominal obligation, owing to higher-than-average Hungarian production costs. According to the official currency rate of 1938, one dollar was equal to 5.15 Hungarian pengös, which would amount to about 1.5 billion pengös in recompensation deliveries. But because of the differences in the price levels one recompensation dollar was really equal to 10.21 pengös in delivered goods. The $300 million in Hungarian deliveries cost 3 billion pengös in 1938 prices, instead of 1.5 billion. In the first year war compensation absorbed 17 per cent of the diminished national income of 1945–46. This proportion decreased to 10 per cent of the national income in 1946–47, and to 7 per cent in the following years.

According to the armistice agreement, Rumania was similarly obliged to pay recompensation to the Soviet Union in six years, with 55 per cent of it in oil and oil products. The Rumanian national economy suffered much less war damage than Hungary but was at a more backward stage of economic growth. Almost 38 per cent of the budget went for compensation in 1946–47, and almost 47 per cent in 1947–48, or about 14–15 per cent of the national income.

The heavy burdens of compensation naturally influenced unfavorably the possibilities of reconstruction in these countries and deprived the economy of important resources. It would be one-sided, however, to judge the effect of the deliveries only from this point of view. The reparational deliveries were heavy burdens but they gave a stimulus to many important fields by initiating production. The Hungarian machine tool industry is an example. Almost non-existent formerly, it was established in the most critical postwar months. In the frame of recompensation the Soviet Union wanted to dismantle 5,000 modern machine tools in the Hungarian industry. However, the Hungarian government suggested that instead of dismantling, they manufacture 3,450 new machine tools. The Soviet Recompensation Committee accepted this offer. The two biggest Hungarian machine factories—the Manfred Weiss Works, Csepel, and the Budapest-Salgótarján Machine Factory—introduced the serial production of machine tools, instead of dismantling. The recompensation duties also gave a stimulus to rebuild the Rumanian oil production and oil processing industries.

Thus the grave burdens of compensation were at the same time a factor in the rapid start of reconstruction. Because the payments were mostly in the form of industrial goods, they provided a stimulus to rapid recovery in 1945–46. Another special feature of these years, connected with the obligations of compensation, was the establishment of joint ventures by the Soviet Union in Rumania, Hungary, Bulgaria, and Yugoslavia. The establishment of such companies was connected with the provision of the armistice agreement which permitted the expropriation of German properties abroad for the benefit of the victorious countries. The German interests in the territory of the former satellite countries were regarded as part of German war compensation to be paid to the Soviet Union. As we have seen in previous chapters, by the end of the war considerable German interests existed in the economy of Hungary, Rumania, and also Bulgaria, though on a much smaller scale. The German-owned shares automatically became Soviet property. In many cases the Soviet state did not keep a portion of some bank or industrial shares, but changed them through interstate agreements, and sometimes these interests in several enterprises were concentrated in a reduced number. Besides these new Soviet-owned ventures, enterprises with mixed interests were also established, serving as a basis for joint companies. For instance, in Hungary the Soviet Union received a 42 per cent former German interest in the firm of Aluminiumérc Bánya és Ipari R. To establish a joint company the Hungarian partner turned over a further 8 per cent of the shares. The Soviet partner paid with the return of shares of another company (Bauxit-Ipar-Rt.) where they had only a minor interest. In the case of joint transportation enterprises, the Hungarian state turned over shares for deliveries of Soviet equipment. Upon the establishment of the Joint Danube Shipping Company, the Soviets delivered towboats of 1,800 horsepower capacity and barges of 14,000 tons load-bearing capacity. A Soviet Hungarian intergovernmental agreement was signed on April 8, 1946, with the establishment of Hungarian-Soviet bauxite-aluminium and oil companies, and also joint ventures in Danube navigation (MESZHART) and air transport (MASZOVLET).

The joint enterprises provided for a 50 per cent interest to each partner. They were under Soviet leadership and enjoyed a privileged legal economic position. The organized network of joint enterprises was not so significant in Hungary, although such enterprises were important in the alumina and aluminium industries and in oil production. By 1948 the complete network was only 3.7 per cent of the whole Hungarian industry (calculated on the basis of the number of employed workers). Water transportation was entirely under joint control, and banking partially.

The joint enterprises achieved much greater influence in the Rumanian economy. As we have seen, the role of foreign capital was more important in the underdeveloped economy of Rumania before the war, and the economic life was much more firmly under their control, than in Hungary. The resolution of the Potsdam Conference concerning the Soviet rights of ownership of German properties and investments created important Soviet shares, especially in some leading raw material industries. Eight big Soviet-Rumanian enterprises were established, in addition to the joint bank, air, shipping and insurance companies. These included iron and metal production, coal mining, and the extraction of oil and natural gas. In coal mining, the basis of the joint enterprise was the mining shares of Petrozseny, which were received from the Hungarian government as reparation. According to some estimates, the share of the joint enterprises reached 35 per cent of the stock value in 1946 of Rumanian large industrial firms and financial institutes. Whatever doubts there may be about the accuracy of these figures, it is true that the influence of joint enterprises was decisive, especially in the key industries, from the point of view of reconstruction and the whole national economy.

In Bulgaria the German properties received as reparation had a leading role only in mining. A joint enterprise was established in 1946 called GORABSO. This enterprise dealt with the mining of nonferrous ores in Rhodope. The other German properties remained exclusively in Soviet hands, mostly in the building material industries and in shipbuilding until 1950 when they were converted to joint enterprises.

Two joint enterprises were operating for a short period in Yugoslavia too. Their origin had nothing to do with German property, which did not belong to the Soviet Union anyway, but with Yugoslav efforts to build up air and water transportation. The JUSTA was organized to establish public air transport; the JUSPDOL, a joint company, for Danube shipping. After two years of activity both enterprises were closed down in 1949 because of the Yugoslav-Soviet conflict.

The reconstruction tasks, based on self-reliance and, in some countries, reparations left open only one financial possibility—an inflationary money policy. The depreciation was already well advanced in the East European countries during the war years. Serious inflation developed in Yugoslavia, Bulgaria, Hungary, and Rumania due to the military operations and to uncompensated deliveries to Germany. During this period the banknotes in circulation increased 42 times in Yugoslavia, 22 times in Bulgaria, 14 times in Hungary, 6 times in Rumania. After such precedents and because of a decreased production level and substantially increased financing requirements, inflation in some of the countries became uncontrolled in the postwar years, especially in Hungary and Rumania. The process is illustrated by the increase in the volume of banknotes in circulation: 0.9 billion pengös were in circulation when the war started in Hungary; 14.5 billion in the spring of 1945; 47.5 quadrillion in July 1946— a volume unprecedented in world history. The real purchasing power of this remarkable amount of paper money was altogether 3.5 million pengös, only a fraction of the value of prewar coin stock. In Rumania the 39 billion lei in circulation in 1939 jumped to 560 billion in May 1945 and to 48,451 billion in August 1947.

Inflation was much more modest in the other countries of the area. The currency reform in Yugoslavia was already in effect in April 1945. Not only were the chaotic monetary relations of the occupation liquidated during the reform, but 292 billion dinar in circulation were reduced first to 6 billion and later to 18 billion as a consequence of strict state measures. The depreciation was extremely moderate in Czechoslovakia. The index of the money in circulation (based on 1938 = 100) was 254 in 1945. The depreciation was slow to the end of 1948. During the same period banknotes in circulation rose only 3.6 times. In Poland the circulation of banknotes increased more rapidly, about 7 times, between the end of 1945 and the end of 1948.

The moderate or extremely rapid inflation was very important in the postwar recovery of the East European countries: it imposed heavy burdens on the population and also created a peculiar inflationary boom. The enterpreneurs wanted to get rid of the rapidly depreciating money, shifted mostly into fixed investments. Capital shortage could be solved by greatly depreciating state credits and by paying off the compensation primarily with uncovered paper-money issue. Where it was almost impossible to control the inflation and depreciation became more and more disruptive for production and for providing the basic needs of the population, it was curbed relatively soon, as for instance in Hungary by August 1946. In Rumania this step was taken during the summer of 1947. After inflation was curbed, there were no longer any important setbacks or stagnation in the rate of reconstruction. Some deflationary phenomena occurred, however, and were accompanied by disturbances in credit and working capital, but the effect of these could not be compared with the crises in stabilization, deflation, and consolidation which followed World War I. The reconstruction did not come to a standstill since the reconstruction plans in 1947 in most of the East-Central European countries not only provided for continuous progress by great concentration of forces and a system of priorities, but speeded it up in some aspects. Planning gave preference to investments of high efficiency. Thus, industrial capacity could be utilized more rationally than previously. A rapid growth in productivity could be achieved even with a relatively lower rate of investment because of the liquidation of bottlenecks caused by war damages. The different plans scheduled the end of reconstruction either by 1948 or 1949. The important indices of the economy, above all the level of the national income and of industrial output, proved that the prewar level was achieved by 1948 or at least by the latter part of 1949, with the exception of Rumania. Even in those countries where the reconstruction plans lasted until 1949, the production level was higher in that year than in the prewar period.

Table 14-2. Indices of Industrial
Production and National Income in
East-Central European Countries, 1948
and 1949 *(1938 = 100)*

Country	Industrial Output		National Income	
	1948	*1949*	*1948*	*1949*
Poland	140	165	117	125
Hungary	107	137	88	124
Rumania	85	114	79	90
Bulgaria	184	245	111	138
Yugoslavia	150	168	103	106
Czechoslovakia	108	122	106	113

Source: Based on *Economic Survey of Europe,*
Geneva, 1949.

The relative speed of the reconstruction process becomes clear if we take into account that in most of the West European countries, although the war damages were not as heavy as in the East, industrial output and national income did not regain their prewar levels as fast. The rate of reconstruction in the East European countries was speeded up mostly by liquidating bottlenecks through flexible planning methods applied in the mixed (private and state) national economies. By putting certain production units into operation it was possible to start operating some other plants. This is evident by the capital coefficient trend. One unit of investment resulted in 2.5 units of increase in national income; for instance, in Hungary in 1947–48. The ratio before the war was generally 1:0.6.

The other important factor in the rapid rate of reconstruction was a relatively large surplus of manpower. This made it possible to mobilize workers into production and also created dynamic growth of output through the increase in employment. (The only exception in this respect was Czechoslovakia. Here the reconstruction required not so much restoring of war damage but the achievement of prewar productivity levels. Hence the reconstruction period had a strongly intensive character.) In Hungary, for example, about 150,000 new workers were mobilized into the manufacturing industry between 1946 and 1948. The increase in employment was 80 per cent while the production increase was from 40 per cent of the prewar level to 107 per cent. (For instance, in the mining industries 40 per cent more workers were employed than before the war, in order to achieve the 1938 production level.) In Czechoslovakia, however, during 1945–46 a 50 per cent increase in production was achieved with only a 10 per cent increase in the number of workers.

Two other general tendencies of the process could be emphasized as special characteristics. While the restored capacities were replaced rapidly, and the prewar production level was almost reached, two structural modifications could be observed. The share of industry gradually increased and the proportion of agriculture declined. While the restoration of industry caused production capacities in most of the countries to surpass prewar levels by 1948–49, agricultural output did not come up to the prewar level in any of the East European countries. In Czechoslovakia, Hungary, and Rumania it reached about 90 per cent of peacetime output, and hardly exceeded 75 per cent in Poland. In Bulgaria alone was agricultural production close to that of the late 1930s.

The other conspicuous feature of structural change was the regrouping within industry. As part of the rapid restoration of industry in general, there was an extremely rapid increase in output of investment goods, with new capacities often substantially surpassing the prewar level. The food sector and light industries lagged behind in all the countries of the area. In Hungary in 1948, the production index for heavy industry was 124 (1938 = 100), food industry only 94, and light industry 86.

The reconstruction process in Czechoslovakia and the other countries was similar. These structural changes were partly the consequences of deliberate industrialization, mostly from 1948, but they were also the inevitable results of economic needs. The reconstruction could not have occurred other than by the most strenuous development of output of investment goods and raw materials because the demands of reconstruction as well as the obligations of reparation in some of the countries called for increased production in these sectors.

The East European countries in general fulfilled the tasks of restoration by 1948–49 and achieved the production level of the last peacetime year. If we regard the reconstruction task in a narrower sense, we could consider it accomplished by achieving the prewar level. However, reconstruction in a broader sense was far from finished. In such fields as agriculture, consumer goods, and services, much more needed to be done. Moreover, the replacement of the lost growth that would normally have been achieved betwen 1938 and 1948 was also a part of the reconstruction. In this sense by the beginning of the fifties many reconstruction tasks remained unsolved and the growth of the economy was strongly influenced by them for a time.

A new phase of economic development opened up after 1949–50 in the East European countries, based on the achievement of the prewar level of output and on the political changes fully accomplished in 1948. The new period was characterized by the socialist economic strategy, forced industrialization, collectivization of agriculture, and adoption of centralized planning based on compulsory directives. All these were inseparably connected with the radical socio-economic transformation and rapid economic growth occurring in Eastern Europe during the last twenty years.

Appendix

Exchange Rates, 1913 and 1925–1938 (U.S. cents per unit of national currency)

	Austria	Czecho-slovakia	Hungary	Poland	Rumania	Yugo-slavia	Bulgaria
1913	K r o n e				lei	dinar	leva
	20.26	20.26	20.26	—	19.30	19.30	19.30
	schilling[a]	korona[b]	pengo[c]	zloty[d]			
1925	14.06	2.97	—	17.74	0.48	1.70	0.73
1926	14.07	2.96	17.56	11.18	0.46	1.76	0.72
1927	14.08	2.96	17.47	11.19	0.60	1.76	0.72
1928	14.07	2.96	17.44	11.21	0.61	1.71	0.72
1929	14.06	2.96	17.49	11.19	0.60	1.76	0.72
1930	14.09	2.96	17.45	11.21	0.60	1.77	0.72
1931	14.02	2.96	17.45	11.20	0.60	1.77	0.72
1932	13.96	2.96	22.36	11.18	0.60	1.64	0.72
1933	15.45	3.82	29.57	14.41	0.78	1.77	1.00
1934	18.79	4.24	29.60	18.85	1.00	2.27	1.29
1935	18.83	4.16	29.56	18.88	0.93	2.28	1.30
1936	18.79	4.01	19.78	18.87	0.74	2.30	1.29
1937	18.77	3.49	19.73	18.92	0.73	2.30	1.29
1938	18.91	3.47	19.24	18.84	0.73	2.31	1.24

[a]Introduced in December 1924. 1 schilling = 10,000 Krone.
[b]Introduced 1919.
[c]Introduced November 1926. 14,000 Krone = 1 pengö.
[d]Introduced April 1924.

Note: After 1933 the actual exchange rates were higher, because of payment of different premiums.

Bibliographical Summary

Introduction

The broad economic historical background summarized in the Introduction—the formation of the peculiar East-Central-European development and its deviation from Western Europe's—is based on a rather rich literature, of which some important works are the following: G. F. Knapp: *Grundherrschaft und Rittergut.* Leipzig, 1897 and *Die Bauernbefreiung und der Ursprung der Landarbeiter in den älteren Theilen Preussens.* I-II. Munich and Leipzig, 1887; J. Nichtweiss: "Zur Frage der Zweiten Leibeigenschaft und des sogenannten Preussischen Weges der Entwicklung des Kapitalismus der Landwirtschaft Ostdeutschlands," *Zeitschrift für Geschichtswissenschaft.* Berlin, 1953. No. 3; S. D. Skazkin: "Osnovnye problemy tak nazyvaiemogo 'vtorogo izdaniia krepostnichestva' v Srednie i Vostochnoi Evrope" (The main problems of the so-called second edition of serfdom in Central and Eastern Europe). *Voprosy Istorii.* Moscow, 1958. No. 2; A. Klima and J. Macurek: *La question de la transition du féodalisme au capitalisme en Europe centrale, 16e = 18^e siècles.* x. Congrès International des Sciences Historiques. Göteborg, Stockholm and Uppsala, 1960. IV; J. Kulischer: *Allgemeine Wirtschaftsgeschichte des Mittelalters und der Neuzeit.* Munich and Berlin, 1929; J. Topolski: *Issledovania po agrarnoi istorii v narodno-demokraticheskoi Polshe. Ezhegodnik po agrarnoi istorii* (Research on agrarian history in the Polish people's democracy). Moscow, 1959; W. Abel: *Die landwirtschaftlichen Grossbetriebe Deutschlands.* Première Conférence d'Histoire Economique. Stockholm, 1960; W. Rusinski: *Hauptprobleme der Fronwirtschaft vom 16. bis zum 18. Jahrhundert in Polen und den Nachbarländern.* Première Conférence d'Histoire Economique. Stockholm, 1960. Particularly useful as a theoretical basis is the work of P. S. Pach: *Die ungarische Agrarentwicklung im 16-17. Jahrhundert. Abbiegung vom westeuropäischen Entwicklungsgang. Studia Historica.* Budapest, 1965. On the specific problems of the Balkans see: W. Miller: *The Ottoman Empire and Its Successors, 1801-1922.* Cambridge, 1923. L. S. Stavrianos: *The Balkans since 1453.* New York, 1963; and *The Balkans in Transition: Essays on the Development of Balkan Life and Politics since the Eighteenth Century.* Ed. by Ch. and B. Jelavich. Berkeley and Los Angeles, 1963.

Part I. The Rise: Transition to Modern Capitalist Economy and the Industrial Revolution

The historical and theoretical problems of the period under review, both the transition from traditional to modern capitalist economy and the structure and growth of modern economy, were based first of all on the following works: K.

Marx: *Das Kapital: Kritik der politischen Oekonomie.* I-III. Hamburg, 1903, 1904, 1909; V. I. Lenin: *Razvitie kapitalizma v Rossii* (The development of capitalism in Russia). Petersburg, 1899; A. Toynbee: *Lectures on the Industrial Revolution of the 18th Century in England.* London, 1887; S. Kuznets: *Six Lectures on Economic Growth.* Illinois, 1959 and *Postwar Economic Growth,* Cambridge, 1964; W. Rostow: *The Stages of Economic Growth: A Non-Communist Manifesto.* Cambridge, 1960; *The Economics of Take-off into Sustained Growth.* Ed. by W. Rostow. London, 1963 and *The Process of Economic Growth.* London, 1960; M. Dobb: *Studies in the Development of Capitalism.* London, 1960; *Problemi storici della industrialisazione e dello sviluppo.* Urbino, 1965; J. Schumpeter: *Business Cycles.* New York, 1964; *Capital Formation and Economic Growth.* Ed. by M. Abramovitz. Princeton, 1955; A. Gerschenkron: *Economic Backwardness in Historical Perspective.* Cambridge, 1962; *Economic Progress.* Ed. by L. M. Dupriez. Louvain, 1955; B. Hoselitz: *Sociological Aspects of Economic Growth.* Glencoe, 1960; P. Bairoch: *Révolution industrielle et sous-développement.* Paris, 1963; W. Hoffmann: *Stadien und Typen der Industrialisierung.* Jena, 1931; W. Sombart: *Der moderne Kapitalismus.* Munich and Leipzig, 1928; M. Weber: *General Economic History.* Illinois. 1950; "The Industrial Revolution and After." Ed. by M. J. Habakkuk and M. M. Postan, in Vol. VI of *The Cambridge Economic History of Europe.* Cambridge, 1965; *A History of Technology.* Ed. by Ch. Singer. Vol. IV-V. Oxford, 1954, 1958.

On the main trends of economic growth in the advanced countries in the period under review there is an abundance of historical literature. It is enough here, however, to refer to the most important comprehensive works comparing East-Central-European and Western trends. The theoretical works mentioned above present many valuable elements for this comparison. In addition, the basic books on England, the pioneer country of modern transformation, were very useful: T. S. Ashton: *The Industrial Revolution, 1760–1830.* London, New York and Toronto, 1948; Phyllis Deane: *The First Industrial Revolution.* Cambridge, 1965; J. D. Chambers: *The Workshop of the World: British Economic History from 1820 to 1880.* London, New York and Toronto, 1961; H. L. Beales: *The Industrial Revolution, 1750–1850: An Introductory Essay.* London, 1958; A. K. Cairncross: *Home and Foreign Investment, 1870–1913: Studies in Capital Accumulation.* Cambridge, 1953; H. J. Habakkuk: *American and British Technology in the 19th Century: The Search for Labour-saving Inventions.* Cambridge, 1962; P. Mantoux: *The Industrial Revolution in the 18th Century: An Outline of the Beginnings of the Modern Factory System in England.* London, 1961; *Studies in the Industrial Revolution: Essays Presented to T. S. Ashton.* Ed. by L. S. Presnell. London, 1960; P. Mathias: *The First Industrial Nation,* Cambridge, 1970.

On Continental Western Europe see: Sh. B. Clough and Ch. W. Cole: *Economic History of Europe.* Boston, 1952; A. Birnie: *An Economic History of Europe, 1760–1939.* London, 1951; J. H. Clapham: *The Economic Development of France and Germany, 1815–1914.* Cambridge, 1955; W. O. Henderson: *The Industrial Revolution in Europe, 1815–1914.* Chicago, 1961; W. Bowden, M. Karpovich and A. Usher: *An Economic History of Europe since 1750.* New York, 1937; W. Treue: *Wirtschaftsgeschichte der Neuzeit, 1700–1960.* Stuttgart, 1962; H. See: *Französische Wirtschaftsgeschichte.* Jena, 1936; A. L. Dunham: *The Industrial Revolution in France, 1815–1848.* New York, 1955; H. Mottek: *Wirtschaftsgeschichte Deutschlands.* Berlin, 1960; R. Cameron: *France and the Economic Development of Europe.* New Jersey, 1963; J. Kuczynski: *Studien zur Geschichte des Kapitalismus.* Berlin, 1958; *Studien zur Geschichte der industriellen Revolution.* Red. H. Mottek. Berlin, 1960; P. Benaerts: *Les origines de la grande industrie allemande.* Paris, 1933; F. K. Lütge: *Deutsche Sozial- und Wirtschaftsgeschichte.* Berlin, 1960; A. Sartorius von Waltershausen: *Deutsche Wirtschaftsgeschichte, 1815–1914.* Jena, 1923; "La rivoluzione industriale," *Studii Storici.* Rome, 1961. No. II.

For the East-Central-European political situation in the first half of the nineteenth century and especially for the general position of the Hapsburg Monarchy see H. Hantsch: *Die Geschichte Österreichs.* Graz, Vienna and Cologne, 1963; E. Zöllner: *Geschichte Österreichs von den Anfängen bis zur Gegenwart.* Vienna, 1961. A Marxist view from the Hungarian side is established by P. Hanák: *Probleme der Krise des Dualismus am Ende des 19. Jahrhunderts.* Studien zur Geschichte der Österreichisch-ungarischen Monarchie. Budapest, 1961.

On the national fight for independence in the Balkans the most comprehensive view is given by D. Djordjević: *Révolutions nationales des peuples balcaniques.* Belgrade, 1965. There is a rather thorough review of the historical development of Rumania: *Istoria Rômâniei.* Vol. IV. Bucharest, 1964. The problem of socio-economic transformation with special reference to the beginnings of capitalist transformation of agriculture and the questions of serfdom in the first half of the nineteenth century in Austria was treated by J. Blum: *Noble Landowners and Agriculture in Austria, 1815–1848.* Baltimore, 1948; also by K. Grünberg; *Studien zur österreichischen Agrareschichte.* Leipzig, 1901. For Hungary see Gy. Mérei: *Mezögazduság és agrártársadalom Magyarországon. 1790–1848* (Agriculture and the agrarian society in Hungary). Budapest, 1948.

For the general theoretical problems of capitalist transformation and especially for the delay between the decline of the traditional system and the rise of the new capitalist economy, see E. Niederhauser: *The Problems of Bourgeois Transformation in Eastern- and South-Eastern Europe.* Nouvelles Etudes Historiques. Budapest, 1965. Vol. I.

Some interesting studies have been presented on the first sign of modern economic development in the Balkans, among them: N. Todorov: "Sur quelques aspects du passage du féodalisme au capitalisme dans les territoires balkaniques de l'empire Ottoman," *Revue des Etudes Sud-Est Européennes.* Bucharest, 1968, I. 1–2; J. Grosul, N. Mohov and P. Sovetov: "Ob osobennostiah perehoda ot feodalizma k kapitalizmu" (On the peculiarities of the transformation from feudalism to capitalism). *Voprosy Istorii.* Moscow, 1965. No. 11; A. Oţetea: "Consideraţie asupră trecerii de la feudalism la capitalism în Moldova şi Ţara Romînească" (On the problem of transition from feudalism to capitalism in

Moldavia and Walachia). *Studii și materiale de istorie medie.* Bucharest, 1960; Dj. Natan: *Stopanska Istoria na Blgaria* (Economic History of Bulgaria). Sofia, 1957. On the same problems in the Hapsburg Monarchy see H. Hassinger: *Der Stand der Manufakturen in den deutschen Erbländern der Habsburger Monarchie am Ende des 18. Jahrhunderts. Die wirtschaftliche Situation in Deutschland und Österreich um die Wende vom 18. zum 19. Jahrhundert.* Stuttgart. 1964; J. Slokar: *Geschichte der österreichischen Industrie und ihrer Förderungunter Kaiser Franz I.* Vienna, 1914; Gy. Mérei: *Magyar iparfejlödés, 1790–1848* (Hungarian industrial development, 1790–1848). Budapest, 1950; J. Purš: "The Industrial Revolution in the Czech Lands," *Historica.* Prague, 1962.

The history of the concept of industrial revolution was treated by G. N. Clark: *The Idea of the Industrial Revolution.* Glasgow, 1953. The concept was introduced by J. S. Mill: *Principles of Political Economy.* London, 1865. See also K. Marx: *Das Kapital.* Vol. I; and F. Engels: *Die Lage der arbeitenden Klasse in England.* Leipzig, 1845. Referring to the main sources of this problem see: *Quellen zur Geschichte der Industriellen Revolution.* Ed. by W. Treue, H. Pönicke, and K. Manegold. Göttingen, 1966.

For the strongly differing interpretations of industrial revolution four different groups may be mentioned. Stressing only the most typical concepts we can refer to the neglect of the revolutionary process in industry by W. Bowden, M. Karpovich and A. Usher: *An Economic History of Europe since 1750.* New York, 1937; G. Unwin: *Studies in Economic History.* Ed. by R. M. Tawney. London, 1927. The second group speaks about industrial revolution in regard to each partial technical innovation in one or another branch of industry, as, for example, E. M. Carus-Wilson: "An Industrial Revolution of the Thirteenth Century," *Economic History Review.* London, 1941. XI. 1. For the industrial revolution as a process of transformation inside industry as a whole see: S. G. Strumilin: *Ocherki ekonomicheskoi istorii Rossii i SSSR* (Problems of economic history of Russia and the USSR). Moscow, 1966.

On the broader interpretation of socio-economic transformation, besides the previously cited works of Marx, Toynbee, T. S. Ashton, P. Bairoch, A. Gerschenkron, and Sh. Clough and Ch. W. Cole, see: J. K. Neff: "The Industrial Revolution Reconsidered," *Journal of Economic History.* New York, 1943. I; V. Jatsunsky: *Industrialisation of Russia before 1917.* Première Conférence d'Histoire Economique. Stockholm, 1960; D. Landes: "Technological Changes and Development in Western Europe, 1750–1914," in Vol. VI of *The Cambridge Economic History of Europe.* Cambridge, 1965; H. L. Beales: *The Industrial Revolution, 1750–1850.* London, 1958; E. Hobsbawm: *The Age of Revolution.* London, 1962. Representing this concept with a systematization of the different interpretations is the valuable study by D. C. Coleman: "Industrial Growth and Industrial Revolution," in Vol. III of *Essays in Economic History.* Ed. by E. M. Carus-Wilson. New York, 1962.

For the Marxist literature and divergences of views in connection with the interpretation of industrial revolution, besides the previously cited works of

Strumilin, Jatsunsky, and Hobsbawm, see: J. Kuczynski: "Zum Problem der industriellen Revolution," *Zeitschrift für Geschichtswissenschaft.* Berlin, 1956. No. 3; J. Purš: *Einige teoretische Probleme der Ökonomie und Politik in den Beziehungen zwischen Ost- und West-Europa vom 17, Jahrhundert bis zur Gegenwart.* Berlin, 1960; G. Mori: "Rivoluzione industriale: storia e significato di un concetto," *Studii Storici.* Rome, 1964, No. I; A. Špiesz: "K problematike počiatka priemyslovey revolúcie na Slovensku" (On the Problem of Industrial Revolution in Slovakia). *Historický Časopis.* Bratislava, 1954; I. T. Berend and Gy. Ránki: "Az ipari forradalom kérdéséhez Kelet-Délkelet-Európában" (Contribution to the problem of industrial revolution in Eastern-Southeastern Europe). *Századok.* Budapest, 1968. No. 1.

Chapter 1. The Demographic Preconditions of Modern Economic Development

On the general demographic problems and the Western European demographic progress rich material is presented in the following works: G. Sundbärg: *Aperçus Statistiques Internationaux.* Stockholm, 1908; M. Reinhard: *Histoire de la population mondiale de 1700 à 1848.* Paris, 1949; *Raum und Bevölkerung in der Weltgeschichte.* III. Ploetz. Würzburg, 1958; D. V. Glass and E. Grebenik: "World Population, 1800–1950," in Vol. VI of *The Cambridge Economic History of Europe.* Also useful in connection with the demographic processes in the nineteenth century are: *Handwörterbuch der Staatswissenschaften.* Jena, 1909; the popular summary by C. M. Cipolla: *The Economic History of World Population.* Baltimore, 1965; *Population Movements in Modern European History.* Ed. by H. Moller. New York, n.d. and Sh. Clough: *The Rise and Fall of Civilization.* New York, 1957.

For the demographic revolution of the British Isles see the works of T. S. Ashton and Phyllis Deane cited earlier. For France see P. Aries: *Histoire de la population francaise.* Paris, 1948. The examination of the countries under review can be based first of all on W. Moore: *Economic Demography of Eastern and Southeastern Europe.* Geneva, 1945. For the Austro-Hungarian Monarchy: *Einige Daten zur wirtschaftlichen Entwicklung Österreich-Ungarns in den letzten 50 Jahren.* Zusammengestellt von der Anglo-Österreichischen Bank, anlässlich ihres fünfzigjahrigen Jubilaeums. (No place and year of publication); M. Pisztory: *Az Osztrák-Magyar Monarchia statisztikája* (Statistics of the Austro-Hungarian Monarchy). Budapest and Pozsony, 1884. For Hungary the best statistical summary is: *Magyarország történeti demográfiája* (Historical demography of Hungary). Ed. by J. Kovacsics. Budapest, 1963. See especially in this volume the study by L. Thirring: *Magyarország népessége 1869–1949 között* (The population of Hungary between 1869–1949). For Russia: A. G. Rashin: "Naselenie Rossii za sto let, 1811–1913" (Population of Russia during a hundred years). *Statisticheskie ocherki.* Moscow, 1956. For Poland there are useful data in the book published by L. Wellisz: *The Problems of Postwar Economic Reconstruc-*

tion of Poland. Washington, 1944. Also useful in understanding the economic and cultural relations of Bosnia-Hercegovina is P. Sugar: *Industrialization of Bosnia-Hercegovina, 1878–1918.* Seattle, 1963. The special problem of emigration was examined in the very informative book by W. F. Wilcox and T. Ferenczy: *International Migration.* Vol. I. Geneva, 1929.

Chapter 2. Agrarian Transformation and Modern Agrarian Development

Besides the previously mentioned comprehensive economic histories of Western European agricultural development see also the valuable data in B. H. Slicher van Bath: *The Agrarian History of Western Europe. A.D. 500–1850.* London, 1963. A useful collection of studies with the aim of popularization is: *Agrarian Conditions in Modern European History.* Ed. by Charles Warner. New York and London, 1966. F. Dovring: "The Transformation of European Agriculture," in Vol. VI of *The Cambridge Economic History of Europe,* deals both with Western Europe and with East-Central Europe. On the agrarian development of East-Central Europe primarily after World War I but partly in the 19th and early 20th centuries an overall picture is given in W. Moore (already cited) and in D. Warriner: *The Economics of Peasant Farming.* London, 1939.

On the emancipation of the serfs and its background in the Hapsburg Monarchy, Rumania, and the Polish territory see E. Niederhauser: *A jobbágyfelszabaditás Kelet-Európában* (The emancipation of serfs in Eastern Europe). Budapest, 1962. In his other study—*A parasztság Európában,* in *A parasztság Magyarországon a kapitalizmus korában 1848–1914* (The peasantry in Hungary in the age of capitalism. 1848–1914) Ed. by I. Szabó. Budapest, 1965, Vol. II— the author is also dealing with the region of the Balkans and treats the question of agricultural development in addition to the institutional and judicial problems.

For the Austrian and Bohemian territory see K. Grünberg: *Die Bauernbefreiung und die Auflösung der gutsherrlich-bäuerlichen Verhältnisse in Böhmen, Mähren und Schlesien.* Leipzig, 1893, 1894; K. Grünberg: *Studien zur österreichischen Agrargeschichte.* Leipzig, 1901. For a comparison with Hungary see P. S. Pach: "A magyarországi és oroszországi poroszutas agrárfejlodés egyezö é eltérö vonásairól a 19. század második felében" (The similarities and differences in agrarian development of the so-called Prussian type in Russia and Hungary in the second half of the 19th century). *Közgazdasági Szemle.* Budapest, 1958. No. 1.

The abolishment of the traditional agricultural system and its remnants in Hungary have been discussed in *Parasztságunk a Habsburg önkényuralom korszakában* (The peasantry of Hungary in the age of Hapsburg absolutism). Ed. by P. Sándor. Budapest, 1951; Gy. Szabad: *A tatai és gesztesi Eszterházy uradalom áttérése a robotrendszerröl a tökés gazdálkodásra* (The transition of the serf system into capitalist agriculture in the Eszterházy estates in Tata and Gesztes). Budapest, 1957. For the comparison with Russia: V. I. Lenin: *Razvitie kapitalizma v Rossii* (The development of capitalism in Russia). Petersburg, 1899; S. Dybrovski: *K voprosu ob obshchinev Rossii v nachale XX veka* (On the problem of the obshchina in Russia at the beginning of the XXth century). *Ezhegodnik po agrarnoi istorii vostochnoi Evropy.* Kiev, 1962; A. Gerschenkron: "Agrarian Policies and Industrialisation, Russia 1861–1917," in Vol. VI of *The Cambridge Economic History of Europe.* Cambridge, 1965. For Rumania: D. Mitrany: *The Land and the Peasant in Rumania.* Oxford, 1930.

The tenant system and its use in Germany and Hungary was examined by J. Puskás: *Die kapitalistischen Grosspachten in Ungarn am Ende des 19. Jahrhunderts.* Studien zur Geschichte der österreichisch-ungarischen Monarchie. Budapest, 1961. For the capitalist tenant system in Russia see the previously cited work of Liashchenko; for Rumania: M. Serbian: *Rumäniens Agrarverhältnisse.* Berlin, 1913.

Regarding mortgage credits: *Handwörterbuch der Staatswissenschaften.* Vol. V. Jena, 1910; Gy. Vargha: *Magyarország hitelugye és hitelintézetei története* (The history of the credit- and bank-system in Hungary). Budapest, 1896; C. Jonescu: *Die geschichtliche Entwicklung und der gegenwärtige Zustand der rumänischen Landwirtschaft.* Berne, 1901; *The Early Banking in the Industrial Revolution.* Ed. by R. Cameron. New York, 1967.

Some of the above-mentioned works also deal with the use of machines in agriculture. Besides these works one may consult V. Slavescu: *Die Agrarfrage in Rumänien.* Halle, 1914. On the special problem of agrarian development in the Balkans see L. Stavrianos: *The Balkans since 1453.* New York, 1958; J. Tomasevich: *Peasants, Politics, and Economic Change in Yugoslavia.* Stanford, 1955; R. Aratinović: *Les ressources et l'activité économique de la Yougoslavie.* Paris, 1930; G. Entscheff: *Die Industrie Bulgariens mit besonderer Berüchsichtigung der Mehl- und Wollindustrie.* Leipzig, 1915. Dealing with later period and containing useful data is the work by G. Molloff: *Die sozialökönomische Struktur der bulgarischen Landwirtschaft.* Berlin, 1936.

For the agrarian development of the Austro-Hungarian Monarchy see in the series *Wirtschaftskunde der Länder der ehemaligen österreich-ungarischen Monarchie,* E. Puteari: *Die Rinder- und Schweinezucht.* Vienna, 1919. 6. Heft; S. Matlekovits: *Magyarország az ezredik évben* (Hungary in the thousandth year). Vol. II. Budapest, 1896; M. Szuhay: *L'évolution des cultures à charrue en Hongrie de 1867 à 1914.* Nouvelles Etudes Historiques. Budapest, 1965: S. Strakosch: *Die Grundlagen der Agrarwirtschaft in Österreich.* Vienna, 1906; *Österreichische Statistik LXXXIII.* Vienna, 1909.

On the urbarian regulation of Maria Theresa see: F. Eckhart: *A bécsi udvar gazdaságpolitikája Magyarországon Mária Terézia korában* (The economic policy of the Vienna Court in Hungary in the age of Maria Theresa). Budapest, 1922; F. Eckhart: *A bécsi udvar gazdaságpolitikája Magyarországon 1780–1815* (The economic policy of the Vienna Court in Hungary, 1780–1815). Budapest, 1958; D. Szabó: *A magyarországi urbérrendezés története Mária Terézia korában* (A history of the urbarian regulation in Hungary in the age of Maria

Theresa). Budapest, 1933. The first famous Hungarian statistician, E. Fényes, in his book *Magyarország leirása* (A description of Hungary) I-II. Pest, 1849, gives valuable data on the agricultural growth in the first half of the 19th century as well as on the different types of land estates and on the division of peasant and landlord estates. The most modern examination of the same problems is J. Varga: *Typen und Probleme des bäuerlichen Grundbesitzes in Ungarn.* Budapest, 1965. The changes in the structure of estates at the end of the 19th century was examined by J. Puskás: *A magyarországi mezögazdaság tökés fejlödésének vizsgálata az 1895. évi uzemstatisztika adatai alapján* (An examination of Hungarian capitalist agricultural development based on the agricultural statistics of 1895). Történelmi Szemle. Budapest, 1960. No. 4.

For Russia and Poland see: P. I. Liashenenko: *Istoria narodnogo khoziaistva SSSR* (The history of national economy of the Soviet Union). Moscow, 1952; P. A. Hromov: *Ekonomicheskoe razvitie Rossii v 19–20 vekah* (The economic development of Russia in the 19–20th centuries). Moscow, 1950; J. Rutkowski: *Historia gospodarcza Polski* (The economic history of Poland). Poznań, 1947; A. Rostworowski: *Die Entwicklung der bäuerlichen Verhältnisse im Königreich Polen im 19. Jahrhundert.* Jena, 1896. For Rumania: J. Adam and N. Marcu: *Studii despre dezvoltarea capitalismului în agricultura României Dupa reforma din 1864* (Studies on the development of capitalism in Rumanian agriculture. After the reform of 1864). Bucharest, 1956; A. Otetea: *Le second asservissement des paysans roumains, 1746–1821.* Nouvelles Études d'Histoire. Bucharest, 1956; A. Oțetea: *Le second servage dans les principautés danubiennes, 1831–1864.* Nouvelles Études d'Histoire. Bucharest, 1960; O. B. Ionescu: *Die Agrarverfassung Rumäniens, ihre Geschichte und ihre Reform.* Leipzig, 1901. For Serbia: N. Konstadinović: *Seljačko gazdinstvo u Jugoslaviji* (The agriculture in Yugoslavia). Belgrade, 1939; J. Tomasevich: *Peasants, Politics, and Economic Change in Yugoslavia.* Stanford, 1955; B. Arsitch: *La vie économique de la Serbie du Sud au XIXᵉ siècle.* Paris, 1936. For Bulgaria: Z. Natan: *Stopanska istoria na Blgaria* (The economic history of Bulgaria). Sofia, 1957.

A Marxist interpretation of the different types of capitalist agricultural development was established by V. I. Lenin. See Sochineniia Tom. 13. Moscow, 1952. This volume contains the two famous articles of Lenin: "The Agrarian Program of Socialdemocrats in the First Russian Revolution in 1905–1907" and "The Agrarian Problem and the 'Marx Critics.'"

A comparative examination of the differences in agrarian development among Eastern European countries was developed by P. S. Pach: "A magyarországi és oroszországi poroszutas agrárfejlódés egyezö és eltérö vonásairól a 19. század második felében" (The similarities and differences of the agrarian development of the so-called Prussian type in Hungary and Russia in the second half of the 19th century). *Közgazdasági Szemle.* Budapest, 1958. No. 1. Also worth consulting is P. Sándor: *A 19. századvégi agrárválság Magyarországon* (The agrarian crisis at the end of the 19th century in Hungary). Budapest, 1958. Besides the previously cited works of Liashchenko and Hromov see, for Russia, N. Egiazarova: *Agrarnii krizis kontsa 19 veka v Rossii* (The agrarian crisis at the end of the 19th century in Russia). Moscow, 1959. For the Balkan countries see: L. Pasvolsky: *Economic Nationalism of the Danubian States.* New York, 1926; J. Evans: *Agrarian Revolution in Rumania.* Cambridge, 1924. A. Otetea: *Consideratii asupră trecerii de la feudalism la capitalism in Moldova* (On the problem of transition from feudalism to capitalism in Moldavia and Walachia). Studii si materiale de istorie medie Vol. II. Dezvoltarea economiei Moldoviei între anii 1848 si 1864. Bucharest, 1963; A. Jaranoff: *La Bulgarie économique.* Lausanne, 1919; and the above-cited work of Z. Natan and A. Stanojević: *Die Landwirtschaft in Serbien.* Halle, 1913. Useful international data on livestock are to be found in L. Gaál: *A magyar állattenyésztés multja* (The past of Hungarian animal husbandry). Budapest, 1966.

Chapter 3. The Establishment of Modern Credit and a System of Transport

On the theoretical problems and Western European trend of processes examined in this chapter, we can refer to the previously cited works dealing with general economic historical problems. In addition some of the main special works are: L. Girard: "Transport," in Vol. VI of *The Cambridge Economic History of Europe.* Cambridge, 1965; L. Knowles: *Economic Development in the Nineteenth Century: France, Germany, Russia and the United States of America.* London, 1932; L. Pressnell: *Country Banking in the Industrial Revolution.* Oxford, 1956; L. H. Jenks: *The Migration of British Capital to 1875.* London, 1927; J. Bouvier: *Le Crédit Lyonnais de 1863 à 1882: Les années de formation d'une banque de dépots.* Paris, 1961; R. Cameron: *France and the Economic Development of Europe.* Princeton, 1961; L. Schwerin von Krosigk: *Die grosse Zeit des Feuers: Der Weg der deutschen Industrie.* Tübingen, 1957–1959. Refreshing views are presented in the previously cited work of A. Gerschenkron and in the study by R. Cameron: *The Early Banking in the Industrial Revolution.* New York, 1967.

From the rich literature dealing with the banking system in the Austro-Bohemian territory we should mention the two studies in the 1957 and 1959 volumes of *Schmollers Jahrbuch* by E. März: *Besonderheiten in der Entwicklung des österreichischen Bankwesens* and *Die historischen Voraussetzungen des Creditmobilierbankwesens in Österreich.* See also E. März: "Die Entwicklung des Bankwesens in den letzten Jahrzehnten der Osterreichisch-Ungarischen Monarchie," in the volume *Die Frage des Finanzkapitals in der Österreichisch-Ungarischen Monarchie.* Bucharest, 1965. The latter volume also contains J. Křížek: "Beitrag zur Geschichte der Entstehung und des Einflusses des Finanzkapitals in der Habsburg-Monarchie in den Jahren 1900–1914." Interesting material is also to be found in the special commemorative publication: *Hundert Jahre Creditanstalt-Bankwesen.* Vienna, 1955; and in *Hundert Jahre der österreichischen Wirtschaft.* Vienna, 1948. Ed. by H. Mayer. There is useful material in the *Tafeln zur Währungsstatistik.* Part II. Vienna, 1904; and in F. Steiner: *Die Entwicklung des Mobilbankwesens in Österreich.* Vienna, 1913. In recent literature see: E. März: *Österreichs Industrie- und Bankpolitik in der Zeit Franz Josephs I.* Vienna, 1969.

In connection with Austria but also a wider area see E. C. Corti: *Der Aufstieg des Hauses Rothschild, 1770-1830.* Leipzig, 1927, and *Das Haus Rothschild in der Zeit seiner Blüte, 1830-1871.* Leipzig, 1928. J. Bouvier: *Les Rotschilds.* Paris, 1966, gives a more modern view but deals less with the Austrian branch of the Rothschild House.

An examination of the Hungarian banking system can be made from the histories of the various big banks: L. Hegedüs: *A Pesti Magyar Kereskedelmi Bank keletkezésének és fennállásának története* (The establishment and history of the Hungarian Commercial Bank in Pest). Budapest, no date; A. Fenyvesi: *A Pesti Hazai Első Takarékpénztár Egyesület 50 éves története* (50 years history of the First Domestic Savingsbank Union in Pest). Budapest, 1890; J. Pólya: *A budapesti bankok története az 1867-1894. években.* (A history of the banks of Budapest, 1867-1894). Budapest, 1895. There are some comprehensive works on the Hungarian banking system as a whole: Gy. Varga: *A magyar hitelügy és hitelintézetek története* (The history of the Hungarian credit-system and banking institutions). Budapest, 1896 and A. Matlekovits: *Das Königreich Ungarn.* Leipzig, 1900. Valuable statistics appear in: *A Magyar Szentkorona országainak hitelintézetei, 1894-1909. években.* Magyar Statisztikai Közlemények. 35. (The banks of the countries of the Hungarian Holy Crown 1894-1909. publications of the Hungarian Statistical Office. No. 35). Budapest, 1913. For the modern literature: V. Sándor: *Nagyipari fejlődés Magyarországon* (The development of large-scale industry in Hungary). Budapest, 1954.

For Polish and Russian banking systems see: E. Piltz: *Poland; Her People, History, Industries, Finance, Science, Literature, Art and Social Development.* London, 1909; W. Kula: *Historia gospodarcza Polski w dobie popowstani owej, 1864-1918* (Polish economic history in the period after the revolt, 1864-1918). Warsaw, 1947; I. Kostrovicka, Z. Landau, and J. Tomaszewski: *Historia gospodarcza Polski 1920 weików* (The economic history of Poland in the 19th and 20th centuries). Warsaw, 1966. Besides the above-cited works of Lenin, Hromov, and Liashchenko, see also: F. Poljanski: *Pervonachalnoe nakoplenie kapitala v Rossii* (The primitive accumulation of capital in Russia). Moscow, 1958; *The State and Economic Growth.* Ed. by H. G. Aitken. New York, 1959; and F. Gindin: *Russkie kommercheskie banki* (The Russian commercial banks). Moscow, 1948. For banking in the Balkans consult: C. Colocotronis: *L'organisation bancaire des pays balkaniques et les capitaux étrangers.* Paris, 1934; H. Feis: *Europe: The World's Banker.* New York, 1965; E. Ene: *Les banques en Roumaine.* Paris, 1915; J. Kirkner: *Industrie Serbiens.* Halle, 1912; P. Ercuta: *Die Genesis des modernen Kapitalismus in Rumänien.* Leipzig, 1941; G. Giorceanu: *La Roumanie économique.* Paris, 1927.

The rise of the modern transport system is a very well explored field of economic history. One can find valuable data in the comprehensive works cited earlier. As special studies, treating the Austrian and Bohemian territory, see: *Fünfzig Jahre Staatsschuld.* Vienna, 1912; J. Grailer: "Das österreichische Verkehrswesen" and A. Gratz: "Die österreichische Finanzpolitik," both in the previously cited volume *Hundert Jahre der österreichischen Wirtschaft;* P. Kupka: *Die Eisenbahnen Österreich-Ungarns, 1822–1867.* Leipzig, 1868.

For Hungary: Gy. Ujhelyi: *A vasútugy története* (The history of railways). Budapest, 1910; S. Matlekovits: *Magyarország államháztartásának története* (The history of public finances in Hungary). Budapest, 1894; *Technikai fejlődésünk története, 1867–1927* (The history of technical development in Hungary, 1867–1927). Budapest, 1927; T. Földi: "A magyarországi vasötépités a külföldi nagytöke profitforrása" (Hungarian railway construction a profitable source of foreign capital) in the volume *Tanulmányok a kapitalizmus történetéhez Magyarországon, 1867–1918* (Studies on the history of capitalism in Hungary). Ed. by S. Pach and P. Sándor. Budapest, 1956.

For Russian and Polish railway construction we relied on the previously cited works. On the formation of modern transport in the Balkans, besides the study by H. Feis, see M. R. Dimtschoff: *Das Eisenbahnwesen auf der Balkan-Halbinsel.* Bamberg, 1894; *Aspecte ale economiei Românești* (Aspects of Rumanian economy). Consiliul Superior Economic Oficiul de Studii, cercetări si îndrumări. Cuvint lămuritor de N. Lupu-Kostaky. Bucharest, 1939; D. Aratich: *Histoire des chemins de fer yougoslaves.* Paris, 1938; J. Bousquet: *Les chemins de fer bulgares.* Paris, 1909.

From the rich literature on swindles as a concomitant of railway construction striking examples are presented in the study of T. Földi cited earlier, and in L. Schönberger: *Die ungarische Ostbahn: Ein Eisenbahnund Finanzskandal.* Vienna, 1873.

About the general economic consequences of railway construction and its theoretical aspects see: S. Pollard: *The Development of the British Economy, 1814–1950.* London, 1962; A. Fishlow: *American Railroads and the Transformation of the Ante-Bellum Economy.* Cambridge, 1965. In the work cited earlier, *The Economics of Take-off into Sustained Growth,* see the article by W. Rostow: "Leading Sectors and the 'Take off.'"

Chapter 4. The Role of the State

The theoretical challenge was made first of all by A. Gerschenkron in his essay *Typology of Industrial Development as a Tool of Analysis.* Deuxième Conférence Internationale d'Histoire Economique. Paris, 1962, and in his previously cited book. The collection of studies edited by H. G. Aitken also gives a many-sided approach. Among the basic works are the studies of B. F. Hoselitz: "Entrepreneurship and Capital Formation in France and Britain since 1770" in the volumes *Capital Formation and Economic Growth* and *The Progress of Underdeveloped Areas.* Chicago, 1952; P. T. Bauer and B. S. Janey: *The Economics of Underdeveloped Countries.* London and Cambridge, 1957; A. O. Hirschman: *The Strategy of Economic Development.* New Haven, 1958. From the recent literature a work that merits great interest is N. Spulber's *The State and Economic Development in Eastern Europe.* New York, 1966.

In the framework of the broadest interpretation there is a connection with the theoretical debate on economic strategy in the Soviet Union during the 'twenties. From the abundant literature let us point out here the study by M. Dobb: *Soviet Economic Development since 1917.* London, 1948, and A. Erlich: *The Soviet Industrialization Debate, 1924–1928.* Cambridge, 1960.

The special role of the state in East-Central Europe in connection with financing railroad construction was examined in a general way in the works mentioned as basic studies on railway construction. One can also refer to the following: *Geschichte der Eisenbahnen der österreichisch-ungarischen Monarchie.* Vienna, Teschen, and Leipzig, 1897–1899, 1909; J. Kaizl: *Die Verstaatlichung der Eisenbahnen in Österreich.* Leipzig, 1855; E. Neményi: *Die Verstaatlichung der Eisenbahnen in Ungarn.* Leipzig, 1890; G. Keller: *Der Staatsbahngedanke bei den verschiedenen Völkern, historisch dargestellt.* Aarau, 1897; *Handwörterbuch der Staatswissenschaften.* Vol. III. Eisenbahnen, Eisenbahnpolitik. Jena, 1909.

The role of the state in industry through customs policy and other forms of intervention in the area under review was examined by F. Hertz: *Die Schwierigkeiten der industriellen Produktion in Österreich.* Vienna, 1910; E. März: *Österreichische Industrie- und Bankpolitik in der Zeit Franz Josephs I.* Vienna, 1969; W. Offergeld: *Grundlagen und Ursachen der industriellen Entwicklung in Ungarn.* Jena, 1914; *Emlékirat a hazai kis- és gyáripar fejlesztéséről* (Memorandum on the developing of domestic small-scale and large-scale industry). Budapest, 1909; J. Szterényi and J. Ladányi: *A magyar ipar a világháboruban* (The Hungarian industry in the World War). Budapest, 1934; V. Sándor: *Nagyipari fejlődés Magyarországon 1867–1900* (The development of large-scale industry in Hungary). Budapest, 1954; I. T. Berend and Gy. Ránki: *Magyarország gyáripara 1900–1914* (The Hungarian manufacturing industry, 1900–1914). Budapest, 1955; J. Kirkner: *Die Industrie und Industriepolitik Serbiens.* Halle, 1913; O. P. Graf: *Die Industriepolitik Alt-Rumäniens und die Grundlagen der Industrialisierung Gross-Rumäniens.* Bucharest, 1927; V. Dinu: *Die Landwirtschaft Rumäniens unter dem Druck der Krisen.* Bucharest, 1933; N. N. Constantinescu: *Aspecte ale dezvoltării capitalismului premonopolist în Romînia* (Aspects of the development of premonopolist capitalism in Rumania). Bucharest, 1957; L. Pasvolsky: *Bulgaria's Economic Position.* Washington, 1929; J. Sakazov: *Bulgarische Wirtschaftsgeschichte.* Berlin, 1929; A. Gerschenkron: "Some Aspects of Industrialisation in Bulgaria, 1878–1939," in the volume *Economic Backwardness in Historical Perspective.* H. Rossovsky also contributes an important idea in stressing the accelerating influence of state intervention; see his study on "Japanese Capital Formation," *Journal of Economic History.* New York, September, 1959.

Chapter 5. Investments and Foreign Capital

The theoretical problems of foreign capital and its Western European connection were treated by C. K. Hobson: *The Export of Capital*. London, 1914; R. Hilferding: *Das Finanzkapital*. Berlin, 1947; V. I. Lenin: *Imperializm, kak vysshaia stadia kapitalizma*. (Populiarny ocherk). (Imperialism as the highest stage of capitalism). Petrograd, 1917; S. Kuznets: "International Differences in Capital Formation and Financing," in *Capital Formation and Economic Growth;* K. Berill: "Foreign Capital and Take off," in *The Economics of Take-off into Sustained Growth*. A. N. Imlah: "British Balance of Payments and Export of Capital," *Economic History Review*. London, 1952. No. 2; Organisation for European Economic Cooperation. *Report on International Investment*. OEEC. Paris, 1950; P. Douglas: "Capital in the United Kingdom," *Journal of Economic and Business History*. 1929–1930. See furthermore the above-mentioned works of H. Feis, R. Cameron, and L. Schwerin von Krosigk.

On the problem of capital import and export of the cis-Leithan part of the Austro-Hungarian Monarchy see H. Benedikt: *Die wirtschaftliche Entwicklung in der Franz Joseph-Zeit*. Vienna and Munich, 1958: Vol. II of *Tabellen zur Währungsstatistik;* J. Křížek: *Die wirtschaftlichen Grundzüge des Österreich-isch-Ungarischen Imperialismus der Vorkriegszeit*. Prague, 1963; F. Fellner: "Das Volkseinkommen Österreichs and Ungarns," *Statistische Monatsschrift*. 1916. The latter is a basic work in the examination of Hungarian capital imports. See also F. Fellner: *A nemzetközi fizetési mérleg alakulása Magyarországon* (The situation of the balance of payments in Hungary). Budapest, 1908. However, an examination for the earlier period as well was developed only in recent years: I. T. Berend and Gy. Ránki: *Nemzeti jövedelem és tőkefelhalmozás Magyarországon, 1867–1914* (National income and capital accumulation in Hungary, 1876–1914). Történelmi Szemle. Budapest, 1966. No. 2; L. Katus: *A kelet-europai iparosodás és az "önálló tőkés fejlődés" kérdéséhez* (On the problem of industrialisation in Eastern Europe and the "independent capitalist development"). Történelmi Szemle. Budapest, 1967. No. 1.

Besides the comprehensive economic histories listed previously special attention should be given to the famous work of S. Prokopowitsch: *Uber die Bedingungen der industriellen Entwicklung Russlands*. Tübingen, 1913. Also to P. Ol; *Inostrannye kapitaly v Rossi* (Foreign capital in Russia). Moscow, 1922; and B. Ischachanian: *Die aüslandischen Elemente in der russischen Volkswirtschaft*. Berlin, 1913.

The most comprehensive analysis of the role of foreign capital in the Balkan countries was given by H. Feis in *Europe: The World's Banker*, and also by E. Kohlruss: *Die französischen Kapitalanlagen in Südosteuropa im Rahmen der gesamten Auslandsverschuldung der südosteuropäischen Länder*. Leipzig, 1934. The activity of foreign capital has an unprecedented role in the economy of the Balkans; therefore, almost every work dealing with the economic history of this region treats this problem. The above-cited monographs, especially the works of N. Lupu-Kostaky, V. Slavescu, C. Colocotronis, L. Pasvolsky, J. Tomasevich, P. Ercuta, J. Kirkner, R. Aratinović, and A. Jaronoff, are important in understanding the influence of foreign capital. In addition, one should consult M. A. Georgescu: *Le régime juridique et financier des capitaux étrangers en Roumanie.* Paris, 1933; O. Constantinescu and N. N. Constantinescu: *Cu privire la problema revoluției industriale în Romînia* (On the question of the problem of industrial revolution in Rumania). Bucharest, 1957; N. Arkadian: *Industrializarea României* (Industrialization of Rumania). Bucharest, 1936; N. N. Constantinescu: *Contribuții la istoria capitalului străin în Romînia* (Contribution to the history of foreign capital in Rumania). Bucharest, 1960; T. Savin: *Capitalul străin în Rômînia* (Foreign capital in Rumania). Bucharest, 1947; M. Lamer: *Die aüslandische Kapitalanlagen in Balkan.* Weltwirtschaftliches Archiv. 1939; M. Simitch: *La dette publique de la Serbie de l'origine à la guerre de 1914.* Paris, 1923; S. Dimitrijevic: *Das ausländische Kapital in Jugoslavien vor dem zweiten Weltkrieg.* Berlin, 1963; S. Curicin: *Pénétration économique et financière des capitaux étrangers en Yougoslavie.* Paris, 1935; D. Kastris: *Les capitaux étrangers dans la finance roumaine.* Paris, 1921; S. Rădulescu: *La politique financière de la Roumanie.* Paris. 1923.

Chapter 6. The Development of Manufacturing Industry and the Modernization of the Economy

There is available vast statistical material and a rather broad literature on the development of manufacturing industry in the Austrian-Bohemian territory. From these works we would single out the following: K. Pribram: *Geschichte der österreichischen Gewerbpolitik von 1740–1860.* Leipzig, 1907; H. Hassinger: *Der Stand der Manufakturen in den deutschen Erbländern der Habsburg-Monarchie am Ende des 18. Jahrhunderts. Die wirtschaftliche Situation in Deutschland und Österreich um die Wende vom 18. zum 19. Jahrhundert.* Stuttgart, 1964. On the first signs of early industrialization see the valuable study of H. Freudenberger: "Industrialization in Bohemia and Moravia in the 18th Century," *Journal of Central European Affairs.* Boulder, Colorado, 1962. Treating the problem more comprehensively is the monograph of A. Klima: *Manufakturní obdobi v Čechách* (The period of manufactures in Bohemia). Prague, 1955.

In regard to the first use of machines, see D. Long: "Philippe de Girard and the Introduction of Mechanical Flax Spinning in Austria," *Journal of Economic History.* New York, 1959; and especially J. Purš: *The Industrial Revolution in the Czech Lands.* Prague, 1962. There is much material in the above-cited work of J. Slokar: *Die Industrie in Österreich;* and in A. Salz: *Geschichte der bohmischen Industrie in der Neuzeit.* Leipzig, 1913.

In the more recent literature see the doctoral dissertation of N. Gross: *Industrialization in Austria in the Nineteenth Century,* University of California, Berkeley, 1966—partly published in *Journal of Economic History,* New York, 1968. This is worth attention for its deep analysis of statistical sources. In the volume edited by W. Weber (*Österreichische Wirtschaftsstruktur gestern-heute-morgen*. Berlin, 1961) is a thorough discussion of the development of Austrian industry by S. Koren. From the older sources see: *Tafeln zur Statistik der Österreichischen Monarchie I–XXI. 1828–1848.* Vienna, 1854; F. Schmitt: *Statistik des österreichischen Kaiserstaates.* Vienna, 1867; J. Czoernig: *Statistisches Handbüchlein für die österreichische Monarchie.* Vienna, 1861; J. Hain; *Handbuch der Statistik des österreichischen Kaiserstaates.* Vienna, 1853. See also the comprehensive economic census of the year 1902: *Österreichisches Statistisches Handbuch.* Vienna, 1904.

About shorter periods or special problems refer to: *Die Entwicklung von Industrie und Gewerbe in Oesterreich in den Jahren 1848–1888.* Vienna, 1888; and H. Brachelli and F. Migerka: *Österreichs kommerzielle und industrielle Entwicklung in den letzten Jahrzehnten.* Vienna, 1873; J. Zapf: *Die Wirtschaftsgeschichte Wien's unter der Regierung seiner K. Und K. apostolischen Majestät des Kaisers Franz-Joseph I, 1848–1888.* Vienna, 1888.

At the 50th and 60th anniversaries of the reign of Franz Joseph and published in conjunction with the jubilee were: *Die Grossindustrie Österreichs,* Vol. I-V, Vienna, 1898 and *Die Grossindustrie Österreichs,* Vol. I-III. Vienna, 1908. These volumes contain detailed descriptions of the development of different branches of industry, and also a history of certain firms.

On the development of Bohemian territory there are the studies of J. Purš: *K otázce průmyslové revoluce v hlavních odvetvích textilního průmyslu v českych zemích* (On the question of industrial revolution in the main branches of textile industry in the Czech territories). Prague, 1954; and *Pouziti parnich strojů v průmyslu v českych zemích v období do nástupu imperializmu* (The steam engines in the Bohemian industry in the period before the beginning of imperialism). Československý Časopis Historický. Prague, 1954. Nos. II and III. On the 20th century see the studies of F. Hertz giving interesting points of view: *Die Produktionsgrundlagen der oesterreichischen Industrie vor und nach dem Kriege.* Vienna, 1917; *Die Schwierigkeiten der industriellen Produktion in Oesterreich.* Vienna, 1910.

Written comprehensively but using very poor material is: H. Benedikt: *Die wirtschaftliche Entwicklung in der Franz-Joseph-Zeit.* Vienna, 1958. On the history of different branches of industry see F. Kreiwang: "Die Papierindustrie"; F. Henderich: "Die Baumwollindustrie" in *Wirtschaftskunde der ehemaligen Österreichisch-Ungarischen Monarchie.* Heft 9. Vienna, 1919; F. Juraschek: "Bauwollproduktion und Handel und Industrie im letzten Dezennium" in *Statistische Monatsschrift.* 1895.

The basic work on national income in Austria is: F. Fellner: *Ausztria és Magyarország nemzeti jövedelme* (National income in Austria and Hungary). Budapest, 1919. Using in some respects revised data: A. Gürtler: *Das Volkseinkommen Österreichs und Ungarns.* Weltwirtschaftliches Archiv. 1918; E. Waizner: *Das Volkseinkommen Alt-Österreichs und seine Verteilung auf die Nachfolgerstaaten.* Metron. Vol. VII. 1928. See furthermore the volumes of *Compass*

Leonhard, part I and II, published yearly at the beginning of the 20th century. For an examination of Hungarian industrialization see the first statistics available from the 19th century: E. Fényes: *Magyarország leirása.* Vol. I–II. (The description of Hungary). Pest, 1847; K. Keleti: *Hazánk és népe.* (Our country and her people). Budapest, 1872; L. Láng: *Magyarország statisztikája.* Vol. II. (The statistics of Hungary). Budapest, 1887; *A Magyar Korona Országainak Gyáripara az 1898. évben.* (The manufacturing industry of the lands of the Hungarian crown in 1898). Budapest, 1901; *A Magyar Korona Országainak Gyáripara az 1906. évben.* (The manufacturing industry of the lands. of the Hungarian Crown). Budapest, 1911; *A Magyar Korona Országainak uzemi és munkásstatisztikája az 1910. évről.* (Firms and workers statistics of the lands of the Hungarian Crown in the year 1910). Budapest, 1915.

We can refer to comprehensive monographs dealing with certain periods of industrialization: Gy. Mérei: *Magyar iparfejlődés 1790–1848* (Hungarian industrial development, 1790–1848). Budapest, 1951; M. Futó: *A magyar gyáripar története* (A history of Hungarian manufacturing industry). Budapest, 1944; E. Lederer: *Az ipari kapitalizmus kezdetei Magyarországon* (The beginnings of industrial capitalism in Hungary). Budapest, 1952; and the already cited works of V. Sándor and I. T. Berend and Gy. Ránki. See also: I. T. Berend and Gy. Ránki: *The Development of Manufacturing Industry in Hungary, 1900–1944.* Studia Historica 19. Budapest, 1960; M. Wiener: *A magyar cukoripar története* (The history of the Hungarian sugar industry). Budapest, 1903; V. Sándor: *A budapesti malomipar története* (The history of mill industry in Budapest). Tanulmányok Budapest Multjából. Budapest, 1954. For good foreign trade statistics see: *Külkereskedelmi forgalmunk 1882–1913* (Hungarian foreign trade, 1882–1913). Budapest, 1923.

For the general problems, interdependence and controversy in the Austro-Hungarian Monarchy see: I. T. Berend and Gy. Ránki: *Das Niveau der Industrie Ungarns zu Beginn des 20. Jahrhunderts im Vergleich zu dem Europas. Studien zur Geschichte der Österreichisch-Ungarischen Monarchie.* Budapest, 1961; P. Hanák: *Hungary in the Austro-Hungarian Monarchy: Preponderancy or Dependancy?* Austrian History Yearbook. Houston, Vol. VII. Part 1. 1967; Gy. Ránki: *Az Osztrák-Magyar Monarchia gazdasági fejlődésének néhány problémája* (Some problems of the economic growth of the Austro-Hungarian Monarchy). Valóság. Budapest, 1968. No. 4; I. T. Berend: *A közép-kelet-európai gazdasági integráció kérdéséhez. Történelmi előzmények.* (On the problem of economic integration in East-Central Europe. The historical background). Közgazdasági Szemle. Budapest, 1968. No. 2. On the economic place of the Monarchy in Europe: I. Svennilson: *Growth and Stagnation in the European Economy.* Geneva, 1954; S. V. Waltershausen: *Die Entstehung der Weltwirtschaft.* Jena, 1931.

About the Russian industrialization, besides the oft-cited works of Lenin, Liashchenko, Hromov, Gerschenkron, and Prokopovitch see: *Otcherki ekonomicheskoi istorii Rossii v pervoi poloviny XIX veka.* (Problems of the economic history of Russia in the first part of 19th century). Ed. by M. K. Rozhkova. Moscow, 1959. In this volume, of special value is the study by V. K. Jatsunsky: *Krupnaja promyshlennost Rossii v 1790–1860 gg.* (The large-scale industry in Russia in the years 1790–1860); R. Portal: "The Industrialization of Russia," in Vol. VI of *The Cambridge Economic History of Europe.* Cambridge, 1965; R. Goldsmith: "The Economic Growth of Tsarist Russia," *Economic Development and Cultural Change.* Chicago, 1961; B. Gille: *Histoire économique et sociale de la Russie.* Paris, 1949; A. Gerschenkron: "The Rate of Industrial Growth in Russia since 1885," *Journal of Economic History.* New York, 1947. Supplement.

For the Polish Kingdom: W. Kula: *Historia gospodarcza Polski w dobrie popowstani owej. 1864–1918.* (The history of the Polish economy in the period after the revolt, 1864–1918). Warsaw, 1947, and the above-cited books by Piltz and Bujak.

As far as industrial growth and the development of national income are concerned, a comparative analysis can be based on the works of S. Kuznets: *Postwar Economic Growth.* Cambridge, 1964; S. J. Patel: "Rates of Industrial Growth in the Last Century," *Economic Development and Cultural Change.* Chicago, 1961. Also very useful are the cited works of W. Hoffman and, for England, J. Chambers.

The distribution of the population around the turn of the century can be ascertained by the data of different censuses. See also: W. Woytinsky: *Die Welt in Zahlen.* I-VII. Berlin, 1925–1927.

For the industrialization of the Balkan countries, see the cited works of O. Constantinescu, N. N. Constantinescu, G. Entscheff, K. Popoff, R. Aratinović, J. Kirkner, Z. Natán, and L. Pasvolsky. Also the following books: A. Strat: *Des possibilités de développement industriel de la Roumanie.* Paris, 1932; N. P. Arcadian: *Industrializarea României* (The industrialization of Rumania). Bucharest, 1936; I. Dumitrescu: *Die Grossindustrie Rumäniens.* Bonn, 1914; J. Sakazov: *Bulgarische Wirtschaftsgeschichte.* Leipzig, 1929; K. Lambrev: *Polozhenieto na rabotnicheskata klasa v Blgaria ot osvobozhdenieto do nachaloto na XX. vek. 1878–1904* (The situation of the working class in Bulgaria from the liberation to the beginning of the 20th century). Sofia, 1954; M. Mirković: *Ekonomska Historia Jugoslavije* (Economic History of Yugoslavia). Zagreb, 1958.

The problems of structure of industry and the role of different sectors were based on the works of W. Hoffman, W. Rostow and S. Kuznets.

Chapter 7. New Trends of Modern Capitalist Development Around the Turn of the Century

For the formation of monopolies and finance capital and their role from the theoretical aspect we used the well-known and above-cited works of R. Hilferding, C. Hobson, and V. Lenin. In addition, V. I. Lenin, *Sochineniia,* Vol. 39 (Notes on imperialism). Moscow, 1960.

For a description of the processes the following work may be consulted: *Die Frage des Finanzkapitals in der Österreichisch-Ungarischen Monarchie.* Bucharest, 1965. In this volume were published the papers and discussion of the Budapest Conference on the problems of Monarchy in 1964. There is an important volume of studies by J. Křížek and E. März, cited above. See also: I. T. Berend and György Ránki: *A monopolkapitalizmus kialakulása és uralma Magyarországon. 1900–1944* (The formation of monopolistic capitalism and its rule in Hungary 1900–1944). Budapest, 1958; *Verhandlungen der Kartellenquete.* Vienna, 1912; J. Varga: *Magyar Kartellek* (The Hungarian Cartels). Budapest, 1913; G. Zsoldos: *Bankkoncentráció* (The concentration of banks). Budapest, 1914; Ch. Allmayer-Beck: *Materialien zum österreichischen Kartellwesen.* Vienna, 1910; O. Jászi: *The Dissolution of the Habsburg Monarchy.* Chicago, 1929; N. N. Constantinescu and V. Axenciuc: *Capitalismul monopolist în România* (Monopoly capitalism in Rumania). Bucharest, 1962; J. Munteanu- Gh. Matei: *Aspecte ale dezvoltării capitalismului monopolist în România* (Aspects of the development of monopoly capitalism in Rumania). Bucharest, 1957; V. Axenciuc: "Les monopoles dans l'industrie de la Roumanie," *Revue Roumaine d'Histoire.* Bucharest, 1965. No. 1; Z. Natan and L. Berov: *Monopolisticheskiiat kapitalizm v Blgaria* (Monopoly capitalism in Bulgaria). Sofia, 1958. See also the three studies of M. Deifter in the *Istoricheskie Zapiski.* Moscow, 1952, No. 38; 1953. No. 43; and 1954, No. 47; and G. Tchiperovich: *Sindikaty i tresty v dorevolutsionnoi Rossii i v SSSR* (Syndicates and trusts in Russia before the revolution and in the SSSR). Moscow, 1927.

Part II. Changes and Stagnation
in the Twentieth Century: 1914–1949

The literature concerning the territorial-political transformation in East-Central Europe, the collapse of the Monarchy, and the formation of new states is extremely rich. Apart from general histories we may mention here the following:
S. Saucerman: *International Transfers of Territory in Europe.* Washington D.C., 1937; H. Hantsch: *Die Geschichte Österreichs.* Graz, Vienna, and Cologne, 1963; E. Zöllner: *Geschichte Österreichs von den Anfängen bis zur Gegenwart.* Vienna, 1961; R. Kann: *Werden und Zerfall des Habsburges Reiches.* Graz, 1962; G. Gratz: *A forradalmak kora* (The age of revolutions). Budapest, 1935; T. Hajdu: *A Magyar Tanácsköztársaság* (The Hungarian Soviet Republic). Budapest, 1969; D. Nemes: *Az ellenforradalom története Magyar országon 1919–1921* (The history of counterrevolution in Hungary). Budapest, 1962; A. Macartney: *Hungary and Her Successors: The Treaty of Trianon and Its Consequences, 1919-1937.* New York, 1937; E. Holzer: *Die Entstehung des Jugoslawischen Staates.* Berlin, 1929.
Other works are *The Cambridge History of Poland.* Ed. by W. F. Reddaway and H. Penson. Cambridge, 1951; H. Seton-Watson: *Eastern Europe between the Wars, 1914–1941.* Cambridge, 1945; *Istoria Chechoslovakii* (The history

of Czechoslovakia). Red. by N. I. Melnikov, A. Nedorezov, and Sz. Prasolov. Moscow, 1960; *Istoriia Jugoslavii* (The history of Yugoslavia). Red. by J. V. Bromlej and L. Valov. Moscow, 1963; *Istoria Bolgarii* (The history of Bulgaria). Ed. by P. Tretjakov and S. Nikitin. Moscow, 1955; *The Balkans in Transition.* Ed. by B. and Ch. Jelavich. Berkeley, 1963; L. S. Stavrianos: *The Balkans since 1453.* New York, 1958.

Chapter 8. The Consequences of World War I: Disintegration and Reconstruction

A vast body of literature is available on the economic consequences of the war. The economic exhaustion, the chaotic economic situation, and the decline of agricultural and industrial production are well documented in the following books, mostly national in scope.

G. Gratz and R. Schüller: *Der wirtschaftliche Zusammenbruch Oesterreich-Ungarns.* Vienna, 1930; K. Rothschild: *Austria's Economic Development Between the Two Wars.* London, 1946; N. Layton and Ch. Rist: *The Economic Situation of Austria.* Report presented to the Council of the League of Nations. Geneva, 1925; J. Szterényi and J. Ladányi: *A Magyar ipar a világháboruban* (The Hungarian Industry during the War). Budapest, 1933; I. T. Berend and Gy. Ránki: *Magyarország gazdasága az elsö világháboru után. 1919–1929* (Hungary's economy after World War I, 1919–1929). Budapest, 1966; J. Faltuš: *Povojnová hospodárska Kríza v rokoch 1921–1923 v. Ceskoslovensku* (Postwar depression in Czechoslovakia in 1921–1923). Bratislava, 1966; R. Olšovsky, V. Průcha, H. Gebauerova, A. Pruszký, A. Dorbý and J. Faltuš: *Přehled hospodářského vývoje Ceskoslovenska v letech 1918–1945* (Survey of the economic development of Czechoslovakia during the years 1918–1945). Prague, 1961; *Central-eastern Europe, Crucible of World Wars.* Ed. by I. S. Rouček. New York, 1946; D. Jovanovich: *Les effets économiques et sociaux de la guerre en Serbie.* New Haven, 1930; K. S. Patton: *Kingdom of Serbs, Croats, and Slovenes—Yugoslavia.* Washington, 1928; V. Dinu: *Die Landwirtschaft Rumäniens unter dem Druck der Krisen.* Bucharest, 1933; M. Mirković: *Ekonomska historija Jugoslavije* (The economic history of Yugoslavia). Zagreb, 1958; H. Prost: *La Bulgarie de 1912 à 1930. Contribution à l'histoire économique et financière de la guerre et ses conséquences.* Paris, 1931; Zh. Natan: *Istoriia ekonomicheskogo razvitia Bolgarii* (The history of the economic development of Bulgaria). Moscow, 1961; Th. Alton: *Polish Postwar Economy.* New York, 1956; T. Taylor: *The economic development of Poland, 1919–1950.* New York, 1952; I. Tomasevich: "Foreign Economic Relations, 1918–1945," in *Jugoslavia.* United Nations Series. Stanford, 1949; R. Aratinović: *Les ressources et l'activité économique de la Yougoslavie.* Paris, 1930.

On the inflation following the war, besides the books cited earlier, one should consult S. Strakosch: *Der Selbstmord eines Volkes.* Vienna, 1922; *Hundert Jahre Creditanstalt.* Vienna, 1956; G. Heidelberg: *Die Wirkung der Inflation und Sanierung auf den ungarischen Geld und Kapitalmarkt.* Budapest, 1927; V. Madgearu: *Evoluţia economiei românesti după războiul mondial* (Evolution of the Rumanian economy after the World War). Bucharest, 1940.

The problem of the war debts, the various loans, and the reparation question are thoroughly treated in the works noted above, especially in the valuable book of K. S. Patton. Also particularly useful are: E. Kohlruss: *Die französische Kapitalanlagen in Südost-Europa im Rahmen der gesamten Auslandsverschuldung der südost-europäischen Länder.* Leipzig, 1934; T. S. Kosoroff: *La dette publique extérieure de la Bulgarie, 1879–1932.* Paris, 1933; X. Netta: *La dette publique de l'État roumain.* Paris, 1935. Relating to the Hungarian reparation question a quantity of dates and notes on secret diplomatic conversations and the like are available in the Országos Levéltár (National Archives), Budapest. We used especially the volumes containing the papers of the Premier Ministry, the Financial Ministry and the paper of Szabóky (Secretary of State in the Financial Ministry).

The literature on the agrarian development is obviously primarily focused on the special problem of land reform, and the situation of the villages after the land reforms. For the general background and effect, see the studies of S. Zagoroff, J. Végh, and A. Blimovich: *The Agricultural Economy of the Danubian Countries, 1935–1945.* Stanford, 1955; D. Warriner: *The Economics of Peasant Farming.* London, 1939. For special calculations on agricultural overpopulation, W. E. Moore: *Economic Demography of Eastern and Southeastern Europe.* Geneva, 1945. Historical events and circumstances are detailed in I. Dolmányos: "A kelet-európai földreformok néhány problémája" (Some problems of the East-European land reforms). *Agrártörténeti Szemle* (Review of Agrarian History). Budapest, 1963–1965. See also N. Spulber: *The Economics of Communist Eastern Europe.* London and New York, 1957. Among the studies concerning different countries, see J. Evans: *Agrarian Revolution in Rumania.* Cambridge, 1924; D. Mitrany: *The Land and the Peasant in Rumania,* London, 1930; H. Roberts: *Rumania: Political Problems of an Agrarian State.* New Haven, 1951. *Etudes Danubiennes: Bulgarie.* Paris, 1935: A. S. Petkoff: *Landwirtschaftsgestaltung und Agrarpolitik Bulgariens unter besonderer Berücksichtigung der Agrarreform der Zeitnach dem Weltkriege.* Sofia, 1941; E. Lipinski: *Development of Agriculture and Industry.* Warsaw, 1955; *Osteurope Handbuch Jugoslavia.* Cologne and Graz, 1955; *Osteurope Handbuch, Polen.* Cologne and Graz, 1955; I. Vazenilek: *Pozemková reformá v Československé republice* (Land reform in the Czechoslovak republic). Prague, 1924; F. Pölöskei and K. Szakács, eds.: *Szegényparaszt és földmunkásmozgalmak Magyarországon* (Movements of poor peasants and agricultural labourers in Hungary). Budapest, 1963.

The drive toward nationalization is examined in the studies *Contribuţii la istoria capitalului străin în Romînia de la sfîrsitul primului război mondial pîenă la iesirea din criza economocă de 1929–1933* (Contributions to the history of foreign capital from World War I to the end of the economic crisis of 1929–

1933). Bucharest, 1960; C. Colocotronis: *L'organisation bancaire des pays balkaniques et les capitaux étrangers.* Paris, 1934; *Österreichs Wirtschaftsstruktur.* Ed. by W. Weber. Berlin, 1964; B. Alexsander: *Das jugoslawische Bankwesen.* Zagreb, 1926; V. Kosak: *Die bankmässige Finanzierung der jugoslawischen Industrie.* Frankfurt, 1938.

Extremely useful in relation to this topic were the papers of the most significant Hungarian industrial and financial enterprises which are available in the Országos Levéltár (National Archives), Budapest. They gave us the broad and interesting picture of the negotiations between Hungarian and Rumanian, Serbo-Croatian, and Czechoslovak firms and the role of Western capital in these affairs. See the papers of Pesti Magyar Kereskedelmi Bank (Hungarian Commercial Bank of Pest), Magyar Általános Hitelbank (Hungarian General Creditbank), and Salgótarjáni Köszénbanya Részvénytársaság (Coal Mines of Salgótarján Ltd). Some aspects of the special prosperity connected with the inflation and the development of production in the period under review are thoroughly and comprehensively examined in the important study of I. Svennilson: *Growth and Stagnation in the European Economy.* Geneva, 1954.

Chapter 9. Reconstruction and Its Inherent Contradictions

The economic cycle and situation in the second half of the 1920s is treated in every economic history dealing with the interwar period. Of the numerous books and articles relating to the economic history of the Western European countries we especially exploited the following: I. Svennilson: *Growth and Stagnation in the European Economy.* Geneva, 1954; C. Clark: *The Conditions of Economic Progress.* London, 1951; *Industrialization and Foreign Trade.* Geneva, 1945; E. Staley: *World Economy in Transition.* New York, 1939; A. Bowley: *Some Economic Consequences of the Great War.* London, 1930; Sh. Clough and Ch. Cole: *Economic History of Europe.* Boston, 1952; C. Day: *Economic Development of Europe.* New York, 1948.

The specific aspects of the postwar economic policies, and the main trends in the customs policy at this time, are traced in: F. Hertz: *The Economic Problem of the Danubian States: A Study in Nationalism.* London, 1947; H. Liepmann: *Tariff Levels and the Economic Unity of Europe.* London, 1938; L. Pasvolsky: *Economic Nationalism of the Danubian States.* New York, 1929; A. Székely: *A Duna medence kereskedelmi politikája a két háboru közé eső husz esztendöben* (Trade policy in the Danube Basin during the 20 years between the wars). Budapest, 1944. Also worthwhile are: N. Layton and Ch. Rist: *The Economic Situation of Austria* and I. Tomasevich: *Foreign Economic Relations*—both already cited—and M. Lamer: *Weltwirtschaftliche Verflechtungen Südslawiens.* Zagreb, 1933 and A. Basch: *European Economic Nationalism.* Washington, 1943.

For the specific countries of the area see on Austria: G. Slavik: *Der Aussen-*

handel und die Handelspolitik Österreichs 1918 bis 1926. Vienna, 1928. More comprehensive: *Hundert Jahre österreichische Wirtschaftsentwicklung.* Vienna, 1948.

For Czechoslovakia very informative studies are: A. Tibal: *La Tchéchoslovaquie.* Paris, 1935; *Die Wirtschaft der Tschechoslowakei, 1918–1928.* Prague, 1928.

On Hungary: I. T. Berend and Gy. Ránki: *Magyarország gazdasága az elsö világháború után* (Hungary's economy after World War I). Budapest, 1966; J. Buzás and A. Nagy: *Magyarország külkereskedelme 1919–1929* (Hungary's foreign trade, 1919–1929). Budapest, 1961; L. Fucsek: *A Dunavölgy államainak gazdasági közeledése* (The economic rapprochement of the states in the Danube Basin). Budapest, 1932.

On Rumania and mostly descriptive: *Die wirtschaftliche und finanzielle Organisation Rumäniens in 1926.* Bucharest, 1927; *Les forces économiques de la Roumanie en 1930.* Bucharest, 1931. On Bulgaria: H. Prost; *La Bulgarie de 1912 à 1930.* On Poland: R. Gorewsky: *Die wirtschaftliche Entwicklung Polens.* Warsaw, 1935.

The problems of capital supply and the necessity of foreign loans for the stabilization of the currency are theoretically examined in the work of J. M. Keynes: *The Economic Consequences of the Peace.* New York, 1921. Also very useful is E. Kohlruss: *Die französische Kapitalanlage,* cited before.

For the history of the various stabilizations, and the various loans of the League of Nations, very instructive studies are *The Problem of International Investment.* Report by the Royal Institute of International Affairs. London, 1937; A. Brown: *Industrialisation and Trade.* London, 1943.

On Austria particularly useful data appear in: *Bericht über die Industrie, den Handel und die Verkehrsverhältnisse in Wien und Niederösterreich während die Jahre 1921 und 1922.* Vienna, 1922. Less detailed but more comprehensive is: K. Rothschild: *Austria's Economic Development between the Two Wars.* London, 1946; *Hundert Jahre Creditanstalt.* Vienna, 1956; W. Weber: *Österreichs Wirtschaftsstruktur gestern, heute, morgen.* Berlin, 1962; L. Pasvolsky: *Economic Nationalism of the Danubian States,* previously cited.

On Hungary: I. Berend and Gy. Ránki, *op. cit.,* deals with the history, economic background and effects of the stabilization. For the history of the loans see: M. Ormos: *Az 1924. évi magyar államcölcsön megszerzése* (The obtaining of the Hungarian state loan of 1924). Budapest, 1963. For economic analysis: G. Heidelberg: *Die Wirkung der Inflation und Sanierung auf den ungarischen Geld und Kapitalmarkt.* Budapest, 1927.

On Bulgaria see the above-cited works of Zh. Natan: *Istoria ekonomicheskogo razvitia Bolgarii* (The history of economic development in Bulgaria). Moscow, 1957; C. Colocotronis: *L'organisation bancaire des pays balkaniques* and H. Prost: *La Bulgarie de 1912 à 1930.* Also on this topic: L. Leschtoff: *Die Staatsschulden und Reparationen Bulgariens 1878–1927.* Leipzig, 1929.

For Rumania see: *La Roumanie économique.* Bucharest, 1928; *Die wirtschaft-*

liche und finanzielle Organisation in Rumänien in 1926. Bucharest, 1927; E. Gyárfás: *A leu árfolyama és a pénzügyi válság.* (The exchange rate of the leu and the financial crisis). Cluj, 1924; D. Gheorghiei: *Fiantele Romăniei după război 1919–1931.* Bucharest, 1931.

The problem of the stabilization in Poland is first examined by the American expert commission: Reports submitted by the commission of American financial experts headed by E. Kammerer. Warsaw, 1926. Also by Górecki: *Poland and Her Economic Development.* London, 1935.

For Yugoslavia the works already mentioned of M. Mirković: *Ekonomska historija Jugoslavije;* and R. Aratinović: *Les ressources . . . de la Yougoslavie.* Also useful is: M. Curicin: *Pénétration économique et financière des capitaux étrangers en Yougoslavie.* Paris, 1935.

For Czechoslovakia the memoirs of the minister of finance, killed by an anarchist, is the most valuable: A. Rasin: *Les finances de la Tchécoslovaquie jusqu'à la fin de 1921.* Prague, 1923. Also J. Faltus: *Provojnová hospodárska kriza* (Postwar economic crisis).

The role of foreign capital and the utilization of the loans are generally estimated by L. Berov: *Le capital financier occidental et les pays balkaniques dans les années vingt.* Etudes Balkaniques. Sofia, 1966.

For Bulgaria: L. Pasvolsky: *Bulgaria's Economic Position.* Washington, 1937. For Poland: L. Wellisz: *Foreign Capital In Poland.* London, 1938, and P. Douglas: *The Economic Independence of Poland.* Cincinnati, 1934.

On Yugoslavia: Curicin: *op. cit.,* and M. Tosk, A. Vejner, P. Rudanko, and G. Strekurev: *The Balance of Payments of the Kingdom of Serbs, Croats and Slovenes in 1926.* Belgrade, 1928.

On Hungary: I. T. Berend and Gy. Ránki: *Capital Accumulation and the Participation of Foreign Capital in the Hungarian Economy after the First World War.* Nouvelles Études Historiques. Budapest, 1965.

In Rumania the economic and financial conflicts with foreign investment and the cutting of old financial ties are treated in the pamphlet of V. Madgearu: *Romania's New Economic Policy.* London, 1930. There is useful data in N. N. Constantinescu: *Contribuţii la istoria capitalului străin* (Contribution to the history of foreign capital) and in C. Colocotronis: *L'organisation bancaire . . . ,* both cited previously.

General descriptions of the economic development of the 1920s and the main indices are given in the very important study of L. Svennilson: *Growth and Stagnation in the European Economy.* Geneva, 1954. In addition see P. Alpert: *Twentieth Century Economic History of Europe.* New York, 1951.

On agricultural problems see D. Warriner: *The Economics of Peasant Farming.* London, 1939; *Les Balkans, leur passé et leur présent.* Belgrade, 1935. Also G. Hudaczek: *Die österreichische Volkswirtschaft und ihr Wiederaufbau.* Vienna, 1946; H. Kalbrunner: *Der Wiederaufbau der Landwirtschaft Österreichs.* Vienna, 1926.

General reviews of the economic development for the various countries are presented in the following studies: *Economic Review,* published by the Oester-reichische Creditanstalt für Handel und Gewerbe. *Aspecte ale economiei romanesti* (Aspects of the Rumanian economy). Ed. by Lupu-Kostaky. Bucha-rest, 1939; J. Taylor: *The Economic Development of Poland, 1919–1950.* New York, 1952; Th. Alton: *Polish Postwar Economy.* New York, 1955. In addition see R. Gorecki: *Poland and Her Economic Development;* P. Douglas: *The Economic Independence of Poland,* cited earlier; Ch. Romanesco: *Le mouvement bancaire en Roumanie depuis 1918.* Paris, 1929; M. Libros: *La situation économique et financière de la Roumanie en 1929.* Bucharest, 1930.

Chapter 10. The Effect of the World Economic Crisis and the Policy of State Intervention

The theoretical and historical problems of the world depression of 1929–1933 became fashionable economic topics, and there is a vast literature on this sub-ject. The reports of the various economic, governmental and international or-ganizations written during the depression, economic histories written later, and theoretical studies are available in great quantity. Besides the special literature referring to the various countries, we shall mention here only a few comprehen-sive and theoretical publications. The best Marxist examination of the world crisis is by the famous Marxist economist E. Varga: *Die grosse Krise und ihre politischen Folgen.* Moscow and Leningrad, 1934. A more general historical and theoretical Marxist interpretation is given by I. A. Trachtenberg: *Kapitalistische Reproduktion und Wirtschaftskrise.* Berlin, 1957 and by L. A. Mendelsohn: *Teoria i istoria ekonomicheskih, krizisov i ciklov.* Moscow, 1964.

Apart from general histories the general background, the course, and the economic and political effects of the depression are discussed in W. Röpke: *Crisis and Cycles.* London, 1936; *The World Economic Crisis and the Way of Escape.* London, 1932; E. Merrill: *Responses to Economic Collapse. The Great Depression of the 1930s.* Boston, 1964; G. Kroll: *Von der Weltwirtschaftskrise zur Staatskonjunktur.* Berlin, 1953; T. Hoffmann: *Die grosse Krise.* Frankfurt, 1952.

An enormous quantity of statistical material, uneven in scope and quality—information on fiscal, industrial, banking aspects in the various countries in yearbooks and other sources—is not mentioned here. Particularly useful, how-ever, was: *Statistisches Handbuch der Weltwirtschaft.* Berlin, 1937. Also I. Svennilson's frequently cited book and the publication of the Royal Institute of International Affairs: *South Eastern Europe. A Political and Economic Sur-vey.* London, 1939.

Concerning the course of the depression in the different countries treated, the most comprehensive and useful publications were the following: for Austria: *Österreichs Wirtschaftsstruktur gestern, heute, morgen.* Ed. by W. Weber, Ber-lin, 1961; *Hundert Jahre Creditanstalt.* Ed. by H. Mayer. Vienna, 1948; *Monats-berichts des Österreichischen Instituts für Wirtschaftsforschung.* Vienna; K.

Rothschild: *Austria's Economic Development between the Two Wars.* London, 1946.

For Czechoslovakia: *Prehled hospodárského vyvoje Ceskoslovenska v letech 1918–1945* (Survey of the economic development of Czechoslovakia during the years 1918–1945). Prague, 1963; A. Tibal: *La Tchécoslovaquie. Étude économique.* Paris, 1935; A. Dobry: *Hospodárska krise ceskoslovenského prumyslu ve vztahu k Mnichovu* (The economic crisis in the Czechoslovak industry in relation to Munich). Prague, 1955.

For Hungary: *Az 1929–1933. évi világgazdasági válság hatása Magyarországon* (The effect of the world crisis of 1929–1933 in Hungary). Ed. by M. Incze. Budapest, 1955; the reports on the economic situation of the Hungarian Institute of Economic Research (Magyar Gazdaságkutaté Intézet) between 1929 and 1933; *Ungarisches Wirtschaftsjahrbuch 1929, 1933.*

For Poland: L. Grosfeld: *Ekonomicheskiy krizis 1929–1933 gg. v Polshe* (Economic crisis in Poland between 1929–1933). Moscow, 1954; Z. Landau and J. Tomaszewski: *Zarys historii gospodarczej Polski 1918–1939* (Outline of the history of Poland's economy, 1918–1939). Warsaw, 1960; F. Zweig: *Poland between Two Wars.* London, 1944; R. Gorecki: *Poland and Her Economic Development.* London, 1935.

For the Balkan countries: V. Slavescu: *La situation économique de la Roumanie et sa capacité de payment.* Bucharest, 1934; E. Grunberg: *L'industrie roumaine et la crise mondiale.* Paris, 1936; Zh. Natan: *Istoria ekonomicheskogo razvitia Bolgarii* (The history of economic development in Bulgaria). Moscow, 1961; M. Mirković: *Ekonomska struktura Jugoslavije* (The economic structure of Yugoslavia). Belgrade, 1962; N. Vuco: *Agrarna kriza u Jugoslaviji 1930–1934* (Agrarian crisis in Yugoslavia 1930–1934). Belgrade, 1968.

Some valuable works treating a particular aspect of the depression, and giving important information on a number of special questions, are: *Austria's Public Finances.* Third Report by the Financial Organisation of the League of Nations. Geneva, 1937; C. Hudaczek: *Die österreichische Volkswirtschaft und ihr Wiederaufbau.* Vienna, 1946; R. Gradowsky: *Polska (Poland) 1918–1939.* Warsaw, 1959; M. Ehrendiener: *L'organisation bancaire en Yougoslavie.* Zagreb, 1936; M. Lamer: *Weltwirtschaftliche Verflechtungen.* Weltwirtschaftliches Archiv 1939; V. Dinu: *Die Landwirtschaft Rumäniens.* Bucharest, 1933; G. Jaranoff: *Wirtschaftsstruktur und Aussenhandel Bulgariens.* Jena, 1940; M. Matolcsy and S. Varga: *The National Income of Hungary, 1924/25–1936/37.* London, 1938; I. Moloff: *Die Sozialökonomische Struktur der bulgarischen Landwirtschaft.* Berlin, 1936; S. Zagoroff, J. Végh and A. Blimovich: *The Agricultural Economy of the Danubian Countries, 1935-1945.* Stanford, 1955.

The complex impact of the crisis relating to the state intervention developing in the early 1930s is theoretically presented in several well-documented studies: H. S. Ellis: *Exchange Control in Central Europe.* Cambridge, 1941; A. Basch: *The Danube Basin and the German Economic Sphere.* London, 1944; N. Montchiloff: *Ten Years of Controlled Trade Agreements.* League of Nations. Geneva,

1935; A. Jovanovich: *Mémoires sur le contrôle des Changes en Yougoslavie.* Paris, 1939; I. Tomasevich: *Foreign Economic Relations, 1918–1941,* in the volume *Yugoslavia.* United Nations Series 1949; S. Obradovitsch: *Zwischen Clearing und Devise.* Leipzig, 1939; I. T. Berend and Gy Ránki: *Magyarország gyáripara a második világháboru elött és a haboru időszakában 1933–1944* (The industry of Hungary before and during World War II, 1933–1944). Budapest, 1958; M. Szuhay: *Az állami beavatkozás és a magyar mezögazdaság az 1930-as években* (State intervention and the Hungarian agriculture in the 1930s). Budapest, 1962; C. Bobtchev: *Réglementation du commerce et politique commerciale en Bulgarie.* Sofia, 1939. Concerning the question of state intervention there is abundant material and information in the works of Zweig, Wellisz, Kohlruss, and Taylor, cited above.

Chapter 11. German Economic Expansion:
Grossraumwirtschaft *in East-Central Europe*

From the abundant literature concerning the Nazi economic policy we shall mention only those which give the best analysis of the East-Central-European Grossraumwirtschaftsproblem, its role and place in the German economy and economic policy: R. Erbe: *Die nationalsozialistische Wirtschaftspolitik 1933–1938 im Lichte der modernen Theorie.* Zurich, 1958; H. Lossos: *Bilanz der deutschen Devisenbewirtschaftung.* Jena, 1940; A. Schweitzer: "Die wirtschaftliche Wiederaufrüstung Deutschlands von 1934–1936," *Zeitschrift für die gesamte Staatswissenschaft,* 1958. No. 4; K. Borchardt: "Ein neues Urteil über die deutsche Währungs- und Handelspolitik von 1931- bis 1928," *Vierteljahrschrift für Sozial- und Wirtschaftsgeschichte.* 46. Band. 1959. No. 4; H. Rittershausen: "Die deutsche Aussenhandelspolitik von 1879 bis 1948," *Zeitschrift für die gesamte Staatswissenschaft,* 1948. No. 1.

The economic connection and interconnection between Nazi Germany and East-Central Europe is presented in: E. Wagemann: *Der neue Balkan.* Hamburg, 1939; H. Gross: *Die wirtschaftliche Bedeutung Südosteuropas für das Deutsche Reich.* Stuttgart and Berlin, 1939; R. W. Kingsmann: *Südosteuropa und Grossdeutschland.* Breslau, 1939; W. Darré: *A Német Birodalom és a délkelet–európai államok együttmüködése a mezógazdaság terén* (Cooperation between the German Reich and the South-Eastern European countries in the field of agriculture). Budapest, 1940; A. Basch: *The Danube Basin and the German Economic Sphere.* London, 1944.

On German economic penetration in Southeastern Europe and German economic policy in addition to the works cited above, we found abundant material in the various archives, especially: Deutsches Zentralarchiv Potsdam, Auswàrtiges Amt, Handelspolitische Abteilung; Public Record Office London; German Foreign Ministry; National Archives Washington; German Foreign Ministry; Magyar Országos Levéltár (Hungarian National Archives) Budapest;

Külügyminisztérium (Foreign Ministry); Gazdaságpolitikai Osztály (Department of Economic Policy).

A variety of studies mainly national in scope are to be found for all the countries. For Austria useful data are presented in the volume *Österreichs Wirtschaftsstruktur,* cited earlier. Also in K. Rothschild: *Austria's Economic Development between the Two Wars.* London, 1946. For Hungary a comprehensive picture is given by I. T. Berend and Gy. Ránki: *Magyarország a fasiszta Németország "életterében" 1933–1939* (Hungary in the economic sphere of Nazi Germany, 1933–1939). Budapest, 1960.

For Bulgaria see: L. Berov: *Kom voprosa za Vnosnotorgovskata orientaciia na bolgarskiia fashizm 1929–1944 gg.* (On the problem of the trades orientation of fascist Bulgaria). Sofia, 1954; G. Jaranoff: *Wirtschaftsstruktur und Aussenhandel Bulgariens.* Jena, 1940; Zh. Natan: *Istoria ekonomicheskogo razvitia Bolgarii* (The history of the economic development of Bulgaria). Moscow, 1961.

For Yugoslavia the works of J. Tomasevich and S. Obradovitch cited earlier.

For Rumania: N. N. Constantinescu: "L'exploitation et le pillage de l'économie roumaine par l'Allemagne Hitlerienne dans le période 1939–1944," *Revue Roumaine d'Histoire.* Bucharest, 1964, and *Aspecte ale economiei românești* (Aspects of the Rumanian economy). Ed. by Lupu Kostaky. Bucharest, 1939; A. Niri: *Istoricul unui tratat înrobitor.* Bucharest, 1965.

Chapter 12. Economic Growth and Structural Changes in the Interwar Period

The rate of growth of economic development in the interwar period is drawn by N. Spulber: *The State and Economic Development in Eastern Europe.* New York, 1966; I. T. Berend and Gy. Ránki: *Magyarország gazdasága az elsö világháboru után 1919–1929* (Hungary's economy after World War I, 1919–1929). Budapest, 1966; M. Matolcsy and I. Varga: *Magyarország nemzeti jövedelme 1924/25–1934/35* (Hungary's National Income). Budapest, 1936; F. Hertz: *The Economic Problem of the Danubian States. A Study on Economic Nationalism.* London, 1947; W. Piper: *Grundprobleme des wirtschaftlichen Wachstums in einigen südosteuropäischen Ländern in der Zwischenweltkriegszeit.* Berlin, 1965; *Enciclopedia Romîniei.* Bucharest, 1940, and the works of J. Tomasevich: *Foreign Economic Relations,* and of Th. Alton: *Polish Postwar Economy.*

The level and the development of the infrastructure are treated in L. Wellisz: *Foreign Capital in Poland;* W. Moore: *Economic Demography of Eastern and Southeastern Europe;* M. Mirković: *Ekonomska struktura Jugoslavije;* J. Moloff: *Die sozialökonomische Struktur der bulgarischen Landwirtschaft;* I. Svennilson: *Growth and Stagnation in the European Economy,* all cited previously. Further useful data are to be found in the journal titled *Les Balkans.*

On agriculture, the calculations regarding the development of production are based on the data of Svennilson. For the land structure and the fragmentation of the landed property see the works of R. Aratinović, Th. Alton, M. Mirković, and J. Moloff—all cited above. Abundant material is also given by J. Tomasevich: *Peasants, Politics, and Economic Change in Jugoslavia.* Stanford, 1955; J. Petricevic: *Untersuchungen über die Betriebsformen der Bauernbetriebe Kroatiens.* Zagreb, 1942.

The capital supply may be followed best in the studies of Tomasevich, Berend and Ránki and in *Az 1929–33-as világgazdasági válság hatása Magyarországon* (The effect of the world crisis in Hungary). Ed. by M. Incze. Also in *Bulgaria.* Ed. by L. Dallin. New York and London, 1957; N. Vuco: *Poljoprivreda Jugoslavije, 1918–1921* (Agriculture in Yugoslavia 1918–1941). Belgrade, 1958; B. Stojsavljević: *Prodiranje kapitalizma u selo 1919–1929* (The development of capitalism in the village). Zagreb, 1963; N. Arcadian: *Finantiare industriei românești.* Bucharest, 1936.

On the level of productivity and technology: E. Lipinski: *Development of Agriculture and Industry.* Warsaw, 1955; M. Szuhay: *Állami beavatkozás és* (State intervention and the Hungarian agriculture in the 1930s). Budapest, 1963; B. Newman: *Balkan Background.* New York, 1945.

The comparison of the production level has been done by S. Zagoroff, J. Végh, and A. Blimovich: *The Agricultural Economy of the Danubian Countries, 1935–1945.* On the agricultural surplus population see the thorough calculations of W. Moore. We also took into consideration the calculations of Rosenstein-Rodan ("Agricultural Surplus Population in Eastern and South-Eastern Europe," *The Economic Journal,* 1943), cited by N. Spulber in *The State and Economic Development.*

The marketing problem is presented by I. Svennilson in *Growth and Stagnation,* and in D. Warriner: *The Economics of Peasant Farming.*

The pattern of European industrial development, the industrial structure, and the level of production and productivity are comprehensively examined in: *Industrial Statistics,* OEEC. Statistical Bulletins. Paris, 1955; *Patterns of Industrial Growth, 1938–1958.* United Nations, New York, 1960; *Industrialization and Foreign Trade.* League of Nations. Geneva, 1945. Statistical data and sources are published in N. Spulber: *The Economics of Communist Eastern Europe.* London and New York, 1957.

A vast body of literature is available on the industrial growth of the various countries in the interwar period. From these we used for Austria the works of K. Rothschild, W. Weber, and *Hundert Jahre österreichische Wirtschaftsentwicklung,* cited before; the publication of the Österreichisches Institut für Konjunkturforschung; and the volume *Austria—Public Finances,* Third Report by the Financial Organisation of the League of Nations. Geneva, 1937.

For Czechoslovakia: *Prehled hospodárského vývoje Československa v letech 1918–1945* (Outline of the Czechoslovak economy): A. Zaubermann: *Industrial Progress in Poland. Czechoslovakia and East Germany, 1937–1962.* London, 1962: *Rozvoj československého průmyslu* (Development of Czechoslovak Industry). Prague, 1962.

On Hungary: I. T. Berend and Gy. Ránki: *The Hungarian Manufacturing Industry, Its Place in Europe.* Etudes Historiques. Budapest, 1960, and by the same authors: *Magyarország gazdasága as I világháború után, 1919–1929* (Hungary's economy after World War I, 1919–1929) and *Magyarorszag gyaripara a második világhaboru elött és a háboru időszakában 1933–1945* (Hungary's industry before and during World War II, 1933–1945), both cited before.

Concerning Polish industrial development consult the works of J. Taylor, L. Wellisz, F. Bujak, E. Lipinski, and E. Piltz. Also R. Gradvaski: *Polska* (Poland), *1919–1938.* Warsaw, 1958; F. Zweig: *Poland between Two Wars.* London, 1944; J. Tomaszewski: *Zarys historii gospodarczej Polski* (An outline of the history of Poland's economy). Warsaw, 1962; A. Kozik: *Razvitie promyshlennosti Polshi* (The development of industry in Poland). Moscow, 1959.

On the Balkan countries: for Rumania the above-cited work of N. Arcadian: *Industrializarea României* (The industrialization of Romania), and N. Kostaky: *Aspecte ale economiei românesti* (Aspects of the Rumanian Economy). In addition, V. Madgearu: *Evolutia economiei românesti dupa razboiul mondial* (Evolution of the Rumanian economy after the World War). Bucharest, 1940; W. Axenciuc: "La place occupée par la Roumanie dans la division mondiale capitaliste à la veille de la seconde guerre mondiale." *Revue Roumaine d'Histoire,* 1966: *Romania.* Ed. by S. Fischer-Galati. London and New York, 1957; and A. Stark: *Des possibilités de développement industriel de la Roumanie.* Paris, 1932.

On Yugoslavia: M. Mirković: *Ekonomska Historija,* R. Aratinović: *Les ressources de la Yougoslavie*—both cited above. See especially M. Kukoleca: *Industrija Jugoslavije 1918–1933* (The industry of Yugoslavia, 1918–1933). Belgrade, 1940. Also: *Enciklopedija Jugoslavije.* Zagreb, 1960, and *Jugoslavien. Osteuropa-Handbuch.* Cologne, 1954.

On Bulgaria: Zh. Natan's comprehensive work previously cited and the interesting article of A. Gerschenkron ("Some Aspects of Industrialization in Bulgaria 1878–1938") and the extensive article of L. Berov: "Kom voprosa za tempovete na kapitalisticheskata industrializacia na Bolgariia" (On the question of the rate of capitalist industrialization in Bulgaria) published in: *Izvestiia na Ekonomicheskia institut na Bolgarska Akademia na Naukite.* Sofia, 1954.

The problem of the national income and the level of income is presented especially in the following volumes: A. Eckstein: *National Income and Capital Formation in Hungary 1900–1950. Income and wealth.* Series V. London, 1956; F. Hertz: *Economic Problem of the Danubian States.* London, 1947; S. Stajic: *Realni nacionalni dohodak Jugoslavije u periodima 1926–1939 i 1947–1956* (Real national income of Yugoslavia in the periods 1926–1939 and 1947–1956). Belgrade, 1957; D. Grindea: *Despre venitul național in capitalism* (National income in capitalism). Bucharest, 1956; and N. Spulber: *The State and Economic Development in Eastern Europe,* cited previously.

The problem of monopoly organizations, the question of the merging of industrial and bank capital, was a fashionable topic of Marxist economic history literature in the 1950s. This explains why almost every East-European country had comprehensive works on the topic, and all general economic histories devoted much consideration to this problem. Disregarding the general works, we wish to refer to the work of R. Wagner: *Panství kapitalistických monopolů v Československu* (The rule of capitalistic monopolies in Czechoslovakia). Prague, 1958; I. T. Berend and Gy. Ránki: *A monopolkapitalizmus kialakulása és uralma Magyarországon* (The rise and rule of monopoly capitalism in Hungary). Budapest, 1958; N. N. Constantinescu and V. Axenciuc: "Les monopôles dans l'industrie de la Roumanie," *Revue Roumaine d'Histoire,* 1965; and A. Vijoli: *Cercetări asupra capitalului financiar în tăra noastră* (Research on the financial capital in our country). Bucharest, 1949. Former non-Marxist works are also available for Rumania: D. Giurescu: *Les Monopoles en Roumanie avant et après la stabilisation.* Paris, 1932; N. Arcadian: *The Cartel System in Romania.* Bucharest, 1938.

On Bulgaria: Zh. Natan and L. Berov: *Monopolisticheskiat kapitalizom v Bolgaria* (Monopoly capitalism in Bulgaria). Sofia, 1950.

No comprehensive work is available for Yugoslavia, but there are a few articles and small works, written mostly in the interwar period: V. Kosak: *Die bankmässige Finanzierung der jugoslawischen Industrie.* Frankfurt, 1938; S. Kukoleca: *Cartels and Their Significance for the Jugoslav Economy.* Socialni Archiv, 1939; B. Machetch: *Etablissements de crédit et banques locales en Yougoslavie.* Paris, 1923; A. Ehrendiener: *L'organisation bancaire on Yougoslavie.* Zagreb, 1936.

For Poland: R. Gradowski: *Polska* (Poland) *1918–1939.*

All these works deal with the role of foreign capital too, but in addition the topic is well treated by V. Banderer: *Foreign Capital as an Instrument of National Economic Policy.* The Hague, 1964; L. Lamer: *Die Wandlungen der auslandischen Kapitalanlagen auf dem Balkan.* Weltwirtschaftliches Archiv, 1938; *Contribuţii la istoria capitalului strain in România* (Contributions to the role of foreign capital in Rumania). Bucharest, 1960; also L. Wellisz: *The Foreign capital in Poland;* S. Curicin: *Pénétration économique;* and J. Tomasevich: *Foreign Economic Relations*—all cited above.

See also S. Dimitrevic: *Das ausländische Kapital in Jugoslawien vor dem zweiten Weltkrieg.* Berlin, 1963.

Chapter 13. In the System of the German War Economy

The Nazi economic policy in the occupied and satellite countries has been elaborated in a certain sense in such scholarly works as *Hitler's Europe.* Ed. by A. Toynbee. London, 1954; partly in A. Basch: *The Danube Basin and the German Economic Sphere,* cited earlier; P. Einzig: *Hitler's New Order in Europe.* London, 1941; I. Witt: *The Economics of Barbarism.* London, 1942; and K. Brandt: *Management of Agriculture and Food in the German-Occupied and Other Areas of Fortress Europe.* Stanford, 1953.

The special literature on Austria's economy in this period is relatively small.

Our data and views are based first of all on the work of K. Rothschild: *Austria's Economy since 1945*. London, 1951. Also useful was *Hundert Jahre Österreichische Wirtschaftentwicklung*, and *Österreichs Wirtschaftsstruktur*, both cited before. Some important information is available in the pamphlet of F. Rominek: *Österreichs wirtschaftliche Ausbeutung. 1938–1945.* Vienna, 1966. The social and economic history of Czech lands during the German occupation is elaborated in the three bulky volumes of V. Král: *Otázky hospodárského a sočialniho vyvoje v Českých zemích 1938–1945* (An outline of the economic and social development in the Czech lands). Vol. I–III. Prague, 1957–1959. A good summary is given of the economic situation in the Czech protectorate as well, as on Slovakia in *Přehled hospodářského vývoje Československa* (Survey of the economic development of Czechoslovakia), cited before. Worthy of attention is the early work of L. Chmeta: *Hospodářska okupace Československa, její metody a dùsledky.* (The economic occupation of Czechoslovakia, its' method and effects). Prague, 1946, written just after World War II as a popular summary. Relating to Slovakia is the work of L. Kovacík: *Slovensko v seti nemeckého finančného kapitála* (Slovakia in the network of German financial capital). Bratislava, 1955; Vl. Baick: *Polnohospodárstvo za Solvenského štátu* (Agriculture during the Slovak state). Bratislava, 1958, and the article of L. Lipták: "Porobenie slovenského priemysla nemeckým kapitálom v čase fašistického panstva" (Subjection of Slovak industry by German capital in the period of fascist rule) in the review *Historický Časopis*, Bratislava, 1955.

On agricultural production in Southeastern Europe during the war period the most comprehensive work is S. Zagoroff, J. Végh, and A. Blimovich: *The Agricultural Economy of the Danubian Countries, 1935–1945.*

For Hungary, apart from statistical publications, the work of I. T. Berend and Gy. Ranki: *Magyarország gyáripara a második világháboru elött és a haboru idöszakában* (Hungary's industry before and during World War II) thoroughly examines and documents the problems of economic life. The same authors devoted a special article to the adaptation of the Hungarian economy to the demands of the German war machine, and the looting of the Hungarian economy by Nazi Germany: I. Berend and G. Ránki: "Die deutsche wirtschaftliche Expansion und das ungarische Wirtschaftsleben zur Zeit des zweiten Weltkrieges," *Acta Historica*, Budapest, 1958.

On Rumania, N. N. Constantinescu's article is available: "L'exploitation et le pillage de l'économie roumaine par l'Allemagne Hitlerienne dans la période 1939–1944," *Revue Roumaine d'Histoire*, 1964. A book with some interesting statistics is: M. Marevschi: *Contributti la istoria finantelor publice a Rominiei 1914–1944* (Contribution to the history of public finances in Rumania). Bucharest, 1957.

For Bulgaria we used the frequently cited work of Zh. Natan: *Istoria ekonomicheskogo razvitia Bolgarii* (The history of economic development in Bulgaria); the article of L. Berov: *Kom voprosa za vans notargovs kata orientaciia na bolgarskiia fashizam* (On the question of foreign trade orientation of Bulgarian fascism). Sofia, 1954, and P. Kircenov: *Nacionalen dohod na Bolgariia* (The national income in Bulgaria). Sofia, 1946.

The economic situation in Poland during the war is presented by the following: St. Protiowski: *Hans Frank's Diary*. Warsaw, 1961; I. Kostrowicka, Z. Landau and J. Tomaszewski: *Historia Gospodarcza Polski XIX-XX wieka* (The history of economy in Poland in the 19th and 20th centuries). Warsaw, 1966; Cz. Madajczyk: *Die deutsche Besatzungspolitik in Polen 1939-1945*. Wiesbaden, 1967.

Some useful data are to be found on Yugoslavian agriculture during the war in the work of Zagoroff, Végh and Blimovich: *The Agricultural Economy of the Danubian Countries,* cited above.

On the economic destruction we used basically: K. Rothschild: *The Austrian Economy since 1945;* F. Nemschak: *Zehn Jahre österreichische Wirtschaft 1945-1955.* Vienna, 1965; F. Heissenberger: *The Economic Reconstruction of Austria, 1945-1952.* Washington, 1953; J. Marczewski: *Planification et croissance économique des démocraties populaires.* Paris, 1956; J. Goldmann: *Czechoslovakia: Test Case of Nationalisation.* Prague, 1948; I. T. Berend: *Ujjáepités és a nagytöke elleni harc Magyarországon 1945-1948.* (Reconstruction and the fight against the big capital in Hungary 1945-1948). Budapest, 1962; *Magyar Gazdasagkutató Intézet 54. számu helyzetjelentése* (54th report of the Hungarian Institute for Economic Research). Budapest, 1947; *Közgazdaság Évkönyve* (Economic Yearbook). Budapest, 1947; *Rehabilitation of the Polish Economy.* Polish Research and Information Service. New York, 1948; Th. Alton: *Polish Postwar Economy.* New York, 1955; *Economic Survey of Europe in 1948.* Geneva, 1949.

Chapter 14. Postwar Reconstruction

The economic historical events as well as the economic problems of the period just after the war (1945-48) involving the whole area are comprehensively treated by N. Spulber: *The Economics of Communist Eastern Europe.* London and New York, 1957; and J. Marczewski: *Planification et croissance économique des démocraties populaires.* Paris, 1956.

The following also relate to the whole period and problems involved but are national in scope: I. T. Berend: *Ujjaépités és a nagytöke elleni harc Magyarországon 1945-1948* (Reconstruction and the fight against big capital in Hungary 1945-1948), cited above; J. Taylor: *The Economic Development of Poland, 1919-1950.* New York, 1953; E. Lipinski: *Development of Agriculture and Industry.* Warsaw, 1955.

Concerning the land reforms, see: J. Kotatko: *Land Reform in Czechoslovakia.* Prague, 1948; *La Réforme agraire en Romanie.* Bucharest, 1946; J. Ganev: *Agrarne reforma v Chuchbian i u Nas* (Agrarian reform abroad and at home). Sofia, 1947; M. Somlyai: "Zemel'naja reforma 1945 goda v Vengrii" (Land reform in Hungary 1945). *Acta Historica.* Budapest, 1967; S. Szakács: *Földos-*

ztás és agrarfejlödés a magyar népi demokráciában 1945–1948. (Land reform and agricultural development in the Hungarian People's Democracy, 1945–1948). Budapest, 1964; S. Zagoroff, J. Végh, and A. Blimovich: *The Agricultural Economy of the Danubian Countries, 1935–1945.*

On the problem of nationalization and capital expropriation consult: J. Goldmann: *Czechoslovakia: Test Case of Nationalisation.* Prague, 1948; *La Tchécoslovaquie en marche vers la socialisme.* Prague, 1948; V. Vinogradov: *Voprosy Teorii i praktiki socialisticheskoi natsionalizatsii promyslennosti* (Theoretical and practical problems of socialist nationalization of industry). Moscow, 1964.

On theoretical problems and the special features of state capitalistic methods as transitory means to socialism see: I. T. Berend: "Der Schutz der Währungsstabilisierung und der staatskapitalistische Weg der Kapitalenteigung in Ungarn. 1946–47" *Acta Historica.* Budapest, 1963. Vol. IX. No. 1–2.

The history of the first reconstruction plans is discussed by Gy. Ránki: *Magyarország gazdasága az elsö 3 éves terv idöszakában. 1947–1949* (Hungarian economy during the period of the First 3 Year Plan, 1947–1949). Budapest, 1963; G. Braibant: *La Planification en Tchécoslovaquie.* Paris, 1948, J. Goldmann and J. Flek: *Planned Economy in Czechoslovakia.* Prague, 1949; G. Kemény: *Economic Planning in Hungary.* London, 1952; C. Bobrowsky: *Dix ans de planification en Pologne. Problèmes économiques des démocraties populaires.* Vol. II. Paris, 1955; *Étude sur la situation et les perspectives économiques de l'Europe.* Geneva, 1948.

On the problems of foreign aid, loans, and foreign trade see: M. Goldmann: *Soviet Foreign Aid.* New York, 1967; Th. Alton: *Polish Postwar Economy.* New York, 1955; A. Zauberman: *Industrial Progress in Poland, Czechoslovakia and East Germany, 1957–1962.* London, New York and Toronto, 1964; the article of V. Sergeiev in *Vneshnaia Torgovlia.* 1961. No. 12; M. Dewar: *Soviet Trade with Eastern Europe.* Oxford, 1951; *Vneshnaia Torgovlia SSSR.* Ed. by D. F. Fokin, Moscow, 1964.

Besides the general comprehensive books and studies dealing with special economic-historical questions mentioned above, the authors relied on statistical information, official plan reports, laws, decrees and statements of top figures of party and government. We should like to emphasize the advantages that we had in being able to study all these topics in the Hungarian archives of banks, firms, government and party institutions.

Index